LINCOM Studies
in Pragmatics

Directives in Young Peer Groups

A Contrastive Study of Reality TV

Hanna Pułaczewska

2012
LINCOM EUROPA

Published by LINCOM GmbH 2012.

LINCOM GmbH
Gmunder Str. 35
D-81379 Muenchen

LINCOM.EUROPA@t-online.de
www.lincom.eu

webshop: www.lincom-shop.eu

Printed in E.C.
Printed on chlorine-free paper

Die Deutsche Bibliothek - CIP Cataloguing-in-Publication-Data

A catalogue record for this publication is available from Die
Deutsche Bibliothek (http://www.ddb.de)

CONTENTS

PREFACE

The following corpus study analyses contrastively directive speech acts in Polish, German and British English produced in groups of young peers living together. The analysed corpora are excerpts from reality TV series produced according to the same formula in all the three languages. The study looks at the social and linguistic aspects of the use and the formulation of directive speech acts.

Its goal is to find out how the speakers of these languages obtain their interactive goals using linguistic means in ways which are typical of a given society. I name the sum of the conventions of socially appropriate coupling of context, occurrence, form and function of verbal communication "interaction style" and attempt a comparative analysis of interaction styles with a view to directive activities. I will discuss how the production and form of directive utterances are conditioned and constrained by social contexts in the three language communities which are studied; and I will discuss the social meaning they carry in particular contexts.

As a component of "rhetorical space", the aspect of verbal interaction distinct from its propositional "content space", social rhetoric articulates and (re)defines the attitude of the speaker to the hearer and other participants of interaction as well as the speaker's conception of their relationship, their respective roles, shared background, the communicative situation and the broader socio-cultural context. In addition to politeness phenomena, social rhetoric includes such differentiators of cultures and languages as culture-specific ways of creating, expressing and sustaining intimacy and distance and expression of affect. I speak of "social rhetoric" rather than "interpersonal rhetoric" in order to mark the difference between my approach and the traditional pragmalinguistic perspective on these aspects of verbal interactions. The latter is insufficient in dealing with interactions in groups because it focuses upon dyadic social encounters, where the speaker and the hearer are the only relevant participant roles.

The contrasts in the interaction styles in Polish, English and German will be analysed on the basis of the strategies and routines of language use in directive speech acts in Polish, English and German. The term "strategy" is used to mean any sort of coupling of the linguistic form, sequential organisation and propositional meaning with illocutionary forces and perlocutionary goals. The term "routine" is used to mean a conventionalised coupling of utterance form with its communicative function.

The analysis was initially guided by the notion of politeness; later, the perspective was extended to include the more general notion of interaction style, but the concept of politeness

1

has remained a crucial point of reference. As it has been studied more extensively than any other area of interpersonal (sic) rhetoric, I will have recourse to the dichotomy between positive and negative politeness, the basic notions of the study of politeness, which have been widely applied in the area of comparative pragmatics. I will test the thesis that the tendencies towards displaying positive and negative politeness are not only different in various cultures but also that they correlate with a culture's collectivist versus individualist orientation; an analysis of this correlation informs a large part of the following study.

The first part of the book, comprising chapters 1 through 4, contains theoretical and methodological considerations. It discusses the deficiencies of the traditional methods of politeness study such as written questionnaires, role plays and role enactment, and advantages of using natural data. It defines basic theoretical notions applied in the study, such as linguistic politeness, negative vs. positive face wants, involvement vs. consideration, collectivism vs. individualism, directive speech acts and their subcategories, participant structure, Head Act and various types of modification. It also sketches the heuristics used in selecting relevant data, classification and interpretation of the material won in this process, and probing interlingual contrasts.

The following empirical part comprises chapters 5 through 7.

In chapter 5, the occurrence of directives of various types in the data corpus and their linguistic forms are analysed quantitatively, and a statistical overview of interlingual as well as intralingual differences is presented. This presentation takes into account situational factors influencing the form of directives as well as the frequencies with which they occur in particular languages and groups of speakers.

A description of selected grammatical, lexical and prosodic devices used in construing directives with focus on those which could not be elicited in earlier studies based on non-natural methods follows in chapter 6.

Chapter 7 focuses on the group aspect of the encounters represented in the data corpus. It discusses how the group context influences the production and form of directives, as well as how directives contribute to establishing and maintaining group bonds. The relationship between these social functions of directives and their linguistic forms is discussed. Next, it is shown how social preferences for individualism versus collectivism in different groups of speakers are reflected in the types and forms of directive speech acts produced in similar contexts

Final reflections and conclusions follow in chapter 8.

I. DATA – METHODS – BASIC CONCEPTS

1. THE CHOICE OF DATA SOURCES

1.1. CULTURAL DIFFERENCE AS AN ANECDOTE

Leech (1983: 150) concludes that "so far, our knowledge of intercultural differences in this sphere [the typological study of cultures and languages in relation to interpersonal rhetoric] is somewhat anecdotal", a view shared by Sifianou (1992: 93) in her comparative work on English and Greek as well as by Marcjanik (1997) who studied verbal politeness in Polish. In spite of a proliferation of studies on requests and conventional routines used in requesting, as well as on the imperative, the claims concerning the trends in the use of strategies and conventions of form are seldom based on any quantitative analysis. For example, according to Thomas (1983: 102), "polite usage in Russian permits many more direct imperatives than does English"; Sifianou (1992: 126) makes similar claims with respect to Greek compared to English, while Tannen (1981) claims that Greeks are less direct in requests than Americans, including in intimate contexts such as family life. Reflecting the researchers' first-hand knowledge of the cultures and languages they discuss, such claims may be biased by their individual and idiosyncratic perspectives[1].

In studies attempting to grasp cultural and linguistic differences in a more systematic way, the questionnaire/role-play/role-enacting elicitation method is typically applied. In these methods, the test persons, native speakers of a language, are asked to produce a verbal input as a response to an instruction which describes a communication situation, the test person's participant role in the interaction, and sometimes also its verbal context. Although it has been used fruitfully in the study of directives, the use of non-authentic data poses serious problems. The following section briefly summarises the deficiencies of this method before presenting the data sources used in this study.

1.2. NON-NATURAL AND PSEUDO-NATURAL METHODS IN THE CROSS-LINGUISTIC STUDY OF LANGUAGE USE

Most works on linguistic politeness are based on a paradigm of politeness research based on elicited non-natural (and pseudo-natural) data. Even the authors who realise the

---

[1] For example, some claims about Polish by Wierzbicka (1985) seem to some other Polish native speakers to be based on an overgeneralisation of what might be her own idiolect, unduly granted the status of a standard way of expression.

deficiencies of non-natural methods view their use as inevitable in contrastive studies (cf. e.g. Márquez Reiter 2000), while trying to overcome some of their limitations.

In non-natural methods, the data is obtained by either questionnaires in which test persons simulate natural speech in oral or written mode; role plays, based on instruction describing the situation to which a verbal response is to be given; or more open, dialogic "role enacting" (pseudo-natural). Although they have been used fruitfully in the study of directives by Held (1996), Dąbrowska (1997), Blum-Kulka, House and Kasper (1989), Le Pair (1996), Fukushima (1996), Márquez Reiter (2000), Kachru (1998), De Kadt (1992) and many others, they all share some deficiencies, visible in intralingual studies as well as cross-linguistic ones.

The main advantages of non-natural methods are the (presumed) constancy of context and illocutionary function which are pinned down by the instruction and its translation; and the amount of compatible data of the same sort which can be collected within a relatively short period. However, these advantages of non-natural methods hardly make up for their deficiencies.

The recognition that the data acquired by means of written or spoken questionnaires as well as by role play do not match spontaneous speech in real conditions led to the development of the methodologies based on the study of naturally occurring speech, such as conversational analysis, interpretative sociolinguistics and spoken language analysis. For the critics of the methods based on the experimental and introspective set-ups, the results gained under such conditions are unrealistic because of non-accountability and the lack of real consequences of imaginary behaviour. The second factor which makes the non-natural methods unrealistic is that they fail to elicit data bound into full discursive contexts. The limitations of written simulation of speech are particularly obvious; quoting Beebe (1985: 11)[2], "... written role plays bias the response towards less negotiation, less hedging, less repetition, less elaboration, less variety and ultimately less talk". This may particularly affect the elements of social rhetoric and obscure rather than expose cultural contrasts. For example, as observed by Müller 1979, different languages may tend towards rhetorical verbosity as a means of defining and sustaining a relationship in varying degrees; such facts are eliminated by the written simulation of speech. Even worse, questionnaires typically test one turn within an exchange – either a topic opener, or a response to a prefabricated topic opener. Hartford and Bardovi-Harling (1992: 45) found that elicited data restricted the range of semantic formulas used to realise a speech act (rejections) as well as multiple turn negotiations typical of natural data. Researchers comparing natural speech with the results of

---

[2] Quoted in Blum-Kulka et al. (1989: 184).

elicited data found that elicited ones yield shorter and less complex data (Beebe and Cummings, 1996; Bodman and Eisenstein 1988; Hartford and Bardovi-Harling, 1992; Weasenforth, 2002).

In addition, both questionnaires and instructions in role plays hint strongly at the responses expected; the scheme applied makes obvious which speech act should be performed and who should perform it[3], which may strongly obliterate actual behavioural differences.

Some authors (e.g. Márquez Reiter 2000) made attempts to overcome the main deficiencies of the non-natural methods, simulating contextuality by elicitation of dialogues rather than singular turns. Even such interactive set-ups, however, share the main deficiencies of both role plays and written questionnaires.

Firstly, the contextuality of such experiments is deficient in that the instructions do not fully specify all the contextual parameters which potentially influence the choice of the linguistic form. Significant aspects of the situational context must either remain unspecified or be "filled in" freely by the test person before verbalising a given speech act. Thus, the task to be performed by the test person is considerably different from the task occurring in a real-life situation, which is to merely verbalise a request in a specific situation.

Secondly, the situations presented to the subjects in the task descriptions tend to be isolated rather than connected to ongoing action. They lack the background of a longer interaction of speaker and hearer, or their common non-verbal activities. Typically, in the questionnaires H and S come together to perform the required exchange and part again. It is doubtful whether this type of situation is a predominant component of social experience in any society[4].

An even more elementary fault of non-natural (and pseudo-natural) methods is that they can supply no data concerning the linguistic co-production of socially meaningful contexts. The differences we can learn about by using them are only on dimensions which we planned to encompass, and designed the instructions accordingly. Generally, the question answered when using the questionnaire method is different from the question answered by using natural data. In the former case, the question is: what do people say when they want to

---

[3] An example of these characteristics of the pseudo-natural method (role playing) can be found in Garcia (1989).

[4] These characteristics of questionnaires and role-playing sometimes result in such counterintuitive claims as the one in an otherwise illuminating study by Dąbrowska (1997: 521) who maintains that "when (Polish) women make a request, they always make use of the polite *przepraszam* (excuse me) as to avoid imposition …" This generalisation is certainly true with reference to requests that open interactions between strangers, which seems to be the main or only type of requests in the questionnaires used by Dąbrowska.

make H do X? In the latter case, the question is: when, how, to whom and for what purpose do people produce (and interpret) directive utterances?

Levinson (1988) differentiates the "alternates view" in which only the questions of the former sort are asked, from the ethnography of speaking view, highlighting the latter type. To illustrate the problem, he mentions the study he once initiated of the differences in class-stratified realisations of same speech functions by shop assistants in shops of different class levels. In this study, an investigator went in to a number of class-stratified shops and produced a standardised initiating piece of dialogue:

> We were hoping, as on the alternate approach, to hold function constant in this highly restricted setting, so that different class-stratified realizations of greetings, requests, offers of service, etc., could be studied … What had gone wrong of course was that, despite the restricted setting, the kinds of speech functions relevant to shops of different kinds had diverged and become irreconcilably different. For in the higher and middle ranking shops there was a quite different definition of the activity or speech event: customer and assistant expect to be paired in an intense and prolonged verbal interaction which will only cease when the customer leaves, satisfied or dissatisfied. In the lower ranking stores, there was no such expectation … even when interaction is initiated by the customer, there are no greetings, and minimal help is given … From these structural facts, the quite different and incommensurable speech functions attended to in verbal interaction naturally follow. With such divergence in function, there was no hope of studying variant realisations of the same function. And so, in the grip of the alternates approach, I abandoned the study. But I now wonder whether this was not a serious error. For if we suppress the differences of speech function, and restrict ourselves to studying circumstances which are strictly commensurable (emphasis H.P.), what we are doing is *divorcing sociolinguistics from the study of social practice* (italics S.L., ibid.: 171-172).

Questionnaires used in the cross-linguistic comparison are clearly based on the alternates view. Márquez Reiter (2000: 59) admits that "cross-cultural research poses a further source of difficulty since people from different cultures may differ in their considerations of role-relationships". Her way out of the dilemma was to ensure that "the situations of role-play were carefully designed and discussed with native speakers in both cultures to try to ensure 'sameness' of context in both languages" (ibid.). However, the very occurrence of "difficulty in producing situations which reflected 'everyday' occurrences in both cultures under the same combination of social variables" (ibid: 62) is a dimension of cultural difference, which the elicitation procedures seek to overcome rather than to expose. Thus, role plays make different cultures look more alike than they really are. Directive utterances are produced in situations arranged by interaction participants in accordance with the logic of their own cultural system. For example, the circumstances in which requests, excuses and apologies actually occur may be different for various cultures.

Role-plays do not help us discover relevant dimensions of cultural difference; predicting what is relevant and what is not rests on the test designer. While looking at the comparative work based on role-plays and questionnaires, I was struck by the fact that situation designed to elicit directive speech acts were such in which either the speaker or the hearer was the exclusive beneficiary of the predicated act. In real-life situations, the objectives of S and H are frequently complementary; they are constituted by, and constitutive of the social bonds between S and H. The design of such questionnaires is implicitly based on a model of communication in which people interact and communicate in order to satisfy needs prior to the interaction and communication; directives are conceived of as having only instrumental, rather than integrative function[5].

With one or two exceptions, all the items (situations) used in the questionnaires I have come across required a single hearer to be addressed. A look at natural data shows, however, that requests, proposals, offers, advice, etc. can also be targeted at groups. The question of difference of linguistic behaviour towards individuals and groups could not be addressed by the traditional study of politeness for that very reason. Similarly, all kinds of directives, apologies, etc. made by a speaker on behalf of a group (such as a married couple, team, or institution) are excluded from analysis. In addition, all the considerations of "face" underlying the approach to directives in the traditionally politeness theory need some adjustment to the fact that we also address directives on behalf of groups and to groups, because "face" is a concept inherently tied to a single individuated self.

Further, it is notable that beneficiaries of naturally occurring directives are frequently not as clear as in invented situations. Consider the following example from the British version of Big Brother:

1-E1[6]. The group are preparing for a dressing-up party. M is alone in the women's bedroom and is putting on a woman's bathing suit.

```
1 M these are so uncomfortable
```

---

[5] For the discussion of instrumental vs. integrative motivation, cf. Earl Stevick (1976).
[6] The indexing of the data quoted follows the original numbering in the full version of this study, an unpublished manuscript available with the author, and is therefore discontinuous.

(F enters the room and sees M)
2 F oh my God # someone come and look # someone come and look # . of
course they are fucking uncomfortable
3 M men wear these
(F grasps a skirt and hands it to M)
4 F <start laughing><put it on # put it on immediately>

In this episode no clear benefit to F follows from the fulfilment of her categorical request to M. The emphatic form of the request (repetition and the imperative coupled with the intensifier "immediately") functions as a humorous expression of F's disgust. At the same time, F is advising M to do something beneficial to himself – changing his unattractive appearance. Apart from this, in the show which the group is preparing to give to the T.V audience, M is going to look better with a skirt on, profiting the group, the audience, and the program makers. F is here appealing to the norm saying that it is better to look good – for all parties involved.

The process of invention of situations in a role-play conceals the existence of "mixed" genres, such as multiple beneficiaries, an advisory element in requests, or requests made for the sake of someone else. Their existence and density of occurrence is, however, a parameter of its own of a potential cultural-linguistic difference. Moreover, all the facts concerning the relation between the form of the utterance and the speaker's intention to benefit persons other than the speaker (or the hearer) are beyond the scope of analysis in the controlled design. The design makes the responses compatible with the assumption that there is one beneficiary who is identical with the speaker (in requests) or, alternatively, with the hearer (in advice), and that the speakers only represent themselves. This assumption is convergent with the social emphasis of research on one-to-one communication (individual speaker, individual addressee), and the resulting focus upon favour-asking as a prominent type of directive activity.

Another observation which puts the dyadic (speaker-hearer) model of interaction in doubt is that people frequently talk in groups continuing, repeating and reformulating each other's directives, as in the following exchange:

2-E1. F1 and F2 are talking to a program maker whom they can only hear and not see.
1 F1 we were wondering # . if it is in any way convenient . to you
2 F2 within your interest # cause there would be so much more fun
3 F1 it would be s::o funny # . so funny tonight # . if we could have

```
just a little bit
4 F2 a lot more
5 F1 a lot more of alcohol and tobacco # . and by the way # . we find
your voice really attractive
```

Such a collective performance will not occur in prefabricated set-ups where the roles are appointed in advance. However, such "collective" realisations of speech acts might function differently in different cultures.

Disadvantages notwithstanding, there is one respect (apart from the ease of analysis) in which the questionnaire method is superior. This concerns the ability of the questionnaire method to incorporate mild hints ("off-record" strategy, utterances interpretable as non-directives) in the analysis of directive speech. As the observer has no direct access to the speaker's intentions, mild hints occurring in natural data usually cannot be classified as intentional directives. As questionnaires and role-plays prescribe the speaker's intention, the realisation of this intention by hints can be incorporated in the analysis without any difficulty. The present study, based on the natural data, is almost exclusively confined to on-record realisation of directives, apart from a few cases in which some contextualisation cues in the subsequent course of interaction allowed me to identify directives in the form of mild hints.

2. THE APPROACH

2.1. ANALYSIS AND COMPARISON OF DATA

The analysis and comparison of linguistic data in this work will be two-fold:

- Qualitative analysis based on methods of the study of politeness, spoken language analysis (Gesprochene-Sprache-Forschung), interpretative sociolinguistics, and stylistics as a receptor of the methods of the latter.
- Statistical comparison of tendencies, applying the concepts of the study of politeness to the analysis of linguistic form while furthering the analysis towards the study of linguistic behaviour as a component of social life. The statistical data is interpreted as a reflection of the interaction between linguistic behaviour and social life, as proposed by the ethnography of communication (Hymes 1972).

Ethnography of communication studies language in its cultural context. Hymes (1972) argues that socio-cultural knowledge is revealed in the performance of speech acts because culturally specific values and norms constrain both the form and content of what is said. He proposes a model for describing the interaction of language and social life, which is based on the study of speech events as components of social life. The objective is "to fill the gap between what is usually put into ethnography and what is usually put into grammar", that is, to show how social norms affect the use and distribution of communicative resources.

Spoken language analysis (Gesprochene-Sprache-Forschung), which was developed within the field of Germanic linguistics, is based, like conversation analysis and interpretative sociolinguistics, on the study of authentic data. One of its foci is the convergence of grammatical structures with communicative acts. Spoken language analysis examines the interaction between syntactic structures and specific conventionalised conversational activities. It analyses the role of syntactic and lexico-syntactic structures in the interpretation of verbal interaction in relationship with prosodic, rhetorical and sequential characteristics of this interaction.

Interpretative sociolinguistics treats the social reality as produced in the course of interaction, and treats verbal interaction as a component in the construction of its social contexts, which in turn make speech interpretable. The object of interpretative sociolinguistics is to examine the verbal processes and strategies used for constructing meanings and the associated contexts of interpretation. Interpretation and production of speech is viewed as based upon revisable inferences developed during interaction by its participants, concerning the speaker's meanings, communicative intentions, and evaluations of the situation by co-participants. Analyses done within the frame of interpretative sociolinguistics assimilate ethnographic information, and may make use of interviews with people with first-hand knowledge of the culture and language under analysis for the assessment of possible interpretations.

The study of politeness derives from the speech act theory and from Brown and Levinson's (1978) seminal study. It analyses the forms and strategies occurring in the realisation of speech acts which carry with them a "threat" to the interlocutor's ego and his or her social image, that is, the ways in which the Gricean conversational maxims of clarity, quantity etc. are violated in such acts; for example, by means of the grammatical form, conversational routines, and indirectness. Regarded as having a high potential of social risk, directive speech acts have been a focus of the study of politeness. This field of study worked out its own analytical categories for dealing with the linguistic form of directive utterances. Some of them will be utilised in the analysis which follows, especially in its quantitative part.

Stylistics is defined by Seltig (1997: 10) as an empirical analysis of the creation and deployment of style reconstructing the participants' perspectives in natural interactions, inspired by methods of interpretative sociolinguistics. Sandig (1986: 31) characterises style as a system which comprises various dimensions of verbal action and differentiates the social significance of what is said by the way in which it is said; similarly, for Keim (1997: 319), style is "the socially meaningful way to perform an act of communication". It is constituted, among other things, by intonation patterns, rhythm, morphology, lexicon, syntax, routine formula, the way of using and verbalisation of speech acts and their sequences, rhetorical questions, metaphor, irony, elements of the contents such as the use of stereotypes, themes, and text patterns, organisation of conversation, conflict avoidance strategies, body language and other non-verbal components of interaction. We can speak of a "style" as opposed to punctual uses of singular resources when they co-occur in bundles, are used to co-define the social context (e.g.intimacy, hierarchical distance) and are not predetermined by regional or social origin of the speaker.

The notion of bundles of co-occurring properties of speech as constitutive of different interaction styles resulted in postulating contrast pairs such as "powerless-powerful" (see e.g. Hosman 1989, Müller 1997), or "involvement-considerateness" (Tannen 1984). There is a high affinity between the aspects of verbal interaction analysed by stylistics, and politeness phenomena, with the traditional distinction between "camaraderie" versus "deference", or positive and negative politeness. However, the study of politeness, in particular in the contrastive mode, has created its own research paradigm which has little in common with interpretative sociolinguistics, as its main sources of data are questionnaires and role plays.

As a result, the study of politeness constitutes a branch of its own rather than an aspect of stylistics. In this work, I will attempt to bridge the gap between well-established concepts of politeness study, and stylistics as the study of actual interaction in its social context of use.

The qualitative analysis needs to be completed by numerical analysis because the contrast in language use is a matter of tendencies and frequencies rather than just a matter of existence or non-existence of a given type of a conversational routine, or a regular appearance versus non-appearance of a given behaviour in a given culture. The analysis of conversational routines appearing in all three languages shows that there are few patterns unique to any given language. Similarly, for almost every episode of use of a certain strategy of interaction in one language, a corresponding episode can be found in other languages. As it is typicality versus exceptionality of linguistic events that is at issue, the qualitative analysis does not suffice for the assessment of similarity and difference. There is also a scarcity of comparative works on requestives (and any type of speech act) based on both authentic and quantifiable material. Reflecting on the video-recorded data which I had at my disposal, I soon realised that comparing sets of arbitrarily chosen episodes would automatically result in confirming my starting hypotheses about any particular difference or similarity in the interaction styles of the three groups. The very act of choosing these episodes would depend on the pre-analytical assumption of their being representative for a given group. Therefore, a detailed quantitative analysis of the available data will be performed as a preliminary step.

The very fact that requests are made, or advice given, more frequently in one culture than another already provides a key to grasping some cultural differences in patterns of verbal interaction. In what follows, an analysis of the statistical distribution of their occurrence in the data offers a glimpse of these differences. It is followed by the analysis of their linguistic realisations.

By comparing three rather than two languages, I venture to avoid ambiguity and a certain circularity of premises and results inherent in a dual comparison, where an identical score of two languages on a given parameter may be interpreted as showing similarity between those languages in a given respect; or as showing that the hypothesised dimension of difference is not a relevant analytical category.

The statistical part of the analysis differs from the following qualitative part in a partial de-contextualisation of the analysed phenomena. This is unavoidable as all counts require a previous "digitalisation" of the "analogue" flow of data by their compartmentalisation into a number of pre-established categories. The statistics concentrate on a particular unit, almost always contained within one turn of interaction and identified as the core realisation of a directive speech act. The regularities examined in this part pertain to the co-occurrence of some pre-defined aspects of the situation with directive speech, and the linguistic form of the so delimited units.

The qualitative analysis which follows makes up for this deficiency and focuses on particular instances of directive utterances embedded in their situational contexts, showing regularities and postulating underlying social norms. The analysis illustrates how directive utterances function within large socially meaningful episodes with view to constitution and expression of relationships.

The qualitative and quantitative analysis of speech will be supplemented by a discussion of some extra-linguistic cultural differences between the British, German and Polish cultures suggested by the analysed data. They are related to factors that are assumed to influence the production, form, and affective significance of directive utterances.

2.2. VERIFYING ANALYTICAL CATEGORIES

The following remarks refer to the limitations on the methods of corpus study claimed by interpretative sociolinguistics, in particular, the claim of the inductive derivation of relevant categories and typologies (of genres, situations etc.) from the corpora under study. Günthner (2000) criticises, among others, Biber (1988) and Paltridge (1997) for defining genres according to pre-conceived criteria (topic, purpose, message form), defined "prior to any comparison of texts" (Biber 1988: 71). The distinction between the two procedures seems to lie to a considerable extent in the presentation itself, and be less the matter of the procedure followed in the study and more of the researcher's strategy in describing his modus operandi. The authors who use "aprioristic" categories start the description at the point at which the categories are fixed, and erase the traces of the creative procedure which led them to the acceptance of these categories as relevant with view to the data to be analysed. The other camp who claim that the categories are "emic" with respect to the corpus under analysis, and have been won inductively[7] on the basis of the data, make the process itself visible: "Die Konturen des tatsächlichen Erkenntnisgangs sollen möglichst wenig verwischt werden" (Kotthoff 1998: 5).

Kotthoff (1998) addresses the issue of the mode of presentation (or non-presentation) of the data-based re-construction of relevant concepts by the analyst, and advocates that in studies that exhibit the process-oriented approach to language (different from a structure-oriented approach) a process-oriented style of presentation should be used, in which the

---

[7] "Abductively" in a corrected version sensitive to the criticism of induction as a viable method of scientific discovery.

14

impression is being avoided that the results won out of the data have been the point of departure for the analysis. While I adopt the process-oriented approach to language working on the data corpus, I will sacrifice process-oriented style to clarity and comprehensibility of presentation there where they cannot be adhered to at the same time.

Günthner (2000) explicitly referred to her hermeneutic procedure of a "double go" through the texts. The first "go through" provided prototypical examples, further criteria of inclusion or exclusion of a particular verbal action in a genre under analysis, and an indication regarding the factors which should be analysed. The "double go" method is likely to result in discovering some categories of analysis on which the interaction participants orient themselves, and, as a result, a socially relevant clustering of the flow of data. This method has also been adopted in the following study.

However, as observed by Günthner, it is hard to show that the induced analytical categories are indeed "emic" in the sense that the participants orientate themselves on them, because both the explicit and implicit validation is frequently not provided during the encounter under analysis. The Utterances in natural speech have multiple illocutionary and perlocutionary facets and the hearers may respond to only one of the recognised intentions (see Levinson 1981). Irony and tease, for example, are not regularly made recognisable as such by the responses to them ("contextualisation cues"). Instead, the researcher is able to interpret the responses because she has recognised the preceding utterances as ironic and attributed the same recognition to interaction participants (see e.g. Drew 1987 on the "po-faced receipts of teases"). Actually, the "discovery" of the relevant analytical categories is located at the researcher's judgement, enlightened by the previous study of linguistics and related branches with their categories and notions prior to the analysis of the corpus at hand, and supported by native speakers' interpretations. Taken to the extreme, the postulate of discovering the categories "in the data themselves" would amount to non-transferability of any concepts to new contexts and corpora, different from their "context of discovery", and block cross-fertilisation between particular research projects; theory would have to be created "from scratch" every time.

2.2.1. EMIC OR ETIC?

The issue of validating analytical categories touches the debate concerning the emic versus etic approach led for the last three decades in cultural anthropology. According to Berry (1969), the emic approach studies behaviour from within the system, examines only one culture, the structure is discovered by the analyst and criteria are relative to internal characteristics; the etic approach studies behaviour from outside the system, examines many cultures comparing them, structure is created by the analyst, and the criteria are considered absolute or universal. A formulation of the emic postulate, implicit already in Malinowski's famous phrase that the final goal is to "grasp the native's point of view", has been provided by Boas (1943: 314, quoted in Jahoda 1983: 22-23): "If it is our serious purpose to understand the thoughts of a people the whole analysis of experience must be based on their concepts, not ours".

The emic postulate has consequences for the role of the interview in the interpretation of data and theory construction. In its strict form, the call for using emic categories requires that they be validated by being available to the awareness of either interaction participants themselves or other members of a given speech community, used as informants and interpreters of data. Yet compliance with this postulate would preclude any insight transcending the level of lay reflection. According to Geertz (1973: 23), even an actor-oriented description "involves interpretation and construction and therefore cannot be identical with the way people themselves experience their lives. Thus to the extent that anthropology entails scientific analysis, an inescapable etic appears to be tacitly conceded" (ibid: 23). The issue of re-constructing the native speaker's perspective is particularly problematic for a contrastive study, because there exists a "limit of awareness" with regard to the motives and structures of one's own behaviour[8] and an even more fundamental limit of awareness of culture-dependence of values and one's own culture's "unquestionables". This reduces the cultural insider's ability of conscious formulation of factors shaping their behaviour.

Rather than embrace Gumperz's (1982) method of interpretative sociolinguistics, where the postulate of using the "emic" perspective appears as the requirement that interpretations and descriptive categories are validated by discussing data with culture's insiders, I adopt here the complementary emic and etic perspectives as defined by their originator Kenneth Pike (1967: 38): "Two units are different etically when instrumental measurements can show them to be so. Units are different emically only when they elicit different responses from people acting within the system." This definition does not imply that the difference in elicited responses should be noticeable to interaction participants or lay observers. An example of measurable distinctions of which culture's insiders are not aware is the use of different politeness strategies in directives when talking to single and multiple addressees, and for different types of beneficiaries, in one or more languages

---

[8] Basically the same "limit of awareness" also manifests itself, for example, in the deficiency of the introspective methods as ways of obtaining data on grammar.

under analysis.

Interviews with representatives of the cultures under study were applied, though, as an auxiliary method in several cases to test judgements of social adequacy of verbal and associated non-verbal behaviours, and verify the analyst's interpretation of some interactions. The categories applied in the following statistical analysis have been postulated as an initial hypothesis and tested against the data as possibly meaningful dimensions of sociolinguistic difference. The hypothesis itself was inspired both by a close look at the data itself and ideas from sociology as well as linguistics. The notions pertaining to the form of directives are taken from syntax, semantics, phonetics and phonology, and the study of linguistic politeness. With regard to the "etic" and "emic" dilemma, intralingual analysis was used as a preliminary step for studying interlingual contrasts. This means an integration of emic and etic perspective into "derived etics" in which etic concepts are tested for their emic relevance, and then cross-cultural measurements are taken on emically different behaviours. "Derived etic" is a notion introduced by Berry (1969) to label a "true" etic, that is, one constructed empirically from an initial emic analysis. In my analysis, directives have been differentiated according to hypothetically meaningful parameters of context (etic concepts such as action types, or participants' structures) relevant to the focus of this work on interdependence versus autonomy. The correlations between linguistic forms and the contextual factors identified are taken to substantiate the "emic" character of the categorisation, i.e., to show that these factors indeed shape the perception of social interactions in particular cultures ("Units are different emically only when they elicit different responses from people acting within the system").

The following strategy was used in the construction of analytical categories to be applied in the statistical analysis:

- Win potential analytical categories through the inspection of data enlightened by introspection, field observation, and concepts from linguistics, cultural anthropology and social psychology.
- Test the validity of postulated analytical categories (e.g. participants' structures) by testing whether they correlate with some other categories (e. g. impositiveness) for language 1 and language 2. If this is the case in both languages, the categories are meaningful for both; describe the different patterns of correlations. If this is only the case for one of them, then the category that is significant (emic) for one language is meaningless for the other. A major intercultural or inter-lingual difference has been located.

2.2.2. HEURISTICS APPLIED

Applied for the needs of the present study, these heuristics led to the following methodology:

- The identification of directive speech in the sample is based on the definition of a directive speech act in Searle (1976) and its refinement in Bach and Harnish (1982). In the former, the speaker intends his or her utterance to be the reason for the hearer performing the action in question. In the latter, a directive should only enhance the probability that H will X, and does not need to be definitely the only reason for it (S may not know whether or not H is going to do X anyway). As "the only reason" condition has been suspended, speech acts in which speakers supported other people's directives by repetition or paraphrase (cases of collective performance of directives) were counted as occurrences of directive speech and included in the data under analysis.
- Proposals, requests and advice as sub-types of directives are ethno-categories taken from everyday speech, but have been refined for analytical purposes. Their "refinement", or technicalisation, meant that the notions were analysed into functional constituents and re-defined so as to make them mutually exclusive, exclude aspects of form (such as that a *request* is usually polite), and exclude the degree of legitimacy, because perceptions of legitimacy are part of what is being compared. The re-definition results in the inclusion of some cases in the category "request" which would be excluded from the highly overlapping ethno-categories of English *request*, German *Bitte* and Polish *prośba* because they are characterised by high legitimacy and, typically, impositive linguistic form (demands).
- The formation of analytical categories was guided by the assumption (based on the data as well as the author's cultural experience) that legitimacy of directive speech acts is perceived differently by the speakers of the three languages in analogical situations; that this difference affects the production of directives and their form; that it reflects the different degrees of individualism and collectivism in the three cultures studied; and that the analytical categories should reflect those recurrent aspects of context which affect the perception of legitimacy. In particular, the analytical category of beneficiary configuration has been postulated as a link between the perception of legitimacy and individualism/collectivism (I/C).
- Syntactic, semantic, prosodic, lexical, and syntactic-lexical categories (conversational routines) were appointed a priori as analytical categories, and

18

checking their correlations with functions and aspects of context was defined as a goal of the analysis.

- The degree of impositiveness of particular linguistic forms was defined in a way aprioristic to the data itself, in a way that agrees with views of other authors quoted insofar they dealt with these forms. The use of impositive forms and non-impositive forms is a variable to be compared.

- Some analytical categories denoting aspects of the context were won by testing the hypothesis that they significantly co-relate with some other analytical categories (occurrences, syntactic formats, impositiveness). They were accepted as relevant if a significant correlation occurred in at least one language. For example, the analytical category "sort of action", differentiating directives into inhibitive vs. initiating has been introduced following Held (1995), and proved to correlate highly with impositiveness versus tentativeness in English and German, while the distinction multiple/single addressee was tested and judged relevant for German only.

2.2.3. INTERVIEWS WITH NATIVE AND NON-NATIVE SPEAKERS

Interviews with native speakers of all the three languages were conducted to provide verification of the analyst's interpretation for several episodes, and evaluations of particular verbal actions in terms of their social appropriateness. For each language, up to five native speakers, including at least one male and one female native speaker were asked to help evaluate the same episodes. All informants were students or young graduates, in age corresponding to the average age of Big Brother participants.

3. THE DATA CORPUS

The analysed sample is a collection of video-recordings and protocols from the reality TV series "Big Brother", broadcast in the years 1999-2004 on German, British and Polish television according to minutely similar formulas, creating very similar frames for spontaneous interactions in all the three languages. The age structure, gender structure and the number of participants, as well as the situational setting including the living conditions and the way of data collection are nearly the same for all three languages.

3.1. SETTING

The data corpus consists of the transcripts of spontaneous interaction in the experimental set-up which is basically the same in all three languages. During the duration of the experiment, an excerpt of the recordings (from the minimum of 25 minutes in English to the maximum of 60 minutes in German and Polish) was shown daily on TV in each of the respective countries. The participants lived in isolation from the outside world in a building called the Big Brother house consisting of a living room with a kitchen cell, two bedrooms, a bath, a shower and a yard or garden. They were not acquainted with each other prior to the program. The show starts with a group of 14 or 12 participants, half of them male; each week one person is eliminated by the anonymous vote of the remaining participants, or the telephone vote of the TV audience. New participants sporadically join the group. The duration of the experiment is between 63 and 104 days. After that time one of the remaining two to four persons wins a popularity contest by the vote of the audience. Video cameras installed in every room except for the toilet and microphones worn by the participants record the ongoing action.

The participants are conscious of being observed, but habituation effects enter early and they behave largely in a spontaneous way. This is manifested by the occurrence of conflicts, threats, swearing, and flirting despite existing relationships outside the experimental setting, involuntary sounds such as belching and farting, and other sorts of uninhibited behaviour such as picking one's nose, intimate shaving etc. The duration of the experiment, as well as its continuity and the omnipresence of the experimental setting, ensures that the participants will not be able to consciously control and denaturalise their behaviour to a high degree even though they are conscious of being observed by a great number of viewers.

It is controversial to what extent the behaviour of the test participants is representative for other contexts and warrants generalised conclusions. A part of this problem, including a certain denaturalisation of behaviour in the mass media context of which the participants have sometimes been suspected, is the usual "observer's paradox" always involved in data collection (we cannot observe, within legal or physical limits, how people or elementary particles behave when they are not being observed). The other is the non-typicality of the living conditions in the Big Brother house where people share a bedroom and do not leave the house for work or study, which results in a quantitatively more intense interaction and psychical tension.

It has been pointed out to me that the conduct of the participants of the experiment is suspected of not being authentic, in the sense of their "showing off" and suppressing less

20

attractive traits of their personalities. While I agree with this, I do not think that it invalidates any of my claims based on the observation of interactions in the Big Brother house. I assume that the behaviour of the test persons in the Big Brother house, as behaviour in any particular (non-extreme) context, is generally in phase with the patterns of behaviour acquired during socialisation, and that an individual does not throw these patterns away, for lack of communicatively meaningful and potentially successful alternatives: "Communication requires that speakers should base their interactions on validity claims that are acceptable to their fellows" (Agozino 2003: 104). While the participants are displaying "better versions" of their "real" selves, they do so in a contest in which the judges are their fellow inmates and spectators. Thus, these attempts in self-improvement are based on the judgements about what is "better" resulting from the hierarchies of values predominant in a given society. Notwithstanding the fact that the Big Brother house creates more opportunities than everyday life (the latter being partly occupied by work and other duties) for playful behaviour meant to entertain, such as wild dances and practical jokes, the acceptability of the public face of each participant depends crucially on its verisimilitude. If being "authentic" means that the housemates should not strive for social acceptance any more than they do outside the media frame, such authenticity is not a necessary prerequisite for social validity.

This is why I assume that although the specific context of the Big Brother show filters out certain ways of behaviour and promotes others, the resulting interaction still does reflect cultural tendencies by preserving most pronounced *differences* between cultures.

To sum up, even if the participants may be to a large extent "showing off" in order to win popularity among the viewers and the cohabitants, the forms of expression in the mundane dialogues in the Big Brother house, centred mainly about the everyday activities of its inhabitants, will tend to be those acquired during socialisation, which are the established means of self-presentation, promoting social harmony and conflict solving between the interaction participants.

To preclude the possible objection that the circumstances in which "Big Brother" was recorded were extreme in the sense of not having even any remotely related real-life equivalents, it should also be pointed out that they resemble the typical ways of modern urban life such as flat and house sharing, students dormitory, and a holiday camp.

3.2. COMPARABILITY OF THE BIG BROTHER SERIES IN THREE LANGUAGES: SITUATIONAL DESIGNS

The eight series of the program analysed in this study came in three slightly different designs:

Design A: "static"

In the static design all the participants formed one group. From time to time, they were given various tasks by the supervisor. The performance of the tasks determined their weekly budget which they could spend on food and luxury items.

Design B: "battle"

In the "Big Brother Battle" design the participants are divided into two competing teams frequently engaging in competitive tasks. Success and defeat determine the living conditions of the teams, such as food, bedroom, access to toiletries, and privileges such as music and alcohol. Design B has not been utilised in Great Britain.

Design C: individual contest

In one British series of the program, the "Big Brother Battle" concept described above as design B was changed so that the competition deciding the membership in the privileged group and the losers group took place individually. This design was utilised only in Great Britain.

The data samples used in the following quantitative analysis of directive activities are excerpts from the Polish and German series involving designs A and B, and the British ones with designs A and C. As the group combat in design B promotes group integration and solidarity and designs A and C do not, it can be argued that the comparison is made between different environments. I was initially impressed by the fact that Great Britain was the only country where Endemol's concept of group battles had not been adopted; rather, "battle" design B had been changed so that the competitions deciding each person's membership in the winners' or the losers' group were fought individually (in the third series). This I interpreted as a symptom of the expectations of the British program editors in regard to the taste of the spectators, favouring individual combat over group scenarios that interlink the fortunes of individuals. Actually, however, the choice of the set-up most probably reflected the fact that roughly at the same time another reality series, "The Survivor", was broadcast on British TV. In "The Survivor", the participants were divided into two groups competing against each other and were referred to as two "tribes". In choosing to change Endemol's original scenario, the editors of Big Brother are likely to have been motivated by the wish to avoid a doubling of the same program design, and the split of the potential audience. Therefore, the assumption that the selection of the respective set-ups reflected the viewers' predilections (as they were estimated by the program producers) concerning group and individual action, and the preferred level of shared responsibilities and team spirit in general, cannot unreservedly be made. A backing for this assumption, admittedly weak though, came from my interviews with five native British viewers, which revealed that all of them viewed the British solution (individual rather than team competition) as more interesting, spicy, and consistent with the basic principles of the game. Nevertheless, the difference between the "battle" design, promoting group solidarity, and the other designs must be taken into account in the analysis. Therefore, different series of the program in each language will be discussed separately in most cases in the following statistical analysis, so that comparisons can be made between the series made within the same design.

3.3. THE SAMPLES

The analysis was based on written transcripts from videotaped material. The transcripts used for the statistical analysis of directive activities contain all the scenes in which directive utterances occurred in excerpts of emitted material covering several weeks. The qualitative part of analysis was based on this material and selected additional scenes.

The choice of material included in the statistically analysed samples was determined by availability and inter-group comparability. Two series of the program were analysed for each language. The excerpts provided comparable amounts of data from comparable periods of the stay in the Big Brother house. The latter criterion was introduced because of the potential effect of the duration of the stay in the Big Brother house upon the patterns of directive activities.

The data used in the statistical analysis of communication between peers include the data samples listed below. The times given in the list refer to interaction, or potential interaction made possible by the simultaneous presence of more than one person in the same room. Comments and editorials, as well as scenes showing empty rooms, single persons, and people in sleep were excluded. The numbers correspond to the cardinal order of the series as they were broadcast on TV, that is, the names used in the media (Big Brother Edition 1, Edition 2, etc.)

- **German corpus G2**, 1999, performed in static design A in which all the participants formed one group, divided into two periods:
  o G2E (E for "early", about 3 hrs, week 1)
  o G2L (L for "late", about 4 hrs, weeks 5 and 6)
- **German corpus G4,** 2003, design B (team competition):
  o G4E (about 4 hrs, weeks 1 and 2)
  o G4L (about 3 hrs, weeks 5 and 6).
- **British corpus E3**, 2003:
  o E3E in static design A (about 5 hrs, weeks 1 and 2)
  o E3L in design C in which the participants compete against each other for better living conditions (about 8 hrs, weeks 3 through 6)
- **British corpus E4,** 2004, design A:
  o E4E (about 4 hrs, week 1 and 2)
  o E4L (about 5 hrs, weeks 5 and 6)
- **Polish corpus P1,** 1999, design A (about 3 hrs, weeks 5 and 6):
- **Polish corpus P3**, 2002, design B:
  o P3E (about 5 hrs, weeks 1 and 2)
  o P3L (about 3 hrs, weeks 5 and 6).

In addition to this part of data, the following materials were viewed and scanned for directive activities relevant to the issues pursued in the qualitative part of the analysis. Several episodes transcribed and discussed in the qualitative analysis come from this part of the material.

- G1 about 3 hours of interaction
- G4 about 60 hours of interaction
- E1 about 1 hour of interaction
- E2 about 1 hour of interaction
- E3 about 45 hours of interaction
- P1 about 1 hour of interaction
- P3 about 45 hours of interaction

To ensure the compatibility of the series which were performed in different designs, the scenes of the contest (where teams were competing against each other in tasks such as boxing, diving, climbing, solving a mathematical problem etc.) were not included in the data. The few exceptions were tasks which required action spread over a longer period of time (several hours), took place within the Big Brother house (rather than on a sport field as usual), and intermingled with other action not specifically connected to the competitive task.

3.4. INTRALINGUAL ADEQUACY OF THE DATA

3.4.1. GROUP IDIOSYNCRASY

The tendencies of the interaction style in a young peer group reflect the group dynamics which are different for each group and depend on a mix of personalities of the participants within the group. The fact that different individuals show different preferences in their style of communication might invalidate any claims based on the assumption of cultural relevance of their linguistic performance. The assumption that there is something to compare interculturally can only be held if the intracultural differences in language use between the speakers of Polish, German and British English overwhelm intracultural differences in language use resulting from differences in group dynamics and individual styles.

The assumption that the idiosyncrasies of particular groups and individuals will not affect the data to such an extent as to override interlingual differences in cultural styles was based on several properties of the data. First, for each language transcripts from two different program series were used; second, there were a relatively high number of interaction participants within each series (twelve to fourteen); and finally, the program producers were cautious to grant some amount of "stage time" to each participant in order to give everybody a fair chance to present themselves to the audience. The latter was crucial for each participant's chance to win the individual competition, constituting one of the main attractions of the program.

My assumption was that particular groups within one language showed similar verbal behaviour, and that the differences were small compared with the interlingual difference. This assumption was verified by a separate analysis of all the samples, whose results will be presented in the statistical analysis.

3.4.2. POTENTIAL SYSTEMATIC SOURCES OF INTRALINGUAL VARIANCE

The data analysed statistically in the three languages differed by some environmental features which might have influenced the level of intimacy and solidarity between the participants, and which might be reflected in the frequency of directive activities as well as the mix of politeness strategies manifested in directive behaviour. The following factors were

25

identified as a potential source of difference in frequency and type of directive activities, and their form:

The set-up in which two groups combat against each other involves team co-operation with a common goal and sharing the outcomes of group action with others, which is likely to promote solidarity and group integration, within the whole group or within particular teams. This might have biased the results of the interaction towards more immediate directive behaviour, presupposing co-operation of the interaction partners. The Polish and German data comes from designs A and B. The British data come from design A, and C in which the participants compete against each other for better living conditions.

The time span of the acquaintance prior to the recorded sample of directive behaviour might influence intimacy, solidarity and group integration.

The number of test participants might have influenced directive behaviour in various ways. More participants might have uttered more recorded directives; at the same time, the group integration might have been positively affected as the participants continually eliminated those among themselves whom they accepted least.

Since the house in which the participants live during the experiment consists of several rooms and a yard, not all participants are present simultaneously in each episode.

The number of test participants in the statistically analysed episodes varies between 14 and 5, and diminishes with time as the test participants eliminate other participants one by one by voting, on a weekly basis. Only in E4L, are there less than eight participants (six and five). The duration of the acquaintance between the participants and the number of the participants are approximately inversely correlated.

The division of each sample, with the exception of P1 for which little early data was available, into two sub-samples from two different stages of the program made it possible to verify the effects of timing on the occurrence and form of directive speech prior to the cross-linguistic comparison of the samples.

3.5. SOCIAL CHARACTERISTICS OF PROGRAM PARTICIPANTS

The information on the participant's age structure and professions has been obtained mainly from the official Big Brother web sites. I greatly appreciate the help of Endemol Deutschland who supplied me with the birth dates of the programs' participants.

The gender mix in all of the groups throughout the program is approximately the same (50/50) for male and female participants at all times. The age structure as well as educational and professional mix are very similar in all the groups (see Appendix 1).

What strongly differentiates the Polish group from the other two is the marital status and parenthood. While the childless single was the preferred type of participant, this tendency is not so strong in the Polish group:

Parenthood: percentage of parents

P1: 27%, P3: 47%, G2: 8%; G4: 17%, E3, E4: no children or no information available.

Marital status: percentage of married participants

P1: 27%, P3: 47%, G4: 14%, E4: 8%, information not available or sporadically available for G2 (where some participants were described as "single" on the program's website) and E3.

I do not regard parenthood, marital status, and the ready availability of information of these social characteristics of the program's participants as a possible source of difference in the linguistic form of directives in themselves. However, these factors are relevant with a view to the program's conception and reception, reflecting the trends and preferences of each culture.

3.6. TRANSCRIPTION CONVENTIONS

#	*tone group boundary*
.	*break of approximately two syllables' length*
..	*break of approximately three to four syllables' length*
_	*break of least five syllables' length*
_ (5 sec)	*long break; the duration is given in brackets*
?	*tone group-final rising intonation*
´?	*tone group-final strongly rising intonation*
!	*exclamative intonation*
^	*high rise-fall intonation (marked when relevant)*
BEGGING INTONATION	*comment about the type of rise-fall intonation*
<u>patrz</u>	*emphatic stress*
---	*not interpretable*
[ ]	*brackets mark beginning and end of overlapping speech*
[[ ]	
[ ]	
[ ]]	*overlapping speech by more than two persons*
(simultaneous speech)	*undecipherable overlapping speech by more than two persons or an unrecognisable number of persons*

<start nasalization><	*beginning of distinguished prosody; description of special features is provided between brackets*
><end nasalization>	*end of distinguished prosody*
>	*end of distinguished prosody and turn end*
(F moves towards the door)	*brackets mark beginning and end of the description of non-verbal actions of an interaction participant*
(laughs)	*para-verbal actions*
…	*omission*
F1, F2	*the first, second etc. female speaker in the scene; the referent is not the same in different scenes unless it is explicitly stated*
M1, M2	*the first, second etc. male speaker in the scene*
F, M	*the only female and male speaker in the scene*
F to M:	*comment naming the addressee of the current turn of talk, inserted if it increased comprehensibility of the interaction*
Steve, Iwona Gałaj	*The names of the participants have been conventionally replaced by other names of the same syllable structure, except for cases in which their phonetic form was crucial for comprehensibility.*
F2-JANE	*identifies a speaker referred to by name in the preceding or following interaction (used when it is not sufficiently clarified by the context)*
1-E3.	*identification of a scene: the running number in the text, sample name*
1-E3. CAMPING	*identification of a scene quoted several times by title*
4/1	*the first part of turn 4 (used when a turn is split into two parts because of a long intervening comment on extra-verbal action)*
`	*pitch fall in the following syllable (indicated when relevant)*
´	*pitch rise in the following syllable (indicated when relevant)*

Brief comments on the context and setting are usually provided, e.g.:

100-E4. F1 and F2 are talking to a program team member whom they can hear but not see.

28

Quotations from the samples in the text are distinguished by a different font (Courier New 9 pt), e.g.: "... as shown by his comment: `the reason why we nominate people # is that they are not a part of the group.`"

The English translation of the Polish and German dialogues is the result of a compromise between a literal (word-to-word) translation and one that is easy to understand. In particular, non-hedged performative verbs, prepositional phrases and language-specific impersonal constructions, including the intransitive use of some verbs which are always transitive in English, are translated literally; word order is largely preserved even if it leads to an ungrammatical translation.

4. BASIC CONCEPTS

4.1. APPROACHING DIMENSIONS OF CULTURAL DIFFERENCE

In reaction to the cultural restrictedness of many theories in linguistics, as well as in other branches of human sciences such as social and personality psychology, proposals have been made that culture be included as a parameter in constructing theories (cf. e.g. Triandis 1986 for social psychology). However, "the concept of 'culture' is too broad and inclusive ... and must be 'unpackaged' ... to be more scientifically useful. One way to proceed is to represent cultures as a set of dimensions ... To build a truly universal theory that takes into account the influence of culture, we must first be able to link observed cultural differences to specific dimensions of culture that are hypothesized to have produced the differences" (Leung and Bond 1989: 133-134).

The basic dimensions of cultural difference affecting the communication patterns may be captured alternatively from either of two perspectives: the social sciences, and pragmalinguistics. The former aims at defining such differences on the level of hierarchies of values and attitudes; the latter starts from the analysis of speech and discovers its basic "cultural" parameters on the basis of verbal behaviour. The direct pragmalinguistic approach is exemplified by House (1996), who analysed non-natural German and English speech samples and identified the following dimensions of pragmatic difference in linguistic performance: directness/indirectness, orientation towards self/others, orientation towards contents/orientation towards addresses, explicitness/implicitness, and ad-hoc form/dependence on verbal routines. The other approach takes the dimensions of cross-cultural differences proposed by comparative anthropology and comparative social psychology as the starting point for an analysis of language samples.

Contrasts between cultures noted by comparative social anthropology are e.g. high vs. low context and polychrony vs. monochrony in approaching time, proposed by Hall and Hall (1980). A quantified comparison of numerous national cultures along a set of dimensions is offered in studies in comparative social psychology by Hofstede (1980), (1991), (2001), and Hofstede and Minkov (2010). The independent dimensions of cultural difference identified by Hofstede and widely accepted in comparative social sciences are individualism vs. collectivism (autonomy vs. interdependence), uncertainty avoidance, power distance, femininity vs. masculinity (relationship maintenance vs. ego-maintenance), and long vs. short-term orientation. These dimensions characterise communities in their social practice, attitudes, and value hierarchies rather than just their linguistic performance.

Within the last decade, social psychology has exerted a considerable influence upon linguists. Numerous authors have applied Hofstede's dimensions of cross-cultural difference to explicate contrasts in language use. Hofstede himself offers remarks about how the dimensions affect language form and usage. For example, in collectivist countries like Japan, where people are integrated into strong, cohesive groups, attempts are made to maintain harmony and avoid direct confrontation. Thus, "the word *no* is seldom used [...] [and] the word *yes* should not necessarily be seen as approval; rather, it may be used to maintain the communication line: *Hai* in Japanese stands not for yes but for 'yes, I heard you'" (Hofstede 2001: 228).

In several recent contrastive pragmalinguistic studies, Hofstede's framework was used predictively to formulate hypotheses, or as an explanatory device to account for observed features of discourses. Smith *et al.* (1998) looked for correlations between the ways to handle disagreement, and the scores on individualism and power distance in companies in twenty three countries. Dekker *et al.* (2008) used differences in power distance, masculinity, uncertainty avoidance and individualism to explain perception of communications in virtual workplaces located in four countries. Koeman (2007) investigated the correlation between individualism and direct communication in television commercials in five countries. Meeuwesen *et al.* (2009) studied doctor-patient interaction in ten EU countries looking for discursive correlates of power distance; correlations that were contrary to the expectations were elegantly explained away. Further contrastive pragmalinguistic studies that applied Hofstede's dimensions to interpret properties of discourses include Katan (2004), Katan (2006), and Cucchi (2010) for Italian and British English, Loukianenko Wolfe (2008) for English and Russian, Guillén-Nieto (2009) for Spanish and British/American English, as well as Hatipoğlu (2006) and Bjørge (2007) for English vs. English as Lingua Franca.

The links proposed in these studies between particular aspects of discourse and the aforementioned cultural dimensions may sometimes appear arbitrary and ad hoc. In the following study, which also seeks to bridge between pragmalinguistics and comparative social psychology, the validity of the proposed connections is substantiated through a careful examination of selected contextually-embedded interactions that follows after a quantitative analysis of tendencies in whole samples. Of the four dimensions of difference identified by Hofstede, it is the individualism/collectivism (autonomy/interdependence) distinction that will be central to this endeavour.

4.2. AUTONOMY AND INTERDEPENDENCE

Autonomy and interdependence, or individualism and collectivism, mean respectively: "preference for a loosely knit social framework in society in which individuals are supposed to take care of themselves and their immediate families only", and "preference for a tightly knit social framework in which individuals can expect their in-group to look after them, in exchange for unquestioning loyalty" (Hofstede 1991).

Individualism/collectivism is a variable concerning a society's tendencies towards a formation of in-groups and in-group bonds, related to the relative importance of duty and freedom as contrary values, and affecting the degree to which each participant of interaction presupposes the other's co-operation on the basis of assumptions about mutual responsibilities of group members towards each other. I assume that this variable relates, in a manner specified in the next chapter, to the application of indirect vs. direct approach as interaction strategies, and thus to negative and positive politeness (based respectively on deference/distance, and camaraderie). Apart from influencing the linguistic form, it can be expected to also influence the frequency with which in-group members address directives towards each other as a result of assumptions concerning mutual responsibilities.

Another dimension of sociopsychological difference which should be mentioned here because it has sometimes been conflated with collectivism and individualism in literature is femininity/masculinity. This variable refers to the degree of preference for typical "masculine" and typical "feminine" virtues – generally, preference for ego-enhancement, achievement, material possessions, money, unequal gender roles, and heroism on the one hand; or caring for the weak, life quality, modesty, equal gender roles, and relationship maintenance, *independent of in-group/out-group considerations*, on the other. The qualification marked in italics is important: an individual or society can show a high preference for maintenance of relationships to others over maintenance of individual achievement, without attaching high value to rights and responsibilities based on group membership.

In what follows I will assume that the respective amounts of autonomy and interdependence inherent in German, British and Polish society are different and that they affect the realisation of directive speech acts in these societies in ways that are predictable and systematic.

Basically, individualism refers to the broad value tendencies of a culture in emphasising the importance of an individual identity over group identity and rights independent of any group membership over rights based on group membership. Individualist and collective tendencies are manifested in everyday family, school, and workplace interaction. In individual societies, interpersonal relationships are established and maintained primarily on the basis of their individual costs and benefits, whereas relationships are judged primarily on their value to the group and only secondarily with respect to their value to the individual in a collectivist culture (Triandis 1995). According to Hui and Villareal (1989: 311), "individualists believe that the self is the basic unit of survival, while collectivists hold the view that the unit of survival lies in a group or several groups". Hofstede (1991) describes individualist societies as such in which "everyone is expected to look after him- or herself and his or her immediate family", whereas collectivist societies are such "in which people from birth onwards are integrated into strong, cohesive in-groups" and "there is an emphasis on affiliation, nurturance, and behaviour is strongly under the influence of roles and obligations" (Triandis 1988: 72). Following Hui (1984), Triandis (1988) distinguishes between *basic collectivism*, in which an individual is born into one large in-group which determines the whole of his or her life and prescribes the norms of behaviour, and *contextual collectivism*, where an individual can be a member of different in-groups exerting influences on one or more behaviours, and can be free to find him- or herself within the network of social relationships. Collectivism promotes relational interdependence[9], in-group harmony, and in-group collaborative spirit (Triandis 1995), while individualism promotes entrepreneur spirit and social change. Factors related to the amount of individualism are, among others, national wealth, population growth and historical roots.

In view of the variety of senses assigned to the notions of "group" and "in-group" in social psychology, it is useful at this point to outline their meanings more precisely. Brown (2000: 3-4) proposes an "intersubjective" definition in which a *group* "exists when two or more people define themselves as members of it and when its existence is recognized by at least one other". The critical factor for the existence of a group is the awareness of a common fate, owing to e.g. the same location, economic activity, threat from other groups, common boundaries, past grouping as one group, minority status (Campbell 1958, Triandis 1990: 53).

---

[9] While some authors speak about "interdependence" and "autonomy" (an individual's need to decide freely) using these terms as synonyms for "individualism" and "collectivism", others seek to establish correlations between collectivism on the one hand, affiliation and succorance on the other (e.g. Hui and Villareal 1989), or collectivism and interdependence (e.g. Markus and Kitayama 1991). As affiliation and interdependence are the main constituent parts of the definition of collectivism, and autonomy and self-reliance are the main constituent parts of the definition of individualism as they are usually defined and as I understand them, the correlation is suspect to circularity. In what follows, I will speak of "collectivism" or "individualism" referring to general preferences of a given culture, and "interdependence" or "autonomy" referring to the attitudes manifested by the interactants in particular situations under study.

Typically, group members show more positive evaluation of other group members than of group outsiders (Brown 2000). A *small group* is distinguished by face-to-face interaction of its members; all the data in the current analysis come from a group of this kind. The notion of *in-group* will be used in what follows in two senses, disambiguated by their particular contexts of use. In the first sense, the notion applies to a highly consolidated small group, where the criteria of consolidation comprise of sharing some goals, attitudes and norms of behaviour, mutual influence upon each other's norms and attitudes, supportiveness, and "social attraction between group members as group members, whatever they are like as individuals" (ibid: 46). In the second sense, frequently but not necessarily co-referential with the former, I will follow Brown's linguistic practice using the notion of an in-group to mean a group of any kind when juxtaposing it with an *out-group*, that is, the people outside the scope of the currently discussed group, who may also form a group of their own.

Major differences between individualistic and collectivist cultures have been summarised by Ting-Toomey (1999: 67):

Individualist cultures	Collectivist cultures
"I" identity	"we" identity
individual goals	group goals
individual emphasis	in-group emphasis
voluntary reciprocity	obligatory reciprocity
management of individuals	management of groups

On the psychological level, "the formation of personal identity is based on two principal mechanisms: individuation and identification ... The processes of cognitive separation and recognition of similarity between the self and others are interconnected with analogous processes concerning perception of the social world. Individuation and identification are the two opposing processes. Individuation ... if applied to oneself, [...] contributes to the growing differentiation of 'I/they'. The process of identification, on the other hand, blurs the boundaries ... Identification ... is a precondition for the development of the collectivism orientation ... It should be acknowledged that the two facets of self-identity develop unequally in different social settings. Some cultures foster individuation, whereas others foster identification ... The fact that both individualist and collectivist assumptions can coexist in a human mind does not deny that individuals and cultures differ widely in this respect. The differences among people can be explained as a result of unequal availability of the two facets of self-identity … Triandis (1989) concludes that 'aspects of the self … are differentially sampled in different cultures' (p. 517)" (Reykowski 1994: 279-280).

Triandis and Vassiliou (1972) worded their description of what makes the Greek rural society more collectivist than the American one in the following way: "In Greece the self is entangled with the ingroup. Achievement is not individual achievement but the achievement of the ingroup. (…) Within the ingroup, influence such as criticism is acceptable … social control is considered good."

The degree of a culture's individualism strongly influences moral stances. Miller (1991) argues that cultures differ to the extent to which they see interpersonal benefits and responsibility as a matter of individual choice (preference) and moral duty. Individualist cultures view the person as inherently autonomous, the individual as primary, duty as a matter of choice and consent. In the alternative view, duty and responsibility is mandatory and natural, rather than an imposition. The cultural focus is "on the desirability and naturalness of mutual support, rather then on the undesirability of constraint" (ibid: 22). Also, in situations of moral conflict, the members of collectivist cultures prefer loyalty to norms resulting from in-group bonds to loyalty to impersonal norms of justice or out-group members (Reykowski 1999: 28-29).

It has been claimed by several authors that the value orientation towards collectivism and individualism is reflected in speech as preference for certain patterns in realisations of speech acts. The following example illustrates this relationship. It has been frequently claimed by linguists from English-speaking countries that the interrogative sentence form as a vehicle of conventional indirectness is inherently polite because it is based on the principle of non-imposition upon the hearer, and saves the hearer's face by letting him or her an easy way out if he or she decides to refuse a request. Thus, by enhancing (or faking) choice and face-saving, conventional indirectness of "whimperatives" (directive questions, interrogative requests) is a means of being polite. An interesting facet of the question of "free choice" given to the speaker and the face-saving role of an interrogative form was pointed out to me by a member of a West African culture which, according to Hofstede's list, is very strong on collectivism. This speaker consistently refused to fulfil requests made (in German) by his family members in the "polite" interrogative form rather than an imperative followed by an illocutionary force indicating device (such as "bitte"). In his eyes, the crucial function of the interrogative was not as much giving the hearer a chance to say "no" but, rather, a denial of the speaker's dependence on the fulfilment of the request by the hearer. This minimised the object of request and the potential indebtedness of the speaker to the hearer, which was inherently impolite. In other words, disguising a request as an interrogation about the hearer's ability or willingness to do X is evaluated as an impolite strategy in which the speaker is trying to save his/her own face, rather than admit dependence on the hearer's action and elevate the hearer relative to the speaker. The direct request cherishes the addressee by admitting the importance of his or her socially expectable co-operation with the speaker. As the value orientation of West African societies is towards stressing interdependence, the strategy of giving choice and claiming self-sufficiency is inherently antisocial. A similar point was made by Wierzbicka (1996) with respect to Chinese family culture. For Wierzbicka, rather than being just conventionally indirect, the "whimperatives" (interrogative directives) do contain an interrogative semantic component consisting in the expression of the awareness on the part of the speaker that the hearer might refuse, and that the fulfilment of the request cannot be taken for granted. She defines autonomy as the right of each individual to choose his deeds freely, unimpeded by others, and says with reference to the Chinese culture that "with family members especially, the message of 'autonomy' would be culturally wrong" (ibid: 321).

Whereas using exclusively "negative politeness" where some amount of positive politeness is expected as a way to acknowledge interdependence might be universally impolite (or unfriendly), I assume that societies differ both in the range of social contexts in which positive politeness should or can be used, and in the proportion of positive (roughly: direct) to negative (roughly: indirect) politeness strategies.

In a study on Greek, Sifianou (1992 b) proposed to view the relatively high frequency of the imperative in realising directives as a reflection of close in-group bonds and the interaction participants' awareness of their respective duties and obligations. Blum-Kulka (1990), who studied directives in parent-child interaction, showed that Israeli parents tend to prefer "solidarity politeness" while American parents tend to prefer conventional politeness. "Asked to 'soften' a directive to a child, Israeli informants invariably responded by a shift in the tone of voice, and a questioning intonation, combining with a signal of endearment added to the name ... American respondents, on the other hand, marked the command for politeness by a shift in strategy from the direct to the conventionally indirect (typically using 'can you' or 'could you')." (1990: 278). The author concludes that "in juggling the needs for independence and involvement, American parents seem to display respect verbally for the child's independence at all ages, while in the Israeli society parents' discourse we find a higher degree of display of emotional involvement".

On the one hand, the extensive presence of directives and the directness in their expression in communication between socially-close peers are likely to be good indicators of the consensus about mutual rights and responsibilities, resulting in a lack of necessity to attend to the hearer's freedom of choice. On the other hand, as interdependence/autonomy interacts with other multiple facets of social conduct, it would be premature to claim that indirectness and lack of imposition reflects the quality of the group bonds, or perception of social distance. Various societies might have developed different means of expressing mutual concern and social closeness, and directive activities are only one among many aspects of their verbal display. This necessitates a contextualised analysis of directive utterances as a missing link between any quantitatively classified data and the causal interpretation of differences in terms of I/C hypothesis.

According to Hofstede (1991), examples of highly individualist societies are the United States, Australia, United Kingdom, Canada, and France. Less than one third of the world's population resides in predominantly individualist cultures. In addition, gender differences exist with respect to individualistic or relational-oriented values: females have generally been found to subscribe to collectivist values more than males who emphasise self-empowerment to a higher degree. In this evaluation, however, the notion of "individualism" seems to be unduly amalgamated with the ego-enhancement labelled "masculinity" or "ego-maintenance", and kept separate by Hofstede 1980, 1983 and 1991. Hofstede and Minkov (2010) ranked West German and British societies 67 and 89, respectively, in his job-related cross-cultural comparison on individualism among 91 countries; Poland scored 60. While I know of no studies comparing British and German subjects with respect to individualism and collectivism outside a work-related context, studies among German and Polish teenagers (Smoleńska and Frączek 1987, Smoleńska and Wieczorkowska 1990, Schonpflug and Jansen 1995) showed that there were striking differences between the two countries, surpassing the differences assessed in Hofstede and Minkov's study. The German teenagers manifested rather clearly an individualist orientation (they tended to subscribe to the view that "In deciding my fate I should take care of my own preferences only"), while the Polish subjects had collectivist inclinations (they tended to subscribe to the view "In deciding my fate I must take into account the well-being of people close to me"). The results of the COS test by Bierbrauer et al. (1994), conducted with German and Polish students whose mean age matched roughly the mean age of the Big Brother participants, showed that the Poles were higher on the scale of collectivism than their German counterparts. In light of these results, the Poles rank highest on collectivism among the three groups under analysis. These findings are supported by the conclusions of contrastive social psychologists applying the methodology of *Kulturstandardforschung*, based on field observations. Boski (2003) notes higher collectivism (or "humanism" as a positively connoted aspect of collectivism) of the Polish compared to the German culture.

As noted by Boski, "die Diskussion über Individualismus und Kollektivismus ist nicht wertfrei zu führen. Für diejenigen, die dem Individualismus positiv gegenüberstehen, ist es eine Lebensart, die mit Frieden, Selbstverantwortung, Selbstkontrolle, aktivem Handeln und Fortschritt in allen Bereichen einhergeht. "[10] The supporters of collectivism stress the human significance of social networking, social responsibility and warm-hearted, close interpersonal bonds ("herzliche, enge persönliche Beziehungen", ibid: 127). Because this discussion is by nature value-bond, the distinction between relationship maintenance ("femininity") and collectivism ("interdependence") cannot be emphasised enough. According to Hofstede (1980), a society's preference towards relationship maintenance over individual pursuits and achievements is not identical with scoring high on collectivism. While altruistic virtues can be practised on the basis of "tandem" bonds, such as love or friendship, in collectivism responsibility is based on joint group membership. A low score on collectivism does not imply any weakness of interpersonal bonds. Rather, it means that the network of social relationships is organised along more or less voluntary bonds between individual persons rather than group bonds. This also means that interpersonal boundaries can be dismantled or lowered without a threat to an individual self only when both sides perceptibly consent, rather than just by the fact that people have been pushed together by their shared background: neighbourhood, workplace, hospital ward, or participation in a Big Brother enterprise.

4.3. DIRECTIVE SPEECH ACTS

Searle (1976: 11) defines directives as speech acts whose illocutionary point is that "they are attempts of varying degrees ... by the speaker to get the hearer to do something". The propositional content is such that the speaker predicates something about a future act of the hearer, the preparatory condition is that the speaker believes that the hearer is able to perform the act and is not going to perform it without the speaker's verbal action, and sincerity condition is that the speaker wants the hearer to perform the act. Directives are realised in the form of utterances identifiable by applicability of such speech verbs as order, request, demand, beg, advice and offer (Searle 1976: 11). Bach and Harnish (1979: 47) defined directives as expressions that "express the speaker's attitude towards some prospective action by the hearer" and they also "express the speaker's intention ... that his

---

[10] "The discussion about individualism and collectivism cannot take place in absence of attributions of value. For those who are well-minded about individualism, it is a way of life associated with peace, self-governance, self-control, initiating action and progress in all fields" (transl. HP).

utterance or the attitude it expresses be taken as (a) reason for the hearer to act." The use of the indefinite article is significant as it eradicates the requirement that the hearer is expected *not* to perform the predicated act in absence of the directive, and replaces it with the speaker's intention to enhance the probability of performing the desirable action by the hearer. Thus, it also includes in directives utterances uttered in ignorance of the actual hearer's intention, or in the co-presence of other directive utterances by other speakers. This less restrictive definition is more compatible with natural data, and has been adopted for the selection of data in this study.

4.3.1. SUB-CLASSIFICATIONS OF DIRECTIVES AND INADEQUACY OF THE DYADIC MODEL OF COMMUNICATION

Markkanen (1985: 23), who analysed requests cross-linguistically, concluded that "finding reliable criteria for a sub-classification in two languages is very difficult, and that no such subdivision is felt necessary" as the criteria of a sub-classification of directives are either vague or language-specific or both. Several other authors, though, have proposed some sub-classification schemes. Leech (1983) differentiates impositives which imply the transfer of goods or services from the hearer to the speaker, and commissives which imply a transfer in the opposite direction. Spearber and Wilson (1986) classify directives into requestive and advisory, on the basis of whether the future action is good for/in the interest of the hearer or the speaker. Edmondson and House (1981) distinguish between suggests and requests on the same basis. Tsui (1994: 100) believes that a distinction is necessary between requests and proposals; the latter commit both the speaker and the addressee to a future action. Aimer (1996), on the other hand, believes that 'proposals' involving both the speaker and the hearer "result from defocalisation strategies or impersonalisation devices and are accounted for on the dimension of politeness or modification", that is, that a separate category of proposals is unnecessary as they are "requests in disguise". She distinguishes between requests (beneficial to the speaker) and advisories; the latter include offers (the future action is to be carried out by the speaker and to benefit the addressee) and advice (the future action is to benefit the addressee and to be carried out by the addressee).

The other criterion of classification of directive utterances is hierarchical distance and obligation. Green (1975) divides directives into orders, demands, requests, pleas, and suggestions along these lines. Pufal-Bax (1986: 676) believes that non-advisory directives constitute a continuum spreading between requests and orders depending on the degree of the addressee's subordination to the speaker or its absence, which determines the addressee's obligation of compliance:

> Thus, requests and orders have the following in common: their main illocutionary point is that X, the addresser, wants Y, the addressee, to do something. This future act by Y is at cost for Y. The difference between requests and orders can be mainly described as follows: in a request, the requesting person benefits from the future act. By contrast, in an order, the person does not necessarily have to benefit from A. With regard to the social aspect, this means that Y complies with a request because s/he wants to do X a favour, who then is indebted to Y. On the other hand, obeying an order means that Y has to perform A by virtue of X having power over Y, and that, as a result, X is not indebted to Y. Thus, requests occur between interlocutors in a reciprocal relationship, or when the addresser is in a less powerful position, whereas orders are given in relationships in which the addressee is inferior.

I believe the speech act theory, and newer approaches inspired by its concepts, to be biased towards the dyadic model of communication, which is reflected in the dyadic account of directives based on a cost-benefit calculus and hierarchical distance. This bias seems to follow from the general predominance in human sciences of the Occidental perspective, with its individualist stand, in the conception of human interaction. The main facet of this stand is the neglect of the group-oriented component of human interaction in favour of its inter-individual, i.e. interpersonal component. Brown (2000) concluded referring to the Ameropean social psychology: "Even the most cursory survey of currently popular textbooks and the main scientific journals reveals that group processes receive very short shrift indeed compared to phenomena associated with dyadic or interpersonal relationships and – increasingly in recent years – individual cognitive processes ... Where group behaviour is discussed, considerable emphasis is often given to its negative or socially undesirable aspects – deindividuation, prejudice, social loafing and 'groupthink' – rather than the more positive aspects of team spirit, intergroup cooperation, group productivity and collective problem solving. Indeed, such is the concentration on the allegedly anti-social nature of groups that one commentator has been moved to suggest, only half-jokingly, that 'Humans would do better without groups' (Buys, 1978)." Brown perceives this tendency as an aspect of a broader ideological trend in the industrialised West where "governments proclaim the virtues of individual enterprise and choice, and denigrate policies aimed at promoting social welfare and collective responsibility ... collective bargaining is being replaced by private contract between employer and employee; the owner of a small business, battling against government bureaucracy, is championed while a group of workers occupying a factory due for closure is ridiculed" (Brown 2000: XIV). The following study seeks to outbalance the cultural and scientific neglect of groups in linguistic pragmatics, as Brown did in social psychology. The study of language use that ignores or neglects the study of groups, i.e. of people acting towards each other in the awareness of being members of same or different groups, is unlikely to help us understanding some important facets of human communication. According to Brown and Turner (1981: 46), "the direct extrapolation of theories about interpersonal behaviour to group contexts is inherently fraught with difficulties and … alternative theories, relating specifically with group behaviour, are necessary".

The individualist bias characteristic of the Occidental human sciences criticised by Brown has been transferred also to the study of societies which show less individualism in their social practice. Two decades ago, writing on the influence of Western focus upon one-to-one relationships, an Indian social psychologist put it this way:

> … many scholars from the Western world working in these countries tend to perceive and value other cultures in terms of their own and impose their own values in their effort to understand a diverse culture. In either case, non-Western cultures and their psychological functioning tend to be viewed through the lens of Western psychological theories … Individualistic orientation that generally characterizes the Western psychology has been taken for granted and is freely used in formulating problems for research. To give only one instance, in tune with individualistic bias … parent-child interactions has frequently been studied to assess its influence on children's linguistic, cognitive and social development. The specific feature of the Indian family setting is ignored. Typical interaction pattern in the Indian system is rarely between individual to individual as such, but it is group or collective-based (Sinha 1980: 159), and 'contextual' … instead of analysing only the influence on parent-child interaction, it is more appropriate to take into cognisance the entire context or 'ecology' in which the development of the child takes place. That is, the roles of cousins, aunts and older relations who frequently act as parental surrogates cannot be ignored … In other words, the total psychological climate of the entire family complex, if not community, in which the child grows has to be analysed … overawed under Western influence, many … scholars have ignored these contextual factors and thereby missed the important causative influence that the 'collective' exerts on the growing child (Sinha 1983: 3).

Sinha (1983) terms this sort of bias "imposed etics" or "Euro-American emics".

Similarly, a linguist's approach to interaction can be influenced by the degree to which he or she perceives the individual as autonomous and co-operation as secondary. One effect of this might be the predominance of the "autonomy perspective" in the contemporary research in pragmatics, whose basic notions have been worked out by writers from English-speaking countries.

Rather than to always result from a hierarchical distance, the obligation to comply to a directive may involve the addressee's social obligations independent of social inequality and resulting from the participation in a "greater whole". For the same reasons, it is not clear that in most interactions the benefit to the hearer and benefit to the speaker are mutually exclusive and disconnected. As our social life is organised by memberships in various groups, it seems typical that the benefits of potentially desirable actions are not confined to one person. An action requested by S from H can be beneficial to both S and H and possibly other individuals through their common membership in a group such as a family, a work-group, a team, an enterprise or a school class. This invalidates classifications based on the dyadic cost-benefit calculus. Pufal-Bax's proposal of viewing directives as occupying a particular position in a continuum spread between the extremes of "order" and "request" does not meet the point either, because the pools of the continuum are defined in accordance with the "debt or authority" hypothesis. This I hold to be amply falsified by the following exemplary interaction:

1-G2. NUDE UNDER SHOWER
M considers breaking a promise given to his mother. F2 has just argued that he should not.
1 M ja # vielleicht überlege ich mir das mal # aber-
yeah # maybe I will have another think about it # but-
2 F1 hör auf # tu's deiner Mami nicht an # [wenn du es versprochen hast?]
stop that # don't do this to your Mum # if you promised?
3 F2 [nein # du hast es versprochen]
no # you promised
4 F3 [versprochen ist versprochen]
a promise is a promise
5 F4 [du hast es versprochen]
you promised

Here, a demand on the behalf of the addressee's ingroup member (his mother) is articulated by members of the current group, perceiving him as obliged to stick to the general rules of moral conduct.

The linguistic research on requests so far represents the view that the needs and wants of the interaction participants are independent of each other, so that people have to use politeness strategies to mitigate their requests because the benefit is theirs and the cost is on the side of the person of whom the action is requested. Questionnaires and role plays typically support the individualistic perspective, as the situations invented in order to test strategies of requesting are commonly situations of one-sided benefit on the part of the speaker.[11] The underlying assumption of the "mitigation" view is that people communicate in order to satisfy needs prior to interaction and communication.

The following examples illustrate the omnipresence in everyday life of directives where the speaker is a non-exclusive beneficiary of a directive utterance. In recommendations aiming at sharing a sensation between S and H the "benefit" to S is a phatic communion with H. (As shown by the data processed in this study, the recommended sensations are not necessarily enjoyable.) Exemplary recommendations are 1-E2. feel the water # how oily it is uttered during a joint bath, and the situation 2-G2. FEMALE PHOTO in which S gives H a photo of a woman which he finds beautiful, saying guck dir das mal an ("have a look at this"). There is no other potential benefit to the speaker than the shared emotion or evaluation. In both cases, S seeks a phatic communion with H and believes that H might also be interested in a phatic communion with S. The difference between a piece of advice and a request, differentiated by the hearer's and the speaker's benefit, is neutralised. This illustrates the difference between the situations created in real-life interactions and questionnaires based on pre-selection, where joint or interdependent targets are absent.

Such considerations invalidate the proposal by Leech, who sees the "direction of transfer" of goods and services as a differentiator of offers and requests. In many cases, however, whenever people engage in a common social activity, the distinction is no longer very relevant, as it is not possible to "objectively" evaluate which way the transfer goes. If S is proposing to have sex or a game of chess with H, the proposal can be worded either as S doing something for H, or H doing something for S, or S and H doing something together. To take another example, in episode 3-E1, a participant reacts to a quarrel between two other housemates saying: I think we should have a game. She is at the same time requesting, advising and offering assistance: requesting the quarrelling parties to stop, advising them to stop, and offering help in putting the conflict to an end through participation in an alternative

---

[11] Cf. Held (1995); Blum-Kulka at al. (1989); LePair (1996).

joint activity.

The very fact of an interaction taking place manifests the interdependence of the aims and objectives of S and H. A request could not be uttered if S did not believe that fulfilling the request, H might realise some of his or her own objectives, such as the integrative need to be useful to others. Similarly, a piece of advice is uttered when S believes that the fulfilment of the directive by H would be convergent with S's preferences, such as the preference for social contacts with healthy and happy individuals.

One may confine the study of directives to the study of personal advice and requests for a personal favour – that is, to those utterances which aim at the exclusive benefit of either the speaker or the addressee. The question is whether examining such utterances and excluding others reveals or obscures basic facts about human communication and differences in cultural styles. The answer may depend on the analyst's world view, influenced by national culture or its particular subculture.

To sum up, the actual complexity of communicative situations exceeds that suggested by the traditional model, in which the interaction takes place between the speaker and the hearer, there is a unidirectional transfer of "goods and services", other participants' roles are underdetermined, and the speaker as well as the hearer represent themselves alone and speak for themselves. In the approaches which developed out of the speech act theory, in-group and out-group considerations are replaced by the concepts of social distance and distance in a hierarchy ("power distance"). These two notions are conceptually focused on an individual participant and the relation between individual participants. There emerges a need to replace these representations by a model sensitive to group aspects of the social context of communication, which would also provide an alternative set of criteria for a sub-classification of directives.

In particular, the rejection of the dyadic communication model is realised in the following analysis by differentiating among several sorts of a "beneficiary structure", and analysing correspondences between forms of directive utterances and their beneficiary structures.

4.3.2. REQUESTIVES: A DEFINITION

Like numerous other works on directive activities, the sub-classification of directives proposed in this study borrows its basic terms from common speech. Common speech classifies directive utterances into various classes such as advice, instructions, requests, suggestions and offers, which unify frequently occurring correlations on several dimensions of contrast. Such classifications are to some extent culture specific but the ones used in the three languages studied here show considerable similarities.

Diagram 1 shows the sub-classification of directives underlying the following analysis. The subdivision of "do-directives" is based on the relations between the "communicative roles" SPEAKER and HEARER on the one hand, and the "performatory roles" ACTOR and BENEFICIARY of the act predicated in the directive on the other. The resulting categories are: *offers*, as far as they are directive (action by S and H, benefit to H), *proposals* (action by S and H, usually for joint benefit), *requests* (action by H to benefit S) and *advice* (action of H to benefit H). The same criteria inform sub-classifications of directives in linguistic studies reflecting the tradition of the speech act theory. They will be utilised in the following analysis together with further distinctions, explained in section 4.3.3.

Requestives, advisories and **requirements** (do-directives) are directives which refer to the alternative between an action and non-action of the hearer. In other words, they are not based on the speaker's certain knowledge about the hearer's intention to perform the action.

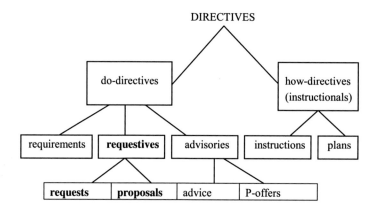

Diagram 1. A sub-classification of directive utterances.

The differentiation between requestives and requirements originates from Bach and Harnish (1982: 47), who elaborated on Searle's (1976) illocutionary acts and defined them as follows:

- requestives (e.g. ask, tell, beg, request, invite, insist):
  "In uttering e, S requests H to A if S expresses:
  - i.   the desire that H do A,
  - ii.   the intention that H do A because of (or at least partly of) S's desire."
- requirements
  "In uttering e, S requires H to A if S expresses:
  - i.   the belief that his utterance, in virtue of his authority over H, constitutes the sufficient reasons for H to A, and
  - ii.   the intention that H do A because of S's utterance."

For the purpose of the following analysis, requestives will be distinguished from requirements and advisories by the following criteria:

Requirements depend on institutionalised or enforced subordination of H to S with respect to the sort of action in question; the fulfilment of the demand is mandatory for the hearer. Typical contexts are institutionalised work, education, sport, and military organisations.

Requestives are directives that
- are not based on institutionalised or enforced subordination of the hearer to the speaker making it mandatory for the hearer to obey;
- are addressed to a hearer who is not the main beneficiary of the action referred to in the communicative act (although the hearer may belong to its beneficiaries).

Advisories are directives addressed to the hearer which fulfil the following conditions:
- there is no obligation on the part of the hearer to follow the directive, e.g. as a consequence of a nurturing relationship in which the speaker has an authority over the hearer;
- the hearer is the main beneficiary of the action referred to in the communicative act.

"Main beneficiary" is the beneficiary whose benefit from the predicated action the utterance strongly focuses upon.

In advisories, H is by definition the main beneficiary; in requestives H may be included among other beneficiaries.

In advice, the action beneficial to the hearer is to be performed by the hearer herself. In P-offers, a joint or coordinated action beneficial to the hearer is offered by the speaker.

Instructionals have sometimes been defined as oriented towards the hearer's benefit (e.g. in Hindelang 1976); it does not however seem to me that the beneficiary identity is relevant with respect to this category. Instructionals (how-directives) pertain to the way to perform tasks whose performance itself is within the scope of an already negotiated consensus, or tasks imposed from without by a superior force[12]. In an instructional, the speaker knows or assumes that the hearer intends to perform (or participate in) an action, whatever its motivation and beneficiary; and refers to the details of this action. The difference between spoken instructions and plans is gradable rather than absolute; it pertains to the level of abstractness vs. descriptive detail, time frame, and the speaker's participation. *Instructions* inform the hearer how, when and where to perform the intended action, alone or in co-operation with the speaker, in order to best achieve its known purpose; the action is simultaneous with, or follows shortly upon the utterance. Prototypical instructions are those which refer to manual manipulation of objects. *Plans* are more abstract, refer to a more distant future and pertain to actions involving the speaker's active participation; examples of plans are specifications of the division of labour in joint activities like preparing a party or a workshop, and formulations of the rules of future co-operation.

Instructionals appear both if the vertical social distance is low, and in authority-based relationships between the speaker and the hearer. In the latter case, they can be attached to a *requirement* to perform an action and specify the details of this action.

The subject of the following statistical analysis is non-advisory directives. Advisories are outside the scope of statistical analysis in this study, while some borderline cases between requestive and advisory directives will be discussed in the qualitative part. Instructionals (how-directives) will be only referred to when this helps to understand cross-linguistic differences in requestives.

Excluded from the scope of this study are requests for turn, requests for permission and requests for information in the form of promptive questions (i.e. without a verb of speaking)[13].

---

[12] Another type of instructional – exemplified by a written instruction of use, cooking recipe, and its spoken equivalents – is an explanation concerning the way to perform an action involving the manipulation and use of physical objects. Such instructionals are directed from an expert (knower) to a non-expert (non-knower) and are based on the assumption that the hearer might be willing to perform the action in question in a non-immediate future, and be in need of knowing the technical detail. Their illocutionary function is to give information; they are non-directive, and outside the scope of this study.

[13] Cf. Pułaczewska 2006, unpublished manuscript (Habilitationsschrift) containing the full version of this study.

4.3.3. INTERACTIVE STRUCTURE OF REQUESTIVE UTTERANCES

The interactive structure of directive utterances pertains to questions such as:

- Who speaks to whom when issuing the requestive utterance?
- On whose behalf?
- What kind of behaviour is the goal of the utterance?
- Whose behaviour?

The dimensions of interactive structure listed below are not a priori concepts but followed from the analysis of the data to hand, i.e., proved to influence the use of certain syntactic and semantic devices pertaining to politeness strategies in at least one of the languages under consideration.

ACTION STRUCTURE

The term "action structure" corresponds to Blum-Kulka's (1990) "goal" of a requestive utterance. The directives analysed in the following study are of two types:

- initiating - asking for *action*
- inhibitive - asking for *non-action,* including
  - terminating (present-based: asking to stop a current behaviour),
  - preventive (future-based),
  - corrective (past-based: asking for a non-repetition of a past behaviour).

PARTICIPANTS' CHARACTERISTICS

Taking all of the participants' demographic characteristics into account in the following analysis was not a viable undertaking. Instead, I chose to concentrate on a distinction which was created interactively by the participants, i.e., the one between plural and singular addressees. This distinction is in accord with the general focus of the study on the individualism-collectivism dichotomy as differentiator of cultures and trends in language use.

PARTICIPANTS' ROLES

The participants' structure of a requestive utterance includes

- the communicative roles of the speaker (S) and the addressee (hearer, H)
- the performatory roles of the actor of the proposed action and its beneficiary.

ADDRESSEE

The requestives under analysis will be categorised according to the number of addressees, distinguishing between SA (single addressee) and MA (multiple addressee).

BENEFICIARY

To replace the individualist perspective on directives by a view stressing interdependence of interlocutors' aims and resulting interdependence of benefits, I will distinguish the following configurations of the communicative roles (S, H) and the performatory role "beneficiary":

- S is included in the beneficiaries of the predicated action
- H is included in the beneficiaries of the predicated action
- there is a third party (that is, a party distinct from H and S) who is a beneficiary.

Considerations pertaining to the beneficiary structure and general language use resulted in the following subcategorisation:

- **proposals** - requestives proposing a joint action of the hearer and the speaker (actor includes both H and S). Exceptions are directives whose beneficiary is the speaker, with or without a third party, and not the hearer of the proposed action – these are requests.
- **requests** - requestives which predicate the action of the hearer and not the speaker, or predicate a joint action of the speaker and the hearer for the speaker's, and not the hearer's, benefit.

Although the non-technical language use initially informed my choice of the labels proposal, request and advice as technical terms, full convergence is not attainable and the technical use of these labels will extend to speech acts which oppose some aspects of their use in general language. "Request" is defined in Longman's dictionary[14] as "an act of asking for something, esp. politely". This definition pertains at the same time to the illocutionary force and the form of request as a directive speech act. In what follows, the term "request" will also be attached to utterances which do not manifest conventional politeness in their linguistic form. Also, the considerations of the obligation of fulfilment on the hearer's part (low obligation seems to be preferred in the general use of "request") had to be excluded from the definition of request as a technical term. Firstly, there are no culture-independent standards for judgements on obligation; secondly, the hearer concludes from the utterance form, among others, the extent to which the speaker perceives the hearer as obliged to fulfil

---

[14] Longman Dictionary of Contemporary English 1987.

the request; thirdly, the relatedness between the perception of obligation and the linguistic form is one of the issues pursued in this study. Therefore, it was necessary to keep them separate on the level of the basic classification of the material to be analysed.

The rejection of a dyadic communication model is reflected in the analytical categories applied. Precisely speaking, it is reflected in the recognition that the beneficiary of the action may be non-identical with the speaker, the hearer, or both. This includes situations of :

- "Group preference" – where the predicated action is meant to benefit the group, and the speaker and the hearer are beneficiaries of the action via their membership in the group; this also includes "norm preference" – where S is demanding from H compliance to a social norm and the focus of the benefit is the internalised norm itself, abstractly related to its source, such as a society. The benefit to the ingroup, as well as the benefit to the speaker and the hearer, is indirect and results from the participation in the wider social context which provides the norm.
- "Other preference" – where S is demanding from H an action beneficial to another person/animal, X, on the ground of S's and H's responsibilities towards X, resulting from a common membership in a group or ingroup (family, work group, sport team, religious community, gender group, mankind) or a nurturing relationship between X and S or H or both (domestic animals).

In addition to the primary classification of requestives into proposals and requests, the following configurations of the communicative roles of speaker and hearer with the performatory role of beneficiary will be distinguished:

- beneficiary equals S
- beneficiary equals H and S
- beneficiary includes H, S, and an external party
- beneficiary is an external party
- beneficiary equals H
- beneficiary includes H and an external party but excludes S

Examples of utterances counted to each category are given below.

Group 1 –S, +H, +EXT Utterances of this group are similar to pieces of advice in which S suggests an action by H to H's own advantage, but also additionally involve an external beneficiary on a par with H.

2-P3 . A group of housemates are sitting on the edge of a hot tub; F1 approaches them in order to join in. It is known to other housemates that M1 and F1 fancy each other.

M2 to M1: wiesz co? będzie jej cieplej # chyba jak będzie tu siedzieć obok
ciebie # wpuść --- tu to myśle że będzie tutaj bardzo ciepło
you know what? # she will get warmer # if she is sitting here next to you # let her in --- and then
I think it will be very warm here
(M1 makes place for F1 to sit next to him)

Group 2 –S, -H, +EXT   Beneficiaries are absent group members and group members who are present
but not addressed, pet animals, (absent) family members, production crew of Big Brother, viewers, or social
norms.

2-E3. M1 is climbing up the wall in order to leave the house.

M2 don't let him # don't let him go # don't let him go # cause he'll hurt
himself # don't let him go

Group 3 +S, -H, -EXT   S is the main beneficiary of the predicated action.

3-E3. F has received bad news.

F can you all just piss off # please # out of my space for the time being

About half of the requestives from this group have the character of requests for
personal favours. The rest are requests, claims and demands of other sorts, such as in the
example 3-E3 above or 5-E3 :

5-E3. F starts talking to M who is standing several meters away about a piece of gossip.

F Tom # . can you tell # . come over here Tom (accompanied by the gesture of
"come to me")

Group 4 +S, -H, +EXT   S shares the benefit from the predicated action with an external
party.

5-G2. M1, M2, F1 enter the room where M2 is preparing the breakfast he promised to make.

M wo ist denn # das Frühstück
where is then # the breakfast

Group 5 +S,+H,-EXT   This group is richly diversified because of the diversity of the situation in which the action proposed might be viewed as being favourable to both parties.

6-E3. The housemates are gathered round the table at dinner time.
```
F we could start with this chicken now
```

Consider also the following example of a relationship-oriented request based on the assumption that H reciprocates S's friendly feelings:

7-E3. F1, F2, M1, M2 move into a new bedroom.
```
F1 to F2: Jane # you can go here
```
(pointing to a bed next to hers)

This group also includes requestives performing a phatic function in which S is asking H to pay attention to some kind of sensory data in a full unit of interaction that can constitute a turn of its own, such as the following:

2-G2. M1 hands a photo of a female to M2.
```
M1 guck dir das mal an
```
have a look at this

Group 6 +S,+H,+EXT   The beneficiary includes the speaker, the hearer and further beneficiaries.
5-P3. A team who lost a competition on the first day plan how to act in order to win further competitions. After urging his team to work harder, M goes on defining the behaviour towards the other team.
```
M z nimi to się będziemy mimo wszystko bratać # bo to nasi ludzie są #
nasza grupa
```
we will chum up with them anyway # because they are our people # our group

This preliminary classification was followed by identifying those clusters of parameters which reflect the degree of interdependence as perceived by the interaction participants. They are defined in chapter 5.1. where the results of the frequency analysis are presented.

4.3.4. INTERACTIVE STRUCTURE AND COLLECTIVISM VS. INDIVIDUALISM

The occurrence of directive activities, by which housemates influence and regulate each other's behaviour, displays assumptions concerning mutual rights and obligations, as well as the speaker's perception of the relationship or relationships within the group. In the following analysis, I characterise and contrast those quantifiable aspects of directive activities in six series of Big Brother that I expect to differentiate between more individualist and more collectivist oriented attitudes of group members. The assumption is that group-orientation, individual-orientation, exerting in-group control, overtaking responsibility for other group members, and an assumption of autonomy are displayed in directive activities. I also assume that the nature of the in-group bonds correlates with the amount of directive activities in general and, even more so, with directive activities representing particular types of interactive structure.

To simplify the general overview, the preliminary classification of directives into six beneficiary groups, presented in the previous section, was followed by identifying two clusters that I assume to capture the relationship between directive activities and the degree of interdependence:

Intervention: directives whose beneficiaries do not include the speaker – clusters beneficiary categories (1) –S, +H, +EXT and (2) –S, -H, +EXT. The sum of these two beneficiary configurations will also be noted as (–S). By producing a directive of that type, the speaker shows that s/he finds it legitimate to attempt affecting the behaviour of the addressee oriented towards a third party. The speaker producing a directive of that type views her- or himself as responsible for the behaviour of other group members towards each other, towards outgroup members, or adherence to social norms; and regards her- or himself as entitled to interfere with this behaviour.

Representation: directives whose beneficiaries include both the speaker and a third party (non-addressee), and may or may not include the addressee. This factor clusters beneficiary groups (6) +S, +H, +EXT and (4) +S, -H, +EXT. Their sum will also be noted as (+EXT, +S). The speaker acts towards the addressee as a representative of a group, sharing the interest in the performance of the predicated act with others.

Another indicator of social orientation is the **number of addressees in directives** - a single addressee (SA) and **multiple addressees** (MA). Frequent production of requestives directed at more than one person is likely to correspond to the speaker's perception of others as groups, approachable *in toto*, and the trust in the possibility to influence behaviour of

53

groups. Accordingly, frequent production of requestives directed at groups will be regarded as a sign of group-orientation.

While all kinds of requestives occurring in interaction certify the assumption by the interaction participants that they may legitimately attempt to influence each other's behaviour, I assume that requestives displaying intervention, representation and multiple addressee are particularly informative as indicators of group-orientation.

4.3.5. ABOUT COST

In the tradition of politeness study, an important contextual factor potentially influencing the linguistic form of a directive is the "cost" of performing the action it predicates. Brown and Levinson (1987) state that perceived imposition is ranked in proportion to "cost" of performing the action by the addressee, while the ranking is also influenced by other variables which can alter the degree of imposition (and with it, the need to use mitigating strategies). The non-natural methods such as role-plays and questionnaires are sometimes designed to check the effect of this factor on form by varying the "cost" of the actions asked for (cf. e.g. Held 1995).

In the natural data, the "cost" of the performance of an action to the addressee spreads through a vast spectrum starting from performing simple acts of perception, and ending in complex actions. In order to find out whether analysing the influence of cost upon the formal structure of directives would make sense for the corpora under study, I undertook a preliminary categorisation of data looking at this property. The corpora did not provide clear criteria for such a differentiation[15]. Requestives representing high cost as it is conventionally understood (such as hosting a stranger, or lending a car) were absent from the data. Requestives of potentially highest cost within the sample were such heterogeneous species as e.g. giving intimate information on oneself to the group (and the cameras), performing in front of the group (and the cameras), or cooking a meal for the group. The estimation of the cost in the first two examples depends on the speaker's (and the researcher's) perception of the addressee's anxiety or desire of public exposure. This estimation is person-specific and culture-specific, and relates to the value a given culture attaches to privacy and secrecy of personal information.

---

[15] It also should be noted that a study by Goldschmidt (1996), conducted in the USA, showed that there is very little interpersonal agreement on the cost and degree of imposition constituted by particular requests for personal favours.

Another type are the "lowest-cost directives", which refer to minimal actions of the speaker, such as, for initiating directives, show, listen, tell, taste, look at something, drink cheers, stretch a hand to support S, or kiss a (female) speaker on the cheek, and for inhibitive directives to stop talking, stop saying something (particular), and talk quietly. In all the groups, non-tentative forms, such as the imperative and the ellipsis, seem to be the only strategy used in their realisations, except in singular cases of sarcastic overpoliteness in corrective inhibitives. In particular, invitations to share a perception (auditory, oligatory, visual, gustatory, and tactile) are always formulated in the imperative.

Because the "minimal cost" requestives are realised in the same ways in all three groups, excluding them from the data would diminish the assessed similarities of linguistic form between the groups. As there is nothing "basic" about any level of cost, no priority is offered here to the questionnaire-type directives, such as requests for personal favours, and they are not treated as a point of reference. Hence, minimal cost directives including basic "attention organisers" are included in the statistically analysed data. Their proportion in particular languages amounts to between 10% and 12%.

Notwithstanding the difficulties with cost assessment, a preliminary analysis showed that while the lowest cost promoted the use of the imperative and elliptical constructions, the negatively polite head acts in all groups were evenly distributed among potentially highest-cost and middle-cost requestives. On the whole, though, research along these lines appeared to be unpromising. This was not a surprise, since the cost concept emerged as part of the study of directives in the dyadic model of communication and becomes diffuse when confronted with ingroup communication. Cost will not be considered in the following statistical analysis.

4.3.6. A MODEL OF PRODUCTION AND INTERPRETATION OF SPEECH

In the model of speech production applied in this study, an *interaction participant* realises his *communicative goal* via an adequately selected *speech act* by generating an appropriate *linguistic form* from among the forms which can be generated by a given *language* (understood as rules applied to inventories). The speech act is selected and the linguistic form generated in a way based on the participant's knowledge of the *context* and guided by his or her *personality* using *pragmatic rules* which are partly based on universal logic and partly language-specific. The pragmatic rules are co-determined by the specific characteristics of a given *culture,* and their criteria of application pertain to *participant characteristics, situation characteristics* and other features of the *context* relevant to the given speech act. The choices made by the interaction participants are his or her *strategy*.

Diagrams 2 and 3 visualise the mutual relationships between the theoretical notions. Diagram 2 shows a general structure where the type of speech act to be realised is left unspecified. Pragmalinguistic conventions affect choices of two kinds: the choice of a particular speech act to realise a given social and communicative goal, and the linguistic form of a given speech act from among forms available in a given language. Pragmalinguistic conventions recommend particular choices for the current configuration of situation characteristics and social characteristics of the participants; these conventions in turn are influenced by the characteristics of a given culture. Individual differences in the choices of linguistic forms from the means provided by language inventory are covered by a notion of personality, which in turn is influenced, but not determined, by predominant tendencies of the given culture. At the same time, pragmatic conventions provide an input to language inventory by lexicalisation and grammaticalisation of recurrent patterns resulting from conventionalisation of responses to recurrent constellations of situational contexts and communicative needs.

Diagram 3 shows the recurrent aspects of context putatively relevant to the production of directive speech acts.

Diagram 2. A model of speech production.

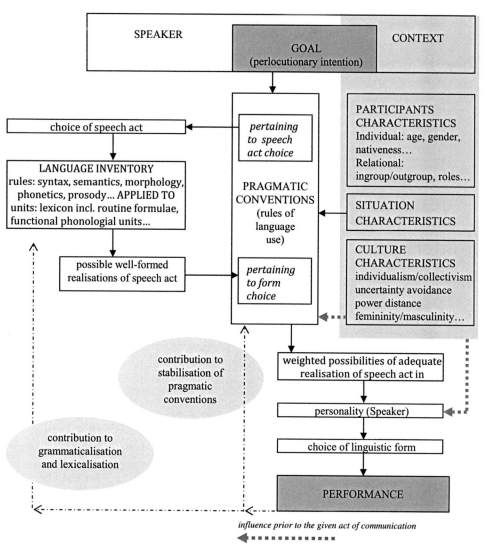

CONTEXT - DIRECTIVE SPEECH ACTS	
PARTICIPANTS CHARACTERISTICS	**SITUATION CHARACTERISTICS**
Individual SPEAKER/HEARER/BENEFICARY/ AUDIENCE: single/multiple, age, gender, education, social status, nativeness …	action type (inhibitive/initiating) cost to hearer cost to speaker benefit to beneficiary legitimacy
Relational SPEAKER TO HEARER HEARER TO BENEFICIARY SPEAKER TO BENEFICIARY	**CULTURE CHARACTERISTICS** individualism/collectivism power distance uncertainty avoidance
INGROUP social roles / OUTGROUP power difference social distance institutionalisation social roles	

4.3.7. DIRECTIVES AND CONVERSATIONAL ROUTINES

The notion of a "conversational routine" applied in the following study pertains to recurrent correspondences between utterance form and utterance function, such that a given function is frequently realised by a given form, and a given function has a high frequency among functions realised by a given form. The fact that the declarative sentence form in general is frequently used for realising directive speech acts cannot be subsumed under conversational routines because of the many functions of a declarative, whereas the use of a declarative sentence in present tense 1st person plural for making proposals ("We will sing a song") constitutes a conversational routine in some languages.

Conventionalized aspects of the form may be:

- syntactic – coupling of a particular function (speech act) with one of basic syntactic sentence types (interrogative, imperative, declarative, etc.),
- morphosyntactic – a specialisation of a particular word form (i.e. mood, aspect, tense of a verb) at fulfilling a particular function,
- syntactic/lexical – when an intention is routinely realized by a certain type of a syntactic construction with some or all syntactic slots filled in by specified lexical material, or a lexical item from a specifiable finite list (sentence builders: lexical phrases that are frames for whole sentences[16]),
- prosodic – when a specific function is routinely realised by an utterance with some specific prosodic features[17].

Language use includes "pre-patterned speech"[18]. The mental lexicon does not only contain single words and fully frozen idioms but also numerous partly lexicalised patterns with fill-in "blanks" for syntactic and lexical completion, which are applied in a stereotyped way in recurrent contexts and which ensure fluency and self-confident behaviour.

In the following study, the notions pertaining to routine function-form correspondences will be applied in the following way:

- Conversational routines – the broadest category, any conventional coupling between utterance form and its function, including the routine use of basic sentence patterns (e.g. imperative, optative) and prosodic patterns to perform particular illocutions (requesting, proposing), and conversational formulae;
- conversational formulae – refer to the specialisation for a given function of phrases containing specific grammatical aspects of words such as e.g. tense, mood, aspect, person of a verb within a particular sentence type, and routine formulae;
- routine formulae – routines containing at least some lexical elements, i.e. syntactic structures such as phrases or sentence types specialised for a given illocutionary function and containing filled lexical entries (slots in sentence/phrase structure).

---

[16] Cf. Nattinger and de Carrico (1992).

[17] Although routinised prosodic features usually accompany other routinised features of the utterance, there are cases when prosody is the main or the only component of a routine. For directives, routinised prosody is the constitutive component of *chanting* as a means of making a group request. "Begging intonation" in Polish can distinguish a request from a requirement.

[18] Stereotyped patterns bound by convention to certain types of situations and functions received various labels such as "bound utterances", "situation formulas", "discoursal expressions", "routine formulae", "fixed expressions", "formulaic expressions" and "conversational routines".

Repeatedly occurring word combinations, such as *you know, I think, sort of* etc., are much more frequent than fully idiomatic ones[19]. Even if the combinatoric meaning is not eliminated, the dominant aspect of a routine formula is the pragmatic function which may transgress the former to a high degree (e.g. "why not VP" in proposals). The utterances which contain routine formulae are interpreted both by semantic-compositional rules and through retrieval of the formulae from a mental lexicon where they are stored as wholes and linked to pragmatic-functional conventions[20].

A number of models exist for the description of conversational formulae, including those in which they are neither lexical units proper nor products of grammar. Aijmer (1984), as well as Pawley and Sider (1984), use a model in which a conversational routine is an abstract sentence stem only partly filled by lexemes and which must be completed by the use of productive syntactic rules. This model will underlie the identification of lexical-syntactic routines in this study.

Explanations for the frequent occurrence of pre-patterned speech have been provided by the study of language acquisition and performance research. Pre-patterned word sequences facilitate language acquisition (Hakuta 1974). Performance research (cf. Kuiper und Haggo 1984) explains the occurrence of routine expressions as a response to the limitation on the access to mental resources during production of speech; the mental retrieval of large "blocks" of speech reduces the combinatoric complexity and the burden on the cognitive system (cf. Aijmer 1996). A different partial explanation of stereotyped speech in general is offered in social anthropology, which regards conventionalised phrases as aspects of ritualisation of human interaction (cf. Goffman 1967).

The use of stereotyped patterns which are conventionally linked to specific intentions guarantees that these intentions will be correctly identified by one's interlocutors. Politeness plays an important role here. In the early discussion of politeness dominated by linguists

---

[19] I.e., such in which the meaning and function of the whole is not equivalent and cannot be deduced from the combinatoric meaning of their component parts.

[20] Manes and Wolfson (1981) concluded in their work about complements in English that complements are conversational formulae because 85% realise three syntactic-lexical patterns (such as "I (really) like NP"). Coulmas (1979: 240) proposed that such phenomena, where the means for realising an illocutionary intention come regularly from a syntactically and lexically limited repertoire, form a class of "recurrent phrases" to be distinguished from "pragmatic idioms". The former are syntactically transformable in the same way as "creative" expressions, and differ from the latter only in the frequency with which they occur as a means in realisation of a given pragmatic function (speech act). Pragmatic idioms, on the other hand, are deficient as far as the relationship between their functional meaning and the "combinatoric" meaning is concerned, syntactical transformability and lexical modifiability. In what follows, we will be dealing with both types of lexical-semantic routines.

from English-speaking countries, the relationship between politeness, pre-patterned speech and conventions of use was treated mainly via the notion of "conventional indirectness": as the direct expression of intentions would frequently endanger both interlocutors' "face" (Goffman 1967), it is replaced by the indirect expression of intentions. Indirect speech is, however, potentially misleading; it ceases to be so when the expression becomes formally stereotyped, and the form linked to the intention by a convention of use (cf. Searle 1975). The principles coupling certain expressions with certain illocutionary roles are specific to a culture as they reproduce the world view anchored in this culture. For example "can/could/will/would you +VERB" functions as a request on the basis of the general principle of Anglo-Saxon culture that it is polite to respect the freedom of the interaction partner and give him or her a choice. Thus, conversational formulae and routines are responsible for the recognition of the speaker's intention by the hearer with the aid of shared cultural norms.

The following study compares the use of particular conversational routines, some prosodic routines applied in realising directives, and the use of positively and negatively polite formulations in all three languages.

4.4. DIRECTIVES AND POLITENESS

4.4.1. LINGUISTIC POLITENESS

The following analysis is based on the claim that individual choices in strategies of interaction are "not random but constrained by overriding stylistic strategies that are conventionalised ways of serving universal human needs" (Tannen 1988: 11). Tannen based her analysis of conversations on the observation by Lakoff (1973) that in realising the social function of language, speakers observe one of the rules that "represent the universal logic underlying specific linguistic choices (i.e. indirectness, preference for particular lexical or syntactic forms) in the form of three principles originally called Rules of Politeness ..." (ibid.) Lakoff's "Rules of Politeness" (later called "Rules of Rapport") include the following alternative or complementary politeness strategies:

- Don't impose (distance, formal politeness)
- Give options (deference, informal politeness)
- Be friendly (or, in an alternative formulation: "Make [the hearer] feel good") (camaraderie).

A similar line of thought developed out of research in sociology represented by Goffman, who builds his notion of deference in interaction on the dichotomous notions of avoidance and presentation rituals, by which people show appreciation to each other. Presentation rituals include salutations, invitations, compliments, and minor services. "Through all of these the recipient is told that he is not an island unto himself and that others are, or seek to be, involved with him and with his personal private concerns" (Goffman 1967: 73). Avoidance rituals, on the other hand, are forms of behaviour oriented toward keeping one's distance from the recipient, privacy and separateness. This dichotomy was further re-conceptualised in accordance with Goffman's metaphorical concept of interaction as a staged performance into the concepts of "positive" and "negative" face wants – roughly speaking, the want to be with others, and the want to be left alone. "Face" is a positive social image an individual claims for him- or herself during social interactions.

Negative face wants have been defined by Brown und Levinson (1978: 67) as "the want of every competent adult member that his actions be unimpeded by others" (ibid: 67). Positive face is "the positive consistent image of 'personality' (crucially including the desire that this self-image be appreciated and approved of) claimed by the interactants" (ibid: 66), and "positive face wants" have been described as "the want of every member that his wants be desirable to (at least some) others" (ibid: 67).

Tannen (1988: 17) comments on the concept of positive and negative face, seeing its origin and its universality in the fact that "human beings are always balancing the paradoxical fact that they are simultaneously individuals and social creatures. They need each other and yet they need to separate." While Goffman's ideas about positive face correspond to Lakoff's concept of "camaraderie", the other two dimensions of rapport established by Lakoff seem to encompass the negative face wants. The fact that it is frequently difficult to differentiate distance and deference in practice gave a primacy to linguistic conceptions based of Goffman's dichotomy.

One of the central aspects of the following analysis is politeness phenomena, conceptualised in terms of the dichotomy between negative and positive politeness, which has made into the cornerstone of the discussions of linguistic politeness by Brown and Levinson's (1979) seminal study. The authors carried out an analysis of the way in which speakers of three unrelated languages, Tamil, Tzeltal and English, departed from Grice's conversational maxims for motives of politeness, and noted similarities in the linguistic strategies that led them towards postulating universality of politeness as a regulative, face-saving factor in social interaction. In Brown and Levinson's (1979: 134) formulation, "negative politeness is the heart of respect behaviour, just as positive politeness is the kernel of familiar and joking behaviour". The linguistic realisations of positive politeness often belong to the normal linguistic behaviour between intimates, "where interest and approval of each other's personality, presuppositions indicating shared wants and shared knowledge, implicit claims to reciprocity of obligations or to reflexivity of wants etc. are routinely exchanged" (ibid: 106). Brown and Levinson's conception of "positive politeness" which equates it with addressing positive face wants has been criticised by Kotthoff (1997) who sees it as unduly overstretched to apply to non-conventionalised aspects of relationship maintenance that are indifferent in her eyes with respect to politeness, such as informality and familiarity. The controversy is in my opinion notational, since there is nothing in principle that would prevent us from using the notion of "positive politeness" to encompass just these aspects of relationship maintenance.

Directness is the degree to which a speaker's illocutionary intent is apparent from the locution (Blum-Kulka et al. 1989: 278). In spite of criticism coming from researchers studying Asian and African communities, who found some claims of Brown and Levinson's model to be based on a restricted socio-cultural pattern and criticised it for "its strong orientation towards British analytical logic and North American social psychology" (Janney and Arndt 1993: 14), it is still a main point of departure for understanding politeness phenomena.

The approach represented in this work incorporates the notions of negative and positive politeness rooted in Brown and Levinson's theory as technical terms into the view of politeness as based on a "conversational contract" (cf. Fraser 1990). In the latter view the linguistic choices made by interaction participants in each stage of interaction inform their interlocutors about their perception of the current state of the relationship between persons involved, or their aspirations concerning a re-negotiation of this relationship. This includes aspects such as social distance, responsibility, leadership, right, duty, authority and subordination. Viewed from the perspective of a conversational contract, expressions of attention to positive and negative face wants when producing directives have a symbolic rather than instrumental role to play in interaction. That is, other than in Brown and Levinson's original conception, they are not merely instruments by which speakers avoid damage to face and maximise their chance of success in reaching local interaction goals, such as the interlocutors' compliance; rather, they are interaction signals applied as means of characterising and shaping relationships themselves. This perspective is consistent with the approach to directives which aspires to analyse them in their role as integrative procedures; and in which the discussion of the social significance of their verbal form is accompanied by the discussion of the social significance of their occurrence.

Relevant to the issue of positive and negative politeness is the claim by Brown and Gilman (1960: 253) that linguistic choices in social interaction are governed by "two dimensions fundamental to the analysis of all social life – power and solidarity". Tannen (1988) associates solidarity with the positive and power with "negative face wants" (cf. Brown and Levinson 1979), and quotes the hypothesis (Dreyfus 1975; Conley, O'Barr and Lind 1979) that indirectness, the strategy guided by negative face wants, is the linguistic choice of the powerless.

While I accept the claim that solidarity addresses positive face wants, the relation between power and negative politeness seems to be less straightforward. First, indirectness, as well as lexical and syntactic choices identified as vehicles of negative politeness, can be observed in interactions where power difference is absent together with familiarity, such as communication between anonymous strangers or role-based communication in institutionalised context between parties equal in power. Second, in many recurrent contexts indirectness seems to be the customary choice of those in power, too (cf. Pufal-Bax 1986). Third, it was noted that in certain speech communities directness is the choice of subordinates in dealing with the superiors, conceived in view of their social role as performing the duties of caregivers, rather than individuals in power principally free to grant or to refute a request. This devaluates the claim of universality for addressing negative face wants (reflected in indirectness) as the linguistic choice of the subordinates. In his study of the South African language Xhosa, Gough (1995) refuted the view that "giving options" is a necessary requirement for deference. In Xhosa, it appears that a performative like *Ndicela ukuba undincede* is deferential through the fact that it overtly acknowledges (a) the speaker as being in a position to need (i.e. petitioner) and (b) the hearer as being in a position to fulfil this need (i.e. the caregiver). Odlin (1989) claims a non-universality of the Western model of social interaction (reflected in the use of modals such as "could" or "can" in requests to superiors) in which people in power "have the power but not necessarily the desire to grand favours". The same point was made by Scollon and Scollon (1983) writing on native Canadian Athabaskan.

These and other studies show not only that power and powerlessness do not translate into indirectness and directness as requestive strategies, but also that indirectness is not necessarily perceived as more polite than its opposite. According to Son Mei Lee-Wong (1994: 508), the indirect request of the form "Could you give me a little salt?" is not necessarily deemed polite in Chinese; "Cultural values and beliefs do not expect S to ostensibly ask H whether s/he could part with a little salt. To query H here would contradict S's sincerity. Using conventionally indirect requests might appear tentative and polite to a non-native speaker of Chinese but to convey tentativeness in this context would be to send a wrong signal to H – that S is not certain if H would give him/her some salt. If that is the attitudinal message S wishes to convey, then H could be offended, that is, S is doubting his/her generosity." Similarly, Son Mei Lee-Wong (2000: 312) found out that "there is no definite preference for indirect requests and such indirectness is not perceived to be the norm of politeness" in PRC Chinese, while Hong Kong and Singapore Chinese, more influenced by their experience of British culture, showed higher percentages of conventional indirectness and more frequently evaluated impositives presented to them as "rude" compared to the Chinese in PRC. De Kapt (1992) noted that the native speakers of Zulu attributed a high level of politeness to performative requests, regarded as highly direct. A study whose results was most at odds with the predictions of Brown and Levinson's model, in which high indirectness corresponds to high politeness, was Lwanga-Lumu (1999) who found that in Luganda (a Bantu language) mild hints and interrogatives of the type "can you x" were regarded as very impolite and straightforward statements of the speaker's want (I want you to x) as most polite.

I believe that the notion of a speech community's collectivism as the opposite of individualism might provide the missing link that can explain much of the apparent inconsistencies in the tests of perceptions of linguistic politeness and its link to (in)directness.

The opinions on the correlation between directness and collectivism are divided and based on disparate sources. The very fact that the attacks against the prominence of negative politeness (roughly corresponding to indirectness) in the discussion of politeness phenomena come from the analysts working on collectivist cultures, such as African and Chinese, suggests that there is an affinity between directness and collectivism. However, a contradictory claim has also been made. Whereas Sifianou (1992) explains the directness of directives in Greek by a high value of ingroupness and preference for positive politeness within ingroups, Tannen (1981) argues that the Greeks tend to represent a highly indirect conversational style in directives. Greece has been described as a collectivist culture among others by Triandis and Vassiliou (1972), Vasilliou and Vassiliou (1973), and Doumanis (1983), while it scored middle on collectivism in Hofstede (1980), and, according to Georgas (1989), some indices show that the urban Greek culture is moving towards individualism. Kim et al. (1996) claim that collectivist cultures will display lower directness and impositiveness, while they conflate individualism with ego maintenance leaving the difference between ingroup and outgroup interaction out of consideration, and base their tests almost exclusively on contexts including high vertical (hierarchical) distance, so that their results may reflect sensitivity to power distance more than anything else[21]. According to Hofstede (1980), sensitivity to distance in social hierarchy is culture-specific and positively correlated with collectivism, which means that behaviour displayed in situations of high vertical distance differs to a higher degree from peer interaction in highly collectivist than in highly individualist cultures. The Japanese, who are considered to be collectivists, have been sometimes claimed to show preference for indirect strategies (cf. e.g. Yamada 1994, Okabe 1983), while Rose (1996) offered counter-examples. Working on natural data, Rinnert and Kobayashi (1999) showed that Japanese speakers used direct requests more frequently than speakers of British English, who preferred indirect strategies; the same tendency was confirmed by Fukushima's (1996) study of communication among equals and Fukushima (2003). House (1996) thinks that the more direct communication patterns of German speakers compared to Americans and the British reflect their higher individualism. However, they scored higher on collectivism than the British in the results obtained by Hofstede.[22]

A concept related to the linguistic choices pertaining to politeness with a specific reference to directives is legitimacy (Blum-Kulka and House 1989: 147). The concept of legitimacy is derived from such ethical concepts as right, privilege and duty, fundamental to

---

[21] Moreover, Kim at al. (1996) only check verbal declarations on whether it is important or not to avoid "intruding on the other person" in particular situations, rather than linguistic production in itself. A further controversial point is that the authors base their assessment of collectivism on generally formulated self-evaluative claims of test participants, rather than judgments of appropriateness of specific social behaviors. In my own research, I was led to the conclusion that claiming adherence to certain values is not a reliable tool for measuring cross-cultural, and even cross-individual attitudes because of a highly subjective understanding of abstract formulations of values. I dropped Grimm's test, successfully used by him in the assessment of changes in individual hierarchies of values, as a cross-cultural assessment method of collectivism for that very reason. For example, the Poles declared a vastly lower priority for "being helpful" than the Germans in their hierarchy of values, while they were significantly more positive about giving financial support to relatives in need, or taking care of aging parents. In fact, the same persons who declared that they would aid relatives and that one should live with aged parents, which are assessment items of collectivism by Triandis (1988), might refute with indignation the verbal concept of "sacrificing one's own interest for one's group", an assessment item of collectivism in Kim et al. (1996), as it might not occur to them that aiding relatives or nursing parents amounts to "sacrificing their own interests".

[22] I object to the view that Hofstede's results, aimed at testing work-relevant attitudes and based on answers to work-relevant questions, can be directly extrapolated to other domains. I have obtained quantified evidence that young educated Polish women are highly individualist in their preference for individual rather than collective performance on achievement-oriented tasks, while their German counterparts are strongly collectivist in this particular respect; the opposite proved true for contexts that did not have an achievement-oriented character. I suspect that in such tasks collectivist tendencies fall victim to ego maintenance (cf. Hofstede 1980), which is high in Polish women, and that the high preference for teamwork declared by the German women is a result, at least as much as a cause, of the image and public appraisal (specific to Germany) of teamwork as a typically female virtue, qualifying women for professional careers.

the anthropological study of social relationships. In some psychological literature, "rights and obligations" are subsumed under the notion of "legitimisation". According to Blum-Kulka and House, high legitimacy is related to the linguistic form "impositive" while low legitimacy is expressed in the linguistic form of indirect requests. (This view is problematic because indirectness can be applied to symbolically conceal power distance and outbalance the injustice of inequality.) Besides the role-specific power (which can, but doesn't necessarily need to, lead to direct and impositive communication style), solidarity, too, can be a source of legitimacy. I propose to amend this conceptual network with the notion of the "ingroup", which transfers it from the dyadic plane of interaction to interaction on the background of a wider network of social bonds. I view the membership in an ingroup as a powerful means of legitimisation of directives, and, hence, a factor influencing the choice of conversational strategies applied.

Keim and Schwitalla (1993) note the contrast in the forms of linguistic realisation of directives in two different female groups: while conventional indirectness was a predominant form in the upper middle class literature group, the imperative was the standard form in the working class handicraft group. Their conclusions concerning the social implications of these two types of linguistic behaviour are opposite to my own interpretation of interactions in the various Big Brother houses. For Keim and Schwitalla, commenting on the handwork group, "bei direkten, verbal unaufwendigen Aufforderungen und Bitten spielt nur die Perspektive der Sprecherin eine Rolle; das negative Face bzw. der Freiraum der Adressatin findet in der Formulierung keine Berücksichtigung ... Die zugrundeliegende Verhaltensregel scheint zu sein: Jede sorgt zunächst für sich. ... D. h. die Frauen sind primär mit der Ausgestaltung ihres eigenen Aktionsraums befasst". The authors note that "komplementär zur hier beobachteten Verhaltensregel ,jede sorgt für sich' gibt es in der Gruppe und darüber hinaus in der sozialen Welt der Gruppenmitglieder die ,Solidaritätsregel'. Diese besagt, dass die Frauen auf die uneingeschränkte Hilfe der anderen rechnen können, wenn sie selbst unverschuldet in Not geraten sind. Wenn jemand jedoch die Notlage selbst verschuldet hat, muss die Betreffende mit harter Kritik und sogar mit der Ächtung der Gruppe rechnen" (ibid: 142). Rather than view these two facts as based on "complementary principles", it is tempting to explain the uninhibited verbal behaviour in making requests in the handwork group as following from the presupposition of cooperation based on the awareness of being engaged in a *group task*[23], eliminating the need for attending to negative face. Requests produced in this context are

---

[23] Even if each woman is working on her own product, the very existence of the group, which is provided space, material and tutorship by the local authorities, is legitimised by the output of the group as a whole.

similar to instructionals produced during joint activities, informing the interaction partner how to optimise her contribution to a joint achievement.

I mentioned before the difference claimed by Levinson between the "alternates view" that deals only with variance of form in realising the same function of speech, and the ethnography of speaking approach, and declared commitment to the latter. The data corpus under study gave me the opportunity to translate this commitment into analytic detail.

While the aforementioned authors concentrate on the influence of the speaker's and the hearer's face wants on the choice of linguistic forms, thanks to some properties of my corpora I am able to take into account the fact addressed by Brown and Levinson (1978) which cannot be encompassed by any elicitation-based approach: "face wants" are not merely reflected in the linguistic forms of utterances, but also in the choice between an action and non-action, that is, between an utterance being produced or not at all. The perfect realisation of the rule "don't impose" is abstaining from requesting, proposing, or giving advice. In peer-to-peer communication where there is no institutionalised role differentiation, directives are uttered because the speaker believes that the hearer does not conceive of herself as an "island for herself", but shares or is inclined to share some goals, interests and mutual or external responsibilities with other people including the speaker. In other words, the commonsensical assumption that the hearer has some positive face wants and might therefore be inclined to co-operate with the speaker is prerequisite to uttering a directive when institutionalised obligations do not apply. Linguistic "positive politeness" is a maximal expression of the speaker's conception of the hearer as having positive face wants with respect to the speaker and the beneficiary, that is, an expression in which these wants are overtly taken for granted rather than merely as possible.

In this study, I largely subscribe by the definition of positive politeness by Rhodes (1989: 249) who describes it as "based on the presumption of co-operation[24], rather than on avoiding or redressing threats to face (negative politeness)". Song Mei Lee-Wong (1994: 509) proposed in the same vain that to be friendly can mean to show solidarity and implies the following principles:

- Do impose within reasonable limits
- Use linguistic forms which express the belief that H will co-operate with S.

More precisely, I assume that the two opposing politeness strategies: politesse – "do not impose – give options" vs. the "positive" politeness (camaraderie) differ by the factor presupposition: positive politeness does not just declare or express solidarity, but also

---

[24] Emphasis by HP.

68

presupposes consensus and non-objectionability of the direct expression of a speaker's preferences. The politesse (negative politeness) does not presuppose consensus (of the hearer with the speaker) as given but as having to be created. Instead, showing regard for the hearer's wishes by offering a choice and minimising imposition, it presupposes the possibility of difference (of wants and aims).

More specifically in the case of request situations, in camaraderie each interaction participant presupposes that the other party has the same goals and aims or is willing to accept the speaker's wants and aims as his or her own, is willing to create benefits to others, and perceives him- or herself as co-beneficiary of such actions. The imperative and stating future acts of the addressee as a matter of fact rather than a possibility are among ways in which the presupposition of consensus manifests itself in directive speech acts.

This definition is culture-independent; that means that no room is created for cultural difference in judgements of what is positively or negatively polite. Instead, cultural differences are assumed to dwell in the relative values of the two types of politeness in different cultures and their adequacy in various types of situations in these cultures.

While writing this book, I became aware of the terminology proposed by Tannen (1984) named the two opposing strategies of verbal interaction "involvement" and "considerateness" rather than manifestations of "negative" and "positive" face wants, or "negative" vs. "positive" politeness; thus, the evaluative connotations of the adjectives could be avoided. I will retain the notion of "impositiveness" and "negative" politeness while speaking of the linguistic form of directives, and adopt Tannen's terms in the interpretative passages dealing with the communicative and interactive behaviour on a more general level. At the same time, the acceptance of Brown's (2000) differentiation between interpersonal (dyadic) and group-oriented aspects of social attitudes led to the following differentiated use of the notions of "involvement" and "interdependence":

Involvement expresses the notion of sharing, responsibility and attempted influence displayed by S towards H(s), but is neutral with respect to group-orientation, and can characterise interpersonal as well as group interactions and relationships.

Interdependence expresses the notion of sharing, mutual responsibility and influence between group members as group members.

I agree with Dąbrowska (1997) that judgements on what is or is not an imposition differ in different cultures. Nonetheless, the terms "impositive" and "imposition" will be retained here as technical terms referring to a forceful statement of a speaker's wants.

4.4.2. POLITENESS, IMPOSITIVENESS AND OPEN CONFLICT

In situations of open conflict, where one or both speakers drop concern for face and indulge in communicative behaviours maximising rather than minimising mutual face risk, the link between positive "face wants" of the speaker and the impositive linguistic devices maximising their directive force is invalidated. Under such circumstances, maximisation of directive force by does not express solidarity, nor any other aspect of positive face wants. Rather than expressing "closeness" in a positive sense, they express "lack of distance" in a sense of disrespect, that is, are applied to hurt the hearer's face wants. They are not negatively or positively polite but impolite. Conversely, in open conflict means of negative politeness which usually serve showing respect for the hearer's negative face wants, such as permission questions and other routine formulae of conventional politesse, are sometimes applied to signalise distancing as the means of hurting the hearer's positive face wants (by accentuating the speaker's own negative face want). Thus, both impositiveness as well as devices of negative politeness have two functions whose interrelatedness is grasped by the spatial metaphor of "closeness" and "distance".

This might provoke the conclusion that the statistical analysis of the Big Brother corpora should exclude open quarrels, where strong impositiveness serves a deliberate violation of the hearer's negative face wants. Directives appearing in situations of open conflict in all corpora are usually inhibitive, either corrective (critical of a past behaviour) or terminating (critical of the present behaviour). However, most corrective or terminating directives found in the statistically analysed corpora are not strongly confrontational, neither are they obviously meant to hurt: such cases are very rare (between two and four occurrences per corpus). Sorting out "impolite" behaviours from the continuum of more or less confrontational prohibitive behaviours included in the corpora would falsify the picture of the differences in the linguistic realisation of initiating and inhibitive directives. This difference results from the principally more confrontational nature of the latter.

4.4.3. POLITENESS STRATEGIES IN DIRECTIVES

Prior todiscussing inter-lingual similarity and difference in the use of politeness in directives, it is necessary to formulate fixed rules of classification linking politeness type with the linguistic form of utterances. This will be done using some of the notions developed by the study of politeness, and amended in a way suggested by the peculiarities of the analysed material. This section introduces the term "head act" as a label for an utterance counting as a realisation of a requestive, that is, the *main strategy* used by the speaker. Several possible configurations are identified of semantic and syntactic features which determine the inclusion of a given utterance in a class of positively or negatively headed directives. Then, *accompanying strategies* such as *internal modifiers* and *supportives* are also identified and linked to positive and negative politeness.

My statistical analysis of politeness phenomena is based on the following assumptions:

- The utterances used for formulating directives are oriented towards impositiveness or negative politeness primarily by way of the head act applied in their verbalisation, and secondarily by the politeness orientation of modifiers which accompany them in the form of supportives (external to the head act) or modification internal to the head act.

- Linguistic forms used as head acts in making directives are either inherently impositive or display negative politeness.

- Modifiers can be oriented towards positive or negative politeness. Modifiers that maximise togetherness and imposition, and such that are typical for informal in-group communication and untypical in formal contexts and out-group communication, are positively polite. Modifiers which minimise imposition are negatively polite.

4.4.4. CATEGORISATION OF HEAD ACT FORMS

The concept of Head Act was applied in Edmondson (1981) and House and Kasper (1981), and has been in use in linguistic pragmatics ever since. The concept of Supportive Moves has been introduced by Edmondson and House (1981). House (1988) applied the notions of Internal and External Modification to speak of various types of modifiers. All these notions have been applied in the voluminous, paradigmatic cross-linguistic study of requests and apologies by Blum-Kulka et al. (1989), based on the questionnaire method, and numerous authors later on, including e.g. Blum-Kulka (1990), Held (1995), Sifianou (1992 b), Fukushima (1996), Le Pair (1996), Márquez Reiter (2000) and many others.

In sub-classifications of the linguistic form of directives, all these authors and many others (an early example being Erwin-Tripp 1979) explicitly or implicitly refer to the dichotomy view of politeness ("positive" vs. "negative"). They recognise the affinity of negative politeness with indirect requestive strategies and positive politeness with directness. House and Kasper (1981) and Blum-Kulka et al. (1989) differentiate the head acts of requests according to the level of directness and assign them to eight or nine different levels. Following House (1988), in Blum-Kulka at al. (1989) this scale of directness is collapsed into three major categories: direct, conventionally indirect, and non-conventionally indirect requests. The three-way partition, which has become paradigmatic and re-occurred in numerous studies, is defined as follows:

a) "The most direct, explicit level realised by requests syntactically marked as such, for example, imperatives, or by other verbal means that name the act as request, such as performatives (Austin 1962) or hedged performatives (Fraser 1975)" (46). The subcategories listed are the imperative, explicit performative (*I am asking you to...*), hedged performative (*I must/have to ask you to...*), locution derivable (*You'll have to/should/must/ought to...*), want statement (*I'd like to...*)

b) "The conventionally indirect level: strategies that realise the act by reference to contextual preconditions necessary for its performance, as conventionalised in a given language (47)." In the coding manual the authors divide conventionally indirect requests into "suggestory formulae" (e.g. *How about ...Why don't you...*) and "preparatory" (280), referring to ability, willingness or possibility as conventionalised in a given language (e.g. *Could/Would you...*)

c) "The nonconventional indirect level, ... strategies that realise the request either by partial reference to the object or element needed for the implementation of the act by reliance on contextual clues (47)", (e.g. *Will you be going home?* as a request for a lift). Requestives of the latter type, called "hints", and can be "strong", when the illocutionary intention of the speaker is obviously implied by the meaning of the utterance in the context given, and "mild", when the illocutionary intention is not obvious. "Mild hints" are to some extent "off record" (the speaker can deny that they realise a requestive intention).

Sub-classification of their linguistic form of directives proposed in earlier contrastive studies (Ervin-Tripp 1976, adopted by House and Kasper 1981 and Blum-Kulka 1987; Blum-Kulka 1989; Blum-Kulka 1990; Held 1995; Fukushima 1996; Sifianou 1992 b; Márquez Reiter 2000) could not be applied to the data at hand without making further distinctions. All of them group together certain types of linguistic expressions occurring frequently in the Big Brother corpora in such a way that at least one of the categories contains utterances realising both negatively and positively polite strategies.

– Sifianou (1992) opts for syntactic criteria as the basic principle of categorisation: she lists imperatives, interrogatives, declaratives, negatives, elliptical constructions, and declaratives in two subtypes – "hints" and other "need statements". However, some syntactic patterns cannot be directly related to impositiveness or negative politeness. Interrogatives, realising indirect strategy and usually associated with negative politeness, can be impositive (e.g. aggressive *wh*-interrogatives, such as *"where is my coffee"* in a re-request for coffee); declaratives can be impositive or negatively polite.

– Blum-Kulka et al. (1989) introduce the category "locution derivables" whose illocutionary intent is "directly derivable from the semantic meaning of the locution" (e.g. an "obligation statement " – a statement of the addressee's obligation to act). However, locution derivables by definition also include subtypes not mentioned by Blum-Kulka. Next to the matter-of-fact declarative in future or present tense (examples: 11-P3. chodź laska # idziemy się kąpać *"come girl # we-go bathing"*, 9-G2. du wirst mir jetzt helfen *"you will help me now"*), they also incude the interrogative in future or present tense referring to the realisation of a speech act (example: 11-E3. so are we going to set up a little camp). The interrogative form signals the speaker's attention to the hearer's preferences while the other subtypes named above do not, and they should not be classified as representing the same type of politeness.

– Also problematic is the category "language specific suggestory formula", comprising utterances which contain a suggestion to do X ("How about cleaning up?"). They were applied e.g. in Held (1988) and Blum-Kulka et al. (1989). They are formulations in which "the illocutionary intent is phrased as a suggestion by means of a framing routine formula" (Blum-Kulka at al. 1989: 280). If Wierzbicka (1985) is correct, though, the form of the "language-specific typical suggestory formula" of one culture can be meaningfully unlike such a formula in another language; the routine formulas develop out of a particular cultural logic and reflect it in their form[25]. Since such differences are part and parcel of the contrasts I aim to analyse,

---

[25] Wierzbicka's insights allow us to expect that suggestory formulas are likely to be interrogative in English, which are characterised by a strong use of negative politeness in the form of consultative devices; and different in Polish:

> It is typical for Polish to use imperative coupled with some diminutives and mitigating intonation for realising requests. In English, an interrogative form is typically used; a number of interrogative conversational routines have been developed for this purpose. Characteristically, Polish has no similar constructions; since in Polish the use of interrogative forms outside the domain of questions is very limited, and since the interrogative form is not culturally valued as a means of performing directives, there was, so to speak, no need for developing special interrogative devices for performing speech acts other than questions, and in particular, performing directives (Wierzbicka 1985: 151-152).

the category "suggestory formula" needs to be amended by taking into consideration differences in the forms of utterances, such as the opposition between interrogative and declarative sentence type.

– Blum-Kulka (1990) assigns negative politeness to indirectness (both conventional and non-conventional) and positive politeness to directness modified by positively polite modifiers. Unmitigated directness is "neutral" as far as politeness is concerned (in the context of parent-child communication). Her contrastive corpus study (comparing American and Israeli cultures) quantifies the data in terms of the respective ratios of neutral (unmodified direct), positive (positively modified direct), and negatively polite (indirect) politeness. Blum-Kulka's pilot study has inspired much of the following analysis. However, neither her premise that unmodified directness is "neutral" in politeness nor the identification of negative politeness with any type of indirectness will be applied here. The former contrasts with my basic assumption that positive politeness is realised by head acts implying the presupposition of consensus, such as the imperative. The latter is counterintuitive because it classifies strong hints (defined below) as negatively polite.

In Blum-Kulka (1990) and other works which adopt the classification of directives from Blum-Kulka et al. (1989), strong hints are, by definition, non-conventionally indirect. In this study, in order to avoid the proliferation of small sub-categories, I extend this term to include impositive directives whose form has undergone some conventionalisation if their propositional content refers to the circumstances rather than the action to be performed. I include mild hints under negative politeness and strong hints under positive politeness, whether conventionalised or not.

An example of a non-conventionally indirect strong hint in declarative is 9-E3:

```
9-E3.
M There is no point arguing.
```

A type of conventionalised strong hint is the "aggressive question"[26]. Two types have been identified on the basis of BB material:

- aggressive wh- questions:

---

[26] The term "aggressive interrogative" was introduced by House and Kasper (1981) in the context of complaint strategies.

74

1-G1.

M wo ^schneidest du "where are you cutting" – an inhibitive request at the hearer to stop cutting the speaker's hair in an undesired way (here with a high rise-fall intonation and emphatic stress)

10-E3.

M where is my coffee – a re-request for coffee

8-P3.

M gdzie jest szlafrok dla Stasia "where is the dressing-gown for Stasio"

- rhetorical realisation future tense interrogative in Polish ("provocative interrogative"):

9-P3.

F będziemy im patrzeć na ręce? "will we be watching their hands" (*watch sb's hands*: an idiomatic expression meaning watching somebody at work.)

An utterance of the form as in 9-P3 is a request or proposal clearly characterising the option predicated in the utterance as unacceptable and condemnable in the speaker's eyes. The opposite is being demanded of the hearers (the hearers and the speaker should help "them" rather than stand and watch "them" at work). This syntactic form (interrogative sentence in second person in requests and first person plural in proposals, future tense, imperfect; I do not mean the lexical idiom) is a conversational routine, coupled with this particular function by a convention of use. The conversational routine is socially inappropriate in situations of high vertical or horizontal distance, and is typical of in-group communication.

In Blum-Kulka's (1990) classification, aggressive and provocative questions would count as indirect requests together with "could-you-x"-questions and realise negative politeness, contrary to impositives (direct requests)[27]. In my classification, they are counted with positively polite requestives.

- Presuppositional wh-question is indirect but positively polite.

---

[27] As long as such constructions realise merely a minute portion of directives in the corpus under analysis, which is the case both in Blum-Kulka's and in my data, the distinction is practically negligible, but this need not be the case for all cultures and corpora.

I define "presuppositional question" as a question asking about the details of the presupposed future action, and thus presupposing that the action will be performed, without a previous consultation with the hearer, for example:

10-P3. F co śpiewamy "what sing-we" (the speaker presupposes a joint action of herself and the hearers, without a prior inquiry whether they want to sing)

- Asking about H having the object of request as a way of performing the request (rather than a way of performing a pre-request, prior to the actual request) is indirect but positively polite.

It presupposes consensus on that H will let S use the object of request if he or she is in possession of this object.

4.4.4.1. CODING MANUAL: HEAD ACT

The classification of directive utterances in the following study is based on various formal, semantic and pragmatic indicators of illocutionary force[28].

My resulting classification of utterances realising directive speech acts follows approximately along the lines by Hindelang (1979), who specifies six semantic dimensions based on modal criteria (imperativeness, possibility/ ability, obligation/ need/ necessity, volition, probability/ impossibility/ certainty) and the notion of performative speech act. Hindelang's classification has been enriched by several additional categories which emerged out of an analysis of the empirical material. The resulting scheme comprises the following categories of form:

Imperative
Go swimming.

Optative
This category includes utterances marked as directives by means of a periphrastic construction involving optative mood, introduced by an optative particle, in Polish:

Żeby+ś   *za dużo nie skakał.*
OPTATIVE PARTICLE + declination suffix 2nd sing   not jump too much
(you-SING should not jump too much)

---

[28] For details, cf. Pulaczewska 2006.

76

Żeby+ście   *mi*   *tam zaraz poszli.*
OPTATIVE PARTICLE + decl. suffix 2nd pl.   dat. ethicus « me »   go-PL there at once
(you-PL should go there at once)

It is a categorical way of expressing the speaker's want, emphasising the assumption that the hearer might want to do something else if not instructed otherwise[29].

Optative also appears as a function of Heische Modus in German, and is applied for making directives in 1st person plural and for the honorific form of address (V-address) because the inflectional paradigm of the imperative is deficient – it misses these two forms. This form of the German sentence will be classified together with the imperative.

Infinitive
Nicht aufstehen. Nie wstawać.

Ellipsis
routine: *Hands up! Cheers!*
situational: *Another one please.*

As all elliptical utterances that occurred in the data had declarative (falling) intonation, there will be no need to distinguish between interrogative and declarative intonation patterns.

Vocative
Johnny! Barbi!

Directive utterances in the form of a bare vocative appear in the corpus as a subtype of elliptical utterances. The vocative merely appoints the actor of the action specified by the co-text or the context. This also includes inhibitive requests aimed at terminating the current activity of the hearer, and requests that H moves into the vicinity of S, typically to make further interaction possible.

---

[29] I assume here that "*żeby*" is not identical with the conjunction of the same form introducing a subordinate clause of purpose. Rather, it is related to the optative particle "*oby*", which also takes conjugation endings, expressing a wish the fulfilment of which is not dependent on the hearer. In my opinion, sentences introduced by "*żebyś*" and "*obyś*" with optative meanings can hardly be subsumed under three basic sentence types registered by Polish grammars – declarative, imperative and interrogative; I am aware of the controversial character of this claim.

Declarative and interrogative:

Realisation (predicates a future action without modal framing)
We start now. You will fetch me some wood.
Gehen wir? Idziemy? Are we leaving?

Deontic (expresses obligation or necessity)
We must finish it right now. Trzeba zaraz to dokończyć.
Müssen wir nicht abwarten? Nie musimy zaczekać?

Competence (expresses ability or lack of constraint)
You could help me doing my homework.
Kannst du mir helfen? Możesz mi pomóc? Can you help me?

Performative (explicitly declares the directive intention by the use of a performative verb)
Proszę zostać. Ich bitte Sie, zu bleiben.
Czy mogę prosić o filiżankę kawy? May I ask you for a cup of coffee?

Preference (expresses volitional modality)
I want you to stay. I would be glad if you stayed.
Wollen wir gehen? Chcemy już iść? Are we ready to go?

Suggestory

I introduce this "waste-bin category" to account for pragmatic idioms that propose a joint action of the hearer and the speaker and do not fit into any other category. They correspond roughly to "language specific suggestory formulae" in House/Vollmer (1988) and Blum-Kulka et al. (1989).

Why not [VP]?
Co byś powiedział na [NP]?
Wie wäre es mit [NP] ?
What about [NP]?
Why don't we [VP]?
I think [NP] is in order.

Hints

The notion of "hint" was applied among others by House and Vollmer (1988) and Blum-Kulka et al. (1989) to denote utterances that indicate an illocutionary force by enforcing non-conventionalised inferences from the proposition ("direct pragmatic implicature"), and fulfil their directive function without mention of the actors and the action to be performed. "Mild hints" with a long inferential path between the semantic meaning and the directive intention realise an off-record strategy and are excluded from this study unless their illocutionary purpose (directive) has been recognised and responded to by the addressees.

Strong hints include both non-conventional linguistic forms and partly conventionalised ones, discussed above in section 4.4.4. (provocative rhetorical questions, aggressive wh-questions, presuppositional wh-questions, questions about H possessing an object as a way of performing a request for this object).

Strong hint
Declarative
Your time is over.
Question about possession, aggressive, provocative and presuppositional question
Do you have scissors?/ Where is my coffee?/ Będziesz tak stać i patrzyć?[30]/ What are we going to sing?

Mild hint
I've finished my beer. / Are you sure that she can manage it alone?

4.4.5. POLITENESS AND HEAD ACT FORM

With the exception of hints, there is a systematic and context-free correspondence between the linguistic form and the politeness of the head act. The politeness type of an utterance can be evaluated on the basis of its configuration of syntactic, lexical, and semantic format. Two types of variation – of sentence type (declarative, interrogative, etc.) and of the semantic/lexical aspects of the utterance (e.g. expression of necessity, ability, etc.) grasp different aspects of similarity and difference. I will speak of the syntactic sentence pattern and semantic/lexical content as "dimensions" of form.

The correspondences between the form and the type of politeness realised by the directive utterances in the data are shown in Table 1.

---

[30] "Are you going to stand and watch?" A conversational routine implying "you should do something rather than just stand and watch".

	Realisation	Preference	Performative	Suggestory	Deontic	Competence	mild hint	strong hint
interrogative								
declarative								
imperative								
imp-decl								
infinitive								
ellipsis								
vocative								
optative								

Table 1. Shadowed fields mark negatively polite utterance forms.

4.4.6. TYPES OF POLITENESS IN MODIFIERS

The notion of impositiveness as the measure of positive politeness functions works less well for modification than for the head act. Modification opens a broad space of strategic nuance. Cultures can differ to the degree in which they create closeness by increasing impositiveness – friendly imperativeness, maternal insistence, and trustful unmitigated declaration of one's own opinion on the one hand; or by other means such as expressions of appreciation, warmth, intimate knowledge, and informality on the other – for example, compliments, terms of endearment, humour and colloquialisms.

The first type will be subsumed under the label "impositive" and the second under the label "confidence/informality". A possible test for distinguishing between the two types is the question whether a particular device can or cannot be applied to hurt negative face wants in an open conflict. This categorisation is basically in line with Kotthoff's (1998:299) observation that intimacy is sometimes expressed by non-attendance to the negative face wants, and her differentiation between stereotyped verbal means of attending to positive face, and non-attending to the negative one. Modifiers of directive utterances which can be used to violate negative face wants, such as "Unverschämtheiten" (cf. ibid.), e.g. vulgarisms, are subsumed here under the label "impositive"; and those which do not carry such a potential, subsumed under the label "confidence/informality".

4.4.7. SUBCLASSIFICATION OF MODIFIERS

Modification of head acts is realised by means of supportives (external to the head act), further classified into interaction markers and supportive moves, and modification internal to the head act or a supportive move.

SUPPORTIVES

Supportives are devices which accompany the head act of a directive. I will distinguish between two sorts of supportives: *supportive moves* and *interaction markers* (complementary speech acts). Moves and complementary acts are discourse analytic categories. The move is a verbal action which carries the conversation forward (Stenström 1994: 36). Complementary acts accompany primary speech acts (such as e.g. requesting, thanking, and apologising) but do not constitute moves of their own.

SUPPORTIVE MOVES

Blum-Kulka et al. (1989) list several types of aggravating supportive moves, such as insults, threats and moralising. None of these has been applied in the following analysis. The following types of "mitigating" supportive moves listed by Blum-Kulka et al. (1989) have been overtaken:

- grounders: give reasons, explanations or justifications
- preparators: specify the character of the speech act which will follow but not its content (*"I would like to ask you a question"*)
- committers: elicit a pre-commitment *("Could you do me a favour?")*
- disarmers (*"I know you hate lending notes, but ..."*)
- promising reward
- imposition minimisers (*"Would you give me a lift, but only if you're driving my way"*)

Further categories of supportive moves overtaken from other authors and utilised in the following analysis are: emphasizers (Brown and Levinson 1987), consultative devices (non-tags; Kasper and House 1981), compliments (Sifianou 1992), steers, whose function is to "steer the discourse towards the subject" (Kasper and House 1981), and availability checks (Fukushima 1996, e.g. *You are going to get up early in the morning # right?*), which will be subsumed here under "steers".

To the categories of supportive moves applied in earlier studies, I added the following ones[31]:

- object minimiser: points explicitly to the small cost of the compliance with the request
- asking for forgiveness
- concession: accompanies directives aiming at terminating or preventing an undesirable behaviour of the hearer, and points out that the restriction is only partial and limited
- specifier: gives further details of the predicated action
- appreciator: expression of appreciation in the course of H following the directive (*'very well # perfect # well done'*)

Contrary to the remaining types of supportive moves, an "appreciator" appears as a reaction to, rather than precedes the hearer's action. However, it may follow immediately in a chain of action in which the performance of the action asked for by S is instantly performed by H and in turn verbally acknowledged and rewarded by S. I counted such verbal rewards to supportive moves of requestives if they follow head acts of directives within the same turn of S's speech. They belong to the immediate context of the head act and function in the same way with respect to politeness as pre-action items.

Positively positive specifiers are those presupposing that the action will be performed as proposed by S, by speaking of it as a matter of fact.

IFIDs ("illocutionary function indicating devices", e.g. *please, bitte*) are also counted as supportive moves by Blum-Kulka; I will count them as interaction markers as they do not have any propositional content of their own.

Next to the positively and negatively polite supportive moves, I also note the existence of supportive moves which neither mitigate nor aggravate the directive they accompany but just provide for the rationality of communication (the interlocutors' mutual understanding of their abilities, goals and reasons), that is, neutral in politeness:

- grounders
- steers/availability checks
- preparators

---

[31] Another class of polite modifiers are hesitators, that is, meaningless sounds such as "yyy" and "eee" inserted between semantically loaded constituents, signalling that the speaker has temporary difficulties finding a formulation but has not yet completed her message and intends to hold turn. This class has not been taken into consideration in the following statistical analysis because it is very rare for politeness-driven hesitators to be distinguishable from "gap-fillers" – effects of word-finding problems coming from different sources.

- specifiers

Grounders are counted as "mitigating devices" e.g. by Kasper and House (1981), Blum-Kulka et al. (1989), and as positively polite by others (e.g. Kotthoff 1999). However, I regard grounders as rational rather than mitigating, and as oriented to politeness by virtue of their meaning. Grounders name the grounds which S has for proposing an action, providing H with additional background knowledge. S assumes that knowing these reasons (new information) will be a reason for H to consent. The reasons themselves may be positively oriented, as in *Give me your sweater because I am cold* (fictitious) and 12- E3. don't let him go because he will hurt himself. In both cases, S believes that naming his reasons will be a sufficient reason for H to perform the required action. Thus, consensus is presupposed concerning what is desirable. In my classification, grounders are positively or neutrally oriented in politeness. They are positive if the S justifies the request e.g. with S's personal need or desire, or a benefit of another group member.

Examples of each subtype of neutrally polite, positively and negatively polite modifiers are given in Appendix 2.

The subcategories of negatively polite supportive moves listed above served as points of reference, but the borders between them were frequently fuzzy. Moreover, mitigating propositions attached to directives in the data are sometimes markedly unique and resent inclusion in any of the above-listed sorts. As negatively polite supportive moves were rare in the data, I chose to not to sub-classify them in the quantitative analysis. Also impositive and neutral supportive moves are so multifaceted that sub-categorising them, apart from the basic distinction regarding the type of politeness, offers little cognitive gain. Categories such as steer, grounder, etc., are too general to offer precise insights[32]; on the other hand, a further

---

[32] For example, supportive moves counted to particular subcategories of positively polite modifiers enhanced impositiveness by various means (the numbers in brackets refer to examples given in Appendix 2):
EMPHASISER
- emphatically articulating speaker's preference (19-E3)
- urging the speaker to immediately comply with the directive (20-E3)
- articulating insistence (21-E3)
- declaring the seriousness of the speaker's directive intention (22-E3)
GROUNDER
- declaring the speaker's will as the source of the directive (24-E3)
- pointing to a social norm as the source of the requestive (23-E3)
- warning of punishment by the speaker in case of non-compliance (25-E3)
PREPARATOR
expressing the speaker's conviction that s/he knows the solution to a problem (26-E3)
STEER

sub-classification of argumentative resources applied in them produces many categories populated by few cases, unable to provide statistically meaningful results (cf. footnote 33 – ten subtypes of argumentative resources listed there represent merely 63 impositive supportive moves occurring in the data). A qualitative discussion of particular occurrences of supportive moves within their discursive frames seems therefore to be a more promising approach in detecting intercultural contrasts and similarities than the quantitative approach.

INTERACTION MARKERS

Interaction markers accompanying directives perform the function of the social organisation of the discourse. They extend the utterance beyond the scope of the phrase expressing the proposition constituting the main speech act, but do not contribute any propositional content of their own; rather, they belong to the "rhetorical space" of the discourse, pointing to the interpersonal or textual environment of a given utterance. They form separate prosodic and syntactic units, apart from some links and summonses co-ordinating the current expression with its preceding co-text and context.

Interaction markers were mentioned with reference to directives by House and Vollmer (1988: 121) who registered the existence of "alerters" as another analytical category next to supportive moves:

"Alerter ("Alarmierer"), mit Hilfe derer wir weitere Elemente, die sich nicht innerhalb des Sprechtaktkerns ("Head Act") auswirken, sondern den Kontext beeinflussen, zu erfassen versuchen. Beispiele sind: Hör mal, Du Judith, Entschuldingen Sie."

Partly following Emondson (1977) who proposes *cajolers* (which increase, establish or restore harmony) and *appealers* (sentence-final tag questions) as subclasses of "gambits", Sifianou (1992) lists *appealers, cajolers* and *alerts* as sub-sorts of "emphathisers", which perform internal modification (I classify them as external modifiers, though). In the following analysis, the position of these elements within a turn was taken into account, which led to the following sub-classification:

- *starters: alerts, links* and *summonses* (discourse-organising devices connecting the utterance to the co- and context),
- *cajolers*, including verbs of sensation and verbs of knowing used outside turn-initial position,

---

- expressing doubt about the purpose of the speaker's current action (1-E4)
- humorously attributing the want to perform the action in question to the addressee, in absence of any evidence (2-E4)

84

- *IFIDS* (illocutionary force indicating devices),
- *tag questions.*

Links and *summonses* are turn-initial components of an utterance which can serve relationship maintenance by marking informality (colloquialisms) or imposition (negation particles). They signal taking turn by the speaker and help him to begin the utterance. *Links* connect the current utterance to the immediately preceding co-text (signalling agreement, disagreement, supplement, reformulation, correction, reservation, etc.). *Summonses* connect the utterance to the context in general, including prior verbal interaction and other properties of the context that the speaker regards as mutually transparent to herself and the hearer[33]. They perform a socialising function by an implicit appeal to the shared expectations of the speaker and the hearer, e.g.:

So what's your name?

as a means to strike a conversation[34].

Question tags are sentence-final consultative devices. They can contain a negation of the main clause or be formulated positively with respect to the main clause: *'Du tust mir jetzt einen Gefallen, ja?' 'You will do me a favour now, right?'*

Negatively polite interaction markers are IFIDs (please, bitte, prosze/prosimy) and question tags. Interaction markers also can be positively polite, either by enhancing informality and confidence (positively polite terms of address such as nicknames and pet names; interjections; starters and tags including verbs of knowing) or by enhancing imposition. The latter function is performed by starters in the imperative, and starters in the form of negation particles articulating discontent with the interlocutor's intention (declared verbally or implied by addressee's behaviour) in utterance-initial position.

Various categories of interaction markers are listed and exemplified in Appendix 2.

---

[33] Links and summonses are clearly distinguishable in a context even if the same lexical items are frequently used in both functions. I initially classed them separately to validate the hypothesis that positive politeness correlates positively with the use of summonses as signals of sharing background assumptions, but it found no support in the data; therefore, they will be amalgamated into a joint category in the following analysis.
[34] The utterance-initial summons refers to the shared awareness of the situational background; it implies that the interaction has already started before, in the non-verbal mode, or that an interaction is expectable in the social context given.

INTERNAL MODIFIERS

Depersonalisation/agent avoidance is the avoidance of stating explicitly that H is the agent of the action to be performed, by using impersonal or speaker-centred constructions when H's action is meant. It is negatively polite.

Hedges are negatively polite elements by which the speaker diminishes self-assertiveness and minimises the object of a directive or avoids its precise propositional specification. *Complex hedges* are fuzzy expressions following the head act such as *and stuff like that/or something/and like/and everything/that sort of thing*, or subjectivity markers such as *I think*. They are peripheral to the sentence (sentence-initial, sentence-final, or marked as disjuncts by prosody if embedded in the sentence) and can form prosodic units of their own, separated from the main phrase. They are similar to interaction markers as they extend the directive without adding new propositional content, and are external to the proposition in the directive. Simple *lexical hedges*, or understaters, are adverbial expressions embedded in the proposition, such as *little, a bit, sort of.*

Other types of negatively polite internal modifiers are: *subjunctive mood* (Konjunktiv in German), *conditional, morphological diminutive, modal adverbial, permission request*, and *polite pessimism* (as in "Are you not coming?").

Positively polite internal modifiers include *colloquialism, humour*, and *referential use of nicknames*, which enhance informality and confidence; as well as *vulgarisms, augmentatives, lexical intensifiers, semantic/syntactic intensifiers*, and *repetition*, all of which enhance impositiveness.

It is controversial whether politeness plural should be counted as negatively or to as positively polite modifiers. On the one hand, it can be viewed as a means of mitigating the impositiveness of a directive and saving the interlocutor's "negative face" similar to defocusing the hearer by using impersonal constructions. On the other hand, it is a means of enhancing informality and confidence by creating and appealing to "we" – a group identity, which is essential to positive politeness. The following reaction to a trespass illustrates the point:

33-P3.
M1 to M2: e # nie **puszczamy** bąków # dobra?
*e # **we** don't fart # all right?*

In what follows, such type of polite pluralisation is termed *solidarity plural* and counted as positively polite modification.

86

Types of internal modifiers which occurred in the data are listed and exemplified in Appendix 2.

II. DATA ANALYSIS

5. COMPARATIVE QUANTITATIVE ANALYSIS OF REQUESTIVES IN PEER GROUPS

The following section consists of two parts. The first part analyses facts concerning the production of requestive utterances and their interactive structure, without mention of form. The second part analyses forms and form differences and their interrelatedness with the interactive structure.

5.1. OCCURRENCE OF REQUESTIVES

In the following statistics, I will analyse figures regarding the production of requestive utterances and their subtypes by the speakers of English, German and Polish. I use the term "production" to refer to their occurrence, and not to their form.

The analysis is preceded by a brief characterisation of particular series, which should provide a preliminary understanding of the interrelatedness between the group dynamics, understood as the development of relationships, and the profile of directive activities within each series and how it changes over time.

As only data from the later stage are available for the first Polish edition of the program, contrasts between different stages in other editions will be examined, to find out whether the data from P1 can be unreservedly compared with the total data obtained from other editions, or whether it can only be legitimately compared to the corresponding (i.e., late) period in other editions.

5.1.1. DEVELOPMENT OF DIRECTIVE ACTIVITIES IN PARTICULAR SERIES

5.1.1.1. DEVELOPMENT OF DIRECTIVE ACTIVITIES IN E3

In this series, after two initial weeks in which all housemates had the same status (design A), the housemates were divided into the winners' group on the "rich" side and the losers' group on the "poor" side with a low standard of living, by means of individual basketball competition. The housemates on both sides could converse freely, but no objects could be passed through. The groups were reselected on a weekly basis (design C).

The introduction of the divide resulted in the rise of individual competitiveness, and the dissipation of the whole group into smaller, temporary alliances, that was reflected among others into the increase of the activity known as "bitching". According to the psychologist accompanying the program, bitching reached "epidemic dimensions" in the "divide" period.

200 cases of bitching occurred alone in the fifth week of the program. Because of the divide, joint activities (other than conversations) involving the whole group were no longer possible. While familiarity of the housemates with each other rose naturally as time passed, the integration of the group as a whole diminished. Individual friendships and courting relationships shaped the patterns of interaction.

There is a striking difference between the two periods in the ratios of proposals to requests, and of requestives (both requests and proposals) addressed to a multiple addressee[35] and those directed at a single addressee. Both proposals and requests to multiple addressees were relatively more frequent in the pre-divide period.

Proposals directed at the whole group or a part of the group (MA) occurred every seven minutes in the first two weeks and just once in 32 minutes in the later four weeks. About one third of proposals at MA in the first two weeks referred to spontaneous joint activities, such as camping in the yard, joint drinking, a practical joke, and symbolic acts during leave-taking. Another large group (about 30%) were proposals concerning storing, eating, and cooking food, prominent integrative activities involving group consultations and decisions. The rest referred to hygiene, the way to deal with tasks and rules set by Big Brother, and miscellaneous topics. In the later period, activities of that type move into the background and interactions reflecting individual relationships including interpersonal frictions find more exposure. (It is possible, though, that the exchanges referring to cooking and hygiene occurred but were not included in the actual TV broadcast as they lost their novelty for the viewer, and because the development of individual relationships required that more attention be turned to exchanges reflecting these relationships.)

The second factor that affected the frequency of requestives in the later period was the decline in the frequency of initiating requests for the speaker's benefit. They occur as frequently as once in 9 minutes in the early period and as rarely as once in 25 minutes in the late period. For comparison, they occurred once in about 22 minutes in both periods of E4. This suggests that the interaction strategy pursued from the start by the housemates in this edition was to form bonds with others on the one hand through proposing joint action to the whole group (proposal to MA), and on the other hand via addressing others individually in matters concerning one's own benefit, including seeking a favour from someone. Both dominant forms of directive behaviour lost some of their prominence, to varied degrees, in the later period.

---

[35] df=1, x^2=12.3, p<0.001 for the ratio of proposals to requests and df=1, x^2=12.8, p<0.001 for the ratio of MA to SA. Cf. Appendix 1.

5.1.1.2. DEVELOPMENT OF DIRECTIVE ACTIVITIES IN E4

In the initial period there occurred an intense effort of the housemates directed towards group consolidation, reflected in a high number of initiatives of group play and fun. As the activities became repetitive and lost their novelty, the vivid start was followed by a period of stagnation.

In the first week, the prevailing sort of request (42% of all requests) was the request to a single addressee for the sake of a larger group including S and H (group 6). Requests from group 6 were produced twice as frequently as in the later period. Requestives from group 3 (speaker's benefit only) formed only 10% of all requestives in the early period.

In the early period, about one quarter of the requests to SA for the sake of a larger group (group 6) referred to the performance of a joint task assigned to the group by Big Brother (peddling in couples on an exercise bike for 72 hours). The remaining three quarters resulted from spontaneously undertaken activities. Even if the requestives referring to the peddling task are not counted, the difference in densities between the early and the later period for this category is considerably large.

Next to requests to a single addressee for the group's sake, frequent in the early period were also proposals of joint action, usually (84%) addressed to MA (multiple addressee), for the sake of a group consisting of the speaker and the addressees (beneficiary configuration 5; see Appendix). They occurred every 10.6 minutes in the early period and every 16.9 minutes in the late period. Again, the figures reflect the fact that in the initial week of their stay in the Big Brother house, the housemates in E4 undertook numerous initiatives aimed at their consolidation as a group, such as games, contests, joint singing, or visiting Big Brother in the diary room.

Requests to a single speaker for the sake of a larger group, and proposals for the sake of the group consisting of the speaker and the addressees reflect largely the same approach to the group, and appear largely within the same interactions. A proposal, implicit or explicit, of a joint action is frequently accompanied by a request to a housemate who is to play a particular role in the joint activity. This is exemplified by the following exchange, where several directives are directed to M3 in the course of preparing a joint visit in the "diary room" (the point of communication between the production team and the housemates):

3-E4. DIARY ROOM

The group have gathered at the entrance to the diary room. The rules say that the diary room can only be visited by one housemate at a time. A button is to be pressed to make Big Brother unlock the door.

```
1 M1 are you all going in
2 F1 yeah # come on
3 F2 no one sit on the chair
4 F3 shall we ring again
(M3 presses the button)
(the group waits for four seconds)
5 F2 only one person go in  (request at underspecified SA, beneficiary +S,+H,+EXT)
6 F1 yeah # only one person go in  (request at underspecified SA, beneficiary +S,+H, +EXT)
7 M2 to M3: press the button again  (request at SA, beneficiary +S,+H,+EXT)
(F1, F2, M1, M2, M4 move a step further from the door, M3 stays by the door)
8 M4 we'll wait here # to hear the bell # we're just gonna wait here
9 M2 just leave it # you just stay there for now (to M3 who is holding a broom; M3
is going to enter the diary room on the group's behalf) (request at SA, beneficiary +S,+H,+EXT)
(An acoustic signal announces the unlocking of the door; the whole group rush into the diary room.)
```

Directives uttered within the frame of joint activities which the housemates agreed to perform resemble instructionals in that they pertain to optimising the contributions of particular housemates in these activities. (Instructionals, though, were defined before as directives uttered in the context where the roles of the instructor and the instructed have been appointed in the earlier course of interaction.) Here, the frequency with which these quasi-instructionals are produced reflects the dynamics of interaction prompting familiarity, informality and a sense of coordinated action by the group.

In both periods, the ratio of requestives addressed at groups exceeds 40%. While inhibitives to single addressees prevail clearly, inhibitives are not infrequently addressed at groups, too (16 items, 30% of all inhibitives).

In this group, the high frequency of requests from group 6 and proposals in the initial period of the relationship reflects the profusion of spontaneous play and fun that was used for group consolidation, and by each individual as the means to become a visible and accepted member of the group. Smaller alliances were not built The creation and confirmation of group bonds, and self-presentation within the frame of the group as a whole was from the beginning the preferred strategy of interaction. Requests for the speaker's sake occur very rarely compared to appeals for action affecting the group. At the same time, individual friendships hardly develop, just as with individual animosities. Clearly, the figures do not ideally reflect all the interaction in the Big Brother house, because the transcripts analysed only cover an excerpt of the action, selected to be shown to the public. On the other hand, though, the selected material is likely to be based on the prominent type of events. Choosing group-oriented behaviour, the participants chose not to distinguish any one person and treat everybody on an equal basis. When more broadcast time was sacrificed in this series to group actions and conversations than to interactions between individuals or smaller subgroups, it may have resulted from the inconsequential character of individual relationships, that is, the lack of strong, emotionalised interpersonal alliances as well as grievances, and, as a result, the scarcity of momentous exchanges between single persons.

Requests from group 6 (for a group's sake) and proposals are the two sorts of requestives that occur in the initial period with a considerably higher frequency than four weeks later, when the bonds are already established, the housemates know each other well, there are fewer persons present, and the dynamics of joint activities decreases.

Notably, the press criticised the change in interaction patterns that took place after the initial few days as a shift from action towards boredom, and the viewership dropped dramatically.

5.1.1.3. DEVELOPMENT OF DIRECTIVE ACTIVITIES IN G2

G2 was implemented in design A. Frequent animosities and differences of opinion occurred early, and escalated with time, leading at a later stage to a split of the group into a formation of fractions supporting one or the other party. Teasing as a distance-diminishing, integrative activity occurred from the very start, especially among the men.

This group stood out by a very low ratio of requestives to multiple addressees in both periods (15 and 17% of all requestives)[36].

5.1.1.4. DEVELOPMENT OF DIRECTIVE ACTIVITIES IN G4

G4 realised the "battle" design B in which the group was divided into teams competing for living standards, living in two areas separated by a division line in the living room, and a fence in the yard. There were no significant differences on the factors intervention, representation, and type of addressee between the early and late period of acquaintance.

This series was distinguished by a high percentage of non-German participants, living in Germany or Switzerland (native speakers of Swiss German). Three foreigners, including a native speaker of German (Somalian), a Hungarian and a native speaker of Swiss German (a Swiss national), and five persons of German origin lived in the house in the first two weeks of

---

[36] Differences from other groups were significant: P1>G2, df=1, x^2=9.2, p<0,005; P3>G2, df=1, x^2=13.6, p<0.001; G4>G2, df=1, x^2=4.3, p<0.05; E3>G2, df=1, x^2=9.4, p<0.005; E4>G2, df=1, x^2=38.5, p<0.001.

the program (sample G4E). In week 5 (sample G4L), the group consisted of six German participants and three non-German participants: the Somalian, a Yugoslavian and a Swiss national living in Switzerland.

The idiosyncrasies of the non-German speakers were reflected not only in their own linguistic production. They may also have affected the directive activities of other participants, in which they functioned either as addressees or beneficiaries, or by their influence upon aspects of group dynamics such as integration, conflicts, alienation, and corrective behaviour.

The impact of the presence of non-German housemates is visible among others in the fact that 22% of all directives in the period preceding the exit of the aforementioned Swiss housemate on the fifth day of the program were produced as a consequence of a row between the Swiss and the Somali housemate (including mediation and further consequences). Another cluster of corrective directive activities concerned the Hungarian housemate F, who behaved in ways judged as deviant or undesirable by some of her team members. In 15 cases within 232 minutes of sampled interaction before her departure, this undesirable behaviour resulted in the production of directives, mainly inhibitive, directed at F. Six further requestives were directed at other persons as a consequence (e.g. in defending F), and 4 were uttered by F in self-defence. These 25 directives amounted to 15% of all directives in the house recorded during the initial 14 days, and enhanced considerably the ratio of inhibitive requestives in the data. One half of all inhibitive requests in the data concerned this housemate as addressee, speaker, or beneficiary. At one point, a reasonable hypothesis was put forward by a German housemate that the difficulties resulted from the fact that the Hungarian housemate "thinks Hungarian" rather than German compared to the rest of her team. Collectivist predilections manifested by this housemate at the outset of the program[37] were rejected by the dominant part of the team and might have initiated the process of her alienation from the group.

Also, uninhibited and distance-diminishing sexual jokes and teasing performed by the Yugoslav housemate frequently resulted in inhibitive requestives on the part of a female

---

[37] The Hungarian housemate treated the whole group from the beginning as her in-group rather than just her team members. She assumed that birthdays would be celebrated by both teams and that the actions and decisions by Big Brother can and should be influenced by the joint action of the housemates. She proposed repeatedly to her team to beg Big Brother to arrange a celebration of the rival team member's birthday which passed without Big Brother taking any notice. The initiative was rejected and judged improper and rather unreasonable by some of her German team members.

German housemate. In sum, the housemates who were not native German speakers were more frequently the focus of corrective and inhibitive directive activities than the German housemates.

To sum up, the interactions between and around the non-German housemates had a considerable impact upon the group dynamic, and the nature of these interactions might raise some doubts about whether the material in this edition reflects the "typically German" traits of the young adults' culture. I accept this sample as a valid and representative source of data, because mono-ethnic youth groups are becoming an exception rather than a rule as a result of world-wide migrations. In 2005, the ratio of foreigners and people who migrated to Germany[38] among German residents in the group age 25 to 30 amounted to 24%[39], and it is higher than that in towns and cities. It would be difficult to find a mono-ethnic group among urban German youths, apart from groups based on nationality as their essential principle (e.g. some ultra-conservative students' associations). I assume that the sample reflected the traits of the present-day German youth culture (influenced as it is by the presence of people with a migrant background) on the basis of the following justification:

- the prevailing majority of the participants were German nationals and native speakers of German;
- the game took place in Germany and within the frame of the German culture;
- the crew producing the program, who acted "behind the curtains", was German (notwithstanding the fact that it may also have included people with migrant backgrounds);
- except for the Swiss housemates, the foreigners and people with migrant backgrounds had spent several years in Germany prior to appearing on the program and can be expected to have adapted the German conventions of language use to a considerable degree;
- among other things, they were selected from among numerous candidates on the basis of their very good command of German and good communicative skills;
- analysing the form of requestive utterances, I took precautions to make sure that the formal properties of directives produced by the speakers who are not native German did not depart to a considerable degree from the rest.[40]

---

[38] I.e., people who currently hold German citizenship but were born abroad.

[39] Statistisches Bundesamt: Bevölkerung mit Migrationshintergrund – Ergebnisse des Mikrozensus 2005.

[40] The housemates for whom German was the second culture showed a weakly significant tendency to the more frequent use of imperative, 66% vs. 48% in requestives by native speakers: $df=1$, $x^2=6.5$, $p<0.025$. This

Courting relationships were numerous and a cross-gender friendship occurred. In-group feeling developed and the tendency to treat the rival team as an out-group was overcome with time, as was visible in the increase of inter-team communication, as well as in singular events such as the participants expressing a feeling of responsibility for peace in the group as a whole, a sacrifice made for a member of a rival team, or expressing interest in a group meeting after the program. The differences in directive behaviour with respect to the "static" series are likely to have resulted in some part from the different design that promoted team responsibility and integration by introducing team goals and team combat.

5.1.1.5. DEVELOPMENT OF DIRECTIVE ACTIVITIES IN P3

This series was implemented in the "battle" design B, but it differed from G4 and E3 as there was no division into "poor" and "rich" territories in the living room and the yard. The housemates were allowed to interact freely, while different sets of house rules were to be followed by the loosing and the winning team.

The interaction showed many indicators of group solidarity such as the use of family metaphors, verbal declarations of friendship and well-being owed to the group or team, "we"-references, planning and taking for granted meetings after the program, frequent references to the housemates who left the Big Brother house, criticising bilateral relationships as drawbacks to team solidarity, giving mostly other-oriented (trespasses against others) or group-oriented reasons when nominating other housemates for eviction (that is, in the weekly secret voting on who is to leave the Big Brother house), and symbolic gestures including rule-breaking as manifestations of group or team spirit.

This did not preclude the development of numerous strong individual relationships, such as intra-gender and cross-gender friendships, courting and sexual relationships, and a teasing relationship.

Requestives from group 6 (the beneficiary is +S,+H,+EXT) are the most frequent type in the early period. Although they are later produced as frequently as before, they become surpassed in frequency by requests for the speaker's own benefit. A close look at the data shows that the increase in the ratio of requestives from group 3 (speaker's benefit) at the later stage is due mainly to the development of a teasing relationship between two housemates, male and female, whose disputes containing calls for verbal activities (such as

---

was however disregarded as it did not produce significant effects in the overall ratio of negative to positive head act politeness, and because the same tendency also occurred in two participants in G2 who had native language skills in German but came from migrant families.

the use of a politeness routine, explaining a pun, clarifying a point) provide as much as one third of all requestives from group 3 in this sub-sample. (These exchanges provide as much as about 20 % of the corresponding bulk in Diagram 9 below, showing frequencies of requestives affecting a single addressee and a single speaker only.)

5.1.1.6. P1: BRIEF CHARACTERISTICS

The data available for transcription came from weeks 5 and 6 of the program. Several indices that occurred during this period suggested that the group integration was lower than in "battle" edition P3, such as a lesser number of nicknames (some housemates were not accorded a nickname at all, and non-distorted standard forms of first name were not infrequently in use)[41], ostentatious indifference of two housemates during the unexpected eviction of a housemate who was popular with the rest of the group, and a discussion of two housemates who commented pejoratively on the lack of group spirit and on other housemates pursuing their own interests only (these two housemates were the last two to leave the Big Brother house, which may have reflected the preferences of the Polish audience, favouring collectivist attitudes).

5.1.2. FREQUENCIES OF REQUESTIVE ACTIVITIES

5.1.2.1. INTRAGROUP CONTRASTS BETWEEN DIFFERENT STAGES OF THE PROGRAM

The measurement showed that for some groups there were some non-trivial intra-group differences between the two periods. There was a weakly significant decline in the proportion of the factor *intervention* (from 12% to 4%, df=1, chi square=4.5, p<0.05), accompanied by a considerable decline in their frequency, for G2. For E3, there was a large and statistically significant decline in the percentage of directives addressed at *multiple addressees*, accompanied by a significant decline in their frequency of occurrence. For E4, there was a significant decline in the proportion of the factor *representation* from 55 to 37% (chi square=8.9, p<0.005), accompanied by a decline in their frequency of occurrence (from 19 to 9 occurrences per hour, or from 3.2 to 6.9 min. mean interval). For P3, the frequency of requestives representing the factor *intervention* nearly doubled[42].

---

[41] The significance of nicknaming in Polish is discussed in section 6.2.1.

[42] The inclusion of the stray cat episode would change the percentage of *intervention* to 19%, *representation* in P3L to 44%, and *addressing groups* to 26%, and increase the frequencies of their occurrence to 3.9, 1.7, and 2.8 minutes, respectively.

The differences confirmed the occurrence of development and change in the quantified aspects of directive activities. In effect, the Polish data P1 should only be compared to the corresponding period in the other samples, as it cannot be assumed to adequately sample directive activities in this series. Consequently, the sub-samples (the early and late period) will be presented separately in several tables in this chapter. Besides, the duration of prior acquaintance will also be tested regarding its impact upon their form.

While acknowledging intra-lingual differences, in what follows I will end up with a comparison totalling all data from any language there where it is necessary to make up for the small sizes of the categories under analysis.

5.1.2.2. INTRA- AND INTERERLINGUAL COMPARISON: AN OVERVIEW

Table 2 and the corresponding diagram below show the frequencies with which requestives occur in particular samples. The figures in the first and second left column refer to the mean frequencies of occurrence in the early and later sample, respectively, of the same series. The figures in the third and fourth columns give the duration of the interaction time (without editorials etc.).

	FREQUENCY (per hour)		TIME SCANNED (minutes)		NO. OF REQUESTIVES		
	EARLY	LATE	EARLY	LATE	EARLY	LATE	TOTAL
E3	33	25	271	477	148	196	344
E4	35	24	266	322	153	128	281
G4	42	34	232	188	164	107	271
G2	31	24	195	255	100	102	202
P3	53	68	314	151	277	171	448
P1	xxx	49	xxx	244	xxx	199	199

Table 2. Mean frequencies of the occurrence of requestive utterances. The shadowing marks the frequencies as *high* (dark), *middle* (lighter) or *low* (white) on a given factor in comparison to the other groups. *Middle:* frequency from 0.67 to 1.33 of the mean of all values.

It should be remarked that I stopped short of including in the sample P3L four consecutive episodes centred around the group trapping, feeding, debating to set free, and finally setting free a stray cat which found its way into the yard of the Big Brother house. These episodes followed immediately the last scene in the statistically analysed sample. They contained a record number of 47 requestives produced within seven minutes, which corresponds to a requestive being produced on average every nine seconds. Although I believe that they reflect some characteristic features of interact tion in this group, and in groups of Polish young adults in general, I opted for excluding them from the statistics as they constituted a distinguished "singularity" in the usual course of action, where requestives were more evenly distributed in time and which I expected to be adequately reflected in the figures. The scene closest to it as far as the number of requestives produced within a short time span is concerned contained twelve requestives uttered within about forty seconds (in the same series). Including the cat episodes in the analysis would further increase the already considerable difference between the average density of requestives in this sample and the German and British samples (increasing the average density of requestives in Diagram 4 from 66 to 86 per hour in P3L). Some of these requestives will however be discussed in the non-statistical part of the analysis.

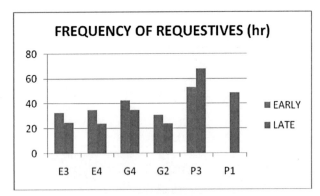

Diagram 4

The interactive style of the speakers of Polish is characterised by a rich presence of requestive speech acts. In what follows I will speak of the rich presence of requestives as an impositive interaction style. (In the chapter on form, I will speak of an impositive communicative style, characterised by the use of direct and positively polite strategies in realising directive speech acts.) I evaluate this result as indicating a higher level of individualism (acknowledgment of other persons' freedom of action) in German and English speakers, and a contrary tendency in the speakers of Polish. A high level of collectivism is reflected in the impositive style based on the presupposition of consensus on group members being entitled to impose on each other[43].

Both "battle" samples, P3 and G4, scored somewhat higher on the density of requestives than the samples in the same languages made in other designs. Sample G4E, where a requestive was uttered on average every 1.4 minutes, came close to the Polish series. This result might reflect chance differences in group dynamics and behavioural patterns in the two German series, resulting from different mixes of personalities who happened to participate together. The other viable explanation is that the team-based design in G4 promoted the production of directives, because it promoted interdependence and group integration, at least within particular teams, through the team members sharing goals, efforts, and outcomes of the competition. This assumption will be further supported in what follows by a closer look at the sorts of requestives produced in each group.

5.1.2.2. PARTICIPANTS' STRUCTURES: REPRESENTATION, INTERVENTION, MULTIPLE ADDRESSEE – INTRA- AND INTERLINGUAL COMPARISON

The following table shows how frequently various groups produced requestives of different sorts, distinguished as indicators of group-orientation of directive activities. The figures specify how frequently requestives of particular subtypes occurred in terms of their mean frequencies and in comparison with the complementary subtypes, that is, as percentages of the whole pool of requestives in the respective samples.

---

[43] Cf. also Sifianou (1998).

FACTOR	ADDRESSING GROUPS				INTERVENTION				REPRESENTATION			
Dimension	Frequency (hr)		%		Frequency (hr)		%		Frequency (hr)		%	
PERIOD	EARLY	LATE	EARLY	LATE	EARLY	LATE	EARLY	LATE	EARLY	LATE	EARLY	LATE
E3	13	5	39%	21%	1	1	3%	5%	7	7	22%	28%
E4	14	11	41%	46%	1	1	3%	5%	19	9	55%	37%
G4	10	9	24%	25%	3	2	8%	6%	15	12	37%	34%
G2	5	4	17%	17%	4	1	12%	4%	8	8	27%	32%
P3	17	18	33%	27%	5	10	10%	15%	24	26	45%	38%
P1	xxx	15	xxx	30%	xxx	5	xxx	11%	xxx	18	xxx	37%

Table 3. Mean frequecies (per hour, rounded) and percentages of requestives containing the factors *addressing groups*, *intervention* and *representation*. Three colours mark the figures as high (dark), middle (lighter) or low (light) on a given factor in comparison to the other groups. Frequency from 0.67 to 1.33 of the mean of all values on the given factor is marked as *middle*; frequency lower than that is *low*; frequency higher than that is *high*. For percentages: if significantly different from the highest then NOT HIGH (low or middle), if significantly different from the lowest then NOT LOW (high or middle), default value: middle.

Both Polish series were characterised by high (in terms of frequencies) and high or middle (in terms of percentages of the whole pool of requestives) scores on these sorts of requestives. The only larger difference occurred in the frequency of requestives showing "intervention", higher in P3L than in P1. This tendency was in agreement with the expectation that team combat might promote integrative interaction, and with the observation of other indicators of group solidarity in both groups (see the description of P3 and P1 above).

The same tendency manifested itself in German "battle" edition G4, which surpassed G2 in the quantity of requestives in general, and in the quantities of directives distinguished as strong indicators of group-orientation, in particular MA requestives. Also in this case, among the two German groups, G4 showed more signs of group integration, while the formation of animosities and group-splitting alliances shaped the interaction in G2.

The German series score low or middle on both "representation" and "addressing groups", and on average high (compared to the English series) on "intervention". G4 occupies a middle position with respect to the occurrence of the distinguished types of directives (intervention, representation and addressing groups), while G2 tends towards the lower end.

Diagrams 5 through 7 show the numbers of requestives of particular sorts occurring per hour of interaction.

The British series E4 and E3 are least similar, and in each of them there is a considerable internal difference on one parameter between the early and the later period. While the attempts to explain why the housemates in E4 reduced "representation" with time must remain speculative, it is tempting to attribute the change in E3 to the change from the design A to the design C, which was based on intensified individual competition and impeded group consolidation. E4 occupies a middle position among all the groups with respect to the occurrence of the distinguished types of directives, while E3 tends towards the lower end.

To sum up, both Polish series contained most directives indicating group-orientation, while the British and the Germans share the middle and lower placement with respect to this property.

The clearest outcome of the analysis is the very infrequent occurrence in the British groups of the requestives representing "intervention". While the Poles and the Germans relatively frequently interfered with the relationships between other housemates or the housemates and outgroup members, this type of behaviour was exceptional among the British. The conclusion is that the British norms of interaction provided relatively little room for interference. Interaction participants were expected to notice needs of others and take care of making their own needs apparent to others, rather than to intervene in relationships and interactions between other people.

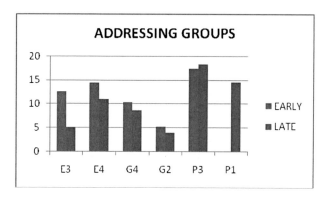

Diagram 5. Frequencies of directives addressing groups per hour of interaction.

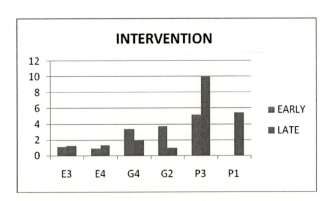

Diagram 6. Frequencies of interventional directives per hour of interaction.

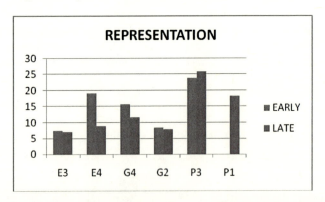

Diagram 7. Frequencies of representational directives per hour of interaction.

The Poles and the Germans differed on that point in that while the Poles did not show any pronounced preference for any type of addressee (41% of requestives of that type were addressed at groups) in interventional directives, the Germans directed them more frequently at single addressees (and only in 17% of cases at groups). The difference in this respect for the total of all German and all Polish data is significant[44]. This relates to the fact that in German nearly half of the interventional directives were inhibitives (correcting or

---

[44] df=1, chi square=5.1, p<0.025

preventing misbehaviour towards others), and in both series and periods, German subjects addressed inhibitive requests generally infrequently at groups (13% of all inhibitives vs. 26% in Polish and 22% in English). The total difference in this respect for the sums of the German and Polish samples is significant[45].

Another interesting perspective on the figures can be achieved by totalling all requestives that concerned the speaker and a single hearer only (as actors or beneficiaries), reflecting directive activities in individual relationships (dyadic encounters), and all those that involve more than two participants, that is, are either addressed at MA (multiple addressee) or include a beneficiary who is neither the hearer nor the speaker (+EXT). The results are presented below (diagrams 8 and 9).

The diagrams show that the differences in the group-oriented requestives (diagram 8) between the Polish and the other groups are more pronounced than for the complementary individual-oriented type (diagram 9). The higher presence of the requestive activities in the Polish series is due mainly to requestives that concern more than two persons as beneficiaries or addressees, which are here assumed to indicate group-orientation.

The diagrams 5-8 also show that in both Polish and German, the "battle" editions P3 and G4 surpassed their counterparts in the "static" design A (G2 and P1) in the frequencies of requestives featuring representation, intervention and multiple addressee, as well as their sum. At the same time, the intralingual differences in the frequency of requestives of the complementary type (SA and –X), concerning the singular speaker and the singular addressee only, were comparatively very small. This suggests that directives of the former type were promoted by the "battle" design favourable to group-oriented attitudes. These non-percentual results are however not amenable to a statistical test of significance.

---

[45] df=1, chi square=5.9, p<0.025

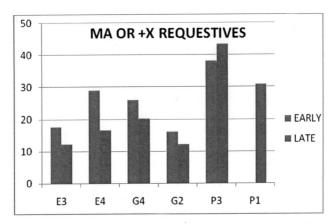

Diagram 8. Frequencies of requestives involving more than two participants per hour of interaction.

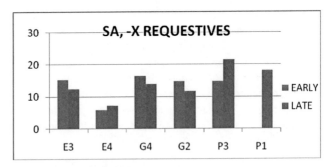

Diagram 9. Frequencies of requestives involving two participants per hour of interaction.

INTERVENTION: TYPE OF ACTION AND ADDRESSEE

Significant differences for the whole pool of requestives comprising all samples occurred between German and Polish within the subcategory "intervention", whose beneficiaries include +EXT (non-S, non-H) and exclude S. 41% of such requests were addressed at multiple addressees in Polish, and only 17%[46] in German, suggesting a stronger group-orientation of such appeals in the speakers of Polish. Utterances of that type were split

---

[46] df=1, x^2=5.9, p<0.025.

between inhibitive and initiating requestives in unequal proportions. In German, 49% of "interventional" requestives were inhibitive, and in Polish only 28%[47]. This suggests that the speakers of German were more strongly corrective in their interventions, while the Poles performed them prevailingly in order to trigger beneficial action rather than terminate misbehaviour.

The British data showed almost the same distribution as the Polish data; this was however inconclusive because of the small number of items in this category in English.

REQUESTS FOR THE SPEAKER'S SAKE TO A MULTIPLE ADDRESSEE

Requests from group 3 are of special interest as they are usually treated as a canonical type of request, with "goods and services" (Leech 1983) flowing from H to S who is the only beneficiary of the predicated action. This triggers intense "face work" in the form of a polite redress on S's part. For that reason, requests for the speaker's sake have typically been the focus of interest in the tradition of study of politeness based on pseudo-natural methods. Only one item, however, in the hitherto mentioned studies concerned a request to a multiple addressee (CCSARP, Blum-Kulka et al. 1989: a student asks people living on the same street for a ride home).

The negligence of requests for the speaker's sake directed at multiple addressees seems justifiable in view of the data to hand: among requests from group 3, only 19% in Polish, 13% in English and 9% in German were of that type. However, the interlingual contrasts that appeared in their production make them worthy of analysis.

The interlingual difference of proportions to the whole pool of requests from this beneficiary group was significant for Polish/German[48]. They occurred on average every 64 minutes in English, every 23 minutes in Polish (with a very small difference between the two series) and every 72 minutes in German, while the German series differ in this respect, scoring 50 for the "battle" series G4 and 112 minutes for G2.

The interlingual contrast between Polish and the remaining two languages is puzzling and the finding could only be interpreted through a thematic and context-bound inspection of the data to hand. A type of utterance in Polish that distinguishes it from the other two languages are relatively frequent requests in the imperative plural for an action which, in the situation given, can be performed by one person only, such as "pass me the salt" in plural rather than singular. (Analogical utterances in English are either hints or speaker-oriented or

---

[47] df=1, x^2=4.3, p<0.05

[48] df=1, chi square=5.8, p<0.025

use an indefinite personal pronoun.) Similarly, utterances such as "stop that" in the imperative plural occur in Polish in reaction to an immediately preceding action by only *one* of two or more hearers; in her reaction, the speaker indirectly attributes the undesirable behaviour to *all* (or both) hearers. The occurrence of this phenomenon isn't merely casual as it recurs in requests from other beneficiary configurations, and in the recorded data not included in the statistical analysis. It will be treated in detail in the qualitative part; at this point it is enough to say that I interpret it as manifesting the perception of a group (or a couple) as a whole rather than as an assembly of individuals. Pluralisation in corrective and terminating inhibitives can also be interpreted as an indirect politeness strategy of softening an implied criticism by defocalising the actual wrong-doer. This interpretation does not go against the claim that it indicates a stronger group-orientation of the speakers of Polish, as this politeness strategy seems to be hardly available to the speakers of German, where the only kind of polite pluralisation used is "we"-plural instead of "you"-singular. Neither did it occur in English, where the plural and singular forms of imperative are morphologically indistinguishable, but the references can be distinguished on the basis of verbal and non-verbal clues (e.g. a term of address, grounder, or eye contact).

It is interesting to note that my child, socialised in Germany, repeatedly objects to corrective and terminating inhibitive requests made in the plural when the actual wrong-doer is another child, much to the interlocutor's confusion whenever this happens during our visits to Poland.

To sum up, I assume that the greater frequency of appealing to groups in requests for the speaker's sake reflects the fact that the Poles more frequently address a group or a couple as a whole rather than appoint a single actor, when an action, or a termination of action, is required of a single person. A more detailed discussion of this language-specific phenomenon will be undertaken in chapter 7.4.10.

OCCURRENCE OF REQUESTIVE SPEECH ACTS: A SUMMARY

The Polish groups displayed the most impositive interaction style, producing requestive utterances more frequently than any other group under study. Another group in which requestives were produced with relatively high frequency was G4 realised in the "battle" edition. This edition involved team competition that promoted the rise of solidarity and group integration at least within particular teams. Also, the Polish "battle" edition P3 surpassed the other edition P1 as far as the frequency of requestives was concerned. This supports the assumption that the amount of directive activities in the peer group context is related to group-orientation and group integrity.

The difference between the Polish and the other groups was considerable for requestives which cannot be accounted for within the model of dyadic encounter, because they involved more than two participants in the three participants' roles (speaker, addressee and beneficiary; "MA or EXT+"). This resulted from the fact that the Poles produced more requestives on behalf of groups in which they were participants, frequently directed requestives to multiple addressees, and frequently interfered between others. The difference between Polish and the other two languages was small or absent for directives uttered in dyadic encounters ("SA and EXT-").

Also, the Polish and German battle editions contained more directives than their "static" counterparts mainly because they displayed more representation, intervention and group address, and only marginally because "dyadic" directives were also more numerous. This additionally supports the thesis that there is a relationship between the production of directives of non-dyadic type and the team spirit.

Another types of requestives produced much more frequently by the Poles than by the other two groups was the request for the speaker's sake (beneficiary group 3) directed to multiple addressee. This can have followed from actually perceiving others as groups, or the politeness strategy of minimising imposition through de-focalising the actual trespasser in inhibitive (terminating, corrective) requestives. This strategy can only be applied when the perception is available of a number of interlocutors as an entity (group) in which actions of individuals represent actions of the group as a whole, and when the speakers assumes that the interlocutors view this perspective as legitimate. As far as this may be viewed as an indicator of group-orientation, the figures indicate the higher group-orientation of the Poles.

The British data stood out in the least frequent production of the requestives from the type "intervention", in which the speaker shows the intention of influencing the behaviour of the addressee towards other person or persons, typically other housemates; this suggests a low social esteem of on-record intervention among the British peers. The Poles showed most intervention. Intervention requestives addressed to multiple addressees were much more frequent in Polish than in German, suggesting a stronger group-orientation of such appeals in the speakers of Polish. The speakers of German produced as many inhibitive as initiating requestives of the interventional type, while the Poles performed them prevailingly in order to trigger beneficial action rather than eliminate misbehaviour.

Several changes occurred in the distribution of requestives between the two stages of the same series. They were inconclusive in themselves, because there was no consistent pattern for different groups within the same language. However, they indicated that both periods should be dealt with separately in order to secure interlingual and inter-group comparability, as only the data from the later period were available for P1.

5.2. POLITENESS STRATEGIES

5.2.1. HEAD ACT POLITENESS: INTERLINGUAL AND INTRALINGUAL DIFFERENCE

One of the goals of the present study is a comparative analysis of the strategies of politeness applied in requestive utterances by the speakers of the three languages under study. The table below shows the percentages of requestives realised by means of negatively polite head acts. In the context under analysis, negative head politeness plays a lesser role than impositive formulations in all languages and all groups. Table 4 shows the intralingual constancy of preferences in different groups of speakers, and the interlingual contrast between Polish on the one hand and the remaining two languages on the other.

% OF NEGATIVELY POLITE HEAD ACTS OF REQUESTIVES					
E3	E4	G2	G4	P1	P3
23%	20%	15%	15%	8%	7%

Table 4. Negatively polite head act in particular series as percentages of all requests and proposals.

The differences between Polish and English are highly significant[49] and suggest a qualitatively different approach to linguistic strategies. The differences between Polish and German are statistically significant but not impressive; also those between German and English are significant[50] while practically meaningless, unless it can be shown that the relatively small total interlingual difference reflects larger differences in some sub-samples selected along specific contextual parameters.

Finally, Diagram 10 illustrates the statistically significant correlation between the mean intervals (the opposite of frequencies) at which requestives occurred in each pooled series and percentages of negatively polite head acts, i.e. the correlation between the impositive interaction style (many directives) and impositive communication style (direct, non-

---

[49] For Polish/English df=1, $x^2=53.0$, p<0.001.

[50] For Polish/German, df=1. $x^2=18.0$, p<0.01. For English/German, df=1, $x^2=7.2$, p<0.01.

tentative formulations of directives).[51] The correlation confirms that more impositive interaction style tends to co-occur with impositive communication style.

CORRELATION IN MEAN INTERVALS AND
% OF NEGATIVE HEAD ACT POLITENESS
OF REQUESTIVES

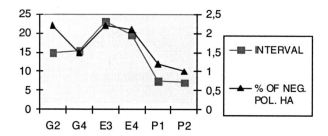

Diagram 10

5.2.2. FACTORS AFFECTING POLITENESS CHOICE

5.2.2.1. INFLUENCE OF INTERACTION STRUCTURE ON HEAD ACT POLITENESS

In view of the differences in the types of directives produced in different groups, the total difference in the politeness strategies used may reflect mainly the influence of contextual factors, rather a stronger preference for positively polite formulations among the Polish subjects in general. While the choice of strategy can be assumed to be strongly influenced by factors not amenable to a statistical treatment, such as personal sympathies and antipathies and the history of previous encounters, I also assume that it is possible to distinguish some directly observable recurrent configurations of context properties which

---

[51] Pearson's product-moment correlation coefficient for the ratio of negatively polite head acts and the mean interval between two consecutive occurrences of requestives is $r=0.87$, $df=4$, $p<0.05$.

111

regularly affect such choices. The analysis of their regular influence on the choice of head act politeness is the subject of the following chapter.

Potential candidates for sources of influence upon the choice of politeness strategies in the head act of requestive utterances are particular properties of interaction structure, such as beneficiary characteristics (+/- H, S, X) and beneficiary configurations, action types (inhibitive vs. initiating), addressee characteristics MA/SA, and actor type (proposal vs. request). Below, the correlations between particular aspects of interaction structure and their combinations, and the proportion of tentative to impositive head acts are put to a statistical significance test.

ADDRESSEE CHARACTERISTICS: MULTIPLE VERSUS SINGLE ADDRESSEE

NEGATIVE POLITE HEAD ACTS – MA VS. SA ADDRESSEE					
df=1	N	MA	SA	x^2	significance
G2	202	29%	12%	6.9	p<0.01
G4	271	28%	11%	12.1	p<0.001
E3	346	24%	23%	0.0	insignificant
E4	281	22%	18%	0.9	insignificant
P1	199	5%	9%	0.7	insignificant
P3	448	9%	6%	0.8	insignificant

Table 5. The effects of addressee characteristics "multiple" and "single" upon head act politeness in requestives. The percentages refer to the percentage of negatively polite head acts.

Table 5 shows how many of the requestives addressed at multiple and single addressees, respectively, were realised in a tentative head act form. The contrast "multiple addressee" versus "single addressee" in formulating requestives seems to be an emic distinction with respect to head act politeness in German, where speakers chose formulating such requests much more frequently in a tentative way when addressing groups (that is, more than one person). The effect is consistent for both groups analysed, G2 and G4. In the other two languages, head act politeness was not influenced by this distinction.

ACTION TYPE: INITATING VS. INHIBITIVE REQUESTIVES

NEGATIVELY POLITE HEAD ACTS – INI VS. INH REQUESTIVES					
df=1	N	INI	INH	x^2	significance
G2	202	16%	12%	0.4	insignificant
G4	271	18%	2%	8.0	$p<0.005$
E3	346	31%	6%	26.0	$p<0.001$
E4	281	23%	4%	10.7	$p<0.005$
P1	199	9%	0%	2.4	insignificant
P3	448	8%	4%	2.7	insignificant

Table 6. The effects of action type "initiating" and "inhibitive" (non-action)
upon head act politeness in requestives.

Table 6 shows that inhibitive requestives were produced very rarely in a tentative form in all three languages. This effect is likely to result from a more confrontational character of requestives of that type, that are usually triggered by a past, present or anticipated action of the addressee that is perceived as inopportune by the speaker. They aim to prevent a repetition or continuation of undesirable behaviour, and therefore might present a high face risk to the addressee. The data shows that when the speakers decided to show their discontent with the behaviour of the addressee, they also almost always disregarded the addressee's negative face wants in the verbal formulation of head acts, and opted for an impositive formulation. The difference between initiating and inhibitive requestives is plain for English, and a strong total correlation occurs also in German, however it is insignificant for one of the German groups. In Polish, although there is a slight nominal difference between both subcategories, it does not reach significance in any series, as the percentage of negatively polite head acts is negligibly small for initiating requestives, too.

ACTOR TYPE: REQUESTS VERSUS PROPOSALS

Proposals of joint action, in which the speaker is not the main beneficiary (these count as requests), were more frequently realised in a tentative way in both English and German. A putative conclusion would be that the type of actor (H in requests, H and S in proposals) is an emic distinction with respect to head politeness in these two languages: proposing to others a joint action with oneself might encourage distance-diminishing impositive strategies to a lesser degree than requesting.

However, a further look at the data is needed before this result can be interpreted, as it might reflect an effect of a co-occurrence of various factors rather than an effect of actor type itself:

- proposals were only exceptionally inhibitive, therefore they were less likely to be impositive than requests (see Table 6 above);
- proposals were more frequently addressed at groups than requests, and the politeness type was influenced by the addressee characteristics multiple vs. single in German (see Table 5 above). Alternatively, the correlation may work the other way round, i.e., the difference between MA and SA head act politeness can reflect the fact that requestives addressed at groups contained a large proportion of proposals (60% in the total of German samples), contrary to requestives to a single addressee which contained a smaller ratio of proposals (ca. 20% for the total of German samples).

To eliminate the influence of the factor "action type" (inhibitive vs. initiating), different actor types (proposals vs. requests) were compared within the subcategory of initiating requestives only. The results are shown in Table 8.

In G2, initiating proposals were more likely to be realised in a tentative way than initiating requests; G4 showed the same orientation while it only approached significance. The results for English suggest that the actor type (request vs. proposal) alone does not consistently influence the choice of head act politeness.

To eliminate the interference of the type of the addressee with the action type, it has been assessed whether initiating proposals and initiating requests to single and multiple addressees differed with respect to head act politeness. As both German series showed a consistent direction of the correlation between actor type and head act choice, I amalgamated proposals from both German corpora in order to obtain an adequate sample size for the smaller category of proposals. The results are shown in Table 9.

NEGATIVELY POLITE HEAD ACTS - PROPOSALS VS. REQUESTS					
df=1	N	RQ	PROP	x^2	significance
G2	202	11%	31%	10.9	p<0.001
G4	271	13%	26%	5.6	p<0.025
E3	346	20%	35%	7.5	p<0.01
E4	281	16%	33%	8.6	p<0.005
P1	199	7%	9%	0.2	insignificant
P3	448	7%	7%	0.0	insignificant

Table 7. The effects of actor type "proposal" vs. "request" upon head act politeness in requestives.

NEGATIVELY POLITE HEAD ACTS - INITIATING PROPOSALS AND REQUESTS					
df=1	N	RQ	PROP	x^2	significance
G2	202	10%	32%	10.7	p<0.005
G4	271	16%	27%	3.4	insignificant
E3	346	30%	33%	0.4	insignificant
E4	281	20%	33%	4.2	p<0.05
P1	199	8%	0%	0.1	insignificant
P3	448	9%	4%	0.1	insignificant

Table 8. The effects of actor type "proposal" and "request" upon head act politeness in initiating requestives.

GERMAN: % OF NEGATIVELY POLITE HEAD ACTS IN INITIATING REQUESTIVES – MA VS. SA ADDRESSEE					
MA	df=1	SA	df=1	x^2	significance
PROP INI	37%	PROP INI	17%	5,2	p<0.025
RQ INI	26%	RQ INI	12%	4,1	p<0.05
x^2	1,2	x^2	0,9	N SA PROP INI=35 N SA RQ INI=35	
SIGNIFICANCE	insignificant	SIGNIFICANCE	insignificant	N MA PROP INI=54 N MA RQ INI=257	

Table 9. Percentages of negatively polite head acts for initiating requestives
sub-classified along types of actor and addressee.

Initiating proposals addressed at a particular type of addressee do not significantly differ from initiating requests addressed at the same type of addressee in the ratio of tentatively formulated head acts. At the same time, both initiating requests and proposals were significantly more likely to be realised by a tentative head act when they addressed to multiple addressees.

In brief, the speakers of German showed more deferent behaviour when addressing a requestive at more than one person. From the factors considered, both action type (initiating vs. inhibitive), and the type of addressee seem to be the true differentiators of strategy choice in German.

BENEFICIARY CONFIGURATION

The assessment of the correlation between beneficiary and preferences in head act choice was conducted in form of a complex chi square statistics. Table 10 shows for each series whether the differences between particular beneficiary configurations in the percentage of negatively polite head acts reached significance. Nominal differences between particular categories do not allow for any conclusions if there are few items in one of the categories, because the less populated categories are more likely to reflect casual fluctuations of form-context pairing. These less populated categories are marked in the table[52]. The results of the chi square test are less conclusive for P1 and G2 than for other samples because of the smaller number of items in these samples.

The nominal differences in the choice of negatively polite head acts among various beneficiary categories are greater if inhibitive directives are sieved out. For initiating requestives only, the results are consistent for both British series (see Table 11). The lack of considerable difference in E3 for the whole pool of requestives (table 10) is due to a higher proportion of inhibitive requestives, mainly reactions to trespasses and practical jokes, in beneficiary 3 (+S, -H, -EXT) configuration in E3.

The results suggest a relatively flat pattern for German, where there was no significant overall effect, and a rather strong dependence of politeness choice on the beneficiary configuration in the other two languages. In both E4 and Polish, requestives for the speaker's own benefit (group 3, +S, -H,-EXT) are more frequently realised using negatively polite head acts than other densely populated beneficiary categories (5, +S, +H, -EXT and 6, +S, +H, +EXT).

Requestives that included an external beneficiary (EXT+) were more frequently realised in impositives than those which did not (EXT-); the difference was significant for both P3[53] and both English series[54]. The same correlation showed for the property (H+) in E3[55] and P3[56]. Neither the properties (EXT+) nor (H+) correlated with impositiveness in German.

---

[52] Tables showing the number of items in each category are available in the Appendix. Figures referring to poorly populated categories do not provide a reliable basis for generalisations.

[53] $df=1$, $x^2=11.5$, $p<0.001$

[54] For E3, $df=1$, $x^2=4.7$, $p<0.05$; for E3, $df=1$, $x^2=9.9$, $p<0.005$.

[55] $df=1$, $x^2=5.9$, $p<0.025$

[56] $df=1$, $x^2=12.5$, $p<0.001$

NEGATIVELY POLITE HEAD ACTS AND BENEFICIARY CONFIGURATIONS

df=5	-S,+H,+EXT	-S,-H,+EXT	+S,-H,-EXT	+S,-H,+EXT	+S,+H,-EXT	+S,+H,+EXT	x^2	significance
G2	0%	0%	20%	4%	17%	17%	8.1	insignificant
G4	50%	12%	12%	6%	22%	13%	7.2	insignificant
E3	0%	8%	29%	8%	24%	21%	9.4	insignificant
E4	0%	20%	41%	9%	21%	12%	18.6	p<0.005
P1	0%	11%	11%	13%	3%	8%	3.0	insignificant
P3	0%	5%	15%	9%	7%	0%	22.5	p<0.001

Table 10. Percentages of negative head politeness for particular beneficiary categories and the significances of the correlation between beneficiary group and head act politeness of requestives. The non-shadowed fields show richly populated categories, containing more than 40 items. The strongly shadowed fields mark categories containing less than 20 items, the weakly shadowed ones mark the categories containing between 20 and 40 items.

INITIATING REQUESTIVES – NEG. POLITE HEADS AND BENEFICIARY CONFIGURATIONS

df=5	-S,+H,+EXT	-S,-H,+EXT	+S,-H,-EXT	+S,-H,+EXT	+S,+H,-EXT	+S,+H,+EXT	x^2	significance
G2	0%	0%	18%	5%	18%	20%	8.1	insignificant
G4	100%	20%	15%	9%	24%	14%	7.2	insignificant
E3	xxx	0%	58%	14%	28%	23%	30.2	p<0.001
E4	0%	29%	65%	15%	22%	13%	41.4	p<0.001
P1	0%	13%	16%	13%	4%	8%	5.8	insignificant
P3	0%	7%	21%	10%	8%	0%	23.9	p<0.001

Table 11. Percentages of negative head politeness for particular beneficiary categories and the significances of the correlation between beneficiary group and head act politeness of initiating requestives. The non-shadowed fields show richly populated categories, containing more than 40 items. The strongly shadowed fields mark categories containing less than 20 items, the weakly shadowed ones mark the categories containing between 20 and 40 items.

As was to be expected, the category that stands out in a particularly frequent selection of negatively polite head act is the category 3 where the main or only beneficiary is the speaker (+S, -H, -EXT). It includes requests for personal favours (which constitute about one third to half of the items in this category in each series) alongside other requests that do not correspond to the notion of favour-asking, e.g. such that are critical of the addressee's behaviour, and requests for a verbal action, such as explanation, clarification, or other specific kind of response.

In Polish, the ratio of requestives realised using negatively polite head acts is negligibly small for beneficiary categories 5 and 6, where both the speaker and the hearer are included in the beneficiary. For P3, which was characterised by strong bonding of the participants, there was also a strongly significant difference[57] between these two beneficiary categories, which differed from each other by the presence or absence of the "external" (EXT+) beneficiary; the presence of external beneficiary promoted impositiveness. For all other series, the difference between beneficiary categories 5 (where the beneficiary was the speaker and the hearer or hearers: S+, H+, EXT-) and 6 (S+, H+, EXT+) was far below significance. The 122 requestives in P3 that could be expected to benefit the speaker, the hearer, and some other (beneficiary category 6) were distinguished by the complete absence of tentative head act forms in their linguistic realisation, while 8% of tentative head acts occurred in the beneficiary group 5. In P1, there occurred 5 negatively polite formulations among 60 requestives from beneficiary category 6 (8%).

To sum up, beneficiary configurations seem to have played a significant role as factors influencing the choice of head act politeness in English, mainly because negatively polite strategy was used more frequently in requests for the speaker's sake than in other types of requestives. There was a strong correlation between the type of beneficiary and politeness of head acts for the larger Polish sample and the sum of the Polish samples. In the smaller sample, negatively polite head acts were more frequently used in requests for the speaker's sake (category 3) than in other categories of considerable size, but the difference did not reach significance (it should be taken into account, though, that P1 contained fewer items and therefore the results of the significance test are less conclusive than for other sample). For German, no correlation occurred between the type of beneficiary and the ratio of negatively polite head acts.

Another interesting correlation is that between the ratio of impositive head acts and the frequency of occurrence of requestives from group 6, possibly the subtype of requestives which is most strongly related to group spirit as it involves the speaker, hearer and some other or others as beneficiaries. Table 12 and Diagram 11 illustrate the correlation between the mean interval of their occurrence and the percentage of negatively polite head acts in

---

[57] df=1, x^2=8.5, p<0.005

118

this category for pooled samples. The correlation is significant for this category and insignificant for other beneficiary categories.[58]

BENEFICIARY CONFIGURATION 6: S+, H+, X+						
group	G2	G4	E3	E4	P1	P3
negatively polite HA in %	20	14	23	13	8	0
frequency (hr)	5	11	5	11	16	23

Table 12. Mean frequencies (rounded) of the occurrence of requestives from beneficiary category 6 and the percentages of negatively polite head acts in this category.

In other words, type 6 is unique in that for requestives of this type, the frequency with which they are produced in particular groups corresponds closely to the preference of impositive head acts in their formulation. It is principally due to the correlation within this group that the overall correlation occurs (see Diagram 10).

BENEFICIARY CONFGURATION 6
(S+, H+, X+)

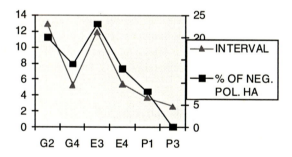

Diagram 11

---

[58] df=4, Pearson's r=0.9, p<0.02

119

5.2.2.2. INFLUENCE OF PRIOR ACQUAINTANCE

The linguistic forms of requestives produced in various stages of the program might be affected by fact that the social distance between the participants diminishes with their time spent together in the Big Brother house. Appendix 4 shows how both periods differ, separately for both action types and in sum.

The only series where negatively polite forms were significantly more frequent in the earlier period of acquaintance than in the later period was E3. The tendency was restricted to initiating requestives and occurred in each of the numerously populated beneficiary configurations. On the whole, though, the results for English were inconclusive, as there was no consistency between the two series under analysis.

The hypothesis that the duration of acquaintance might affect the type of politeness used was not confirmed for German and Polish, i.e. no change associated with period occurred in general. However, there was a significant difference[59] between the two periods for the beneficiary configuration 3 (speaker is the main or only beneficiary) in G2, agreeing with the hypothesised direction (less negative head politeness in the later period). In G4 (the "battle" series), distinguished by stronger group bonds that were already formed at the beginning, no such influence occurred. The percentage of negatively polite head acts in this beneficiary category was low already in the early period (13%), a tendency that continued in the later period (11%).

To recapitulate, the increase in the time of acquaintance from several days to four weeks alone did not strongly correlate with choices of head act politeness, while some effects occurred for some groups and some subtypes of directives. Compared to other contextual factors, the period of acquaintance seems to have played at most a secondary role in increasing the preference for impositive head acts. An exception is requests for personal favours (see section 5.2.5).

5.2.2.3. HEAD ACT POLITENESS: A RECAPITULATION

The results show that impositives were strongly preferred in the formulation of requestive speech acts in all groups under study; the preference was strongest in the Polish subjects and weakest in the British. The German speakers displayed more linguistic deference towards multiple than towards single addressees. Both English and German

---

[59] The difference between G2E and G2L, beneficiary configuration 3: for all requestives (31% vs. 4% negatively polite head acts) df=1, x^2=16.2, p<0.001; for initiating requestives (30% vs. 0% negatively polite head acts), df=1, x^2=21.9, p<0.001; for inhibitive requestives, df=1, x^2=3.5, insignificant.

speakers chose deferent formulations less frequently in inhibitive requestives than in initiating ones. English and Polish proved to vary their strategies of Head Act politeness with beneficiary configurations; in particular, requestives concerning the speaker's exclusive benefit showed considerably more negative politeness than requests potentially beneficial also to the addressee(s). Within the periods measured (zero to several days, vs. four to six weeks), no language showed a clear-cut influence of the time of acquaintance upon the choices of head act politeness.

The preferences for positively polite head act choices in particular groups correlated positively with the densities of requestives. Among particular beneficiary categories, this correlation turned out to be significant for beneficiary category 6, oriented towards a group benefit concerning the current interlocutors plus some other(s). The production of directives from this category can be expected to represent to a high degree a group-oriented, rather than merely interpersonal, perception of the relationships in the Big Brother house.

The results suggests that there is an affinity between the preference for the impositive style of communication (positively polite formulation of directives) in a group on the one hand, and the impositive and group-oriented interaction style on the other.

The analysis showed that the following of the postulated parameters of the context correlated to some degree with the frequency with which negative head act politeness appeared in requestives in particular languages:

GERMAN
ACTION TYPE INHIBITIVE/INITIATING: Negative head act politeness appeared less frequently in inhibitive requestives.
ADDRESS TYPE SINGLE/MULTIPLE: Negative head act politeness appeared more frequently in requestives directed at a multiple addressee.
BENEFICIARY CONFIGURATION: On the whole, beneficiary configuration did not correlate with head act politeness. It showed some minor effects in combination with the duration of prior acquaintance. The result was not consistent for both series.
PRIOR ACQUAINTANCE: There was no definite effect of the prior acquaintance upon head act politeness. While some influence seemed to occur in combination with beneficiary configuration, the result was not consistent for both series. With time, the group G2 which started with a high ratio of negatively polite head acts in beneficiary configuration 3 became more like the other group where negatively polite heads occurred rarely from the very start.

ENGLISH

ACTION TYPE INHIBITIVE/INITIATING: Negative head act politeness appeared less frequently in inhibitive requestives.

BENEFICIARY CONFIGURATION: Beneficiary configurations of requestives showed a strong correlation with the type of head politeness used. Beneficiary configuration +S, -H, -EXT was distinguished by a high ratio of negative head politeness, especially for initiating requestives.

PRIOR ACQUAINTANCE: There was no consistent effect of the prior acquaintance upon head act politeness. With time, the group which started with a high ratio of negatively polite head acts became more like the other group where negatively polite heads occurred rarely from the very start.

POLISH

BENEFICIARY CONFIGURATION: This was the only contextual factor which correlated with the type of head act politeness used in P3. Beneficiary configuration +S, -H,-EXT was distinguished by a relatively high ratio of negative head politeness, and beneficiary configuration +S, +H, +EXT by the contrary tendency. The result is not clear-cut because the small sample P1 failed to show the correlation.

5.2.3. INTERLINGUAL COMPARISON OF REQUESTS AND PROPOSALS: LINES OF COMPARISON

Three different types of requestives will be distinguished in the following analysis: *initiating requests, inhibitive requests*, and *proposals*. This major subdivision has not been introduced a priori with respect to the data analysis but results from the analysis itself. It is based on the observed major intralingual differences between these types of requestive utterances. The differentiation between *proposals* and *requests* is based on strong intralingual contrasts in the syntactic-semantic patterns in utterances in which they are realised. The differentiation between *initiating* and *inhibitive* requests is based on significant differences in the choices of politeness strategies in the head acts of initiating and inhibitive requests, which occurred in two languages under study (English and German).

The quantitative comparison will include the following aspects of similarity and difference:

- the basic syntactic patterns and semantic dimensions of head act;
- most frequent language-specific conversational routines;
- occurrence of modifiers;

-   politeness types in head act choice and modification;
-   politeness orientation of the whole directive act, based on the orientation of the head act and its modifiers.

5.2.4. PROPOSAL

5.2.4.1. IDENTIFICATION OF PROPOSALS

INTERACTIVE STRUCTURE OF PROPOSALS

In a rough conformity with the folk etymology which provided the lexical item used as a technical term in this study, proposal is a directive which predicates a shared or complementary action of the speaker and the hearer. The addressee of a proposal may be a single individual or a group. The beneficiary of the joint action of the speaker and the hearer action may be the speaker, the hearer, and other entities.

The following two special cases will be excluded from samples of proposals:

• The speaker is the main or only beneficiary. In this case, a proposal also fulfils the criteria of a *request*. Proposals of this type will be analysed within the appropriate subspecies of requests. That means that two aspects of participants' structure - beneficiary and actor characteristics - have been weighted against each other; it has been accepted that the property of a directive "benefit to the speaker alone" maximises its weight (face threat), and is therefore likely to have a far stronger influence upon the choice of a socially appropriate conversational routine than the criterion of the speaker's participation in the proposed action.

• The hearer is the main or only beneficiary. In this case, the proposal is also at the same time an *offer* and *advice*.

Before setting out to analyse the linguistic forms of proposals, a more precise delineation of the boundaries of this category is needed, taking into account the consequential distinction between spontaneous proposals and instructionals uttered in pre-planned activities.

REQUESTIVES AND BORDER LINES TO NON-SPONTANEOUS DIRECTIVES: INSTRUCTIONS AND PLANNING

Requestives as defined in this study are speech acts which concern the alternative between the joint action and non-action, or a choice of the course of a joint action to be followed out of few directly given alternatives. Other sorts of statements referring to a

common action of the speaker and the hearer (resembling proposals) or the hearer's actions (resembling requests) are on the one hand instructions, and on the other suggestions uttered during discussions planning details of future actions. Instructions and planning, forming together the class of *instructionals*, concern the *how*-aspect of the actions to be realised. They will be excluded from the analysis as they may show different tendencies in language use than spontaneous directives: "Task-oriented discourse ... opens up a further area of variation that is often unrecognised, and that is the possibility that, while the language itself is relatively unplanned and spontaneous, the underlying task that governs significant elements of the discourse may be highly planned. Plannedness and spontaneity, then, is
not merely dependent on whether a text has been written out beforehand; a distinction has to be made between language arising from planned activity, and language that is unplanned at this level" (Delin 2000: 219).

INSTRUCTIONS

Instructions pertain to the technical details of the action to be immediately performed and imply a division of roles: the speaker is entitled to instruct the hearer how to perform the action, in view of his or her evidently higher expertise, a better perspective on the current situation, the roles being fixed by an exterior authority (including e.g. social rules of gender or age conduct and formal contracts), or a prior role negotiation. The negotiation of roles is typically implicit and takes place if there is no obvious ground for one participant instructing the other rather than the other way round. Typically, one of the interaction participants signalises the willingness to assume alternatively

- the role of the instructed: by asking a question about the "how" of the planned action,
- the role of the instructor: by merely producing a directive utterance.

When the role division is initiated by the instructor, if the hearer is in accord with this role distribution he or she will simply make it visible by performing the action according to the instruction; otherwise, a further role negotiation may take place. If the role of the instructor is not firmly attributed to one person by authority, job contract or expertise, the roles of the instructor and the instructee can be exchanged during the interaction.

The utterances initiating a joint action and at the same time signalising the willingness to overtake one of the complementary roles in its performance are regarded in this study as proposals, whereas further utterances within same transactions, realised on the basis of the accomplished distribution of roles, are regarded as instructional directives. The following example clarifies the point:

50-E3. The group are unpacking their food supply.
1 M hey Baba # are we starting with dinner already
2 F yeah
3 M chicken or lamb
4 F chicken or lamb # what do you want
5A M **hands up for chicken # hands up for lamb**   (PROPOSAL; M   signalises
                                                       overtaking command)
5B M # **hands up for chicken first**   (INSTRUCTION)
(M lifts his hand)

Instructions accompanying a joint action of the speaker and the hearer(s) based on a consensus reached in role negotiation are excluded from the analysis in the following section. It has been observed that they display a higher proportion of imperative and elliptical constructions than spontaneous proposals.

PLANNING

In the Big Brother houses, discussions concerning the details of non-immediate future action which the participants (tacitly or explicitly) agreed to (or were told to) perform are a frame for multiple suggestions made by the discussion participants. Statements suggesting a particular course which should be taken in performing an action, e.g. the succession of steps or role division, differ from spontaneous requestives: they are situated in a larger frame, fixed upon the topic of joint action and inviting the participants to express their opinions. Typically, the group discussions concern the group tasks given to the group by Big Brother, such as preparing a shopping list or performing a play. All the participants are equal, and initiatives concerning dealing with the task are to be expected. The preliminary task of the group is to establish how to perform the action in question. Apart from the tasks coming from an external source, planning processes also occur within group tasks which the test participants gave to themselves.

The set-up of having to plan how to perform a necessary activity, or one which has been agreed upon, is markedly different from the spontaneous production of requestives made outside such a frame. With the task-solving goal of the co-operation pre-established, the formal features of the directive statements uttered during such "planning sessions" might be very different than those of more spontaneous directives. In at least one of the Big Brother corpora (the British one), the former tend to be more direct and forceful, which seems to follow from their high legitimacy in a group discussion; thus, mixing the two types might obliterate significant intercultural differences. Therefore, proposals and requests made during task-solving discussions are excluded from the interlingual analysis in the following section. However, intralingual differences between planning and spontaneous proposals will be briefly discussed.

5.2.3.2. PROPOSAL: HEAD ACT

HEAD ACTS IN GERMAN

The inflection paradigm of the German imperative misses a morpho-syntactically marked inflectional form of the imperative 1st plural. The imperative is formed in a periphrastic way using Heische-Modus in adhortative function, based on a finite verb in the present subjunctive, identical with the indicative present for weak verbs, and verb raising to the sentence initial position; e.g. *"Gehen wir* morgen ins Kino." The illocutionary potential of this form in case of action verbs is that of a directive, and the personal pronoun "wir" can only be interpreted as a hearer-inclusive reference. As a substitute form of the imperative necessitated by a gap in the inflexional paradigm, this form was counted as an imperative syntactic sentence type.

In spoken German, the present indicative frequently replaces the future tense in declarations of intention (including those that perform the illocutionary function of directives), e.g. "Wir gehen morgen ins Kino" rather than "Wir werden morgen ins Kino gehen". Both forms have been included in the "realisation declarative" category.

The distribution of proposals among the various syntactic-semantic dimensions in both G2 and G4 series is similar, and the differences do not approach statistical significance. The detailed distribution of proposals among all distinguished syntactic-semantic dimensions in G2 and G4 is given in Appendix 2. The following dimensions occur most frequently in both series (Table 13).

G4		G2	
realisation declarative	38%	realisation declarative	29%
imperative	14%	imperative	21%
deontic declarative	16%	preference interrogative	14%
preference interrogative	10%	competence interrogative	7%
competence interrogative	10%	deontic declarative	7%
ITEMS	50		42

Table 13. The most frequent syntactic-semantic dimensions in the two German series, G2 and G4.

The differences are statistically insignificant. I assume that the similarity of the results confirms that the data may be regarded as representative in spite of the small sample sizes, and justifies the pooling of the samples from both series in the interlingual comparison.

Syntactic sentence types and semantic dimensions summarised in the interlingual comparison in the following section provide a pattern of similarity and difference in the formulation of directive speech acts independent of their wording (lexical items used). The table below provides an additional level of description, including the routine form-function correspondences of three types, from conversational routines (the most general) through conversational formulae to routine formulae (cf. Chapter 4.3.6). Table 14 presents examples of conversational routines used in German proposals.

CONVERSATIONAL ROUTINE	SEMANTIC DIMENSION/SYNTACTIC SENTENCE TYPE
	DECLARATIVE/REALISATION DIMENSION
(1) wir + VP (verb: 1. pl. indicat. present)	wir machen jetzt ein Spiel # wenn du jetzt den Roten ziehst # mach die Augen zu # dann gewinnst du *we play now a game # if you draw the red one now # close your eyes # that you'll win*
	IMPERATIVE
(2) VP (verb: 1 pl. subjunct. present) + wir	genau # schreiben wir erst mal auf *exactly # write-we first down*

127

	REALISATION INTERROGATIVE
(3) VP (verb: 1. pl. indicat. present) + wir	Walter # wenn du schon genug Tiere getötet hast # spielen wir noch mal Backgammon? *Walter # if you have already killed enough animals # play-we-FUTURE backgammon again?*
	INTERROGATIVE/PREFERENCE DIMENSION
(4) wollen wir + VP (verb: infinitive)	wollen wir noch mal ne Welle machen oder was? *do we want to make a wave again or what*
(5) sollen wir + VP (verb: infinitive)	sollen wir alle zusammen Fliegen töten wieder? *shall we kill the flies together again*
	COMPETENCE DECLARATIVE
(6) wir können + VP (verb: infinitive)	wir können auch alle mal ausgehen und winken *we can also all just go out and wave*
(7) man könnte + VP (verb: infinitive)	aber so spaßeshalber könnte man das durchziehen # oder? *but just for fun one could carry this through # right ?*
	DEONTIC DECLARATIVE
(8) wir müssen + VP (verb: infinitive)	die Lattenröste sind bei euch # die Matratzen sind bei uns # wir müssen dies jetzt umräumen *the frames are with you # the mattresses are with us # we must now rearrange this*
	ELLIPSIS
(9) Applaus für NP	Applaus für uns # wir waren super heute *applause for us # we were great today*

Table 14. Conversational routines which occurred in German proposals.

The routine "wollen wir VP" and "sollen wir VP" formulae specialised for the function of making proposals were both counted to the category of preference interrogative, in view of the similarity of form and the results of interviews conducted with four native speakers, all of whom confirmed that they are very close or identical as far as their approach towards, and the impact upon the interlocutor(s) is concerned. One speaker supposed that selecting one or the other by the speaker might be a matter exclusively of a regional preference. While the strategy used in both of them is an enquiry about the addressee's view of the predicated action involving an inclusive *we*-reference, the compositional meaning of the two phrases differs as a result of the difference in the lexical meanings of the modal verbs. While the deontic modal "soll" suggests that the speaker is going to treat the interlocutor's opinion as binding and obliging to himself, symbolically lifting the addressee to the position of superiority, the volition modal "wollen" expresses the identity of the speaker's and hearer's preferences: the speaker's desire to VP is conditional upon the hearer wanting the same (cf. also Dolnik 2005). Due to this difference in the compositional meaning, the volition modal in the plural was regarded as a preference interrogative (enquiry whose contents is "do you want to X with me") accompanied by "solidarity plural" (internal modifier expressing "confidence/ informality").

HEAD ACTS IN ENGLISH

Table 15 below shows the distribution of proposals in English between the most frequently occurring syntactic-semantic dimensions in E3 and E4. The differences between the two series did not approach significance; the results justify the pooling of the two samples in the cross-linguistic comparison. Table 16 presents examples of conversational routines used in English proposals.

E3		E4	
imperative	18%	imperative	20%
deontic declarative	18%	deontic declarative	13%
realisation declarative	14%	realisation declarative	15%
ellipsis	7%	ellipsis	11%
ITEMS	84		61

Table 15. Most frequent syntactic-semantic dimensions in the two British series, E3 and E4.

CONVERSATIONAL ROUTINE	SEMANTIC DIMENSION/SYNTACTIC SENTENCE TYPE
	IMPERATIVE
(1) let's VP	girls # let's work as a team
	PREFERENCE INTERROGATIVE
(2) shall we VP?	shall we go and set up our tent in the garden?
	DEONTIC DECLARATIVE
(3) we should VP	we should really get it out for him and just put it out # shouldn't we
(4) we're going to have to VP	what we're going to have to come up with # we're going to have to do something every week the same

(5) it should be NP	may be it should be like a non-shoe area
(6) (we) need to VP	we need to make it last for two weeks
(7) we have to VP	we have just to pack it into the little things without lids
(8) we've got to	we've got to cook all that meal
	REALISATION DECLARATIVE
(9) we'll VP	we'll put a little ranch here # shall we
	SUGGESTORY INTERROGATIVE
(10) why don't we VP	why don't we fry off the meat
	SUGGESTORY DECLARATIVE
(11) I think NP is in order	I think a bottle of red is in order
	REALISATION INTERROGATIVE
(12) are we going to VP	so are we going to set up a little camp # Camp David like
	COMPETENCE DECLARATIVE
(13) we could VP	we could start with this chicken now
(14) we can VP	so can we do it tomorrow # or we can do it tonight
	COMPETENCE INTERROGATIVE
(15) can we VP?	can we sort it out # then?
	ELLIPSIS
(16) hands up for NP	hands up for chicken # hands up for lamb # hands up for chicken first

Table 16. Conversational routines that occurred in English proposals.

HEAD ACTS IN POLISH

Peculiar to Polish is the "imperative-declarative" category, whose existence has not been noted before in any study of Polish grammar; it is analysed in more detail in chapter 6 (cf. also Pulaczewska 2005). At this point, it is enough to say that it is a periphrastic form of the imperative using the imperative auxiliary "chodzić" (chodź/chodźcie) in proposals, followed by a declarative statement in the indicative future, as in the following examples:

Chodźcie jej to powiemy.
come-IMP-2.pl. her this tell-INDICATIVE-FUTUR-1. pl. (let's tell this to her)

Chodź jej pomożemy.
come-IMP-2.sing. her help-INDICATIVE-FUTUR-1. pl. (let's help her)

The use of the auxiliary imperative in the same clause as the indicative of the main verb amounts to a violation of the rule "one sentence – one inflected verb form" and seems to form a syntactic anomaly peculiar to Polish and possibly other Slavic languages. The reasons for claiming that both inflected verb forms belong to the same clause are prosodic (lack of prosodic tone group boundary) and syntactic (omitting the initial imperative in the sentences above results in ill-formedness; the indirect object occupies the middle position between the two verbs).

Table 17 below shows the distribution of proposals in Polish between the most frequently occurring syntactic-semantic dimensions in P1 and P3.

P1		P3	
realisation declarative	43%	realisation declarative	39%
imperative	27%	imperative	19%
imperative-declarative	9%	imperative-declarative	11%
deontic declarative	9%	ellipsis	10%
ITEMS	44		70

Table 17. Most frequent syntactic-semantic dimensions in the two Polish series, P1 and P3.

A weakly significant difference occurs in the use of ellipsis; other differences are insignificant. I do not regard the difference in the use of elliptical utterances as being of relevance as they include cases of situational ellipsis, whose predicative meaning is determined by the context. Its occurrence in place of other impositive, consensus-presupposing patterns is likely to be determined by a degree to which the proposal is embedded into the current action, and the resulting presence or absence of contextual cues to interpretation. I interpret this result as justifying the pooling of the two samples in the cross-linguistic comparison.

Table 18 presents examples of conversational routines that occurred in Polish proposals.

CONVERSATIONAL ROUTINE	SEMANTIC DIMENSION/SYNTACTIC SENTENCE TYPE
	REALISATION DECLARATIVE
(1) VP (verb: 1. pl. indicat. present)	już nie gramy # nie? *play-INDICATIVE-PRES.-1ˢᵗ. pl. no more # right?*
(2) VP (verb: 1 pl. indicat. future)	to pójdziemy tam *then go-INDICATIVE-FUTUR-1ˢᵗ. pl. there*
	IMPERATIVE
(3) VP (verb: 1. pl. imp.)	to może przeprowadźmy próbę *then perhaps conduct-IMP-1. pl. a test*
(4) chodź/chodźcie (verb: 2. pl. imp.) + infinitive clause	chodźcie najpierw wynieść te śpiwory *come-IMP-2.pl. first carry out-INF the knapsacks*
	DECLARATIVE-IMPERATIVE
(5) chodź/chodźcie + VP (verb: 1. pl. indicat. future)	chodź się młody wykąpiemy # bo dziewczyny chciały wejść do wiesz # do żakuski *come youngster bath-INDICATIVE-FUTUR-1ˢᵗ. pl. # because the girls wanted to get into you know # into the jacuzzi-DIM*
	DEONTIC DECLARATIVE
(6) trzeba + VP (verb: perfective infinitive)	trzeba zaśpiewać *one-must sing*
	COMPETENCE INTERROGATIVE
(7) możemy + VP (verb: perfective inifinitive)	a możemy wziąć Romka? *and can we take Romek?*
	COMPETENCE DECLARATIVE
(7) moglibyśmy + VP (verb: perfective infinitive)	ale moglibyśmy sobie powiedzieć przynajmniej sport # prawda? *but we could tell each other at least about sport # right?*
(9) możemy + VP (verb: perfective infinitive)	możemy się sprawdzić *we can test each other*

Table 18. Conversational routines which occurred in Polish proposals.

CROSS-LINGUISTIC COMPARISON: SYNTACTIC-SEMANTIC PATTERNS, POLITENESS STRATEGIES

The details of the summary results for all the three languages are presented in Table 19.

PROPOSAL	GERMAN	ENGLISH	POLISH
IMPERATIVE	**17%**	**19%**	**22%**
IMP-DECL	**x**	**x**	**10.5%**
ELLIPSIS	**5%**	**9%**	**6%**
DECLARATIVE	**56.5%**	**44%**	**55%**
realisation	34%	14.5%	42%
preference	0%	1%	1%
deontic	12%	16%	6%
competence	9%	7%	2%
suggestory	1%	1%	0%
performative	1%	0%	2%
strong hint	0%	5%	3%
INTERROGATIVE	**20%**	**28%**	**6%**
realisation	3%	6%	3.5%
preference	12%	13%	1%
deontic	2%	0%	0%
competence	0%	4%	1%
suggestory	1%	2%	0%
strong hint	1%	2%	0%
mild hint	0%	1%	1%
ITEMS	92	145	114

Table 19. Types of politeness and syntactic sentence types: proposals.

N-: negatively polite, P-: positively polite.

A simplified overview of the distribution of directives between various syntactic patterns and politeness strategies in all the series is available in Appendix 8. The most frequently occurring syntactic-semantic utterance types are shown in Table 20.

The results show that the most frequent combination of sentence type with politeness strategy used in the expression of proposals in all three languages was the positively polite declarative. The second most frequent pattern is the imperative, while it is much more frequent in Polish (including the imperative-declarative) than in the other two languages. In Polish, negatively polite interrogatives play a marginal role, contrary to English and German

133

which show similar amounts of negatively polite interrogatives and imperative constructions.

After the two forms of the imperative in Polish have been summed up, the following differences proved significant in simple chi square statistics:

PROPOSALS ENGLISH	%	PROPOSALS POLISH	%	PROPOSALS GERMAN	%
imperative	19	realisation declarative	42	realisation declarative	34
deontic declarative	16	imperative	22	imperative	17
realisation declarative	14	imperative-declarative	11	deontic declarative	12
preference interrogative	13	deontic declarative	6	preference interrogative	12

Table 20. Most frequent syntactic-semantic patterns in particular languages: proposals.

- the imperative in Polish is significantly more frequent than in the other two languages;[60]
- interrogative constructions are significantly more frequent in English and German than in Polish[61];
- the realisation declarative is significantly less frequent in English than in the other two languages;[62]
- the deontic declarative is significantly less frequent in Polish than in English;[63]
- the preference interrogative is significantly less frequent in Polish than in the other two languages;[64]
- the competence declarative is significantly less frequent in Polish than in German, the difference between Polish and English approaches significance;[65]
- the competence dimension is significantly less frequent in Polish than in English;[66]
- negatively polite head acts are significantly less frequent in Polish than in the other two languages.[67]

---

[60] For Polish/English, df=1, x^2=6.6, p<0.025; for Polish/German, df=1, x^2=6.0, p<0.025.
[61] For Polish/English, df=1, x^2=20.7, p<0.001.; for Polish/German, df=1, x^2=8.6, p<0.005.
[62] For Polish/English, df=1, x^2=24.9, p<0.001; for English/German, df=1, x^2=13.0, p<0.001.
[63] df=1, x^2=6.0, p<0.025
[64] For Polish/English, df=1, x^2=13.5, p<0.001; for Polish/German, df=1, x^2=11.4, p<0.001.
[65] For Polish/English, df=1, x^2=3.82, insignificant; for Polish/German, df=1, x^2=5.3, p<0.025.
[66] df=1, x^2=6.6, p<0.01
[67] For Polish/English, df=1, x^2=23.6, p<0.001; for Polish/German, df=1, x^2=15.0, p<0.001; for German/English, df=1, x^2=0.6, insignificant at 0.05.

The cross-linguistic differences in the use of negatively polite versus impositive head acts for totalled samples[68] are illustrated in Diagram 12.

Perhaps the most illuminating finding resulting from this analysis is that the most frequent conversational routine used in expressing proposals in both German and Polish is the realisation declarative, a statement of the performance of a joint activity as a matter of fact, that did not occur at all or occurred very rarely in earlier comparative studies on directives, based on questionnaires and pseudo-natural methods (e.g. Márquez-Reiter 2000, Blum-Kulka et al. 1989, House 1988, Fukushima 1996), and in the corpus-based study of English by Aijmer (1996). The following examples illustrate the naturalness of occurrence of these forms in the context of ongoing non-verbal interaction, and also go some way towards clarifying why they might be difficult to detect using instruction-based elicitation procedures, typically employing contexts that are poorly specified, have a dyadic structure and involve neither joint action nor shared interests of the interaction participants as the background for the current exchange:

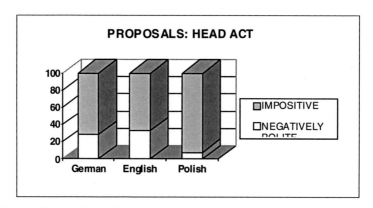

Diagram 12. Proportions of impositive and tentative (negatively polite) head acts in proposals.

---

[67] The intralingual differences between particular samples in the use of negatively polite vs. impositive head act forms were very small (below 4%) and insignificant.

3-G4. F1 is sleeping at a "forbidden" time, risking the punishment of her team. Her team captain F2 consults M1 for advice on how to react.

F2 was mache ich dann

what shall I do then

M1 was sollst du machen # . wir machen alle zusammen # wir machen jetzt alle zusammen # wir sind ein Team

what can you do # we all do it together # now we all do it together # we are a team

(M1, M2, F2 walk to the bedroom to persuade F1 to get up.)

34-P3. BACKGAMMON

M1 and F1 are playing backgammon, watched by F2, F3, M2, M3.

1 Big Brother: Andrzej Banasik # Wielki Brat zaprasza do pokoju zwierzeń

FIRST NAME+SECOND NAME # Big Brother invites to the diary room

(M1 stands up, walks towards the diary room)

2 F1 kto będzie grał?

who will play

3 M2 to M3: Obulon graj

Obulon-NICKNAME play-IMP

4 F2 poczekamy

we will wait

In turn 3, M2 asks M3 to step in for a player who is temporarily absent. In turn 4, F2 makes a counter-proposal by stating that the group will wait for M1 to come back.

The results also show a relatively large diversity of forms in English, where the three most frequent syntactic-semantic dimensions amounted to about half of all the proposals, and a higher stability of form-function correspondence on Polish, where they made up about three fourths of all proposals, with German falling in between.

The measure of the differences collated in the figures presented above shows them to be not only statistically significant but also pragmatically relevant because they amount to different habits of language use. To disregard these differences might be consequential for communication in cross-cultural encounters, and result in acquiring an unintended personal image by speakers transferring the strategy of politeness from their respective speech communities to others, via showing preference for conversational routines which are rarely selected in the language of the interlocutor. An English speaker might be puzzled by the amount of proposals produced in the form of a statement of action as a fact (realisation declarative) in Polish and German, that are higher on impositiveness than the imperative (an assumption that has been confirmed by a pair of informants, a male and a female one, from each language). A young speaker using impositive formulations in his or her peer ingroup as universally as is common in Polish might be sometimes perceived as tactless and overconfident by a speaker of German or English. A speaker using tentative forms as frequently as is typical for English or German in a Polish young peer ingroup might be perceived as undermining the presupposition of consensus characteristic for such interaction, lacking enthusiasm, feeling insecure, and creating an unnecessary amount of interpersonal distance.

Finally, learners of Polish might be tempted to unnecessarily search for equivalents for patterns and strategies frequently used in their languages, such as preference interrogative, producing awkward forms not functional in Polish. While the German routine formula "wollen wir VP" translates well into Polish even if it was not used in the data at hand, the formulae "shall we VP" and "sollen wir VP" are not literally translatable.

SPONTANEOUS PROPOSALS VERSUS INITIATIVES CONCERNING PRE-FORMULATED TASKS

The preceding analysis does not include discussions and negotiations concerning tasks appointed to the housemates by the program designers, or arranging details of complex acts they decided to perform. As defined earlier, such directives belong to the category of instructionals. They refer to joint tasks whose performance itself is within the scope of an already established consensus, be it as a result of an overt negotiation within the group, or because of known obligations towards an external superior.

In the English sample, initiatives to solve problems posed by tasks the housemates received from Big Brother occurred 41 times within four episodes. Two episodes were concerned with planning the order in which to participate in a competitive task, one with selecting a housemate to leave, and one with a strategy to be followed during a quiz organised by Big Brother.

Table 21 shows a simplified overview of semantic and syntactic means used in formulations of head acts of proposals pertaining to the details of the action to be performed, produced in the frame of a group discussion.

137

ENGLISH PLANNING – HEAD ACT TYPE	
realisation declarative	32%
imperative	24%
deontic declarative	10%
ellipsis	7%
preference declarative	7%
realisation interrogative	7%
preference interrogative	7%
suggestory interrogative	5%
ITEMS	41

Table 21. Forms of head acts of *how*-proposals:
planning joint activities in group discussions in English.

Spontaneous isolated proposals include more interrogative constructions than initiatives bound into structured planned discussions about the action to be performed. In the latter, interrogatives are applied as means of testing H's principal willingness to perform the action together with S. In discussions, the cooperation is presupposed and the ratio of interrogative constructions drops in favour of declarative constructions. In particular, the ratio of the realisation declarative rises significantly[69]. The resulting distribution of these non-spontaneous initiatives among different syntactic-semantic dimensions is very similar to that of German spontaneous proposals. The difference with respect to Polish spontaneous proposals is also small and lies only in a more frequent use of the preference dimension in English. Realisation declaratives, stating a future act as a matter of fact, were the most frequent syntactic-semantic format both in Polish and German spontaneous proposals, and in English task-bound (non-spontaneous) initiatives. In brief, the behaviour of the British speakers when they were engaged in task-driven activities and discussions resembled the behaviour of the Polish and German speakers while producing spontaneous proposals. An engagement in task-solving made the occurrence of initiatives expectable and necessary, and legitimised the presupposition of consensus.

In Polish, 42 utterances expressing task-bound problem-solving initiatives occurred within four episodes. Three of them concerned the planning of performances. Of these, two

---

[69] df=1, x^2=6.9, p<0.01.

constituted a task given to the housemates by Big Brother, and one was undertaken by the participants of their own will, but they all posed the same sorts of challenge to the planners. The fourth discussion was concerned with decision-making concerning a competitive task. In these four episodes, 79% of the utterances referring to the actions of one or more housemates were formulated as the realisation declaratives (compared to 42% for spontaneous proposals). This may have resulted partly from the nature of the performance-planning, where the task was to work out complex plot-based events which promoted narrative techniques in the presentation of ideas (present and future declarative).

As with English, the difference in the use of the realisation declarative between spontaneous proposals and directives in the discussion on tasks in Polish was highly significant[70]. The intralingual differences justify the separate treatment of spontaneous proposals and request on the one hand, and discussion-framed initiatives on the other, in the cross-linguistic comparison.

The small size of the sample of discussion-bound directives in German (n=20) precludes any conclusions.

5.2.4.3. PROPOSAL: POLITENESS OF MODIFICATION - AN OVERVIEW

A further factor to be considered in analysing politeness strategies applied by interaction participants is the type of modification optionally accompanying the head act. Politeness of modifiers may counter the strategy used in the head act, resulting in an utterance in which both strategies are applied side by side, thus observing at the same time the involvement expressed by means of friendly impositiveness or informality/confidence signals, and considerateness that demands attention to the addressee's negative face wants.

The occurrence of modification in proposals independent of the type of head act is visualised in Diagram 13. The difference in the use of negatively polite modification was highly significant for Polish and German[71] and weakly significant for English and German[72]. The differences in the use of positively polite modification were insignificant.

A further level of analysis is addressed by sub-categorisation of modifiers into interaction markers, supportive moves, and internal modifiers. The use of modifiers in proposals at this and at the most detailed level of sub-categorisation is shown in Appendix 5. The differences in the particular categories of modifiers could be traced back to the particularly high frequency of use or otherwise of a few devices in each language, such as:

---

[70] $df=1$, $x^2=16.3$, $p<0.001$.
[71] $df=1$, $x^2=14.2$, $p<0.001$
[72] $df=1$, $x^2=4.6$, $p<0.05$

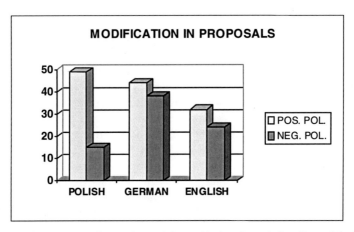

Diagram 13. Percentages of proposals containing positively and negatively polite modification.

INTERACTION MARKERS

informality/confidence:

-     frequent use of starters (including vocatives, verbs of sensation, and colloquial links/summonses) in Polish

impositiveness:

-     Verbs in the imperative occur in German, "*komm/kommt*" (accompanying head acts in the imperative and the realisation declarative). In Polish, some verbs that frequently appear accompanying proposals have undergone grammaticalisation, and utterances which contain them were counted as periphrastic forms of the imperative (imperative-declarative); about 10% of all proposals had this form. This figure is close to the percentage of German proposals containing an imperative verb increasing impositiveness of the utterance, typically in the utterance-initial position.

negative politeness:

-     slightly more frequent use of question tags in English than in German and Polish

SUPPORTIVE MOVES

-     Neutral and positively polite supportive moves were more frequent in English than in the other two languages. A substantial difference occurred in the use of grounders by the British and the Poles. This suggests a more elaborate conversational style of the speakers of English, in which requestives are grounded in the form of explicit justifications, or complex introductory moves. The Polish and the German speakers used simpler introductory strategies instead, such as verbs in the imperative specialised for the starter function, or links and summonses.

INTERNAL MODIFIERS
- frequent use of lexical hedge in German (*mal, einfach, ein bisschen*)
- relatively frequent use of subjunctive (Konjunktiv) in German
- use of complex hedges in German and English
- non-use of hedges in Polish
- frequent referential[73] use of nicknames and colloquial terms in Polish
- frequent use of humour in German
- frequent use of colloquialisms in German and Polish.

Table 22 below shows how frequently the two types of head acts were accompanied by modifiers showing the same, and the competing type of politeness strategy.

In English, positively polite modifiers occurred infrequently in proposals implementing tentative head act strategy, compared to proposals containing impositive head acts, and compared to the other two languages.

---

[73]i.e., non-vocative

PROPOSAL	GERMAN	ENGLISH	POLISH
POS HA			
positive modifiers	45%	40%	50%
negative modifiers	32%	24%	15%
unmodified	33%	47%	40%
NEG HA			
positive modifiers	54%	21%	44%
negative modifiers	50%	33%	11%
unmodified	31%	58%	44%
ALL HA			
positive modifiers	48%	34%	49%
negative modifiers	37%	27%	15%
Unmodified	33%	51%	40%
UTTERANCE			
positive politeness	49%	51%	78%
negative politeness	13%	26%	4%
both types	38%	23%	18%

Table 22. Co-occurrences of head act politeness and politeness of modifiers in proposals[74].

As a result of a combination of head act politeness and modification, three subtypes of utterances can be distinguished when considering politeness:
- those that show only positive politeness (unmodified and positively modified impositives)
- those that show only negative politeness (unmodified and negatively modified tentatives)
- those that contain elements of both types of politeness.

---

[74] Percentages do not add up to 100% because some items contain both types of modification.

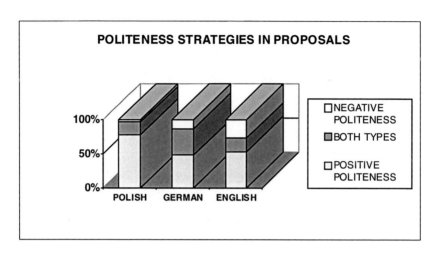

Diagram 14. Occurrence of politeness strategies in proposals: head act and modification.

While the Poles proved consistently to be low on negatively polite strategies both in the head act and in modification, if the type of modification is taken into account a difference between German and English can be seen which is not visible on the basis of head act politeness alone. Proposals involving exclusively a negatively polite strategy were less frequent in German, because negatively polite head acts were more frequently accompanied by positively polite modifiers than in English. The difference in the use of negative politeness only between German and English was significant[75].

Examples of positively polite modifiers accompanying tentative head acts are given below:

4-G4.
F wollt ihr ein bisschen **quatschen**
*do you want to **chat-COLLOQUIAL** a bit*   preference interrogative/colloquialism
26-G2.
M **hei** # soll- # sollen wir es mal Spaßes halber durchziehen?
***hey** # should we do it just for fun?*   preference interrogative/interjection

---

[75] df=1, x^2=6.0, p<0.025

143

The data suggests also that in English as in German, a negatively polite modification tended to accompany negatively polite head acts somewhat more frequently than positively polite ones. The difference was insignificant for proposals alone, but its orientation is the same for requests, and it proved significant for the total pool of requestives. This finding is similar to the findings by Kasper and House (1981), based on role plays.

5.2.4.4. SUMMARY: PROPOSALS

A notable interlingual similarity consisted in the fact that the most frequent combination of sentence type with politeness strategy used in the formulation of proposals in all three languages was positively polite declaratives, while interlingual differences occurred in the choice of the second most frequent pattern, which was negatively polite interrogatives in English, the imperative (including imperative-declarative) in Polish, and both of these for German.

In each language, there were just three to four prominent syntactic-semantic head act patterns; each of them was used in 10 or more per cent of proposals. The most frequent type of head act in both Polish and German was the realisation declarative, which was rare in English. The Poles stood out in the particularly frequent use of the imperative. Modal framing and the interrogative turned out to play a negligible role in Polish, while they were frequently used in English and German. The British data showed a more even distribution of proposals among several among several of the most frequent patterns; and used a greater number of different routine formulas. The distribution of English directives made within the frames of task-oriented discussions based on a general consensus about the joint action to be performed is not distinguishable from that of spontaneous proposals in German, due to the more frequent use of the realisation declarative in such discussions compared to spontaneous proposals in English. The latter tendency occurred also in Polish.

All groups showed a strong preference for impositive rather than negatively polite head acts.

Compared to the other two groups, the Poles proved to be consistently reluctant to use negative politeness in both head acts and modification. The Germans used negatively polite head acts about as frequently as the British, but modified them more frequently with positively polite modifiers such as humour, solidarity plural, and interjection, among others, so that the percentage of proposals realised only by means of negatively polite strategy was lower than in English. The German stood out by frequently mixing both politeness strategies within the same utterance, and the frequent use of humour and lexical hedges. The British showed a more elaborate conversational style in which proposals were more frequently accompanied by negatively polite or neutral supportive moves, and they were somewhat less prone to use colloquialisms than the other two groups. Polish was distinguished by a minimal presence of hedging devices, and a frequent use of colloquial and nicknaming terms in addressing and in references to other housemates.

5.2.5. REQUEST

5.2.5.1. DEFINITION AND PARTICIPANTS' STRUCTURE

In a rough conformity with the folk etymology which provided the lexical item used as a technical term in this study, request is a directive which the addressee is not bound to comply to by an external authority, and which predicates an action of the hearer which does not aim in the hearer's own exclusive benefit, or which predicates a joint action of the speaker and the hearer for the speaker's exclusive benefit. The addressee of a request may be a single individual or a group. The beneficiaries of the action may be the speaker, or the speaker and the hearer, and/or others.

5.2.5.2. LINES OF COMPARISON

Requests will be analysed separately for two action types: initiating and inhibitive. This is because they differ intralingually in the use of the impositive and tentative head act strategies in English, as well as German. If we were to analyse them jointly, a higher use of impositive strategies would occur just in those data samples which happen to contain a higher proportion of inhibitive directives; this could obliterate meaningful interlingual differences.

An intralingual comparison corroborated the lack of a considerable difference between the two series in each language, confirming the assumption that the data is representative in spite of a relatively small sample size. This justified a pooling of the samples. Unless specified otherwise, the figures in the tables below refer to pooled samples comprising data from the two series of the program for each language. Figures referring to a particular series are given in Appendix 7.

5.2.5.3. REQUEST: HEAD ACT

SYNTACTIC-SEMANTIC DIMENSIONS

The total results for the three languages are juxtaposed in Table 23. The following interlingual differences in the use of particular syntactic sentence types and particular syntactic-semantic dimensions proved significant in simple chi square statistics:

INITIATING REQUESTS
- The competence interrogative was significantly more frequent in English than in the remaining two languages.[76]
- The performative declarative was repeatedly used only in Polish; the difference was significant.[77]
- The preference interrogative was significantly more frequent in English than in Polish.[78]
- The competence declarative was significantly more frequent in English than in Polish.[79]
- Interrogative constructions were significantly more frequent in English than in the other two languages[80].

INHIBITIVE REQUESTS
- Strong hints in declaratives were most frequent in German[81]. For all inhibitive strong hints (interrogatives and declaratives), there occurred a weakly significant difference between German and English[82].
- The infinitive occurred more frequently in German than in Polish[83].
- The deontic declarative occurred more frequently in German than in Polish[84].
- Declarative sentences occurred most frequently in German.[85]

The distribution of inhibitive requestives among different syntactic-semantic patterns is almost the same for Polish and English.

---

[76] For Polish/English, df=1, x^2=33.7, p<0.001; for English/German, df=1, x^2=29.1, p<0.001.
[77] For Polish/English, df=1, x^2=10.1, p<0.005; for Polish/German, df=1, x^2=9.3, p<0.005.
[78] df=1, x^2=7.1, p<0.01
[79] df=1, x^2=7.1, p<0.01
[80] For Polish/German, df=1, x^2=32.5, p<0.001; for German/English, df=1, x^2=20.9, p<0.001.
[81] For Polish/German, df=1, x^2=5.4, p<0.025; for German/English, df=1, x^2=8.7, p<0.005.
[82] df=1, x^2=4.0, p<0.05
[83] df=1, x^2=6.8, p<0.01
[84] df=1, x^2=7.9, p<0.005
[85] For Polish/German, df=1, x^2=5.5, p<0.025; for German/English, df=1, x^2=4.5, p<0.05.

Tables 24 and 25 summarise the differences in the use of "conventional indirectness", a negatively polite strategy of referring to preparatory conditions (modal frame) for the performance of the predicated action. Whilst the German and the British opted for this strategy with roughly the same relative frequencies for proposals, in German its use is very rare in requests, and in Polish it proves negligible for both types of requestives. The differences between English and the other two languages are significant[86]. The difference between Polish and German is statistically significant but, in practice, meaningless.

In conventionally indirect inhibitive requestives, the only preparatory condition referred to is competence, i.e., framing of the proposition in alethic modality (ability/possibility). As shown in Table 25, the use of this strategy was rare in all three languages.

---

[86] For Polish/English, df=1, x^2=51.3, p<0.001; for English/German, df=1, x^2=20.6, p<0.001; for Polish/German, df=1, x^2=6.0, p<0.025.

	INITIATING REQUESTS			INHIBITIVE REQUESTS		
	GERMAN	ENGLISH	POLISH	GERMAN	ENGLISH	POLISH
IMPERATIVE	**60%**	**57%**	**66.5%**	**47%**	**63%**	**66%**
IMP-DECL	**x**	**x**	**0.5%**	**x**	**x**	**0%**
INFINITIVE	**2%**	**x**	**2%**	**7%**	**x**	**1%**
ELLIPSIS	**6%**	**4%**	**7%**	**11%**	**10%**	**10%**
VOCATIVE	**3%**	**2%**	**0.5%**	**2%**	**4%**	**3%**
DECLARATIVE	**20%**	**14%**	**15.5%**	**27%**	**16%**	**14.5%**
realisation	*5%*	*2%*	*3%*	*1%*	*2%*	*2%*
preference	*4%*	*2%*	*1%*	*3%*	*5%*	*3%*
performative	*0.3%*	*0%*	*3%*	*0%*	*0%*	*3%*
suggestory	*0%*	*0%*	*0%*	*0%*	*0%*	*0%*
deontic	*5%*	*5%*	*4%*	*8%*	*3%*	*1%*
competence	*3%*	*3.5%*	*0.5%*	*3%*	*0%*	*0%*
mild hint	*1%*	*1%*	*1%*	*0%*	*2%*	*1%*
strong hint	*1%*	*1%*	*3%*	*11%*	*4%*	*3%*
INTERROGATIVE	**9%**	**23%**	**8%**	**6%**	**7%**	**5%**
realisation	*5%*	*3%*	*4%*	*0%*	*1%*	*0%*
preference	*1%*	*3%*	*0.5%*	*0%*	*0%*	*0%*
performative	*0%*	*0%*	*0%*	*0%*	*0%*	*0%*
suggestory	*0%*	*0.3%*	*0%*	*0%*	*0%*	*0%*
deontic	*1%*	*0%*	*0%*	*0%*	*0%*	*0%*
competence	*2%*	*13.5%*	*2%*	*3%*	*3%*	*2%*
mild hint	*0.3%*	*0.3%*	*0.5%*	*0%*	*0%*	*0%*
strong hint	*0.3%*	*3%*	*0.5%*	*2%*	*4%*	*3%*
ITEMS	292	318	388	89	164	145

Table 23. Syntactic-semantic dimensions in the realisation of initiating and inhibitive requests.

HEAD ACT TYPE	GERMAN	ENGLISH	POLISH
COMPETENCE	5%	17%	3%
declarative comp.	*3%*	*3.5%*	*0.5%*
interrogative comp.	*2%*	*13.5%*	*2%*
VOLITION (interr.)	1%	3%	0.5%
DEONTIC (interr.)	1%	0%	0%
TOTAL	7%	20%	3%

Table 24. The use of negative politeness based on preparatory conditions: initiating requests.

HEAD ACT	GERMAN	ENGLISH	POLISH
COMPETENCE	7%	3%	2%
declarative	*3%*	*0%*	*0%*
interrogative	*3%*	*3%*	*2%*

Table 25. The use of negative politeness based on preparatory conditions: inhibitive requests.

GERMAN
INITIATING REQUESTS

The distribution of initiating requests among various syntactic-semantic dimensions in both series is very similar (see Appendix 7), and the differences do not approach statistical significance. The figures in Table 36 show the predominance of the imperative. Other dimensions which occurred with considerable frequency (larger than 5%) were realisation, deontic, preference and competence, split between the interrogative and declarative sentence forms, as well as elliptical constructions. 13% of initiating requests were realised using negatively polite head acts; the difference of 6% between series G2 and G4[87] did not approach significance.

Table 26 provides an overview of the most frequently used conversational routines.

---

[87] Special caution has been taken with respect to participants in G4 whose primary linguistic and cultural background was other than German or Swiss, and who acculturated in Germany as teenagers or young adults (a Somalian, a Hungarian, and a Yugoslavian). Fifty-two initiating requests uttered by those speakers were analysed separately to make sure that their presence does not considerably affect the profile of tendencies in the head act form. The differences were suggestive but statistically insignificant, and the utterances they produced are included in the sample.

CONVERSATIONAL FORMULA	SEMANTIC DIMENSION/SYNTACTIC SENTENCE TYPE
	IMPERATIVE
(1) VP (verb: 2 sing./pl. imper.)	zeig mal von hinten
	show from behind
	DECLARATIVE/COMPETENCE DIMENSION
(2) (du) kannst + VP (verb: infinitive)	dann kannst du auch sagen # was ich gesagt habe
	then you can also say # what I said
	INFINITIVE
(4) VP (verb: infinitive)	aufstehen
	stand up
	INTERROGATIVE/REALISATION DIMENSION
(5) VP (verb: 2 sing. indicat. pres.) + du	gibst du mir mal Feuer # bitte
	give you me fire # please
	INTERROGATIVE/COMPETENCE DIMENSION
(6) kannst du + VP (verb: infinitive)	Harry # kannst du mir das mal zeigen
	Harry # can you show it to me
	DECLARATIVE/REALISATION DIMENSION
(7) du + VP (verb: 2. sing. indicat. pres.)	du passt auf mich auf
	you supervise me

Table 26. Conversational routines that occurred in German initiating requests.

INHIBITIVE REQUESTS

The findings were consistent for the two German groups. In both series, the imperative was consistently the strongly prevailing head act form, and ellipsis came second. The German data differed in the use of tentative and impositive head acts in inhibitive and initiating requests. Inhibitives were rarely formulated using negatively polite head acts (7%) compared with initiating requests (13%). This results from the more frequent occurrence in inhibitives of the strong hint[88] and the infinitive[89]. Examples are given below:

---

[88] df=1, x^2=25.0, p<0.001
[89] df=1, x^2=6.2, p<0.025

INFINITIVE	28-G2.
	M nicht die Lampe kaputt machen # weil eh-
	NEG break-INF the lamp # because erm-
STRONG HINT	5-G4.
	F das ist kein Aschenbecher
	this is no ashtray

ENGLISH

INITIATING REQUESTS

The pattern that stood out among initiating requests in English was the imperative. The second most important dimension is competence, mainly in interrogatives. The findings were consistent for both groups. The figures verify the absolute primacy of the imperative in the British groups, an unexpected finding in view of the wide-spread conventional image of British speakers as tending to use indirect strategies of requesting. 29% of initiating requests in E3 and 20% in E4 were realised using tentative head acts; the difference was below significance.

INHIBITIVE REQUESTS

Imperatives were as frequent as in initiating requests; the other frequent form of head act was ellipsis. The ratios of negatively polite head acts amounted to 6% and 4% in E3 and E4, respectively, and were significantly lower than for initiating requests. The speakers showed a reduced attention to the interlocutors' negative face wants relative to initiating requests, and opted almost always for an impositive head act strategy when they decided to confront them by producing a corrective, preventive or terminating request.

Table 27 exemplifies conversational routines used in English requests.

CONVERSATIONAL FORMULA	SEMANTIC DIMENSION/SYNTACTIC SENTENCE TYPE
	IMPERATIVE
(1) VP (imperative)	show me # show me # show me
(2) don't + VP (infinitive)	don't shout me down # cause you are the one # that shouts
(3) let's + VP (infinitive)	Let's get on with it # will you
(4) don't	Oh Melissa # oh don't
	PREFERENCE DECLARATIVE
(5) I do not/don't want you to/to + VP	I don't want you to shout again

	DEONTIC DECLARATIVE
(6) you should + VP	I think # you should really try # and come over here next week # maybe
	REALISATION INTERROGATIVE
(7) will you + VP	will you just say # hello to my mum # for me
	COMPETENCE DECLARATIVE
(8) you can + VP	you can sit on the sofa
	COMPETENCE INTERROGATIVE
(9) can you + VP	can you let us in please
(10) could you + VP	erm # yes please # but could you get me some of my own tea
	PREFERENCE INTERROGATIVE
(11) do you want to + VP	Jane # do you want to have a go?

Table 27. Conversational routines that occurred in English requests.

POLISH

INITIATING REQUESTS

The distribution between different head act patterns was about the same in both groups. The imperative prevailed strongly, and ellipsis came second while it realised only a small percentage of all directives (about 7% of the total sample of initiating requestives). The figures quantify the predominance of the imperative and marginality of other dimensions. 92% of initiating requests were realised using impositive head acts; the difference between the two series was below 1%.

INHIBITIVE REQUESTS

Inhibitive requests in Polish have almost always been realised in an impositive head act form. Conventionally polite interrogatives constitute only 2% of the sample, and competence declaratives did not occur. The imperative dominates strongly, and the only other pattern appearing with relatively high frequency (10% of the sample) is ellipsis. Other syntactic-semantic dimensions are less than 4%.

Table 28 gives examples of conversational routines that occurred in Polish requests.

CONVERSATIONAL ROUTINE	SEMANTIC DIMENSION/SYNTACTIC SENTENCE TYPE
	IMPERATIVE
(1) VP (verb: 2 sing./pl. imper.)	okulary oddajcie
	give the glasses back
	INFINITIVE
(4) VP (verb: infinitive)	to wyłazić wszyscy # już
	then get out everybody # right now
	INTERROGATIVE/REALISATION DIMENSION
(5) VP (verb: 2. sing. indicat. pres.)	to co # raz dwa trzy i wstajecie?
	so what # one two three and you stand up?
	DECLARATIVE/REALISATION DIMENSION
(7) VP (verb: 2. sing. indicat. pres.)	już szybko # idziesz szybko # raz dwa
	quick # you go quick # in no time
	DECLARATIVE/DEONTIC DIMENSION
(6) trzeba + VP (verb: infinitive)	trzeba tego mopa wziąć # I tam powycierać w tym # łazience
	one-needs to take this mop # and clean the # the bathroom
	DECLARATIVE/DEONTIC DIMENSION
(7) masz + VP (verb: infinit.)	masz ryknąć
	you-sing. are to roar
	DECLARATIVE/DEONTIC DIMENSION
(8) musisz/musicie + VP (verb: infinitive)	musicie zaśpiewać
	you-pl. must sing something

Table 28. Conversational routines that occurred in Polish requests.

HEAD ACT POLITENESS

The differences between English and the other two languages in the preference for positively polite head acts in initiating requests were highly significant[90]. The small difference between Polish and German reached weak significance[91]. There was no significant

[90] For Polish/English, df=1, x^2=34.1, p<0.001; for German/English, df=1, x^2=12.7, p<0.001.
[91] df=1, x^2=4.0, p<0.05

interlingual difference in the use of negatively vs. positively polite head acts in inhibitive requests.

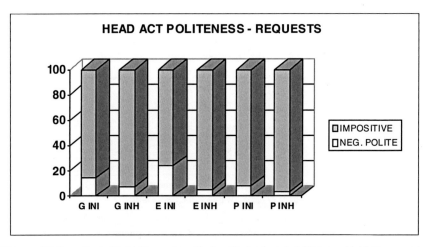

Diagram 15. Proportions of impositive and negatively polite head acts in initiating and inhibitive requests.

A simplified view of the forms used in particular languages divided into positively and negatively polite ones is presented in Appendix 8.

Although the British showed a weaker preference for positive head act politeness than speakers of the other two languages, a much more illuminating finding is the predominance of the imperative as a conversational routine used in realising initiating and inhibitive requests in all three languages under consideration, and marginality of negatively polite head act strategies. As this finding goes against the view of the British subjects as showing a high preference for conventional indirectness, confirmed by studies of English directives based on non-natural methods (Blum-Kulka et al. 1989, Fukushima 1996), as well as a corpus study by Aijmer (1996), this result appears to be in need of further qualification. This may be due in part to the general difference in the social contexts under analysis: there are only young peers living together in Big Brother, while encounters between strangers and formal contexts are included in other studies. The other relevant factor is the previously emphasised distinction between various types of beneficiary. Contrary to non-natural studies, communication in a peer group contains only a relatively small portion of requests whose sole beneficiaries are speakers themselves. The assumption that conventional indirectness is a preferred interaction strategy found some support in English but it was strictly limited to a still smaller subset of such requests, that is, requests for personal favours to the speaker. This type of request is discussed in section 5.2.5.5. Requests with other beneficiary configurations show the opposite tendency.

5.2.5.4. REQUESTS: MODIFICATION

The use of modifiers in initiating and inhibitive requests at the most detailed level of sub-categorisation is shown in Appendix 6. The following overview summarises the most considerable differences in the use of particular devices in the three languages.

INTERACTION MARKERS

informality/confidence:

- frequent use of starters, comprising terms of address, verbs of knowing, verbs of sensation and colloquial links/summonses in initiating requests in Polish; the exception was the interjection, which occurred very rarely in Polish;
- frequent use of positively polite terms of address (colloquial, nicknames and pet names) in Polish; at the same time, the use of terms of address in general (including neutrally polite terms) was about the same in all three languages;
- very rare use of positively polite terms of address in inhibitive requests in English

negative politeness:

- other than in the other two languages, in Polish negatively polite interaction markers add up to a somewhat higher figure in inhibitives than in initiating requests[92]; in particular, the use of IFID (*proszę*) in Polish in initiating requests was more frequent in inhibitives;
- rare use of question tag in inhibitive requests in English

SUPPORTIVE MOVES

impositiveness:

In both initiating and inhibitive requests, supportive moves of the impositive type were least frequent in English, while their use in inhibitive requests was enhanced relatively to initiating requests in all three languages.

INTERNAL MODIFIERS

negative politeness:

- very frequent use of lexical hedge in German (*mal, einfach*);

---

[92] df=1, x^2=6.3, p<0.025

- no use of morphological diminutive in English and German vs. its sporadic occurrence in Polish
informality/confidence:
- very rare use of positively polite terms in references to persons in English and German
- frequent use of humour in German
impositiveness:
- frequent use of lexical intensifiers in German;
- more frequent use of augmentatives/expletives in German and English inhibitive requests than in Polish;
- very frequent use of repetition in English and Polish inhibitive requests and its very rare use in German.

REQUESTS: POLITENESS OF MODIFICATION – AN OVERVIEW

Table 29 shows how frequently impositive and tentative head acts of initiating and inhibitive requests were accompanied by positively and negatively polite modifiers. The category "positively polite modification" comprises the subcategories "informality/confidence" and "impositiveness". As in the case of proposals, also for initiating and inhibitive requests, there is a tendency for negatively polite modifiers to co-occur with negatively polite head acts rather than positively polite ones. The difference is significant for all three languages for the total pool of requestives.[93] At first glance, this disproportion might suggest a dichotomised choice of interaction strategies, but a detailed look at the data shows that the reason for the more frequent use of negatively polite modifiers to modify tentative head acts, which already signal attention to the addressee's negative face wants, is the use of verbal routines. In routine formulas realised by negatively polite head acts, a negatively polite modification such as a conditional/subjunctive mood, passive voice, polite pessimism, modal adverbials, and some types of negatively polite prefacing supportive moves, such as disarmers and preparators, are integrated with conventionally polite interrogative sentence forms, and once the choice of the head act politeness is made the accompanying modification comes along.

---

[93] For German, df=1, x^2=9.0, p<0.005; for English, df=1, x^2=22.1, p<0.001; for Polish, df=1, x^2=14.8, p<0.001.

INITIATING REQUEST	ENGLISH	GERMAN	POLISH
POS HA			
pos. pol. modifiers	37%	52%	56%
neg. pol. modifiers	21%	37%	12%
unmodified	50%	29%	36%
NEG HA			33
pos. pol. modifiers	27%	46%	45%
neg. pol. modifiers	44%	51%	39%
unmodified	42%	33%	30%
ALL HA			
pos. pol. modifiers	34%	51%	55%
neg. pol. modifiers	26%	39%	14%
unmodified	48%	29%	36%
UTTERANCE			
positive politeness	60%	54%	80%
negative politeness	18%	7%	5%
both types	22%	38%	15%
INHIBITIVE REQUEST	ENGLISH	GERMAN	POLISH
POS HA			
pos. pol. modifiers	53%	53%	64%
neg. pol. modifiers	17%	30%	16%
unmodified	38%	33%	31%
NEG HA			
pos. pol. modifiers	22%	50%	0%
neg. pol. modifiers	44%	83%	60%
unmodified	44%	0%	40%
ALL HA			
pos. pol. modifiers	51%	53%	62%
neg. pol. modifiers	19%	34%	18%
unmodified	38%	30%	32%

UTTERANCE			
positive politeness	78%	65%	81%
negative politeness	4%	3%	3%
both types	18%	31%	16%

Table 29. Occurrence of modifiers in initiating and inhibitive requests[94].

The occurrence of modification independent of the type of head act is visualised in Diagram 16 below[95].

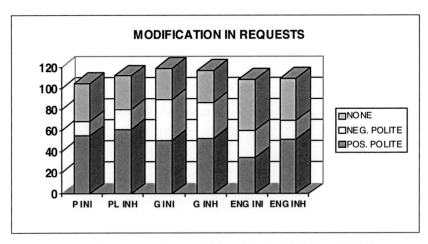

Diagram 16. Occurrence of politeness-relevant modification in initiating and inhibitive requests.

The diagram shows that the finding that the intralingual differences between initiating and inhibitive requests were minor compared to the interlingual differences between particular pairs of languages. Negatively polite modification occurred most frequently in German, both in inhibitive and initiating requests. Modification of English inhibitive requests resembles closely that of requests (any type) in Polish, suggesting that a similar tendency

---

[94] The figures referring to the occurrence of modifiers do not add up to 100% because some items contain both positively and negatively polite modification.
[95] The figures add up to more than 100% because some utterances contain modifiers of both types.

occurs here as for the head act choice, where the British opted for impositiveness more frequently than in initiating requestives and the difference from Polish was only slight. In German, a very similar distribution of politeness-relevant modifiers occurred in requests for both action types.

INTRALINGUAL DIFFERENCES: INITIATING AND INHIBITIVE REQUESTS

In all three languages, the percentage of impositive modifiers was higher in inhibitive requests than in initiating ones. This tendency matched the preferences in the choice of head act in English than in German, while in Polish tentative forms were very infrequent in both action types and the small nominal difference was below significance. This result can be traced back to the increased use of few particular linguistic devices in each language.

In Polish, the intralingual difference resulted almost mainly from the more frequent use of impositive internal modifiers in inhibitive requests, in repetition in particular. However, a significant intralingual contrast occurred in the use of negatively polite interaction markers in Polish between inhibitive and initiating requests (question tags and IFID *proszę*). They were applied in about 9% of inhibitive requests and 4% of initiating requests[96], reducing preference for the "impositive only" type of strategy in inhibitive requests.

Remember though that one aspect of displaying deference in the Polish data has been excluded from consideration in this chapter due to the difficulty of consolidating lexico-morphological ("digital") and supra-segmental ("analogue"[97]) characteristics of messages. Rather than express deference and dependence on the addressee's good will by means of negatively polite lexical interaction markers, Polish depends in this respect heavily on intonation and developed a language-specific intonation pattern functionally equivalent to lexical IFIDs such as *please* and *bitte* (cf. section 6.4.1.).

---

[96] df=1, x^2=4.8, p<0.05
[97] This metaphor refers to the difference between properties that are either present or absent, and those whose occurrence is a matter of degree.

INITIATING REQUESTS	ENG	GR	PL
INFORMALITY			
INTERACTION MARKER			
starter (turn-initial)			
vocative (pos.pol.)	0.9	2.1	5.7
colloquial	3.5	2.1	2.1
nickname/humorous	1.9	2.7	5.7
INTERNAL MODIFIERS			
colloquialism	3.5	6.5	5.9
humour	2.5	5.1	4.9
nickname (non-vocative)	0.3	0.3	3.4
IMPOSITIVENESS			
INTERNAL MODIFIERS			
lexical intensifier	0.9	10.6	3.9
NEGATIVE POLITENESS			
INTERACTION MARKERS			
IFID (please. bitte. prosze)	5.3	7.9	1.9
INTERNAL MODIFIERS			
lexical hedge	11	28.4	4.4
morphological diminutive	0.0	0.0	2.1
NEUTRAL IN POLITENESS			
vocative	19.2	14.4	5.9
voc. initial	13.5	8.9	4.4
voc. non-initial	5.7	5.5	1.5

INHIBITIVE REQUESTS	ENG	GR	PL
INFORMALITY			
INTERACTION MARKER			
starter (turn-initial)	3.7	11.3	6.2
vocative (pos.pol.)	0.0	3.4	5.5
interjection	3.7	7.9	0.7
vocative non-initial	3.7	6.7	8.3
pet name	0.6	3.4	1.4
colloquial	2.4	2.2	2.8
nickname/humorous	0.6	1.1	4.1
INTERNAL MODIFIERS			
colloquialism	3.0	7.9	9.7
humour	3.7	7.9	2.1
nickname (non-vocative)	0.6	1.1	9.0
repetition	16.5	1.1	16.6
IMPOSITIVENESS			
INTERACTION MARKERS			
imp. verb of sensation	0.0	3.4	2.8
other imperative	4.9	4.5	4.1
SUPPORTIVE MOVES			
steer/preparator	1.2	7.9	3.4
INTERNAL MODIFIERS			
augment./vulg.	14.0	11.2	6.2
lexical intensifier	0.0	12.4	3.4
NEGATIVE POLITENESS			
SUPPORTIVE MOVES			
all types	3.0	6.7	1.4
INTERNAL MODIFIERS			
lexical hedge	6.7	21.3	3.4
NEUTRAL IN POLITENESS			
vocative	19.5	14.6	8.3
voc. initial	14.6	10.1	5.5
voc. non-initial	4.9	4.5	2.8

Table 30. Largest interlingual differences in types of modifiers.

In English, both internal modifiers and supportive moves of impositive types were more frequent in inhibitives than in initiating directives. The types of supportive move that occurred with significantly higher frequencies in inhibitives were phrasal and sentential emphasisers[98]; the remaining difference resulted from a slight (on its own insignificant) over-representation of impositive grounders. The type of internal modifier more frequent in inhibitives was augmentative/expletive, while this was due mainly to the use of just one particular inhibitive routine formula based on an expressive verb. (cf. section 6.3.2.).

In German, similarly as in English, a considerable difference between initiating and inhibitive requests occurred in the use of impositive supportive moves and augmentative forms/expletives; both were more frequent in inhibitives. Besides, there was a significant difference in the use of repetition in inhibitive and initiating requests: in inhibitives, it occurred just once in the whole sample (for a discussion, see section 6.2.).

Appendix 6 shows the occurrences of particular types of modifiers in initiating and inhibitive requestives. Outstanding interlingual contrasts are shown in Table 30. Case studies of the use of these particular types of modification follow in chapter 6.

Finally, Diagram 17 shows the types of politeness occurring in inhibitive and initiating requests, resulting from a mix of politeness in the head act and modification.

To sum up, the speakers of English proved as direct and inattentive to negative face wants of interlocutors when producing inhibitives as the Poles. In German, the percentage of requests showing both types of politeness is considerably higher than in Polish and in English due to the frequent occurrence of negatively polite modification in German, in particular, lexical hedges, accompanying as many as 27% of all requests, and confined to just a few lexemes.

---

[98] df=1, x^2=7.4, p<0.01

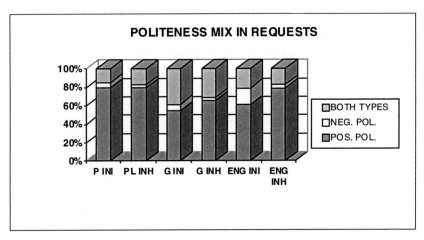

Diagram 17. Types of politeness in requests: initiating and inhibitive.

5.2.5.5. REQUESTS FOR PERSONAL FAVOURS

Requests for personal favours constitute a half or more of all the initiating requests beneficial prevailingly to the speaker, and a small portion of the total pool of requestives in each language, 9% of German and Polish samples and 7% of the English samples. They are considered as a category of their own in the analysis because they are regarded as having a high face-threat potential and treated as the prototypical sort of requests in the mainstream linguistic studies of politeness.

The size of the samples is small (between 43 and 61 items). Therefore I refrain from quoting the exact distribution of the samples among various syntactic-semantic patterns and will only comment on some outstanding differences in this respect.

REQUESTS FOR PERSONAL FAVOURS: HEAD ACT

Table 31 shows the type of head act politeness for particular samples of requests for small personal favours. It also shows intralingual differences between the early and late phases of the program. The percentages given refer to the ratios of negative head politeness in the samples. The right column shows significances of differences between particular samples within the same language, and between particular phases within the same language.

Intralingual differences between particular groups were insignificant.

The two stages of the program differed in the amount of negatively polite strategy in head act choice only in German. The rise in the proportion of impositive head acts in the later stage of the program suggests that the German participants needed some time to start treating each other as intimates who can be addressed prevailingly by distance-diminishing linguistic forms in this type of relatively face-threatening directive activity. At the same time, the Poles rarely use negatively polite strategies from the very start. It seems that for the German subjects, the duration and the resulting quality of personal acquaintance was the

REQUESTS FOR PERSONAL FAVOURS			
% of negatively polite head acts			df=1
German	ITEMS	%	SIGNIFICANCE OF DIFFERENCE
G2	19	37%	x^2=0.28
G4	24	29%	insignificant
G EARLY	18	56%	x^2=7.46
G LATE	25	16%	p<0.01
English			
E3	28	79%	x^2=0.24
E4	18	72%	insignificant
E EARLY	29	76%	x^2=0.00
E LATE	17	76%	insignificant
Polish			
P1	24	17%	x^2=3.13
P3	37	35%	insignificant
P EARLY	23	30%	x^2=0.59
P LATE	38	26%	insignificant

Table 31. Percentages of negatively polite head acts in requests for personal favours.

determining factor in defining each other as intimates, which shaped politeness strategies used in such requests. The Poles, on the other hand, might have defined the relationship as close and permitting distance-diminishing language forms on the basis of the social situation alone (living together in a peer group), in advance of a high degree of actual personal acquaintance. This suggestion correlates with the observations concerning the housemates' first encounters in various Big Brother houses (see chapter 7). After viewing these episodes, informants from all three countries characterised the German participants during this

163

encounter as generally more stressed, watchful, and reserved than the Poles and the British. However, the period of acquaintance hardly affected the use of politeness in the remaining types of requestives, which heavily restricts the validity of this claim.

A closer look at the data suggests that the higher ratio of positively polite head acts in the later stage of the program does not result alone from using different head act choice in the formulation of requests for similar actions, but also from the emergence of requests that were unlikely to occur in the early stages of acquaintance and definitely unlikely to be formulated in any tentative form. The latter kind occurs in the following episode:

6-G4. M1 has been evicted from Big Brother house and is just about to leave.
35 M2 Ich will dich sehen Alter # wenn ich rauskomme # will ich dich stehen sehen # ne?
I want to see you old man # when I get out # I want to see you stand there # right?
...
45 F1 hol mich nächste Woche ab # ja? hast du gehört? hol mich nächste Woche ab
pick me up next week # right? have you heard that? pick me up next week

In this scene, the housemates staying in the house anticipate their future eviction and demand to be picked by M1 upon leaving the house. This demand whose fulfilment might require a massive amount of effort on the addressee's part is at the same time a declaration of friendship and intimacy, and expresses a strong expectation that M1 considers the relationship in the same way. Here, the distance-diminishing form corresponds to the message implicit in the request.

Similarly, according to five native speakers of German, the following request that occurred on day 67 of the program was unlikely to occur in its early phase.

29-G2. MAKE PLACE
M1, M2, M3 are in the hot tub. M4 enters and gets into the tub.
1 M1 to M2 so # geh erst mal in die Ecke # na los #. zack # geh drüber
well # first go to the corner # off you go # quick # move over
(M1 shows M2 where he should move to)
2 M2, M3-TOM (laugh)
(M2 moves to the place shown by M1)

3 M1 es gibt hier feste Regel # was sagst du Tom # so geht das nicht
there are firm rules here # what will you say Tom # one can't do it this way
4 M3 (laughs)
(M1 goes to his usual place, which M2 made available)

Paradoxically, while the demand that M2 make room for M1 in the latter's favourite place in the hot tub constitutes a high face threat to M2, it is less likely to be realised in a linguistic form acknowledging distance in the relationship between the speaker and the addressee, because the acknowledgement of such a distance would be likely to block the very production of the requestive. Out of five native speakers who watched the episode, three regarded it as very rude and two pointed out that it was devoid of any real aggression and took place within the frame of positive politeness, and that the unusually high degree of impositiveness gave it a humorous undertone by an overt transgression of the usual principles of diplomacy in interaction.

The Polish and the German samples share a high overall ratio of positive politeness, while the English subjects prevailingly choose to use negatively polite head acts. The differences between Polish and German on the one hand, and English on the other, are highly significant[99]. The imperative constituted about one third of the head acts in the German and half of the Polish data, and only as little as one sixth in English. 60% of all items in English were competence interrogatives of the form *can you/could you + VP*, which occurred in 9% of the German and 6% of Polish items. If the Germans and the Poles opted for using a polite interrogative, it usually had the form of the realisation interrogative, as in the following examples:

30-G2. M1 and M2 are in the hot tub. M2 is about to leave and M1 is holding an empty beer bottle.
M1 Denis # nimmst du die Flasche mit?
Denis # take-INDICATIVE-present-2. sing. the bottle with you
36-P3. F1 is in the hot tub, talking to F2.
F podasz mi ręcznik?
give-INDICATIVE-future-2. sing. me the towel

The claim that conventional indirectness is a typical means of making requests in English, based on the application of non-natural methods (e.g. in House 1996) and confirmed

---

[99] For Polish and English, df=1, chi square=24.0, p<0.001. For English and German, df=1, chi square=17.0, p<0.001.

165

by intuitions of native speakers, is strongly supported in the data, while at the same time it is shown that such requests constitute only a very small portion of all requestives in natural, action-bound speech.

A further aspect of head act politeness choice in requests for personal favours (RPFs) is its relation to the choice of head politeness in other types of requestives. In Table 48, RPFs are contrasted in this respect with the remaining requestives.

LANGUAGE	RPF	OTHER	x^2	SIGNIFICANCE OF DIFFERENCE
German	33%	13%	11.1	$p < 0.001$
English	76%	17%	87.5	$p < 0.001$
Polish	28%	5%	42.4	$p < 0.001$

Table 32. The ratios of negatively polite head acts for the "requests for personal favours" subcategory and the remaining types of requestives.

Requests for personal favours stand out in that they are realised less frequently than other types of requestives using an impositive head act, in all languages under consideration. The nominal difference is most striking for English, and most moderate for German. While the Poles chose head acts of RPFs very similar to the Germans, on other types of requestives they seem to diverge as widely from the German as from the British. The difference between English and German for the category "other" is insignificant.

The category "other" in Table 32 also contains inhibitive requestives that are generally less frequently realised using negatively polite head acts, while very few of them are present among requests for personal favours. A comparison between requests for personal favours and other requestives from the "initiating" subcategory produces a somewhat more moderate albeit still strongly significant nominal difference in all three languages. A detailed comparison will not be undertaken at this point as initiating requests, inhibitive requests and proposals are discussed in detail in the preceding chapters.

REQUESTS FOR PERSONAL FAVOURS: MODIFICATION

The complex chi square significance test showed that the use of modification to accompany positively polite head acts was significantly different for Polish and German[100] and for English and German[101]. The German subjects showed a stronger tendency to modify

---

[100] df=3, chi square=9.1, $p < 0.05$
[101] df=3, chi square=8.2, $p < 0.05$

impositive head acts by negatively polite modifiers than speakers of the other two languages. No significance could be certified to the differences in modification accompanying negatively polite head acts. The modifiers include:

in English - negatively polite: subjunctive, lexical hedge ("just"), preparator "can you do me a favour", and IFID "please"; positively polite: repetition, grounder ("that's my place"), colloquialism, interjection, and a colloquial term of address ("mate");

in Polish – subjunctive, diminutive in the predicative phrase (*masz ogieńka?* "have you got fire-DIM?"), tag (*okay?*) and a post-posed IFID in the form of a hedged performative in subjunctive mood (*mógłbym cię prosić* "could I ask you?", one occurrence) on the negatively polite side, and on the positively polite side first and second grade diminutives of first names, diminutive of a term of endearment, repetition, colloquialism, referential use of nickname, appealer (*wiecie co?* "you know what?"), compliment, and imperative starter (*weź mi to zrób*, "take-AUXILIARY-IMP do it for me");

in German – subjunctive, lexical hedges (*mal , erst mal*), IFID (bitte), preparator (*du könntest mir den Gefallen tun* "you could do me a favour"), and question tag (*ja?* "yes?") on the negatively polite side, and emphasiser (*na los* "off you go"), grounder (*ich will es schon so* "I want it this way"), positively polite term of address (*Alter* "the old one"), imperative starter (*komm* "come"), and an anglicism as a colloquial summon (*okay*) on the positively polite side.

IFIDs (*please, bitte*) were used in 16% of German RPFs and 30% of English RPFs, and only once in Polish. The difference between German and English did not approach significance.

However, a non-lexical IFID in the form of "requestive intonation", which will be discussed in the next chapter, was used in about 18% of Polish RPFs. This is a subjective rating verified by pitch analysis in all cases where the quality of the recordings allowed this. Generally, the presence and absence of requestive intonation is a matter of degree, and tests conducted with 7 native speakers showed that they did not always agree on its presence or absence (on average, every two test persons agreed with each other in this respect only for 10 out of 14 utterances presented to them). Therefore, it is not reflected in the diagrams and tables.

G2+G4		N= 43
pos. polite HA	unmitigated	12%
	positively mitigated	31%
67%	negatively mitigated	38%
neg. polite HA	unmitigated	14%
	positively mitigated	2%
33%	negatively mitigated	16%
E3+E4		N= 46
pos. polite HA	unmitigated	4%
	positively mitigated	17%
24%	negatively mitigated	2%
neg. polite HA	unmitigated	37%
	positively mitigated	11%
76%	negatively mitigated	35%
P1+P3		N= 61
pos. polite HA	unmitigated	20%
	positively mitigated	46%
72%	negatively mitigated	22%
neg. polite HA	unmitigated	10%
	positively mitigated	8%
8%	negatively mitigated	13%

Table 33. Modification accompanying positively and negatively polite head acts in German, English and Polish.[102]

---

[102] Percentages do not add up to 100% because some items contain both types of modification.

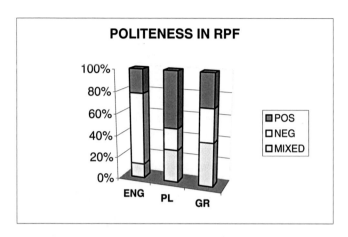

Diagram 18. Requests for personal favours containing only positive, only negative, and elements of both types of politeness in the head act or its modification.

As a result of the combination of head act politeness and modification, three subtypes of utterances can be distinguished with respect to politeness:
- showing positive politeness only (unmodified and positively modified impositives),
- showing negative politeness only (unmodified and negatively modified tentatives),
- containing elements of both types of politeness.

Diagram 18 shows the distribution of requests for personal favours among these three types. It shows that the use of negatively polite modification results in a different distribution of RPFs in Polish and German among the three types of politeness strategies. The difference appears mainly in the rare use of a negatively polite modification by the Poles in impositives (requests realised by impositive head acts), reflected by the size of the "positive politeness only" category. German and English speakers are more alike in their infrequent use of positive politeness not accompanied by any negatively polite mitigation. However, the difference in this respect between Polish and German drops to zero if the role of the requestive pitch pattern in Polish is taken into account.

5.2.5.6. SUMMARY OF REQUESTS

In all three languages, the imperative was a predominant form in which requests were made. Like in proposals, also in requests the Poles showed the strongest preference for impositive head acts and positively polite modification. Negatively polite head acts constituted a small portion of requests, and were used most frequently in English initiating requests.

English showed the most frequent use of conventionally polite modal framing (a reference to "preparatory conditions"), mainly in the form of competence interrogative, referring to the possibility/ability of the speaker to perform the predicated action, in initiating requests. English initiating requests differed in this respect on the one hand from the same type in Polish and German, and on the other from the complementary type in English; inhibitives were, in all three languages, very rarely realised by means of tentative head acts.

The Poles differed least in the head act choice for inhibitive and initiating requests, which were realised using the same syntactic-semantic formats and politeness strategies. The slight difference between the two action types was marked by the increased use of impositive internal modifiers or, alternatively, negatively polite interaction markers in inhibitives. In other words, the Poles decided to signal a deferent (*proszę cię/was*) or consultative (question tag) attitude somewhat more frequently in situations where the presupposition of consensus was weakened by the fact of reacting critically to the hearer's acts or plans; the difference, however, was slight. In the other two languages the difference between the two action types was marked both by impositive modification and by stronger preferences for impositives in head act choice in inhibitive requests.

German was distinguished by the frequent use of declarative strong hints and the infinitive in inhibitive requests. The infinitive can also be used in Polish with the same function but was hardly made any use of. (The differences in the applicability of the infinitive to form requests in Polish and in German are discussed in chapter 6). Also, the Poles showed nearly no use of deontic declaratives in inhibitive requests, which was relatively frequent in German.

The tendencies that occurred in the head act choice were partly in line with those that occurred in the use of politeness-relevant modifiers, in particular, those which maximised the illocutionary force by increasing impositiveness. Modifiers of this type were more frequent in inhibitives than in initiating requests in all three languages. The speakers of English used them less frequently than the other groups in initiating requests, while in

170

inhibitives, they were used with approximately the same frequency in all three languages (from 51% to 59%).

The use of modifiers signalling informality and confidence was highest in Polish, mainly due to the routine use of nicknaming and colloquial forms of addressing and referring to other housemates, while it was lowest in English, where colloquialisms were rarer than in the other two languages.

A frequent use of negatively polite modifiers occurred in German, which resulted in a high percentage of the mixed type of politeness strategy, in particular, a high percentage of impositives modified by means of negative politeness. This was due mainly to the use of lexical hedges, that is, a small number of particles serving the mitigating function. Such devices were used very rarely in Polish, whilst the speakers of English used them with a moderate frequency in initiating requests, and very rarely in inhibitives.

The use of negatively polite supportive moves, such as disarmers, imposition minimisers, preparatory and consultative devices (non-tags) was very limited in all groups, whilst the Poles used them even less frequently than the other two groups. The differences between German and English on the one hand and Polish on the other were significant.[103] As was to be expected, there were no differences in the use of neutrally polite moves, applied to indicate the relationship between requestives and their discursive and situational contexts.

Due to the increased use of negatively polite modifiers by the Poles in inhibitives (compared to initiating requests) and the increased use of positively polite head acts in English inhibitives (compared to initiating requests), English and Polish showed almost the same mix of politeness strategies in inhibitives.

While German and English are more similar to each other when all requestives are taken into account, the situation changes radically when requests (and "demands") for personal favours are concerned. German and Polish become more alike, and English, which strongly opts for conventional indirectness, mainly in the form of the competence interrogative, constitutes the negatively polite end. On the other hand, English and Polish are alike in that they both differentiate rather strongly between requests for personal favours and other sorts of requestives. In both languages negatively polite head act forms are used more frequently in the former. The difference in the orientation of head act politeness between Polish and German is considerable for requests in general, but meaningless for RPFs; the difference in head act politeness between English and German is considerable for

---

[103] For Polish/German, df=1, x^2=6.0, p<0.025 and for Polish/English, df=1, x^2=8.0, p<0.005.

RPFs, but meaningless for other kinds of requestives. In this subtype of requestives, the Poles move towards the negatively polite end of the spectrum, and towards the German, but the difference between English and the other two languages increases because the British shift even more radically towards the negatively polite end. The difference between Polish and German is retained in the more frequent use of lexically realised negatively polite modification accompanying impositive head acts in German, but it appears as negligible if the mitigating function of pitch pattern in Polish is taken into account.

The results confirm the claim by House (1977, 1984, 1996) that the Germans are more direct and impositive in their directive behaviour than the British, but at the same time restrict the validity of this claim in the context of peer group interaction to these particular type of requestives (RPF), which only make out a fraction of directive activities undertaken in real communication. The Poles, who showed in general the most radical preference for impositive forms, differ only slightly from speakers of German when it comes to making an RPF. The occurrence or otherwise of differences in interaction styles shown in directive activities proves to be highly sensitive to the difference between acts perceived as the addressee "doing something for the speaker" and other types of acts.

6. SELECTED GRAMMATICAL, LEXICAL AND PROSODIC PROCEDURES IN THE CONSTRUCTION OF DIRECTIVES

This chapter deals with selected strategies, lexical, prosodic and syntactic devices available and applied in producing directives in the particular languages under study. The presentation complements the inter-lingual pattern of similarity and difference supplied by the statistical analysis.

The types of head acts discussed in this section illustrate the following types of interlingual contrasts in form-function correspondences:

- A syntactic form routinely used in language A to realise a given communicative intention is absent in language B. (Here: the imperative-declarative sentence type specific to Polish.)
- A syntactic form routinely used in language A to realise a given communicative intention exists in language B but is not used to realise this communicative intention in B; there may be exceptions in the form of a number of fully lexicalised routine formulas realising the same function in B, but the pattern is not productive. (Here: the infinitive clause in German and Polish vs. English.)
- A form routinely used in language A to realise a given communicative intention can be produced according to the rules of grammar in language B and used to realise the same intention on the basis of its semantics, but is not routinely used in this function. (Here: unhedged performative with *prosić/ask* in Polish and English.)
- Lexically and semantically similar conversational routines are used in language A and language B in different syntactic forms and applied in different sequential contexts in discourse. (Here: the performative in Polish vs. the cleft performative English; neutral vs. persuasive emphatic formulation.)
- A conversational routine used in language A to realise a given communicative function exists in language B and is used to realise the same communicative intention, but the set of contextual restrictions on its socially or grammatically appropriate application is different in two languages; conditions of applicability may intersect in two languages. (Here: the infinitive in German and Polish.)
- A conversational routine used in language A to realise a given communicative exists in language B and is used to realise the same communicative intention, but the speakers of the two languages show different preferences in their choices of verbal forms, which results in its more frequent occurrence in A. (Here: the realisation declarative in Polish and German vs. English.)

The boundaries between social appropriateness vs. grammatical correctness are fuzzy as grammaticalisation processes operate on socially conditioned language use. The restrictions on contextual appropriateness can be lifted by fictionalisation, i.e. evoking a social context different from the actual context by using verbal forms ill-fitted to the actual context. (Here: the infinitive in German and Polish.)

The following selective analysis of modifiers pertains to those which

- show major contrasts in frequency of use; little attention, though, will be paid to negatively polite lexical imposition minimisers because of the availability of thorough studies examining in detail the semantics and conditions of use of lexical items and routine formulas which appear in this modifying function[104];
- are language-specific because of different habits of usage or rules of grammar in one of the languages under study;
- are (morpho)syntactically different or occur within different syntactic structures while being semantically and functionally equivalent;
- have different implications in interpersonal space while having the same semantic and (morpho)syntactic structure;
- invite inferences by departing from standard contextually appropriate articulation of a directive utterance in a language-specific way, while either the standard or the form of changes show interlingual difference.

6.1. SOME LANGUAGE-SPECIFIC HEAD ACT FORMS

6.1.1. INFINITIVE

A bare infinitive is available for the formulation of directive utterances in both Polish and German. In English, the use of *to* + infinitive in directives is restricted to the lexicalised routine "not to worry". The pattern is not productive.

The infinitive is an impositive and depersonalised form of directive typically associated with institutionalised hierarchical communication, e.g. military commands or ward/prisoner communication. Another typical context of its use is anonymous signs of inhibitive content

---

[104] Among others, Thurmair's (1989) and Nekula's (1996) studies of German lexical modifiers, Hentschel's (1986) study of several discourse particles in German, Schoroup's (1982) treatment of some hedging expressions in English, Hansen's (1998) study of discourse particles in English and Aijmer's (1996) study of modifiers such as *please, just*, and other lexical softening devices in English directives.

regulating behaviour at public places, depersonalised by underspecified authorship and a generalised addressee. In the context of non-hierarchical communication, depersonalisation of the predication by using an infinitive is prototypically used in instructionals by people authorised to issue them in role-based exchanges, involving differentiation of social and associated communicative roles. In a peer context, the infinitive can be a signal of the role appropriation, marking that the speaker overtakes the instructor's role in a co-operative task, as in the following examples:

31-G2. M1 is taking a shower. The housemates agreed to use it in relays as soon as he has finished, because of the limited amount of hot water.

(M1 comes out of the shower)

(M2 gets into the shower)

M1 der nächste fertig mache (extra loud, to invisible people in the next room)

the next make-INF ready

1-G3. The housemates are sitting on the sofas in the living room as ordered by Big Brother. F has been appointed by Big Brother to read a written instruction to the group.

F Mikros anlegen # Mikros anlegen

put-INF the microphones on # put-INF the microphones on

Because of the aforementioned implications for the relation between the speaker and the addressee, serious, non-playful uses of the infinitive are frequently accompanied by modification. Modification fills interpersonal space and restores the social equilibrium. In the following data, it takes the form of a consultative device:

7-G4. EVALUATIONS

M2 to F1: zuhören # okay?

listen-INF # okay?

In the next exchange, the infinitive has been modified by the use of the appealer *hör mal* and an extensive explicit justification naming the reasons for the directive:

2-G1. The housemates have been given one hour to collectively prepare a shopping list of groceries, and are discussing how much milk should be bought. F has been appointed by Big Brother to write the order down.

M to F: **aber ein bisschen beeilen** # **hör mal** # sonst kommen wir mit einer
Stunde gar nicht hin # wenn wir schon bei Milch so lange daran bleiben
but hurry up-INF a bit # listen-IMP-2. sing. # otherwise we will not manage within an hour # if we already
need so long for the milk

In the following German data, the infinitive marks friendly criticism:

31-G2. M1 and M2 are trying to close M1's suitcase.
M1 **und diesmal nicht auf meine Finger setzen** # okay? (tries to close the locks)
leck mich am Arsch # stop # stop stop # das ist schon wieder eine mission
impossible
and don't sit on my fingers this time # okay? fuck # stop # stop # stop # this is again a mission impossible

The utterance contains a consultative device ("*okay?*") and also utilises multiple signals
of informality, confidence and intimacy, such as a colloquial Anglicism in the tag question
(okay?), vulgarism (leck mich am Arsch) and pop culture collocations (mission
impossible, a coinage borrowed from the title of an action film and TV show), as well as
an urgency signal (repetition: stop # stop # stop), signalling jointly that the speaker is
not trying to assume a position of authority but acting within the positively polite attitude of
"cameraderie".

As the modifying devices populate interpersonal space, their use balances out the
depersonalisation immanent in an infinitive construction, and the utterances above stop
short of signalling the assumption of authority or overtaking command on the speaker's part.

When used in a non-hierarchical peer group context, the infinitive frequently carries
with it a playful connotation implying that the speaker assumes a depersonalised authority
position with respect to the hearer. In such cases, it is likely to be accompanied by
contextualisation cues that help the hearer to identify the intended impact of the utterance in
the interpersonal space. The playful mode of interaction where the infinitive is used as a
means of enacting "authority" is exemplified by the following Polish data.

37-P3. SOLDIER
F ("team captain") and M, from the same team, are having a conversation.
F (removes fuzz from M1's face)
M (moves his face away)

F e:p # nie odsuwać mi się   tu # żołnierzu (laughs)
e:p # not get away-INF   *INTENSIFIER # soldier*

The use of the infinitive is a part of a role play in which F is M's superior in an institutionalised context by addressing M as "soldier", a term of address used by superiors in addressing the lowest ranks in the armed forces.

In the following data, speaker F becomes attentive to the playful mode of speaking which she introduced by using the infinitive verb form in a directive, and exploits further this potential of the infinitive by way of its overtly playful application – "foreigner talk".

3-G1. F and M are painting pictures. M comes up to F and takes some paint out of the can. Some of M's paint cans are already empty.

F ja # mit Gefühl # nicht so viel machen # . du gucken deine Becher da ganz vorne
well # with feeling # not do-INF that much # you look-INF your bowls over there quite in the front

F points out to M that he is using too much paint for a picture, and that he should deal with it more "sensitively". The initial use of the infinitive is continued in the second part of the utterance in "foreigner talk", of which the (ungrammatically used) infinitive is a typical aspect, and which allows here nothing other than a playful and humorous interpretation as both F and M are native speakers of German. Code-switching to "foreigner talk" contextualises the preceding occurrence of the infinitive as not being meant as a mark of actually assuming authority by the speaker or a serious reproach. It cues the interpretation of the interaction as located on the humorous plane, and helps to maintain camaraderie.

Foreigner talk and foreigner's talk (talking like to a foreigner, and talking like a foreigner with little command of German) as a means of humorous fictionalisation of the speaker's identity occurs repeatedly in the German material, and it always includes the (sometimes ungrammatical) use of the infinitive as its constitutive component.

The use of the infinitive as a means of depersonalisation of the addressee to mark a critical-aggressive attitude in Polish is exemplified in the following exchange, where the emotionalised attitude of the speaker is additionally expressed by the use of a moderately vulgar interjection *kurde*:

177

38-P3. WIN TODAY

The losing team wakes up in a cold nasty bedroom which is a part of their "punishment" for the defeat in a competition.

F zimno się zrobiło

it's got cold

M no to wygrywać dzisiaj # to będziemy mieli kurde ciepło

then win-INFINITIVE today # then we will have it INTERJECTION-vulg. warm

A peculiarity of the infinitive in Polish is that in non-prototypical contexts it is restricted in its ability to be applied to plural addressees. In P3. WIN TODAY, the infinitive clearly redirects the requestive utterance to the whole group present, rather than just F whose utterance triggered M's reaction. In German peer-to-peer communication, the infinitive can be addressed to either plural or singular addressees. Polish puts a heavy restriction on directing infinitive directives to a single addressee[105]. It only takes place in role-based, prototypical contexts such as a medical examination (e.g. *oddychać- nie oddychać*, "breathe – not breathe"), military exercise, or a sporting competition where the judge is giving instructions to a player. Addressing a singular addressee in other types of contexts using the infinitive consists in the use of an infinitive clause followed or preceded by the verb *proszę/prosimy* ("I/we ask"); the result is a complex performative sentence. The Polish translations of the German utterances above, if uttered to a singular addressee, sound deviant, i.e. drastically inappropriate and confusing unless complemented by *proszę*[106]:

*Tylko tym razem nie siadać mi na palcach.
not to sit on my fingers this time
Tylko tym razem na palcach mi nie siadać proszę.
not to sit on my fingers this time I ask-please
*Nie brać tak dużo.
Not to take that much
Nie brać tak dużo proszę.
not to take that much I ask-please
*Tylko lampy nie stłuc.
not to break the lamp

---

[105] The same was noted by Marek (1973).
[106] Cf. ibid.

Tylko lampy nie stłuc proszę.
not to break the lamp I ask-please

The only scene in which this pragmatic rule is apparently violated in Polish is P3. SOLDIER, in which the prototypical context for using a bare infinitive, hierarchical communication in the armed forces, is being evoked and enacted:

```
37-P3. SOLDIER
F e:p # nie odsuwać mi się        tu # żołnierzu (laughs)
  e:p # not get away-INF          intensifier # soldier
```

After performing the initial clause in the infinitive (nie odsuwać mi się tu), the speaker has two options available. She could finish the sentence adding the main clause *proszę*, and, thus, turn the preceding clause into a subordinate infinitive clause of a performative directive: *nie odsuwać mi się tu proszę* ("I ask-please not to get away"). Alternatively, she can transfer the utterance onto the playful "as-if" plane by adding a counterfactual form of address which introduces a role-based "hierarchy". The latter becomes her actual choice (żołnierzu "soldier"). The evocation and enactment of the military hierarchy (F is the captain and M is the soldier) by F makes the use of the infinitive possible in addressing a singular addressee. This deployment of the infinitive is analogical to its use within the frame of German "foreigner talk"; in both cases, typical contexts of its use are playfully evoked and fake identities assumed.

While the infinitive (outside the role-based contexts mentioned) is applicable to plural addressees only, *proszę + infinitive* clause can be addressed to singular and plural addressees. Thus, the grammatical form does not fully capture the feature +/-singular of the addressee but it is sensitive to this feature, which partly makes up for the absence of an inflectional ending formally marking the grammatical number of the addressee(s). The speaker can mark an utterance as directed at group addressees rather than a singular addressee merely by the choice of the infinitive without *proszę*.

To summarize, the ways in which the infinitive is applied in requestives in the context of a young peer group seem to be similar in German and Polish, and to follow from its identical prototypical contexts of use (institutionalised hierarchical communication) and corresponding prototypical uses in both languages, which are order and instruction. Its functions are:

- a playful, openly counterfactual assumption of authority by the speaker

- sarcastic criticism
- a signal of the role appropriation, marking that the speaker overtakes the role of the instructor in a co-operative task
- a signal that the speaker conceives of him- or herself as articulating an objective necessity, which endows him or her with the right to use a form typical for communication with instructees and subordinates.

What distinguishes the two languages is the limitation of the infinitive in Polish to plural addressees in absence of a formal subordination relationship, and the corresponding lower frequency of use (cf. the statistical part). The contexts in which infinitive constructions are used in Polish directives constitute a subset of the German contexts.

The observation by German learners of Polish that the infinitive construction can be used in Polish in directives, in situations such as P3. WIN TODAY, may easily produce confusion concerning the scope of its application. The transfer of its use to the same set of contexts in which it is used in German, that is, including singular addressees in a friendly relationship, may produce a communication dissonance. It is an example of a situation where the similarities bring dangers of misinterpretation of intentions and confirmation of clichés, in this case, a cliché of a German person as coarse and prone to issue commands in a military style. When confronted with an inappropriately used infinitive, a Polish native speaker is unlikely to realise that the infinitive is in fact used inconspicuously in requestives among friends in Polish under only slightly altered conditions, that is, in requestives directed at groups of addressees, and recall connotations evoked by this usage. Where the absence of structural similarity precludes mistaken generalisations, in this case in the English-Polish language pair, premature overgeneralisations are less likely to occur because in the absence of pragmatic transfer, the learner is likely to depend on more extensive observation, verbal inquiry, and formal instruction.

6.1.2. PERFORMATIVE DECLARATIVE

Performative formulations in requestive utterances within the peer group occurred on the basis of performative verbs: Polish *zapraszać* ("invite"), German *einladen* ("invite"), Polish *prosić* ("ask for") and English *ask (for).*

EINLADEN/ZAPRASZAĆ

The rare use of these items results from their specific propositional contents: they are used in references to actions of a specific type, involving the addressee's relocation in space. *Einladen* occurred just once in the data, and was modified by the passive voice:

8-G4. M1 and M2 are sitting on the blue table; F is passing by.
M1 to F: du bist herzlich eingeladen # auf den blauen Tisch
you are heartedly invited # to the blue table

Its Polish semantic equivalent, *zapraszać*, occurred three times, none of them in the first person singular. The plural or impersonal form was used in all three cases:

72-P3. RESTAURANT
1 F1 grupa restauracji czerwonych zaprasza na posiłek
the chain of restaurants run by the Red invites for a meal

60-P3. NICKNAME
7 M2 zapraszamy na pokoje
we invite to the parlours

73-P3. TALK SHOW 1
4 F2 panna Rudi Rudowolska z Rudowolic # zapraszamy
Miss Ruddy Ruddyhaired from Ruddyhairtown # we invite

All uses of *zapraszać* contained elements of "as-if", i.e. a fictionalisation of the social context: an archaism (na pokoje, "to the parlours") in 60-P3. NICKNAME, and staged role-plays involving fictitious identities in the remaining two scenes. The deployment of forms different from the first person singular, observable in both languages, might serve the pragmatic function of distinguishing the performative as a playfully exalted means to predicate the addressee's change of location from actual invitations, which are more complex social acts involving offers on the speaker's part.

ASK/PROSIĆ

In English, performative formulations in head acts of requestive utterances with *ask* are used

- in the form of hedged performatives such as *may I ask you/I would like to ask you to VP*; their non-occurrence in the data testifies to their formal character making them less appropriate in the context of peer group communication;
- in cleft constructions involving the raising of the infinitive clause to the subject position:

```
4-E1.
M I have given you an opportunity a moment ago # not to drag yourself in
any more # and all I'm asking you now # is to be honest about the papers
```

The use of this routine formula is strongly emphatic; this is achieved by minimising the object of the request to imply that the compliance can be expected because it only requires minimal concession on the part of the addressee. It only occurred in situations involving a certain degree of conflict between the interlocutors. The same routine occurred as an emphatic preface followed by a syntactically complete head act:

```
52-E3.
F [please don't shout at me]
M I just said before people start eating it # without sugar # they should
try it first # because we have to ration things around here
F but they eat
M because those two don't like porridge as it is # and putting sugar on
it won't make much difference
F can you # all I'm asking # can you not shout at me please
```

In Polish, the performative construction *proszę + INFINITIVE CLAUSE* was only used in an utterance addressed by a housemate to Big Brother and in role playing, where the housemates staged encounters involving social distance (e.g. presenter/interviewee in a talkshow, security worker – clients, and other playful interactions involving honorific forms of address). Thus, its occurrence in the corpus of peer interaction does not contradict the general recognition that the standard frame for using this performative verb in head acts of requests is situations involving social distance or authority. The following exchange includes the playful use of the performative construction accompanied by the honorific form of address. Speaker F2 switches from the honorific to the T-form of address in reaction to the addressees' non-compliance with a directive and at the same time replaces the performative construction with the imperative:

39-P3. M1, M2, F1, F2 are sitting at a table. M1 and F1 are having an argument using honorific forms of address.

1 M1 czy pani jest ciemna masa?
are you-HONORIFIC thick (literally: a dark mass)
2 F1 [ja nie # ale pan chyba tak]
me not # but you-HONORIFIC possibly yes
3 M1 no to proszę:-
than I-ask-please
4 F2 proszę nie obrażać # to jest jasna masa
I-ask-please not to be offensive # this is a thin one (literally: a bright mass)
5 M2 główny sędzia tak jakby sobie poszedł
the main judge # has like left
6 M2 tak # zajarać # o zara przyjdzie
yes # to have a smoke # o # he is coming soon
7 F2 proszę się- # a pan proszę się nie wymigiwać # od odpowiedzi
I ask-please # and you-HONORIFIC I ask-please not to avoid # the question
8 M1 jakiej odpowiedzi?
what question
9 F2 na temat
about the subject
10 M1 na jaki temat?
what subject
11 F1 czy pan ma: pretensje
whether you-HONORIFIC are having a problem
12 M1 na jaki temat
what subject
13 F2 do garbatych # że ich dzieci sa proste
about hunchbacks # having children that are straight
(F1 stands up and turns away from the table)
14 F2 to F1: proszę posprzatać za sobą
I-ask-please to tidy up after oneself
(F1 walks away from the table)

183

15 F2 Ma:rta: # ale weź posprzątaj za sobą
FIRST NAME # but AUX-IMP tidy-IMP up after yourself

Throughout the conversation, the use of the honorific form of address is accompanied by the use of *proszę* complemented by an infinitive clause. The playful fictionalisation of the social relationship plays a face-saving function, preventing the argument between M1 and F1 from exploding, and mitigates the directives produced during the conversation. In turn 15, F2 uses the addressee's first name and switches to you-sing. when repeating the request made in 14. Abandoning the formal *proszę* and using the serial imperative (cf. section 6.1.3.) instead, the speaker signals the abandonment of the role-play and, thus, emphasises that the directive is meant seriously and directed to F1 as her real self, rather than part of the game.

The only case where the speaker used the performative verb *prosić* in the head act without playfully evoking the fictional frame involving the honorific address was the following utterance 40-P3:

40-P3. The team is getting up in the morning. Music sets in. F starts dancing and stops after a few moments.
M to F: no dalej # dalej prosimy
more of this # more of this ask for-INDICATIVE-1. pl.

In this utterance, the plural rather than the singular of the performative verb, *prosimy*, was used, implying that the speaker assumed to be speaking on behalf of himself and others. This suggests that the plural form does not connote social (horizontal) or hierarchical (vertical) distance as the singular form does. The finding is significant because just as with the use of the infinitive in the head act, the applicability of the performative routine formula in the head act also turns out to depend on the differentiation between plural vs. singular (as grammatical categories), and single or multiple (as semantic categories) occupancy of a participant's role. The type of the addressee (single or plural) decides about the applicability of the infinitive, while the type of the "author" (speaker and the people whose concern the speaker is assuming to be voicing) seems to decide about the applicability of the performative ("prosimy"). This suggests a strong dependence of context-sensitive grammatical choices on grouping vs. individuating aspects of the utterance context as perceived by the current speaker in Polish.

In Polish, a performative clause was also used as a modifier, similar to E3 above attached as a disjunct to the main proposition, and creating a strong emphasis, too. In this function, though, other than in English (all I am asking) it was necessarily followed by a pronominal object "you" in singular or plural (*proszę cię/proszę was,* "I am asking you"); these forms do not mark distance. At the same time, the use of the infinitive clause in the complement as in E1 above (all I'm asking you now # is to be honest) necessitates the use of the pronoun in the performative VP in English, while it is not used in Polish (proszę posprzątać za sobą, "I am asking to clean after oneself").

In inhibitive requests, the performative occurred in Polish in the form of the routine formula *proszę cię/proszę was* ("I am asking you-sing./you-pl."), standing alone. The formula has the pragmatic force of a reproachful request aiming at making the addressee refrain from a current or planned activity. The reference is provided by the context and co-text. The semantically equivalent routine expression *ich bitte dich* is functional in German, but it did not occur in the data in the function of an inhibitive request[107].

To sum up, while *prosić* retains its functionality as a full verb usable for building performative requests, it is only used in this function in role play in which the interlocutor assumes a socially distant relationship, co-occurring with the honorific form of address (*pan/pani,* "Sir/Madam"), or in plural. It occurs also in a modification of requests in peer communication, where it builds a clause of its own taking a direct object in the form of the personal pronoun in the second person, and is strongly emphatic. In English, the semantically equivalent *ask* occurs in cleft constructions either in the head act or as a supportive move, and is strongly emphatic in both cases. Performative constructions based on the semantically equivalent verb *bitte* did not occur in the German corpus.

6.1.3. OVERSEEN PATTERNS: IMPERATIVE-DECLARATIVE AND SERIAL IMPERATIVE IN POLISH

In spoken colloquial Polish, directives in the imperative, proposals for a joint action in the future tense, requests in the future tense, and offers in the future tense are frequently preceded by an imperative of *dać* ("give", imp. 2. sing. *daj,* imp. 2. pl. *dajcie*), *wziąć* ("take", imp. 2. sing. *weź,* imp. 2. pl. *weźcie,* imp.1. pl. *weźmy*), and *chodzić* ("walk/come", imp. 2. sing. *chodź,* imp. 2. pl. *chodźcie,* imp. 1. pl. *chodźmy*[108]). The syntactic peculiarity of these constructions lies in the fact that on the surface of the utterance, two inflected verbs seem to co-occur within one predicate phrase. The first of them is in the imperative, and the second

---

[107] In both German and Polish, it can either realise an inhibitive request or function as an interaction marker prefacing a critical response to the addressee's earlier verbal contribution.
[108] Morphologically, the imperative form *chodź* is derived from *chodzić,* meaning "walk", a verb whose mode of action is imperfective/progressive, but the meaning of the imperative form is "come" rather than "walk".

either in the imperative or declarative. These constructions, frequent in colloquial speech, are absent from descriptive grammars of Polish because of the prescriptive bias of Polish linguistics; they have been discussed in detail in Pułaczewska (2005, 2006).

6.1.3.1. PERIPHRASTIC IMPERATIVE: IMPERATIVE + DECLARATIVE CONSTRUCTION

DAĆ

Dać (primary lexical meaning: "give", mode of action: perfective) is used regularly as the finite verb in directives similar to the English "let" and German "lassen", meaning "allow". The imperative form of *dać* is complemented by an infinitive clause, as in the following examples:

41-P3.
F dajcie nam się porozbierać z tego
let-IMP-2. pl. us take-INF all this off

42-P3.
F dajcie jej się przebrać
let-IMP-2. pl. her change-INF clothes

Apart from this regular imperative use, *dać* also appears in the initial position in a request from H (hearer) to allow S (speaker) to perform an action, formulated as a declaration, in the indicative mood and future tense, of a future action by S. Frequently, this declaration of the future action by S is an offer on the part of S to do something for H. In this configuration, *dać* serves as a marker of the directive function of the utterance, attaching the imperative mood to a sentence whose predicative content is formulated in the indicative future. The verb phrase of *dać* in the imperative merges syntactically with the following verb phrase in the indicative, resulting in constructions such as the following:

43-P3.
M daj   złożę ci
give-IMP-1.sing   *I will put it together you-DAT*   *(let me put it together for you)*

44-P3.
F daj ci zmienię baterię
give-IMP-2. sing I will change the battery for you (*let me change the battery for you*)

This utterance includes two inflected verb forms: *daj* ("give/let" perf. imperative 2. sing.) and *zrobię* ("do" indicative perf. fut.1ˢᵗ sing.).

Rather than being attached to the rest of the utterance as a disjunct, *daj* is integrated into it in terms of both prosody and syntax. Its omission may result in an ill-formed syntactic construction, like in 44-P3, where a weak form of the personal pronoun occurs as the object of the predicate "złożyć" (put together) although a clause cannot begin with the weak form of a personal pronoun: "*ci zmienię baterię" ("you-weak-DAT I will change the battery") is ill-formed. A further indicator of a syntactic merger is the absence of a tone group boundary between the two verbs; the utterance is realised as one tone group.

CHODŹ/CHODŹCIE

The construction "*chodź/chodźcie* + declarative" is widespread in colloquial Polish. In the analysed sample of 114 spontaneous proposals of a joint action, 12 were realised in this form. The sample contains utterances where this construction performs an auxiliary function as a semantically empty grammatical marker of a directive intention, utterances in which *chodź* retains its lexical meaning as a verb of movement, and intermediate cases.

In the following directive, the verb *chodź* is applied in its lexical meaning:

45-P3.
M to chodź coś zjesz
come-IMP-2. sing. will eat-IND-fut.-2.sing. something
(come you will eat something)

The next example, 46-P3, illustrates the same sort of syntactic and prosodic merger of two verb phrases as that described above with reference to *daj/dajcie*, with the weak form of the personal pronoun in the dative (indirect object) falling between the two verbs. "*Ci pokażę" is ill-formed and requires completion by a clause-initial element. The utterance is preceded by S showing a dance, stopping, explaining it verbally to H and taking H by the hand:

```
46-P3.
```
F chodź ci pokażę
come-IMP-1. sing. I will show you

In the examples below, any remaining trace of the lexical meaning has disappeared:

```
47-P3.
```
S and Hs are sitting at a table and having dinner.
F chodźcie wypijemy za Czerwonych
come-IMP-2. pl. we will drink a toast for the red team

```
48-P3.
```
S is standing close to H.
F chodź pomożemy ci # ty wnoś rzeczy # a my pakujemy
come-IMP-2. sing. we will help you # you carry in-IMP-2. sing. the things # and we pack

```
3-P1.
```
M chodź sobie posłuchamy muzy
come-IMP-2. sing. we will listen to the music

In the scene following 3-P1, the speaker and the addressee are shown listening to music in the same place; no change of place was implied.

6.1.3.2. SERIAL IMPERATIVE: IMPERATIVE AUXILIARY + IMPERATIVE CONSTRUCTION

WEŹ/WEŹCIE/WEŹMY as an auxiliary directive verb

A frequently occurring form of request in the imperative is created by prefacing a VP containing a main verb in the imperative with the imperative form of *wziąć* ("take", perfective). Similarly, as in the case of *dać*, sentence-initial *wziąć* can change the word order in the sentence. The items which would otherwise follow the second (main) verb as elements of its predicate phrase now occur between two verbs:

```
49-P3.
```
12 F ty # <u>weź</u> sobie umyj te buty
you # take-IMP-2. sing. clean-IMP-2. sing. yourself the shoes

188

50-P3.

F weź	ją	zamknij	tam	w kąciczku
take-IMP	*her*	*lock-IMP*	*there*	*in the corner-dim.*

(lock her [a mouse] in the corner)

The sentences "*sobie umyj te buty" ("yourself wash-IMP-2-sing. the shoes"), starting with a reflexive pronoun in front, and "*ją zamknij tam w kąciczku" ("lock her in the corner") starting with a weak pronoun, are ill-formed (unless the reflexive and weak pronouns carry emphatic stress)[109].

The same spectrum of semantic bleaching as for periphrastic imperative could be observed for the construction "*weź*+ imperative". In 50-P3, the lexical meaning of weź ("take") is still present, which is, however, not the case in the sentence fragment in 51-P3, nor in the following two examples, where the second verb is accompanied by a negation:

51-P3.

M weź	opowiedz co on-
take-IMP-2. sing.	*tell-IMP-2. sing. what he-*

52-P3.

F weźcie	się	ze mnie nie śmiejcie	
take-IMP-2. pl.	*PRONOUN-refl.*	*at me not laugh-IMP-2. pl.*	*(don't laugh at me)*

4-P1.

F weźcie	nie zadawajcie pytań	
take-IMP-2. pl.	*not ask questions*	*(don't ask questions)*

In 51-P3, the predicated action to be performed is reporting and in the following utterances, ceasing to laugh and ask questions. The sentence meanings do not include the lexical meaning of *weź/weźcie*.

52-P3 illustrates a relocation of the reflexive pronoun *się* attached to the main verb "laugh" (*śmiać się*) and incapable of occupying the clause-initial position, to the position

---

[109] The accusative of the feminine 2nd singular personal pronoun lacks the differentiation between the strong and weak morphological forms. *Ją* can occupy the sentence-initial position if it is stressed. The masculine weak form of the accusative, *go*, cannot occur with emphatic stress and cannot occupy a clause-initial position.

before *śmiać,* similar to the relocation of the direct object discussed before. *"*Się ze mnie nie śmiejcie"* ("*PRONOUN-refl. at me not laugh-IMP-2. pl.") is ill-formed.

DAWAJ/DAWAJCIE in the serial imperative

Basic forms: imperf. infinitive *dawać,* imperf. imperative 2nd sing. *dawaj,* imperf. imperative 2nd pl. *dawajcie*

Lexical meanings: "give","allow"

The imperative of the imperfective verb *dawać* in directive use performs the function of urging and encouraging a person to perform or continue an action, as in the following authentic utterance:

56-P3.
M dawaj Stachu # walimy im po garbach i do domu
give FIRST NAME # we beat their backs and go home

Its function in these utterances is to urge the hearer to perform or continue an action, and to do so immediately and quickly. It can also co-occur with other verbs in the imperative, as in the example below:

57-P3. S and X are packing H's clothes; S is holding H's bag and urging H to put clothes into it.
F dawaj wsadzaj
give-IMP-2. sing. put-IMP-2. sing. in   (come on put it in)

Dawaj(cie) followed by a clause containing a finite verb form is used in situations where the request concerns immediate physical action. Contrary to *weź,* which can co-occur also with abstract verbs and verbs expressing complex action, one could hardly use *dawaj* while requesting somebody to make tea, or write an essay. The action described by the verb following *dawaj* is to be performed at once and at the same place. It is typically used while the speaker and the addressee are performing a physical action together, as in the example above.

The status of *dawaj* with respect to the apparent "syntactic anomaly" discussed above (two inflected verb forms in one clause) is less clear than that of other "appellative verbs". *Weź(cie), daj(cie)* and *chodź(cie)* can appear within the same tone group as the finite verb forms that follow them, and trigger a change in the word order (object/predicate) as discussed above, which indicates a syntactic merger; *dawaj,* on the other hand, seems to be a disjunct loosely attached to a sentence and a verb forming a clause of its own, rather than an auxiliary. It resembles German and English utterance-initial appellative expressions in the form of verbs in the imperative, which are applied as prefaces to directives and enhance their directive illocutionary force: *komm/kommt* in German and *come on* in English.

6.1.3.3. SUMMARY OF FORMS AND FUNCTIONS

The following summary lists the formats of sentences, and the corresponding illocutionary functions of utterances, containing two inflected verb forms (imperative + indicative future; imperative + imperative), where the first verb occurs with a reduced or absent lexical meaning.

1. Type of directive: REQUEST FOR ACTION/DEMAND; the action is to be performed by ADDRESSEE

   weź + S (finite verb: IMP singular)
   weźcie + S (finite verb: IMP plural)
2. Type of directive: PROPOSAL; the action is to be performed by SPEAKER AND ADDRESSEE
   chodź(cie) + S (finite verb: IND fut. 1st person plural, inclusive)
3. Type of directive: OFFER/REQUEST FOR PERMISSION; the action is to be performed by SPEAKER
   daj(cie) + S (finite verb: IND fut. 1st person plural, non-inclusive)
   daj + S (finite verb: IND fut. 1st person singular)
4. Type of directive: REQUEST; the action is to be performed by HEARER
   dawaj + # + S (finite verb: IMP singular)
   dawajcie + # + S (finite verb: IMP plural)
5. Type of directive: PROPOSAL; the action is to be performed by SPEAKER AND ADDRESSEE
   dawaj(cie) + # + S (finite verb: IND pres. 1st person plural, inclusive)

Of these, (1)-(3) can be regarded as auxiliary imperative verbs integrated into the sentences they preface, while *dawaj(cie)* in (4) and (5) is a main verb, or an inflected appellative interaction marker loosely attached to a sentence as a disjunct.

6.1.4. REALISATION DECLARATIVE

The imperative is frequently assumed to be the most direct type of directive, and very low in the hierarchy of negative politeness. According to Blum-Kulka (1987), only strong hints have been judged as less negatively polite in Hebrew as well as in English. Little attention, though, has been paid to the realisation declarative. It was not included in the test used by Blum-Kulka (1987) to establish the hierarchy of negatively polite syntactic forms of directive utterances, and it hardly occurs in data collected by means of non-natural methods. The preceding statistical analysis shows that the realisation declarative, stating the predicated action as a matter of fact in future tense or narrative present, is a frequent form of directive speech. About 43% of proposals in Polish, 25% in German and 16% in English were realised by this syntactic pattern. In requests, predication of the future action of the addressee as a matter of fact was exceptional and amounted to between 2% and 5% of the data.

In English, the existence of the emphatic imperative[110] involving the use of 2nd person personal pronoun precludes the interpretation of the following requests as cases of realisation declarative, even if the resulting surface structure is not distinguishable from a statement of fact in the present simple tense for verbs other than *to be*, as in the following examples:

```
53-E3. SPELLING[111]
M let's test each other on spelling # Ron you test us on spelling
```

```
54-E3. BASKETBALL
M okay # you decide who's the crappiest out of yous five
```

Directives classed as occurrences of the realisation declarative in English were confined to statements morphologically marked for tense and aspect, such as the following:

```
97-E3. GROUP HUG
The housemates are planning to perform a group hug.
10 F1 to F2: you are going in the middle
```

```
4-E4. BOXING MATCH
F and M1 have just finished a boxing match and are quarrelling about the result.
M2 to F and M1: we will have a rematch # --- Lenox Lewis and Mike Tyson
```

---

[110] The emphatic imperative consists of the second person pronoun and the infinitive present form of the verb, e.g.: *You be quiet.* Its use has been discussed among others by Aijmer (1996). The emphatic imperative consists of the second person pronoun and the infinitive present form of the verb, e.g.: *You be quiet.*

5-E4. SPOON

(simultaneous talk)

(M stands up and fetches a spoon from the kitchen)

M spoon (hands a spoon to F) Natasha # **you are speaking**

Realisation declaratives are strongly impositive, as they imply that the speaker does not acknowledge the possibility of the addresses' non-compliance. However, the co-participation of the speaker in the action predicated in a proposal, paired with the usual contextual embedding in a current joint action of the hearer and the speaker, and "we"-reference makes the use of realisation declaratives inconspicuous in proposals, as in the examples below:

55-E3. RINSING BEDSHEETS

M1, M2 are washing bed sheets in the garden.

M1 we'll rinse this one # then

(M1, M2 rinse a bed sheet together)

4-G1. PARTY

M1, M2, F1, F2 are picking up bottles of beer and wine they have just received from Big Brother.

M1 Wein aufs Bier # das gönne ich dir # wir fangen vom Bier an

wine upon beer # this I recommend to you (a popular rhyme) *# we start with beer*

Also requests predicating the action of the addressee are not perceived as bossy if they are framed within the context of joint activities:

9-G4. WER BIN ICH

M1 has just finished mimicking some prominent German celebrities.

1 M2 wir könnten spielen "wer bin ich" und du bist Robert Lempke

we could play "who am I" and you are Robert Lempke

2 M1 ich kann Lempke nicht so gut # ich kenne ihn nicht so gut

I can't do Lempke too well # I don't know him so well

3 M2 **dann machst du halt Hans Rosenthal nach # und wir spielen trotzdem das Spiel # dalli # dalli dalli**

then you mimic Hans Rosenthal # and we play the game all the same # off you go # off off[112]

---

[112] "Dalli": a directive particle introduced into German by TV host Hans Rosenthal in the 1970s.

```
33-G2. ROPE
```
M1, M2, F1 are in the yard talking. M1 is untangling a rope; M2 is standing close to him.
```
1 M1 ich werde es einmal ganz ausrollen #..jetzt wirst du mir mal helfen
```
I will unroll it first # now you will help me
(M2 approaches M1 and stretches a hand towards him)
```
2 M1 du wirst jetzt hier mal am Knoten # .. ziehen # . jetzt entrollen
wir das mal erst mal
```
now you will this nod # pull # now we unroll it first

The form of the request in G2. ROPE implies that M1 is assuming a position of authority with respect to M2 and overtakes the command. Five native speakers of German agreed that while M1 left no doubt that he was the one to take the instructor's role in the co-operative task, it did not sound excessively impositive in the given situation. From eleven respondents representing the three languages under study, only one British respondent (male) and one German respondent
(female) evaluated its use in requests as potentially mildly unpleasant for a particularly sensitive hearer, while three out of four British respondents perceived it as "typically German". Asked what legitimised the use of this form in this particular situation, the native German respondents named

- the current involvement of M1 in the action for which assistance is asked,
- the current fixation of M1's attention upon the action itself rather than M2,
- the fact that M1 and M2 were engaged in a conversation prior to the request,
- the fact that M2 took the edge off the commanding tone by adding a "we"-reference to a joint action of himself and the addressee in the last sentence (`jetzt entrollen wir das mal`), framing the request into a proposal of joint action.

When a request in a realisation declarative is not clearly framed into a proposal of a joint action, the lack of the assumption of authority on the speaker's part can be realised as in infinitive directives by the use of mitigators referring to interpersonal space, such as consultative consensus-seeking signals. In the following example, the realisation declarative is mitigated by the appealer *weißt du* ("you know") and asking intonation as a marker of a consensus-seeking strategy:

34-G2. M1 is standing in front of the shower where M2 is showering. M2 has paid for five minutes of hot water from the coin-operated water distributor.

M1 to M2: ei # du # wenn du die fünf Minuten nicht brauchst # sagst du bescheid # dann machen wir eine Reihe # .. **weißt du?**

INTERJECTION # you # if you don't need the five minutes # you tell-INDICATIVE-PRESENT us # then we will queue up # you know?

There is a relatively long break before the appealer weißt du? which suggests that it was an added on reflection after the speaker became aware of the impositiveness of the preceding utterance, formulated in a realisation declarative.

The realisation declarative with its matter-of-factness can also be used in a reassuring and supportive way as in the following data:

10-G4. After a lost match, M1 offended F who reacted with fury and stopped talking to him afterwards. M2 has been trying to mediate in the conflict. M1 who tried in vain to apologise to F is explaining his behaviour to M2.

1 M1 ja # aber weiß ich nicht # das ist doch klar # aber kannst doch mal reinstecken # sie kann auch zu mir sagen # du Wichser # du Arschloch # ich weiß das geht bei mir hier rein # _ da raus # und dann spiele ich wieder # das war doch ein Spielstress

yes # but I don't know # it is clear isn't it # you can just deal with some things # she can say to me as well # you jerk # you asshole # I know this goes in here # out there # and then I go on playing # this was just game stress

2 M2 ja # das weiß [ich # Stress]

yes # I know # stress

3 M1 # [im Spie::l]

in a game

4 M2 [---]

5 M1 [--- wie auf dem Fußballfeld] # [---]

like on the football field

6 M2 [ja # ja okay] und **das erzählst du ihr morgen # du redest ganz normal**# . und [du brauchst dich mor-]

yes # okay # and you'll tell her this tomorrow # you will talk quite normally # and you don't need tomo-

The addressee, M1, is facing a conflict with another housemate, and the speaker points out to him a possible reasonable way out of the problem. The lack of actual imposition upon the addressee in turn 6 is the function of its contextual embedding. Rather than from the speaker's own incentive, the use of the realisation declarative follows from a dialogic exchange in which M1 expresses difficulty in coping with the situation. Rather than impose his will on M1, M2 is taking over the initiative and proposing a solution. The presupposition of compliance functions here as a distance-diminishing endeavour signalling a supportive attitude.

Six respondents representing the three languages under study (two from each language) agreed that sudden, topic-opening and in particular interaction-opening occurrences of a realisation declarative predicating the hearer's action are perceived as strongly impositive and bossy unless accompanied by a considerable amount of modifying devices. Contrary to this, proposals and requests framed in joint current activities of the speaker and the hearer (in episodes E3. RINSING BED SHEETS, G2. PARTY, G4. WER BIN ICH) were not perceived as violations the hearer's negative face wants. Evidently, the concern for these wants is lowered by the fact of having already entered a cooperative action with others. Still, a language-specific difference in the status of the realisation declarative in proposals has been made visible in the statistical results: it was the most frequent form in which proposals of a joint action were made in Polish as well as in German, unlike English where conventional indirectness was preferred. The difference cannot be due to the use of the emphatic imperative in English instead (as in "you test us on spelling") because the latter occurred rarely (2% of English proposals).

6.2. POSITIVELY POLITE MODIFIERS: MAINTENANCE OF INFORMALITY AND CONFIDENCE

6.2.1. TERMS OF ADDRESS

The size of the samples varied from 95 requestives accompanied by terms of address (vocative) for German, to 135 in Polish. The frequency of the occurrence of terms of address is similar in all the groups; they were used in approximately 16-18% of all requestives. Also the distribution of vocatives between the turn-initial position, in which a term of address functions as an alert (attention getter) and frequently appoints the current addressee, and other positions in the sentence is very much the same in all groups; about half of all vocatives were turn-initial.

196

The following analysis of interlingual differences in the use of terms of address is focused upon the preferences for the neutral vs. positively polite forms. Its prerequisite step was to single out forms of address different from the standard formal and informal forms of the first name, which I suppose to be emotionally neutral in communication of young peers using the T-form of address. Other forms of address, such as pet names (terms of endearment), creative and nicknaming terms involve a radically greater amount of face work. Such forms are usable only in informal relationships, and express a positive attitude towards the addressee. They are potential distance-diminishers, i.e., devices of positive politeness, with the rare exception of gender-switching augmentative forms of address in Polish that can be used to express intimacy or to offend.

6.2.1.1. POSITIVELY POLITE TERMS OF ADDRESS

In P3, in the "battle" design, 80% of all terms of address accompanying requestives were positively polite, compared to 54% in P1, 27% in E3, 23% in E4, 47% in G2 and 28% in G4. I regard the high percentage of positively polite terms of address in the P3 "battle" edition as being related to the high group integration in this group. Positively polite terms of address are considerably more frequent in P3 than in P1 that also showed fewer indicators of strong group bonds. In German, stronger group bonds did not correspond to an increase of positively polite naming in requestives; they accompanied requestives less frequently in the G4 "battle" edition which contains more indicators of group bonds than in G2. The difference was due to the more frequent use of affectionate and colloquial terms of address in G2; nicknames were used with approximately the same frequency. While affectionate terms of address are more likely to reflect positive emotions related to individual addressees, nicknaming might play a particular role in indicating ingroup bonds.

6.2.1.1. FIRST NAMES

First names occur in their official, full forms and in colloquial versions, classifiable into:

- augmentativa (Polish)   Grzegorz → Grzech, Magda → Madzior
- diminutive, pet names   Wojciech → Wojtuś, Katarzyna → Kasieńka
                           Madgda → Madziorek, Adel → Delly, Jade → Jady,
                           Kate → Katie
- truncated, informal   Elisabeth → Beth, Katherine → Kate
- hypocoristic   Christian → Chris, Manuela → Manu, Daniel →
                           Dani, Wojciech → Wojtek, Anna → Anka, Ania
- acronyms   PJ (initials) → [pidʒei]

The category "augmentative" is peculiar to Polish. Polish derivational morphology is highly productive in the field of augmentation, diminutive, and gender-switching. Morphological diminutives are built by derivation of 1st, 2nd and 3rd grade_(e.g. *Katarzyna* → *Kasia* → *Kasieńka* → *Kasienieczka*), allow gender switching (*Małgorzata* → fem. dim. *Gosia* → masc. dim. *Gosiaczek*, neutr. dim. *Gosiątko*), and can be derived from augmentative forms (fem. *Madgda* → masc. augm. *Madzior* → masc. dim. *Madziorek*).

First names constituted 39% of terms of address accompanying requestive utterances in Polish, including diminutive and augmentative forms which amounted to about 11% of all terms of address. Not included are creative distortions of first names and their foreign counterparts, which were regarded as nicknames (e.g. *Piotr* → *Pietia, Picia, Piter*). In German, 65% of terms of address were first names. In English, 76 % of all terms of address in requestives were first names, including less than 2% of diminutive forms.

The perception of first names and norms of self-introduction show interlingual differences. In the Polish ingroups, the extremely frequent use of nicknames and "creative deviations" from first names pushes the truncated informal versions of the first names towards neutrality in relationship space; real ingroup intimacy is expressed by the non-use of the standard informal forms of first names. In other words, as the positively polite end is already occupied by nicknames and creative deviations, the informal versions of first names can hardly be claimed to express or add to the ingroup feeling and intimacy. In Polish, the informal variants (*Wojtek* from *Wojciech*, *Asia* or *Aśka* from *Joanna*, etc.) are the ordinary form of T-address whenever they are available, which is the case for the prevailing majority of first names; first names that do not build truncated colloquial variants are rare. As confirmed by four native respondents, the informal forms are in use from the very start of any acquaintance whenever a T-form of address is used, and are almost invariably used in self-introductions; this was also the case in the data under analysis. In German, both full and truncated forms were used in self-introductions. Some available truncated forms did not occur in the early stage of the acquaintance (*Chris, Dani*), so that the transition from the full to truncated form seemed to mark a shift in the relationship itself; and some of the available standard truncations were not used at all (e.g. *Gabi* from *Gabriela*). Two native speakers, male and female, confirmed that the form used in self-introduction depends on the personality of the persons introducing themselves; using informal, truncated forms signals more openness, that is, the preparedness to form an intimate relationship. The respondents thought that the switch to the truncated form during an acquaintance signals a claim to knowing someone well and involves giving oneself the right to call them forms different than those used in more distanced relationships. Also in English, some truncated forms were not used in self-introductions and the initial period of the acquaintance, and so seemed to require and express a certain degree of familiarity between the speaker and the addressee (e.g. Spens from Spencer, Soph from Sophie). On the other hand, the differentiated approach to first names is manifest also in their use by the show's editors who introduced the housemates to the public, among others on the Big Brother website where the portraits of the housemates were publicised, and which, at least for the German and the British programs, set the standards of their naming in the media. In Great Britain, some truncated and diminutive forms, both standard and non-standard, were the only forms by which the housemates were presented to the public. In B3, the truncation "Sandy" was used to refer to a male participant whose full first name was Alexander, and another Alexander was addressed as "Alex"; in B4, a little known truncation, "Nush", was used to refer to a female whose full name was Anoushka. Thus, informality was already signalled in the medial frame of the whole event in the British version. The situation was made even more complex in English by the fact that some forms were not identifiable as truncated with certainty because of institutionalised availability and actual practice of giving children first names that are identical with "informal" versions of traditional names (e.g. Kate, Soph, Johnny may be truncated/affixed versions of Katherine, Sophie, and John, or full forms of first names). A female participant in B4 was only known to the public as "Sissy", which might have been a pet form of the female first name Elizabeth as in German, a nickname, or, which is unlikely but not impossible, a full official name.

In German, the housemates were presented on the website using their full official first names. The Polish show's editors chose to publicise on the website the informal or, in rare cases the formal versions of the first names, followed by surnames.

Because of their different value in the interpersonal space, I counted the truncated (Spens, Chris, Soph) forms as positively polite forms of address in German and English unless they were used by the show's editors as the official standard (Kate, Nush, Sissi, Sandy, Johnny, another Soph), on the basis of the assumption that such forms conveyed an "extra" on face work and familiarity relatively to a neutral standard of an informal encounter. In Polish, they were counted as standard forms neutral in politeness. Diminutive and augmentative versions of first names, as well as their creative distortions, were classified with positively polite terms of address on the same condition. The acronym PJ was categorised with forms neutral with respect to politeness.

When the naming practices in a group diverge from the use of the standard form of the first name as the usual term of address, the "neutrality" of this form in politeness becomes questionable. This is visible in the fact that it may be used to signal distancing from the addressee. While some forms, such as pet names, are distance-diminishers par excellence, there exist no specific forms of address to express the intention to increase the distance to the addressee. However, the standard form of the first name was used in Polish twice in the distance-creating function. It was only possible to recognize this aspect of the use of the standard name within its situational context, including more than the current encounter between S and H. The context included the prior encounters between S and H, as well as other interactions within the group. Terms of address in the fuction of distance-creating and distance-diminishing devices are strongly context-sensitive and can usually be interpreted only against the background of detailed information about the relationship and its social embedding, including a wider perspective than the one provided by a dyadic model of social and verbal interaction.

58-P3.

1 M przygotuj się # bo mogą być cztery osoby # Agata
prepare yourself # because they might want four persons # Agata
2 F ja ci coś powiem **Mariusz** # _ y: ja bym w tym momencie nie chciała z tobą rozmawiać
I will tell you something Mariusz-*STANDARD FIRST NAME # erm I would't want to talk to you right now*

To identify the implications of the use of the first name in turn 2 of this exchange, it must be taken into account that speaker F had always been calling hearer M by his nickname during prior interactions, confirming the standard set by the group. In this dialogue, the standard form of address paves the way for the message of distancing and adds up with the propositional contents of the next move, where F proclaims that she is not willing to talk to M. An intentional hurt is aimed at H's positive face, and its means is S's emphasis on her own negative face wants. The function of the hearer's first name in turn 2 as an evocation of negative face wants becomes visible when the context is widened to include the whole history of interactions within the group, where naming a person by the standard (full or truncated) form of his or her first name is an exception rather than a rule, and constitutes only about 20% of all terms of address accompanying requestives in this Polish series.

The next data which covers an excerpt from a row between a female and a male housemate displays a linguistic awareness on the part of the speakers concerning the role of naming as a means of expressing distance and closeness:

59-P3. F has just shouted at M reprimanding him for spreading rumours about her.

1 M dziękuję za występy

thank you for the show

2 F ale nie występy Ken # nie występy # rozumiesz?

no show Ken-NICKNAME # no show # do you understand?

3 M a dla ciebie Mariusz

and for you Mariusz-FIRST NAME

4 F gdyby- # gdyby nie- # wiesz co

if # if not # you know what

5 M ewentualnie Mariusz

in the best case Mariusz-FIRST NAME

6 F Przepiórski jedynie co # . tylko i wyłącznie

Przepiorski-SURNAME only # nothing else

F uses M's nickname in turn 2. In turn 3, M uses the standard form of his own first name as the means of distancing pointing out that he does not want F to use his nickname. F takes up in turn 6 by pointing out that even the first name does not correspond to the distance she wants to keep from M.

6.2.1.2. NICKNAMING

The Polish groups show the greatest diversification and inventive spirit in naming practices, while an interlingual difference occurred between the two groups. In P3, five of the housemates made known to the group the nicknames they bore outside Big Brother house, and four of these were adopted by the group. Ad-hoc production of further nicknames and creative aberrations of first names continued throughout the program. Some of them took ground and were used recurrently, and of some, there are only single instances within the available data. The findings point in the same direction as other indicators of group integration in P3 that are unparalleled by P1, such as symbolic gestures and verbal declarations of friendship addressed at or referring to the group or team; family metaphors; frequent occurrence of requests for the sake of both the speaker and an external beneficiary, in which the speaker spoke in the name of a group or a person whom s/he assumed to share his or her objective; and more frequent addressing of inhibitive requests at groups, indicating the perception of a group as the unit to be blamed for trespasses.

In P3, all housemates become bearers of between one and five nicknames. The nicknames refer to occupation (Student, Chemik "chemist", Hydro – abbreviation from "hydraulik"=plumber), family role (*mamuśka* "mummy", *ojciec* "father", *tato* "daddy", *matka* "mother"), geographic origin (*Harnaś*: a chief of a group of mountaineers in the Tatra Mountains where the housemate came from), physical characteristics (*makabra* "macabresque", *Kruszyna* "the crumble" about an overweight woman, *Chuda* "Skinny"), or personality traits (*Zołza* "shrew", *Stasio* – a male name given to a woman because of her manly behaviour). In P1, four housemates received a single nickname and one received three, all of them derived from first names.

In G4, the web portraits of nine out of seventeen participants included nicknames used by some of them prior to joining the program, but only two of them, both first-name based, were actually adopted by the fellow housemates in the program (Naddl from Nadia, Gabi from Gabriel). One nickname was offered in the web portrait but not adopted by the group in G2. No pre-existing nicknames were offered in the British series.

In the German and British series, up to three housemates were bearers of stable nicknames, and no housemate received more than one nickname. In E3, three housemates were endowed with nicknames. They were derived from the bearer's physical characteristics (*Skinny*), personality (*Baba* "baby" for a young and childish female housemate), and first name (*Spencer* → *Spanky*). In G4, there were three occurrences of stable nicknames. One of them was based on the first name and the other two referred to the referent's nationality and were only used by the housemate who had coined it, and who was the same person on both occasions. *Schweizer* directly named the addressee's country of origin, and *Ketchkemed* denotes originally a Hungarian town and referred to a female housemate who came from Hungary.

Name-based nicknames occurred in all three languages and were foreign versions or novel aberrations of first names (*Pablo, Pawulo* from *Paweł, Naddl* from *Nadia, Chrischi* from *Christian, Jo-Jo from Johnny*), diminutives and other aberrations of established nicknames (*Kensa, Kenio, Henio* from *Ken*, the male equivalent of Barbi, *Frycia* from *Frytka*), or aberrations of second names.

Nicknames create intimacy and mitigate directives. They render criticism milder, diminish or eradicate the conflict potential of inhibitives, and signal non-aggression, as in the following example:

56-E3. F1 is standing at the kitchen sink shouting to the persons behind her.

```
1 F1 can I just say one thing # . I think that when you wash up # you
should really wash up properly # because so far # we've had to rinse
everything we used # either by bubbles or by dirt
```

2 M1 I agree # _ cause we've got to do everything again # and Lynn's painting the sink now # so # . we need to get one of them undone # we've got to drain the pasta
3 M2 to F2, F3 : (puts on an angry facial expression) do some more work # will you (smiles)
4 F2 **shut up # Skinny**

The term "Skinny" in F2's response constitutes a humorous abuse, or banter, based on the assumption that there is enough shared background between the speaker and the hearer for the latter to identify the speaker's intention to signal closeness rather than hostility. Through the use of an ad-hoc nickname, F2 signals that she has recognised the playful tone of M2's preceding move and disambiguates her utterance as non-aggressive. F2 had been calling M2 by his first name before.

The following episode from P3 illustrates the role of nicknaming as a positively polite modification of seriously meant inhibitive directives:

60-P3.
M ale ty ostatnio się marudna zrobilaś # dupa będzie lana # zobaczysz
you have been whining quite a lot lately # the bum will get a beating # you will see
F nie wiem czy mi się chce pracować z takimi ludźmi
I don't know whether I feel like working with such people
M zastanów się czy tym ludziom się chce z tobą pracować
think about whether these people feel like working with you
F no i jest równo (curse deleted by Big Brother editor)
so we are even
M dwie uwagi # po pierwsze bądź mniej wulgarna # . **Stasia!** # _ po drugie # przestań gadać o tych Mercedesach i tych wszystkich
two remarks # firstly be less vulgar # Stasia-NICKNAME # secondly # stop talking about this Mercedes stuff and all that

Using the nickname *Stasia* with emphatic stress, M at the same time makes the message more emphatic and expresses his confidential attitude towards F, thus enhancing the chances of her acceptance of the criticism. For the full interpretation of this scene, it is relevant to know that some time earlier M gave F the nickname "Stasio", which is a male first name (diminutive and colloquial version of Stanisław). Its female version "Stasia" is a creative departure that in this particular situation might be mildly pointing to the fact that F is expected to behave in a more feminine way and abstain from using vulgar language. That the uses of the male and the female version of the nickname are indeed differentiated by an implied reference to gender is noticeable in other situations in which M is using one or another in dependence of what personality traits of F he is currently exploiting or referring to. As time passes, M discovers more feminine traits of F and turns away from using the male version of the nickname, while hanging on to the message of familiarity by not giving up the use of the nickname itself.

The following data contains an explicit reference to nicknaming and displays the feeling on the part of the members of Polish group P3 that the context of interaction makes the use of nicknames more appropriate than the use of standard names:

```
61-P3. NICKNAME
```
The housemates greet a female newcomer to the house.

```
1  F1 Monika (shaking hands with M1)
2  M2 Monika # [jaką] masz [ksywę]
```
Monika # what's your nickname-COLLOQUIAL
```
3  F1 wiesz # nie mam # .. [jeszcze]
```
you know what # I have none # yet
```
4  F2 [(laughs)]
5  M3 [zaraz] coś wymyślimy
```
we will cook one up right away
```
6  M2 trzeba wymyśleć
```
one-must cook up
```
7  M2 zapraszamy na pokoje
```
you are welcome to enter our parlours

Blum-Kulka (1990: 278), in comparing interactions in American and Israeli families, observes that Israeli parents modify their directives to the children more frequently by the use of intimate forms of vocative rather than by conventional indirectness. "*Israeli parents use a wide variety of innovative nicknames, yielding a rich repertoire of emotively colored terms of address per child at every meal.* For example, a child named Jonathan, who was 10 at the time of recordings, was variously addressed by his parents as [jonatan]/[joni]/[onton]/[jonti] and [ontik] (emphasis in original)." The author interprets this style as a continuation of Eastern European Jewish traditions, combining "the dictum of directness, derived from the early Zionist ideology of shunning European formal politeness

... with the language of familial affect, so typical of description of Jewish traditional family life in Eastern Europe". As the same patterns appear in non-Jewish ingroups within Polish society and seem to be typical for Polish family life in general, I doubt whether these phenomena have their origin in the Zionist ideology, but this is not at issue here. Blum-Kulka evaluates the naming practices as highly relevant indicators of cultural difference between the American and Israeli culture: "Nowhere are these differences better expressed than in the use of naming practices", and comments that "Nicknaming serves here as a distance-minimiser; it strengthens solidarity by indexing affect (ibid.)." Blum-Kulka and Katriel (1991) contend referring to nicknames that "their crystallisation as part of the familial code both reflects and reinforces the existence and the continued cultivation of a shared family history, sketching the boundaries of the family as a social unit and enhancing the sense of solidarity among its members."

Both Polish groups also used nicknames in referring (4% in both P1 and P3, vs. between 0 and 0.7% in all the other series), which I evaluate as a strong indicator of group bonds. The referential use of nicknames points to shared insider knowledge of the referent, expresses the perception of the relationship between the speaker and the referent as based on familiarity, and presupposes the same familiarity on the part of the addressee.

OTHER TERMS

Other forms of address besides nicknames and first names included:

- pet names – Polish *Misieńku* "little teddybear", *Misiaczku* "little teddybear", *Misia* "she-bear", *maleństwo* "little thing", *kochanie* "darling"; English *baba, honey*; German *Schatz* "treasure", *Baby, Mäußchen* "little mouse", *Mäubär* "little mause-bear"
- colloquial terms – Polish: *młody* "the young one", *stary* "the old one", *laska* "lass", *chlopaki* "boys", *ludzie* "people"; English: *girls, guys, mate*; German: *Mann* "man", *Leute* "people", *Jungs* "boys", *Alter* "the old one";
- humorous and playful terms – Polish: *pani* "madam" (V-address fem. sing.), *drogie panie* "dear ladies", *panowie* "gentlemen" (V-address masc. pl.), *żolnierzu* "soldier", English: *special boy*, German: *Großkotz* "Boaster" (lit. "Big Puke"), *Mister Bigkotz, little Walter*, Polish: second name, unreal (phoney) first names – *Mirka, Paula, Stasia*, German: *Mudammed*, figurative first name – *Louis* (the addressee's first name is Harry; this ad-hoc nickname might be an allusion to the first name via an implicit reference to the famous Harry Louis)
- 2. sing. personal pronoun.

6.2.1.3. PHONEY FIRST NAMES

A rare usage shared by Polish speakers was the ad-hoc singular use of "phoney" first names, such as sing. *Mirka, Paula,* pl. *Mirki* that simply did not belong to the addressee(s) in addressing a female hearer or hearers. The hearers accept this sort of nicknaming without a comment. A phoney first name in plural occurs once in referential use, where the female housemates are referred to by a male speaker as *Mariolki* (to jest przecież pokój dla Mariolek, "*this is evidently a room for Mariolas*"). This use, that signals informality and playful interaction modality, seems to be foreign to the British conversational logic. The application of unreal first names is similarly restricted in German, where an ad-hoc nickname in the form of an unreal first name can be used figuratively, that is, when this is justified by an association with the addressee; the name *Louis* was used in addressing a person called Harry, probably via association to Harry Louis. A phoney name was applied by a German native speaker of Moroccan descent in G2, and in contrast to the uncommented uses in the Polish group, attracted enough attention to be overtly responded to:

35-G2. Day two. F1, M1, M2 get into the room, M3, M4 are preparing breakfast.
1 M1 wo ist denn # das Frühstück (approaching M3)
2 M3 ja # . setzt euch # . Mudammed
3 M1 was für Mudammed
4 F1 Muddamed (laughs)
5 M1 to M3: Kathrin # war es jetzt richtig
6 F1 [(laughs)]
7 M1 [Kathrin] # (laughs)

The use of the phoney first name *Mudammed* by M3 in turn 2 elicits overt verbal responses from two housemates, M1 and F1. M1 recognises the playful use of the phoney name by M3, and reacts to it in turn 5 pretending that he forgot M1's first name. He attributes to M3 a female name which could not possibly be M3's real name, just as M1 attributed to him a name restricted in its use to the members of the Moslem minority, which M3 does not belong to. F1 laughs about both uses of phoney names. The initial use of the phoney name is followed by a sequence of utterances by other speakers commenting upon it, stretching over five turns. The attention offered to it in the responses marks it as quite unusual, in contrast to Polish where phoney names are accepted without comment. Two native German respondents confirmed that naming a person with a false first name on purpose is difficult to interpret, and can be perceived as an offence. The Polish respondents quoted a number of names that can be used to playfully address persons to whom they do not properly belong, such as *Zenek, Stefan, Franek, Henryk, Henio, Tadziu, Tadek, Kazik, Ziuta, Gienia, Stacha, Krycha, Henia, Franka, Frania* and *Zocha*. The types of utterances in which they are likely to be used are playfully denigrating admonitions, requests and comments on the addressee's behaviour. This use of first names is not wide-spread, and some native informants denied that they have ever encountered it while, paradoxically, they agreed with those who didn't on the names which they would use in this function. The phenomenon itself, or the names usable, may also be specific to some regions[113].

6.2.1.4. LOCATION OF TERMS OF ADDRESS

Differences appear in the limitations on sequencing terms of address within a syntactic phrase and a tone group. In English as well as in German, they are either pre-posed or occupy a final position in a clause, as in the following:

```
57-E3.
M please mate # you can pour us another drink
```

```
58-E3.
M you might as well just lift it # because let's face it # it is not hard
to lift the top guys #. and that way # it's easier # and it's safer # you
know
```

```
59-E3.
F Jade # you can go here
```

In Polish, the positions before and after the main clause are most frequent, but the middle position in a clause and a tone group is within the range of possibilities:

```
64-P3.
F weź Mirka z soba jeszcze dwie kanapki # okay?
```
take Mirka with you two more sandwiches # okay?

---

[113] The phoney names which actually occurred in the data (Paula, Mirka, Mirki, Mariolki) did not occur among the items proposed by the native informants, all of whom lived in the Łódź region. The speakers who used them in the program came from the Wrocław and Poznań regions.

65-P3.
F chodź **tato** tutaj
come daddy here

The terms of address occurring in a clause-middle position are not parenthetical but prosodically integrated with the tone group that frames them.

6.2.2. HUMOUR

Humour is regarded in social psychology as a powerful means of consolidating groups and diminishing interpersonal distance (cf. e.g. Brown and Levinson 1978:104, 111; Bogardus 1942; Coser, 1962; Goodrich, Henry and Goodrich, 1954; Kaplan and Boyd, 1965). "The comraderie generated through such a play may function to strengthen social bonds and foster group cohesiveness" (Long and Greasser 1988: 57).

Numerous authors recognised the social role of humour according to lines making clear its affinity with positive politeness. There is a general consensus that "humour can be used to organise social distance" (Graham, Papa and Brooks: 1992), and that its role in the process is that of distance diminisher. The following summary from Graham, Papa and Brooks (1992: 166) pins down the essential functions of humour in relationship management:

> A number of researchers have studied the relationship between humor and group cohesiveness. For example, Kaplan and Boyd (1965) suggested three functions of humor that may lead to increased group solidarity: integration, adaptation, and accommodation. These functions of humor may enhance morale by decreasing social distance among group members, forestalling conflict, providing common ground, and by controlling deviance from group norms. Pogrebin and Poole (1988) extended this perspective by presenting three functions of humor that operate within a group's subculture to increase cohesion among members. First, humor allows group members to share common experiences and to probe the attitudes, perceptions and feelings of other group members in a non-threatening manner. Humor helps define the working ideology of group members, providing examples of informal standards and expectations for behavior. For example, a sarcastic response to inappropriate behavior may help define group norms. Second, humor promotes solidarity through mutual teasing that allows group members to realize that they share a common perspective.

Vinton (1989) reported that humour may help socialise new members into an organisation, as it creates bonds between employees. Humour "is a form of symbolic activity that reinforces the social structure and the subculture of the group"; person-focused joking "performs a social function of defining and reinforcing relationships between people" (ibid: 167). Attardo (1994: 324-5) offers a description of the functioning of humour as a tool to facilitate interaction and strengthen ingroup bonding: "If two speakers laugh together about the same subject, they share a certain degree of 'affinity' ... or share the knowledge of some scripts upon which the humor is based ... and so their reciprocal attitude will tend to be more familiar. In short, this type of humor has a 'bonding' effect. This is also the case for the use of jokes as repairs for face-threatening acts". Being "an invitation to demonstrate membership and solidarity" (Kotthoff 1998: 285), humour counts as a device of positive politeness (Lakoff 1973, Brown and Levinson 1978).

Longman's dictionary defines humour as "what is funny and makes people laugh". Defining humour is a challenging task that has been approached from different angles, resulting in a proliferation of psychological, sociological and linguistic theories of humour. Studies conducted within non-linguistic disciplines such as sociology and psychology seem unable to capture the nature of comical effects. The linguistic approach that seems to be "ideally equipped to capture some important aspects of humour, such as its importance and organization in conversation and more broadly in communication" (Attardo 1994: 331) is interpretative sociolinguistics. Kotthoff (1998) offers insights into the mechanism of generation and evaluation of humour, and substantiates the claim that it lies within the subject matter of linguistics.

In directives, humour occurred in the form of directive jokes, which were not meant to be followed and are not included in the statistically analysed data, and as an element of seriously meant requestives. I will distinguish between these two basic functional relationships between humour and directive utterances: humorous modification of directives, where the humour is used as a positively polite modifier in a directive that actually aims at an action by the hearer, and the opposite relationship where humorous directives are produced that are not meant to be followed and constitute themselves "global" modifiers of the whole interaction. Directives that are not meant seriously are global in the sense of affecting the whole tone of interaction and communication, diminishing distance and expressing shared background and camaraderie. The third and more complex case are teases, which typically constitute longer interactions, where both types of directives may occur side by side.

In what follows, humorous elements within seriously meant directives will be discussed, and joking directives will be mentioned in passing. As the mechanisms of humour have been a topic of a separate linguistic analysis (Kotthoff 1998), a comprehensive treatment of ironic and comical effects will not be undertaken. Rather, an indication is given of which sorts of elements were counted to the category of humour-based modification in the statistical analysis.

In some cases, comical effects are evidenced by a hearer's response (laughter, humorous response) and, thus, can be interpreted in accordance with the conversation-analytical dictum that all the claims of the analyst concerning the speaker's intention and its interpretation should be validated by the co-occurring cues and hearer's responses or further course of the conversation. However, the dictum itself has become a subject of ardent criticism (cf. e.g. Günther 2000). As Draw (1987) showed in his article on "po-faced receipt of teases", humorous remarks are not always marked as such by the speaker, and the hearers can (and frequently do) choose to respond to the message communicated on a serious plane rather than signal the recognition of a joke. This is a manifestation of the more general constriction on the possibility to validate the speaker's intentions in, and the hearer's interpretations of, a given conversational contribution on the basis of reactions to this contribution: the hearers can choose to react to one or some, but not necessarily all of the many co-existent recognised or putative intentions of the speaker. As a result, the detection of humorous elements in the data was based on my subjective evaluation.

6.2.2.1. DIRECTIVE JOKES

Directive jokes, which were not meant to be followed, occurred rather rearly in the British editions (about once every 75 minutes and once every 42 minutes in E3 and E4, respectively), and more frequently in German (about every 21 minutes in both series) and Polish (about every 30 and every 15 minutes in P1 and P3, respectively). These tendencies are similar to those which occurred in the humorous modification of authentic directives, where English scored lowest, mainly in requests, and the difference between the German and the British subjects was weakly significant[114]. Examples are given below:

6-E4.
M1 to M2: what club are we going to tonight?

---

[114] df=1, d^2=6.3, p<0.025

60-E3. The housemates do not know the answer to the quiz question about who who had the starring role in the Harry Potter films.

```
F1 I know exactly what he looks like
M1 can I have a look
F2 yeah # draw him a picture
```

66-P3. F, who lives in Wrocław, is leaving the Big Brother house.

```
M Aga # powiedz we Wrocławiu że telewizja kłamie
```
Aga # tell them in Wrocław that television lies

Directives of this type were not considered in the statistical part of the analysis.

6.2.2.2. HUMOROUS MODIFICATION OF DIRECTIVES

SUMMARY OF FORMS

Laughter as a signal of speaker's attitude
Unusual conceptualisations of the situation:
  - *Augmentative*
  - *Euphemism*
  - *Motherese*
  - *Diminutive*
  - *Metaphorical paraphrase*

Other cases of a non-prototypical relationship between term and referent
Double meaning with a sexual connotation
Word play and language distortion
Paradox declarations of the effect of compliance with the directive
Dramatisation, fictionalisation, code-switching and self-styling effects:
  - *Playful abuse*
  - *Playful threats, intimidations and acts of violence*
  - *Playful offence*
  - *Violation of social norms: a speaker's self-styling as a negative character*
  - *Role enactment*

LAUGHTER AS A SIGNAL OF THE SPEAKER'S ATTITUDE

In the data below, laughter serves as an explicit contextualisation cue helping to identify the speaker's attitude:

```
61-E3.
1 F1, F2 (laugh)
2 F3 stop laughing (laughs)
```

```
62-E3. M throws a roll of toilet paper at F.
F stop that # it hurts (laughs)
```

In the examples above, laughter communicates that the inhibitive is not meant to communicate resentment, even if it is meant to be complied with as in 62-E3. It can also undermine the illocutionary force of the utterance, resulting in a message not meant seriously, as in 61-E3 above.

ATYPICAL CONCEPTUALISATIONS OF THE SITUATION

A humorous effect can be created by referring to aspects of the situation from an unusual perspective (e.g. augmentative, euphemistic or metaphorical) and double meaning hinting at a sexual connotation.

AUGMENTATIVE

```
38-G2. M is busy killing flies.
F to M: Peter # wenn du schon genug Tiere getötet hast # spielen wir noch
mal Backgammon?
```
Peter # when you have killed enough animals already # shall we play backgammon again?

The comical element consists in offering an extraordinary perspective on flies by naming them "animals", which they are biologically but not by virtue of common language use. Thus, F re-conceptualises the addressee's killing of the flies as an act of brutality against animals. A further comical effect arises out of the contrast between the semantic content of the subordinate clause, and the composed and relaxed way in which the utterance is being produced, and the contrast between the brutality of serial killing of animals and the innocence of having a game of backgammon.

Motherese

63-E3.
F Betty! **wakey wakey!**

The speaker introduces a comical element in the form of a euphemistic attitude towards the addressee expressed by a routine used in dealing with children.

Diminutive

39-G2.
M1 to M2, M3, M4: aber so spaßeshalber könnte man das durchziehen oder? wenn ich heute Abend ins **Bettchen** gehe-
but just for fun one could carry it out # right? when I go to bed-DIMINUTIVE tonight

The speaker introduces a comical element in the form of a euphemistic attitude towards his bed and, implicitly, towards himself.

METAPHORICAL PARAPHRASE

5-P1. M and F are standing, M embraces F.
M na pierwszym piętrze czy na parterze?
on the first floor or the ground floor?

M uses a building metaphor in proposing an erotic caress and letting F decide how far it should go.

OTHER CASES OF A NON-PROTOTYPICAL RELATIONSHIP BETWEEN A TERM AND ITS REFERENT

As metaphor is a gradual rather than all-or-nothing phenomenon, some lexical choices that involve a distortion of the usual perspective do not clearly qualify as metaphors, but share with them the application of a term to an atypical referent:

40-G2. F1, F2, F3 are appealing to M to have a try on a mechanical bull that all housemates are obliged to practice riding in turns.
1 F1 --- Großkotz # einmal die Sieben # **wir wollen ihn fliegen sehen**
the boaster # once number seven # we want to see him fly
2 F2 **wir wollen ihn fliegen sehen**
we want to see him fly

Falling from the bull is re-conceptualised as flying.

DOUBLE MEANING WITH A SEXUAL CONNOTATION

67-P3. While the group are sitting at the edge of the hot tub, M1 is suggesting that M2 should make room for F1 to sit close to him so that she gets warm. F1 and M2 feel attracted to each other.
1 M1 to M2: wiesz co? tu będzie jej **cieplej** # chyba tu gdzie ty siedzisz # wpuść ją --- (points to a place next to M1)
you know what? she might be warmer here # here where you are sitting # let her in ---
2 M2 (makes room for F1) tu to myślę że będzie tutaj <u>bardzo</u> ciepło
here I think it is going to be <u>very</u> warm

While M1 ostensibly pretends to refer to warmth in its standard meaning related to temperature, it is plain that he is referring to a sexual tension.

WORD PLAY AND LANGUAGE DISTORTION

68-P3.
F oj # duper klaper # i nie maruder
oi # set your ass down # and don't whine

F creates a Germanism by adding the German derivational suffix –*er* to Polish roots: a vulgar noun (*dupa* "ass" → *duper*) and colloquial verbs (*klapnąć* "bang down", "sit down" → *klaper; marudzić* "whine" → *maruder*). The comical effect is co-created by evoking the stereotype of German as a language of unmediated direct commands; for a hearer not knowing German, an impression arises of a directive in German infinitive or imperative.

PARADOX DECLARATIONS OF THE EFFECT OF COMPLIANCE WITH THE DIRECTIVE

Humorous modification can also be realised in supportive moves. One type of supportive move noted by the research on politeness is promising a reward for the predicated action. In the following data, the "promise of reciprocation" is made that does not actually lie in the addressee's interest, because of gender asymmetry in matters of availability and desirability of body exhibition. In the preceding stretch of interaction, M is molesting F to show him her breasts.

65-E3. M and F are lying in their beds in the dark next to each other.
1 M I just want to check your breasts out # let's have a look # go on
2 F no (shakes her head)
3 M please
F (shakes her head)
4 M I'll show you mine (mimics showing his chest to F)

Obviously, the prospect of seeing M's breasts can hardly motivate F to comply. Similarly, a "promise" of an undesirable outcome of the addressee's compliance modifies the requestive in the following data:

11-G4.
F Mario # ich habe niemanden der mich kuschelt # machst du das? . dann sage ich's dem Tom
Mario # I don't have anybody to cuddle with # will you do that? # then I will tell Tom

F requests a cuddle from M, but undermines the illocutionary force of her utterance by announcing that she is going to mention it to her boyfriend in the Big Brother house. This is obviously a good reason for the addressee not to comply. This way, she goes some way towards withdrawing the realism of the directive. The resulting message is indeterminate between a real and joking request, making it easy for the addressee to opt out of compliance by choosing to react to the message as a joke.

DRAMATISATION, FICTIONALISATION, CODE-SWITCHING AND SELF-STYLING EFFECTS

The form of humour that co-occurs with seriously meant directives is hardly ever "what makes people laugh", but a humorous undertone realised by the broadening of the referential frame to include at the same time a serious communicate of the directive intention, and an extra plane of playful deviation from plain speech. Besides simple occurrences of an extra meaning or perspective, such as in the examples above, this creative expansion is realised in directives in all forms of "speaking in someone else's voice", violations of the rules of proper conduct (cf. Willer and Groeben 1980), self-irony, and intentional mannerisms created by exaggeration of some aspect of one's own or other people's style of talking.

<u>PLAYFUL ABUSE</u>

Playful threats, intimidations and acts of violence

```
42-G2.
1  M (laughs)
2  F hör auf (hits M)
```
stop that
```
3  M (laughs)
```

```
69-P3.  BROOM
```
M approaches F, intending to play a trick on her; F is holding a broom.
```
F odejdź ode mnie # bo cię uczeszę (swings the broom)
```
get away from me # or I will comb you

In 42-G2, F's fake aggression is contextualised by the harmlessness of the hit (confirmed by M's continued laughter), and the lack of balance between the reason (trespass: laughing at F) and the effect (hitting). In brief, the interpretation of threats and aggressive behaviour accompanying directives as being humorous is cued by the lack of realism of the threats, and the interactants' prior knowledge of what constitutes an appropriate serious response to a given situation.

Playful offence

```
43-G2.  Several housemates, including the addressee, are waiting to ride a mechanical bull; F1 is watching.
F1 --- Großkotz # einmal die Sieben
```
the boaster (literally: Big Puke) # once number seven

Playful abuses are strong means of manifesting positive politeness. According to Kotthoff (1988: 311), "unhöfliche Scherze funktionieren ... als Vertrauensbeweise", while she does not count them as positively polite but chooses to emphasise that they violate both negative and positive face wants. Kotthoff recognises that the transgressions of the norms of politeness function as an indicator of familiarity, "ein Index für eine noch vertrautere Stufe im Umgang mit einander, die man Familiarität nennen kann" (ibid: 299), but actually stops short of explaining the mechanism of the paradox. In brief, the transformation of impoliteness into a proof of trust is based on the same operation of mind as the recognition of its humorous character. It consists in the belief and intention of S that H will disbelieve the appearance of S's malevolence in the light of his or her better knowledge about S's benevolent attitude towards H. In other words, S shows that s/he expects H to reject current evidence rather to reject the general belief that S doesn't hold any ill will toward H and is unwilling to harm or hurt H. The display of this expectation shows S's trust in the robustness of the relationship and the good knowledge of S by H. Obviously, the staging of S's malevolence must be in itself unconvincing in order to eliminate the risk that it be taken at face value and backfire on the relationship; this creates the need for cues that indicate that the abuse is not authentic (cf. e.g. the lack of realism in F's threat in 69-P3. BROOM).

The directives accompanied by playful abuse can be meant seriously in their propositional content, but frequently it is not clear whether they are meant to be followed, or merely a means of staging a playful confrontation between the speaker and the addressee (and paradoxically confirming their relationship). The means and ends are not always possible to tell apart; humorous abuse can be applied in order to modify a seriously meant directive, but in some cases the engagement in a playful confrontation can be more important than the propositional content of the directive and its realisation; the social act of playing is not necessarily subordinate to any goal achievement.

SPEAKER'S SELF–STYLING TO A NEGATIVE CHARACTER

In humorous self-stylisation, the speaker plays with with forms of utterances produced in order to get the hearer to understand that next to communicating propositional meaning, she is consciously trying to convey non-genuine information about her personality. The hearer is expected to distinguish between pretence and reality, and at the same time to realise that this achievement was intended by the speaker and based on the contextualisation cues intentionally built in by the latter.

12-G4. M1, F1, and F2 from the winning team are on the yard. It is M2's birthday, who is from the losing team. Big Brother did not provide the housemates with any means and opportunities to celebrate. F1 has repeatedly proposed that her team members appeal to Big Brother on his behalf, and has just again began talking about the topic.

1 M1 was will sie schon wieder
what does she want again
2 F1 ne # der hat Geburtstag # und das isch-
no # it is his birthday # and it is
3 M1 oh lass ihn doch mal # ja gut # er hat Geburtstag # ist ne arme Sau
was geht uns (laughs) # **was gehen uns die Armen dieser Welt an**
leave him alone # all right # it is his birthday # he is a poor loser # what do we care # what do we care about the poor of the world

As a member of the privileged "winning" team, M1 is ostentatiously acting in an anti-social way, generalising his unwillingness to act on M2's behalf as a violation of the dictum that the socially privileged are expected to care about the weak.

One form of self-stylisation, akin to a playful threat, is exaggerating the categorical tone of a directive. The contextualisation cues applied to disambiguate the speaker's intention in interpersonal space vary from explicit laughter, through irregular prosody and inconsistent mimics, to hyper-impositiveness that cannot be taken at face value.

66-E3. WASHING DISHES
F1 and F2 are cooking in the kitchen. F3, F4, M1 are behind them in the living room.
1 F1 (shouting to the persons behind her) can I just say one thing # . I think that when you wash up # you should really wash up properly # . because so far # we had to rinse everything we used # ---
2 M1 to F3, F4 (frowns) do some more work # will you (smiles)
3 F2 shut up # Skinny

The categorical tone of the demand co-constituted by the accompanying frown in turn 2 is disambiguated immediately afterwards by the speaker's smile. The whole utterance is disambiguated as generated in an "as-if" voice, which is not the speaker's own. This signals that the utterance is a humorous pseudo-directive "global interaction modifier" rather than a humorously modified directive. F2 recognises the intention and responds in the same vain.

The next exchange illustrates the type of situation where disambiguation of the speaker's attitude as being humorous through a smile or laughter is not provided by the speaker himself. Laughter as a form of face redress and a signal of recognition of the speaker's non-aggressive intention is shifted to the response of the audience present (in this case, M3).

44-G2. TUB RULES

M2, M3 are bathing in a round tub. M1 gets into the tub.

1 M1 so # geh raus aus meiner Ecke # na los # geh rüber
right # go out of my corner # off you go # go there

(M1 shows M2 where he should move to)

2 M2, M3 (laugh)

(M2 moves to the place showed by M1)

3 M1 es gibt hier feste Regeln # was sagst du Tom # so geht das nicht
there are firm rules here # what do you say to that Tom # it doesn't work like that

In turn 2, M2 and M3 show through their laughter that they have interpreted M1's impositiveness as having a humorous aspect. M2 protects his negative face by showing that he interprets the utterance as involving an "as-if" plane, and therefore not abusive, and M3 confirms this interpretation, supporting M1's positive face and protecting M2's negative face. M1 confirms the humorous intention by apparently seeking confirmation through M3, referring to the "firm rules", and interpreting M2's behaviour (occupying M1's favourite place before M1's arrival) as a breach of these rules. *So geht das nicht* is a conversational formula expressing a critical attitude towards the interlocutor's trespass. Actually, no trespass has occurred. The violation of negative face wants is enacted by the speaker without redress, which is provided instead by the audience and the victim (addressee). They show that they interpreted the utterance as an intentional playful breach of the rules of negative politeness, based on the assumption of familiarity and trust in a shared background. As concluded by Zajdman (1995: 329): "A humorous FTA (face threatening act) may be performed by violating negative face within the frame of reference of positive politeness".

Face-redressing responses signalling the recognition of hyper-impositiveness as being humorous do not necessarily involve laughter, and can also be kept in a pseudo-serious convention, as in the following scene from Polish edition P3. The speaker, M1, exaggerates traits of his personality and idiolect that are already known to the hearers, such as a tendency to boss others around and issue categorical demands, and the hearer, M2, responds to the recognised humorous intention.

70-P3. COMMAND
Big Brother has instructed M1 to gather all housemates at the table.
1 M1 chodźcie do stołu # tera ja przejmuję stery
come to the table # now I overtake the steering wheel
2 M2 ciekawe # co tu się będzie działo
I wonder what we are looking towards
3 M1 dalej wszyscy siadać
off you go sit down-INFINITIVE everybody
4 M2 czytaj
read-IMP
5 M1 polecenie szóste
instruction number six
6 F1 czyta:j
read-IMP

In turn 1, M1 announces emphatically that he is now in charge. M1's self-centred comment leaves no doubt that a self-caricature is offered; as in episode G2. TUB RULES, the hearers have already spent enough time with M1 to become familiar with his caricatured property, a competitive and highly self-confident behaviour. In turn 2, M2 responds to the hyper-impositive stylisation anticipating that the group are facing an unprecedented and extreme course of events now that M1 has overtaken control. M1 upholds his self-stylisation as an authoritarian ruler by starting his command in turn 3 with the adverbial intensifier dalej ("off you go"), emphatic intonation, and opting for the infinitive, that connotates authority, in the head act. In urging M1 to read in turns 4 and 6, M2 and F2 verify their non-serious interpretation of M1's earlier utterances: they are neither impressed by his bossy manner nor do they take offence, and they boss him in return.

In the data above, the speakers are producing humorous effects through self-characterisations that do not depart from the actual social roles and relationships constituted by the social context of the encounter.

ROLE ENACTMENT AND CODE-SWITCHING

A further step towards fictionalisation of the context of a directive speech act is the departure from the linguistic norms defined by the nature of the relationship or the social identity of the participants. In this type of directive utterance, the speaker actually wants the hearers to perform an action, but enacts an imaginary social role, attributing a complementary role to the hearer within a fictitious frame. The frame may be generated by the directive itself, or created in advance and confirmed by the directive utterance. Invoking a fictitious plane of interaction is frequently realised by using joking or playful terms of address that index social roles.

67-E3. F is going around showing everyone a wart on her finger and accusing other housemates of having infected her.
M let's have a look # lets have a look # **ma'am** (laughs)

The comical effect of using the contextually inappropriate form of address "ma'am" (madam), originally a term of deference used in addressing "high society" women, is enhanced by F's not-ladylike performance, behaving in a direct and loud manner.

In the following directive, the element evoking a fictional frame is a counter-factual term of address. It attributes to the hearer the role of a soldier, and thus refers indirectly to the speaker's role of the "team captain", which implies a hierarchical relationship and turns the request into a military command:

71-P3. SOLDIER
F1 and M1 are sitting close and talking, as they look into each other's faces; F1 is M1's group captain.
(F1 touches M1's cheek)
(M1 turns his face away)
(F1 grasps M1's cheek and pulls his face back to her)
F1 e:p # nie odsuwać mi tu żołnierzu (laughs)
e:p # not move-away-INF soldier
(F1 removes fuzz from M1's face.)

Unlike the data above, where the fictionalisation is grounded in F's role of the "team captain", in the following directive the fictional roles of a soldier and a boss are generated on the spot:

221

72-P3. M1, M2 and M3 are chasing F around the house and trying to catch her.

M1 to M2: żołnierzu # proszę na tam # prawe skrzydło

soldier # I'm asking to move to the # over to the right wing

Other terms of address referring to enacted, fictional social roles were *mamuśka* "mummy" and *tato* "daddy".

In the following exchange, directive utterances occur within a fictional enacted frame. The losing team are ordained to serve luxurious food to the winning team, and invent a playful packaging to turn it into a fancy event, a comic enactment of a "restaurant frame".

73-P3. RESTAURANT

The losing team are to serve a luxurious dinner to the winners in the living room, and are preparing a show to surprise them. F1 from the losing team approaches the winning team waiting in the other room.

1 F1 grupa restauracji czerwonych zaprasza na posiłek

the chain of restaurants run by the Red invites you for a meal

2 F2 dziękujemy bardzo

thank you very much

3 F1 to bardzo proszę dwójkami powolutku # powolutku # //powolutku// (extra loud, emphasis on each syllable)

then I ask-please in pairs slowly-DIM # slowly-DIM # slowly-DIM

(several persons speaking, the winning team are walking in pairs towards the dining room)

4 F1 bardzo proszę dwójkami powolutku # powolutku # //powolutku//(extra loud, emphasis on each syllable)

I ask-please in pairs slowly-DIM # slowly-DIM # slowly-DIM

5 F1 (looks at her fake gun) mi się gana sypie

my gun-COLLOQUIAL is falling apart

6 F2 (laughs)

7 M1 (joins the group) o:

oh

8 F1 to M1: dwójkami # cicho

in pairs # quiet

9 F2 to M1: dwójkami (laughs) # cicho # powolutku

in pairs # quiet # slowly-DIM

10 F3, F4 (laugh)

11 M2 dwójkami niestety nie możemy # bo jest nas siedmioro
in pairs we cannot unfortunately # because we are seven
12 F1, F2 (laugh)
13 F1 jeden się sklonuje # i to natychmiast
one will clone himself # and I mean right now

The playful frame is introduced in turn 1 by reference to "a chain of restaurants". It seems that the reference to a chain, rather than a single restaurant, gives an American touch to the frame and justifies by connotation the role played by F1, that of a member of a security service, visible in the fact that F1 is wearing a self-made gun. The speaker represents the losing team. The directives in turns 1, 3, 4, and 9 are motivated by real circumstances and objectives. F1 needs to delay the winning team from entering the dining room in order to give her own team enough time to prepare the planned spectacle. These objectively motivated directives are accompanied by extra instructions which only aim at maintaining the playful frame itself, such as insisting that the instructees form a procession and walk in couples, in turns 4 and 6. The final directive in turn 12 absurdly predicates an action impossible both in reality and within the enacted frame, and represents the use of humour as a global discourse modifier.

One of the humorous aspects involved in the enactments of fictional roles are intentional mannerisms, that is, departures from the speaker's own and socially appropriate way of speaking, providing for the characterisation of the enacted persona. The directive in turn 12 is formulated as a categorical demand (realisation declarative) emphasized by a routine formula containing the time adverbial i to natychmiast ("immediately"). It is obviously not meant to be followed, but to characterise the harsh manners of the fictive persona enacted by the speaker, the "security ward", by her way of talking to her "charges".

To sum up, directive activities in the context of enactment of fictitious frames are characterised by co-occurrence of real directives, rooted in the requirements of the real situation, with directives rooted in the requirements of the situation on a fictional plane, that are not necessarily meant to be followed and are aimed at maintaining the frame itself, including such that aim at characterising the enacted personae.

The honorific addresses "pani" and "pan" ("Madam" and "Sir") indexing social distance are repeatedly used in Polish as a means of fictionalising the encounter. The data below exemplifies the use of "pani" within the scheme of "role enacting" arranged by the housemates, where they pretend to be participants of talk shows being interviewed.

223

74-P3. TALK SHOW 1

F1, F3, F4, M1, M2, M3, M4 and M5 are enacting a TV studio audience watching a series of talk show interviews; F2 enacts the show's host.

1 F2 naszym następnym gościem będzie
our next guest will be

2 F3 Rudi
Rudi (an ad-hoc nickname based on the adjective root rud- *"ruddy-haired"; applied to a ruddy-haired referent)*

3 F4 Rudi
Rudi

4 F2 panna Rudi Rudowolska z Rudowolic # zapraszamy
Miss Ruddy Ruddyhaired from Ruddyhairtown # welcome

5 (applause by the group)
(F1 walks up to F2 and sits down on the interviewee's seat, in front of the "audience". She is wearing dark sun-glasses.)

6 F3 pani ^zdejmie te okulary # bo pani jest jakaś-
you-HONORIFIC take the glasses off # as you-HONORIFIC are somewhat-

7 F4 tak # proszę zdjąć okulary # bo pani jest <[mało-]
yes # I am asking to take the glasses off # as you-HONORIFIC are little-

8 F2 [nie: # ja-]
no: # I-

9 M1 [jest pa]>ni mało czytelna # proszę to zdjąć
you-HONORIFIC are not well exposed # I am asking to take it off
(F1 takes the glasses off and puts them on the floor next to her)

Throughout the episode, speakers F2, F3, F3, M1 are using the honorific form third person singular (V-address) when addressing F1, signalling social distance and, thus, evoking the "as-if" plane of interaction. The form of the directive in turn 6, pani zdejmie te okulary bo pani jest jakaś, is characteristic of "grocery market talk". It differs from the standard analytical imperative used with honorific address by the non-occurrence of the initial hortative particle "niech". It sounds strongly demanding, is very unlikely to be used in any formal or public situation, and bears social connotations of low education and a social milieu in which F3 is not likely to be at home. This usage illustrates humour of mannerisms, that is, speaking in a way that is recognisably inconsistent with the speaker's normal sociolect. The directive is uttered by a member of the audience within an enacted

224

frame of a talk show interview. It is very unlikely that a member of the studio audience would spontaneously utter any directive at the interviewee, so its very occurrence defies the enacted frame. It is rooted in the actual situation in which the interviewee is really supposed to answer intimate questions about herself and the speaker wants to be able to observe her emotions. By using both the counterfactual form of address and a syntactic pattern which she could not be using if speaking as her real self, F3 makes it clear that she is enacting a role, and creates a focus on the enacted frame. This balances out the authenticity of the speaker's motivation in producing the directive, and prevents the enacted fiction (studio interview) from being deflated by evoking the authentic, non-fictitious context. By emphasising the fictional aspect of the situation, the utterance form protects the addressee's negative face threatened by the demand of greater self-exposure: as everybody is just enacting a role, the "real self" of the addressee is not at stake and face concern is made redundant.

The use of a formal term of address and an appropriate syntactic re-adjustment of the sentence form occurred frequently in Polish, accounting for about 50% of all cases of humorous modification. It frequently occurred over longer stretches of discourse by several interlocutors in turn. Sometimes, fictionalisation of the social relationship by the use of the honorific form performed the function of blunting interpersonal frictions through transferring them onto a counter-factual plane, as in the following episode:

76-P3. M1, M2, F1, F2 are sitting at a table. M1 and F1 are having an argument using a V-form of address.

1 M1 czy pani jest ciemna masa?
are you-HONORIFIC-fem. thick (literally: a dark mass)

2 F1 ja nie # ale pan chyba tak
me no # but you-HONORIFIC-masc. possibly yes

3 M1 no to proszę:-
then I am asking

4 F2 proszę nie obrażac # to jest jasna masa
I am asking not to be offensive # this is a thin one (literally: a bright mass)

5 M2 główny sędzia tak jakby sobie poszedł
the main judge # has like left

6 M2 tak # zajarać # o zara przyjdzie
yes # to have a smoke # o he is coming soon

7 F2 proszę się- # a pan proszę się nie wymigiwać # od odpowiedzi
I am asking # and you-HONORIFIC-masc. I am asking not to evade # the question

M1's critical remark in turn 1 constitutes a strong injury to the interlocutor's personality, while the offence is blunted by feigning fictitious selves through the use of a socially inappropriate form of address, pani (you-HONORIFIC-FEM.). Real social faces that are exposed to injury by mutual aggression are thus withdrawn. The group witnessing the argument catch to the fictionalisation, reducing face injuries to both parties. Reprimanding M1 in turn 4, F2 uses a performative declarative with *proszę* that clearly implies honorific address and a formal relationship, and she uses the counter-factual, honorific form of address in turn 7. M2 re-construes the dispute in turn 4 as a point-scoring game by referring to M4 as "the main judge". The scene culminates in the victory being humorously granted to "the senior private on retirement, Mariusz Borski" by M2.

In German, which also differentiates between the T-form and honorific form of address, the playful use of the latter did not occur. Instead, the fictionalisation of self takes the form of foreigner talk and a foreigner's "broken" speech. These two procedures seem to perform similar functions within the discourse of each language, respectively, one of them being humorous mitigation of "face-threatening acts" such as inhibitive directives, criticism, rejection, etc. The same fictionalisation device also occurs in directive jokes that are not meant to be pursued, which serve as a "global positively polite interaction modifier" of discourse. The scene below illustrates the function of "foreigner's talk" in German.

45-G2. M1 found a medallion while looking through F's photos. F is a native speaker of Turkish and German. M, a native speaker of German, is of Moroccan origin.

1 M1 das kannst du mir jetzt schenken
now you can give this to me
2 F na # das ist meine
no # this is mine
3 M1-FEDAR <start high pitch><du hast gesagt # Fedar [Fedar arkadasch><end high pitch> (laughs)]
you have told me # Fedar Fedar arkadash
4 F [aber das ist meine] # <start Turkish pronunciation><nix arkadasch # aber du geben erst mir deine Klamotten # und dann können wir gucken # du weißt Türken besser handeln als Marokkaner>
but this is my # <start Turkish pronunciation><no-COLLOQUIAL arkadash # you give-INFINITIVE me your clothes # and then we will see # you know the Turks better bargain than the Moroccans

In turn 2 F rejects M1's plain request to give him the medallion, and in turn 3 M1 insists by referring to an earlier utterance by F (not aired on television, possibly invented by M1 in this instant), in which she called him arkadasch, Turkish "friend". M1 implies that this earlier declaration of friendship enhanced his right to expect that F will comply with the request. M1 signals that this expectation and his pretended disillusionment are not meant seriously through using a high pitch voice and making a sad face. In effect, the utterance sounds like a complaint of a child disappointed with a broken promise. The following laughter further contextualises the utterance as an "as-if". F overtakes the playful tone and rejects the request indirectly by producing a humorous response. She rejects the appeal to friendship (nix arkadasch) and proposes a deal obviously disadvantageous to M1: she will think about the request but not before M1 has given her his clothes. At the same time, F switches to a parody of "foreign talk" (Turkish German, "Türkendeutsch"), marked by flat rhythmical intonation, exaggerated stress on stressed syllables, wrong word order, marked pronunciation and the replacement of inflected verb forms by the infinitive. The idea of a deal is thus explained by reference to F's Turkish and M's Moroccan origin, and the stereotypes in which fondness of trade and bargaining is a characteristic trait of the Turks and Arabs. F fictionalises her social background by using a parody of a sociolect which is not hers. She declares that the Turks are better at bargaining than the Moroccans, implying that she interpreted M1's earlier appeal to friendship as a bargaining strategy. Referring to the M1's Moroccan background, F implicitly proposes a play in which F and M1 play foreigners communicating in German which they only know imperfectly. This is confirmed in F's next turn, which is a reaction to an (inaudible) intrusion by a German observer:

7 F to M2: was du reden dazwischen # wir sprechen hier von Kollega zu Kollega
what for you cut-INF in # we are talking here from colleague to colleague

M1 plays along, and the bargaining game including a travesty of "Türkendeutsch" continues for several turns.

Unlike the speakers of Polish and German, the speakers of English very rarely applied conventionalised code-switching fictionalisation devices – I found only one clear-cut example of this device in all the recorded data. The assumed identities fictionalised the speaker's age, the addressee's gender and the kind of relationship between them:

7-E4. M is reading in the garden, F enters
M sit down # sit down son # tell your old man a story

The code-switching which takes place here and cues a fictionalisation goes from the speaker's own to a different chronolect.

HUMOUR: CONCLUSION

Humour and fictionalisation frequently serve as a conventional way of downplaying the speaker's responsibility for directive action in Polish and in German. Humour as a way to mitigate directives was applied least frequently in English. In particular, the British very seldom used conventionalised code-switching fictionalisation as a means of creating ironic distance between their real selves and the actual situation in which requestive utterances were produced.

6.3. POSITIVELY POLITE MODIFIERS: ENHANCING IMPOSITION

6.3.1. REPETITION

Repetition proved to be a frequently applied means of emphasis in Polish and English, in particular in inhibitive requestives. About one sixth of the requests of that type contained a reduplication of verb, verb phrase, emphatic, negation or affirmative particle, elliptical routine, term of address, or adverb of manner.

Cases of repetition occurring in the data occur in several functions:

     i.   In the service of the maintenance of the channel of communication, to assure that the addressee acknowledged the directive.

     ii.   As a means of persuasion when the addressee has been reluctant to comply after the first formulation of the message.

     iii.   As a means of emphasis, when there is no sign of the addressee's reluctance to comply before a repetition:

          a. Part of the message is repeated in a new tone group.

          b. A single lexical item is repeated within the same tone group.

Functions (i) and (ii) are frequently difficult to differentiate especially when they are embedded in simultaneous talk. Of these, (i) is obviously irrelevant to interpersonal rhetoric. The following analysis focuses upon function (iii).

Examples of repetition in the function (iii) are given below. For iii. (b), numerous different uses have been quoted in order to illustrate the exceptionally high productivity of repetition in Polish[115].

---

[115] Cf. also Pułaczewska 2009.

REPETITION IN A NEW TONE GROUP

ENGLISH

71-E3.
F **go # go** Andy

72-E3.
M **don't let him # don't let him go # do- # do- # don't let him go #** cause
he'll hurt himself # **don't let him go**
73-E3.
F I'm excited # **shut up # shut up**

GERMAN

13-G4.
M **komm mal her # komm her** # ich halte dir das Handtuch so
come HEDGE here # come here # I will keep the towel for you

14-G4.
F ei Junge du hast es voll darauf # **mach weiter # mach einfach weiter**
hey boy you really feel the blues # go on # simply go on

15-G4.
M und jetzt mit Jan # **alle zusammen # alle drei zusammen**
and now with Jan # all together # all three together

POLISH

79-P3.
M **przestań** # Zołza **przestań** # nie chcę się z tobą kłócić
stop that # Zolza stop that # I do not feel like arguing with you

80-P3.
M no **co ty # co ty # co ty** # złaź z tego stołu
*what do you think you are doing # what do you think you are doing # what do you think you are doing # get
off the table*

229

Co ty ("what you") is a colloquial routine formula articulating the speaker's disagreement with the current or immediately preceding action of the addressee, refuting a statement, or responding negatively to a question; the formulation implies that the addressee's action, statement or question went against common sense. (Also *no co ty, no coś ty.*)

81-P3.
M to F: **gdzie # gdzie** z tą dupą
where # where with this ass

Gdzie z + NP ("where with NP") is a colloquial routine formula of a terminating or preventive inhibitive very plainly articulating the speaker's disagreement with the placement of an object at a particular location by the addressee.

This use of repetition is commonplace in all three languages under analysis. Peculiar to Polish is the convention of reduplication of a term of address to express a reproachful and critical attitude towards the addressee:

82-P3.
M weź # **Madzia** # **Madzia** # przestań
AUX-IMP # Magda-DIM # Magda-DIM # stop that

6-P1. Big Brother offered M1 a chance to make a sacrifice and be rewarded by with a bottle of beer for each housemate. M1 is considering the offer. M2 insists that M1 take the offer.
M2 to M1: piwko # ty nie świruj # **ty ty**
beer-DIM # don't be silly # you you

REDUPLICATION WITHIN A TONE GROUP

POLISH

83-P3.
F **idź** po te poduszki jeszcze # . **idź idź** kochanie
go fetch the pillows # go go darling

84-P3.

M **właź właź** # ty # właź pierwsza tutaj
get in get in # you # get in first

85-P3.

F1 to F2: Andrzej # **zobacz zobacz** (pointing at M)
Andrzej # look look

86-P3.

F halo # panie # nie spać # **chodzić chodzić**
hello # mister # not sleep # move move

87-P3.

M **czekaj czekaj czekaj** # żebym kogoś nie uderzył
wait wait wait # OPTATIVE I not hit someone

88-P3.

F **poczekaj poczekaj poczekaj**
wait wait wait

89-P3.

F **dawaj dawaj**
go on go on

90-P3.

M **drugi drugi** # **dawaj dawaj**
the next the next # go on go on

91-P3.

M **jazda jazda** # bo nie ma czasu
off off # there is no time

92-P3.

F **nie nie nie** # proszę wytłumaczyc mi- # wytłumaczyc mi tę kwestię
no no no # I am asking to explain to me # to explain this issue to me

93-P3.

M cicho cicho # nic nie mów

quiet quiet # don't say anything

The reduplicated elements include: verb in the imperative and the infinitive, negation particle, adverb, and routine as well as situational ellipsis.

ENGLISH

In English, reduplication within the same tone group was limited to the routine formula *wakey wakey* and the negation particle: *nono, nonono, nononono*. A tone group boundary may occasionally be nearly unobservable in verb reduplication in a fast rate of speech.

GERMAN

In German, reduplication appeared in affirmative and negation particles: *nene, nenene, jaja*, inhibitive elliptical routine: *Moment Moment,* and the colloquial adverbial particle *dalli*:

16-G4.

M dann machst du halt Hans Rosenthal nach # und wir spielen trotzdem das Spiel # dalli # **dalli dalli**

then you mimic Hans Rosenthal # and we (will?) play the game all the same # off you go # off off

The data is inconclusive because "dalli", an emphatic particle expressing a sense of urgency, is a relatively recent neologism, which still has the status of a quotation rather than a lexical item for the generations of speakers aware that popular TV host Hans Rosenthal coined the term. The expression "Dalli dalli" was the title of Rosenthal's TV show in the 1970s. It also was used in the show as a signal for the invited guests to start acting, and was articulated with a tone group-internal reduplication. It is likely to have been adopted in this form from Polish (where "dalej", literally: "further", is used in the function of "go on", "hurry up", and "off you go"). Nowadays "dalli" is used by children and teenagers as an emphatic particle with and without reduplication, without any awareness of its origin as the name of a show.

To sum up, although the iconic principle of emphasis through reduplication seems to play some role in all three languages under analysis, its frequent occurrence in the one and only sporadic presence in the other two languages suggests its higher productivity in Polish. In particular, the verb reduplication within the same tone group seems to be confined to

Polish and is a likely candidate for a language-specific pragmatic routine. Peculiar to Polish is also the pragmatic routine of the reduplication of a term of address to articulate a reproachful attitude in inhibitives.

6.3.2. AUGMENTATIVE AND EXPLETIVE

The term "augmentative" is used here to refer to forms of expression that carry a maximising or pejorative expressive meaning, for which alternative forms neutral in expressive meaning are also available. Augmentatives and vulgarisms were the only type of impositive modification which occurred more frequently in inhibitive than in initiating requests in German as in English. Their use in inhibitive requests in these two languages was higher than in Polish.

Vulgarisms and augmentatives occur almost exclusively in imperative constructions. While the application of the notion of (positive) politeness to these inherently "impolite" maximising devices may sound counter-intuitive (see Kotthoff 1998), it follows from the definition accepted here of positive politeness as comprising all aspects of the utterance that are recurrently used as intimacy markers and expressions of involvement. The following data exemplifies such use of vulgarisms and augmentative forms in inhibitive requests in German.

17-G4. M1 has just declared he is going to leave the Big Brother house.
M2 to M1: mach kein **Scheiß** # bleib hier # es sind ehe nur noch zwei Tage # die wirst du auch noch schaffen
don't do any shit # stay here # it is just two days # you will manage this too

The attitude of commitment is made plain by the predicative content of the utterance: the speaker tries to persuade the addressee to stay in the Big Brother house. The utterance implies that M2 values M1's presence, forcefully addressing the latter's positive face wants. The vulgarism intensifies the expression of involvement by signalising the strong emotions of the speaker caused by the news, and maximises the expression of criticism of the addressee's intention to leave, thus upgrading the appeal to his positive face.

In the next data, a vulgarism and augmentation are embedded in a playful threat with which the speaker expresses concern and a sense of responsibility for the group after his departure from the Big Brother house:

18-G4. LEAVE-TAKING

M is just about to leave Big Brother house.

M soll ich euch was sagen? das war für mich hier # die schönste Zeit
meines Lebens bei euch # echt # bleibt so wie ihr seid # ehrlich es ist
absolut geil # bei euch # ihr seid eine super Truppe # ne? bei den
Battles Gegner ist okay # wenn ihr euch hier in de Haare kriegt # ich
komme hier rein # und jedem einzelnen von euch **verhaue ich den Arsch**
can I tell you something? for me this here was # the most beautiful time of my life with you # really # stay as
you are # honestly # it is absolutely great # you are a great team # right? # it's okay to be an opponent in the
battles # if you start being at loggerheads in here # I will come in here # and spank the ass of every single
one of you

Similarly, a playful threat frames the use of the augmentative in the following data:

19-G4. KLAPPE HALTEN

F to M: ja # jetzt echt **die Klappe** # sonst komme ich dir hinterher
right # now you mouth-AUGMENTATIVE really # otherwise I will come up to you

The threats expressed in G4. LEAVE-TAKING and G4. KLAPPE HALTEN above are both
obviously unrealistic: M in G4. LEAVE-TAKING cannot enter Big Brother house after his
departure, and F in the other data cannot threaten the addressee with physical violence in
view of her weaker physical posture.

In the next data, laughter contextualises the attitude of the speaker using the
augmentative form of inhibitive as not unfriendly towards the addressee:

46-G2. RESOZIALISIERUNGSTAG

1 M1 to M4: wir haben uns einen Resozialisierungstag für dich ausgedacht
we have been planning a social reintegration day for you
2 M2 ach # den kannst du dir in die Haare schmieren # Mann
eh # you can get stuffed with that # man
3 M4 was für einen Resoziali^sierungstag
what a   social reintegration day
4 M2 (laughs)
5 M1 **halt's Maul** # Mann (laughs)
shut you mouth-AUGMENTATIVE # man

234

The expressions *halt das Maul* (shorter: *halt's Maul*) and *Klappe* (elliptical from *halt die Klappe*, "hold your mouth") are inhibitive routines. The lack of an aggressive or seriously critical intention in turn (5) is made obvious by the speaker's laughter. The examples above illustrate the fact that vulgarisms and augmentative expressions in Big Brother material are hardly ever used in real conflict. Rather, they occur in playful threats (19-G4. KLAPPE HALTEN), a friendly persuasion that aims among others at the addressees' own benefit (17-G4. PERSUASION, 18-G4. LEAVE-TAKING), or mark a playful modality as expressions of fake indignation and fake conflict markers in reactions to teasing (46-G2. RESOZIALISIERUNGSTAG).

In English, among 23 cases of augmentation in inhibitive requests, there were 15 uses of the routine formula *shut up*, equivalent in its predicative meaning with the German formulae as discussed above. As in German, the routine was used almost exclusively outside real conflict, and frequently expressed the speaker's positive emotions towards the addressee. It was used to stop the addressee from making self-derogatory assertions, or predicting a course of events unfavourable to himself, as in the following:

74-E3. EVICTION
F and M are lying on their beds and talking about M having been nominated as a candidate for eviction from Big Brother house.
1 M I just know # I so know # I'm up for evico
2 F Ron # you're not
3 M yeah I am # I'm so up for eviction
4 F why # what have you done
5 M sometimes it gets to the point that
6 F Ron **shut up**
7 M ---
8 F I know it's not going to touch me # . trust me (extends her hand out to M)

The strong inhibitive in line 6 is followed by a declaration of involvement in turn 8. F asserts her intuition that she is not going to be affected by the nominations. This is a way of objecting to M's prediction that he will be evicted from Big Brother house, and implies that F would experience his eviction as a personal loss. The following physical gesture of making M hold hands reinforces the message of assistance.

The data below further illustrates other non-aggressive applications of *shut up*:

75-E3. F1, F2, and F3 are sitting at a table, M is standing a short distance away.
5 F1 tell us
6 F2 who fancies who
7 M I can't spill the beans
8 F1 does he fancy # .eh # . Jane
9 M who
10 F1 Emil
11 M who fancies Jane
12 F3 Emil
13 F1 it's either Emil-
14 F2-JANE shut up # please shut up

F is embarrassed about becoming the object of romantic gossip in her presence, and tries to preclude further comments. The co-occurrence of *please* in this data marks the use of *shut up* as a polite request. The co-occurrence with *please* occurs repeatedly in the data.

Briefly, "shut up" in English occurred in almost all cases within friendly and non-abusive interaction, where it was meant to socialise rather than to signal a conflict. The formula equivalent in predicative meaning, "shout your mouth", appeared once in the data and carried the message of hostility and true criticism.

To sum up, in German as in English the increased use of augmentation and vulgarisms in inhibitive requests compared to initiating ones did not result from a stronger confrontational tone of the latter. Generally, augmentation and vulgarisms did not carry unfriendly overtones. They were frequently used to express support, diminish distance, and mark positive sentiment towards the addressee.

In Polish, there are several augmentative expressions corresponding in their predicative meaning to the English *shut your mouth* routine: the reflexive verb *zamknij się*, and expressions that contain augmentative nouns referring to the mouth: *stul mordę/stul pysk/zamknij pysk/zamknij mordę*. None of them is readily available for use in a casual or joking manner as in the British *shut up*. The only occurrence of one of them in the Polish data resulted in a reprimand by a bystander:

94-P3. THREAT
Day one. The losing team, which includes F, M2 and M3, is preparing to sleep in their bedroom. The winning team are is allowed to stay outside their bedroom. M1 is a member of the winning team.
1 M1 <start singing><czer-wo-ni-to-si-ła-sił> (sings his team's chant outside the room)

```
2 M2 jeszcze mamy czas # nie?
```
we still have some time # right
```
3 M3 piętnaście minut
```
fifteen minutes
```
4 F to M1: <starts shouting><ale stul mordę już>
```
but shut your mouth-AUGM. already
```
5 M2 cicho # _ ^Pa:ula          REPROACHFUL INTONATION
```
quiet # Paula-FANCY NAME

In turn 5, M2 reacts to the vulgarism F uses in the preceding turn with a corrective inhibitive, reflecting the low social acceptability of the former.

My observations of cross-cultural encounters confirm that some German learners of Polish with well-developed language skills actually assume that the Polish semantically and syntactically congruent translation of "shut up", *zamknij się*, carries the same expressive meaning as its German equivalents (*halt's Maul, Klappe* as an abbreviation from *halt die Klappe*), that is, that it functions as an expression of social closeness, and use it in accordance with this assumption, confusing the addressees and observers. The Polish pragmatic equivalent of the *shut up* routine, applied to express social closeness in a playful mode of communication, seems to be the elliptical routine formula *cicho* ("quiet"), used by M1 in turn 5 of the above quoted exchange, or its full form *cicho bądź/bądźcie* ("be quiet"), syntactically and lexically non-congruent with the German and English expressions discussed above. It was used in the context of a humorous role-play, as in the following example:

```
72-P3. RESTAURANT
8 F1 to M1: dwójkami # cicho
```
in pairs # quiet
```
9 F2 to M1: dwójkami (laughs) # cicho # powolutku
```
in pairs # quiet # slowly-DIM
```
10 F3, F4 (laugh)
```

Non-equivalences, as depicted above, or "pragmatic false friends", constitute a problem area in language learning. They cannot be deduced from any general rules and principles, but need to be learned one-by-one as "small facts" (cf. Fillmore 1980) of linguistic pragmatics. At the same time, they carry a considerable conflict potential because of the spontaneous emotional response to linguistic expressions which mark aggression or other types of negative affection in the native speaker's language, or whose syntactic-semantic equivalents mark aggression or other types of negative affection in the learner's language. A non-native speaker assuming that a Polish translation of the British and German inhibitive routines discussed above can be used to evoke a joking and casual mode of interaction runs the risk of a cross-cultural misunderstanding; and a native Polish speaker confronted with their playful non-aggressive use in the other two languages is helped by an early realisation of their different expressive value.

6. 4. NEGATIVELY POLITE MODIFIERS

6.4.1. "PROSZĘ" IN POLISH: AN EQUIVALENT OF "PLEASE" AND "BITTE"?

The extremely rare use of the conventional politeness marker "proszę" in Polish noted in the statistical analysis suggests the a lack of its functional equivalence with the German "bitte" and English "please". Syntactically, rather than function as a polite modifying particle, *proszę* retains the character of a performative verb. When used in the modifying function, it formed a clause containing a reference to the addressee ("you") in the form of the direct object:

```
95-P3.
F kochanie # nie klnij # proszę cię
```
darling # don't swear # I am asking you

The alternative "poproszę" in the future tense is used in the same way:

```
96-P3.
M Olga # usiądź na chwileczkę poproszę cię # co
```
FIRST NAME # sit-down-IMP for a moment-DIM I am asking you # what

Interestingly, the use of a lexical IFID is in theory also required in Polish when making requests for personal favours and the phrase "magic word" is used to refer to it jokingly and in educational contexts in all three languages. The lines below are the final part of a lengthy dialogue in which the addressee of a directive utterance is trying to persuade the previous speaker to use the lexeme "proszę" in no less than 39 turns of talk. The interaction takes place in the context of a cross-gender teasing relationship.

97-P3. PER FAVORE

33 F no zrobisz Ojciec tej kawy
so will you make this coffee Father-NICKNAME
34 M no tak ale
well but
35 F signore?
signore (Italian honorific term of address)
36 M te kluczowe- # te kluczowe słowo
the key- # the key word
37 F please # per favore
please (English request IFID) # per favore (Italian request IFID)
38 M ale w Polsce jesteśmy
but we are in Poland
39 F weź # ˆzrób mi # Ojcuniu # ˆzrób   BEGGING INTONATION
AUX-IMP # make me # Father-DIMINUTIVE # make

Rather than conform literally to M's request and use the "literal" translation of the "key word", which she had already named before in English and Italian, F takes into account the fact that, as rightly pointed out by M in turn 38, the interaction takes place in Polish and in the Polish cultural context, and adopts her utterance accordingly. The negatively polite lexeme is replaced by the negatively polite begging rise-fall intonation in the head act and the term of address, and positively polite forms of expression are used, such as an auxiliary imperative and a nickname in the diminutive as an appeal to the comradeship between S and H.

A contrast between Polish on one side and and both English and German on the other is the differentiation that exists in Polish between the singular or plural form *proszę* vs. *prosimy*. This property is shared by other performative verbs of polite speech acts: apologising (*przepraszam/przepraszamy*), thanking (*dziękuję/dziękujemy*), and in conversational formula used for responding to thanks (*proszę/prosimy*). In contrast to German where the corresponding items turned to non-inflected "politeness particles" (*Entschuldigung, danke, bitte*), in Polish they have remained verbs and must be specified for the number. As a result, thanking, apologising, making requests and responding to thanks can be marked as being performed by the speaker representing other persons, too, without adding any measure of formal complexity to the utterance.

6.4.2. "REQUESTING INTONATION" IN POLISH: AN EQUIVALENT OF "PLEASE" AND "BITTE"?

Haverkate (1988) suggested that intonation contours of speech acts should be investigated cross-culturally in order to assess their contribution to politeness. "More specifically, prosodic research should concentrate upon the question of whether imperative sentences, which in not a few languages may have not only order but requestive force, are marked for distinct patterns of intonation corresponding to each of these impositive functions. Requestive types of intonation, then, would have the specific function of expressing negative politeness" (ibid.: 399). Prosodic modifiers have not been taken into account in the preceding statistical analysis of modification because of the conceptual difficulty in providing a unified quantitative treatment of supra-segmental ("analogue") and segmental ("digital") aspects of verbal behaviour. While many attempts have been undertaken to isolate the "meaning", or the communicative function, of various intonations in English (cf. e.g. Jassem 1983), for Polish and German precise statements concerning the contribution of intonation patterns to the message are rare. A routine association of specific prosody with an utterance function has been described by Günther (2000) for reproaches in German ("vorwurfsvolle Stimme"). Marek (1973) attempted a comparative analysis of intonation of Polish and English imperative sentences and requests, but the description offered is formulated in very general terms.

The verbalisation of politeness in Polish in imperatives and elliptical utterances expressing requests for personal favours can be performed by means of a distinct prosody. A specific falling intonation contour of the utterance, involving a pitch drop of one octave within the head act, marks an appealing attitude of the speaker, and thus signals deference by emphasising dependence and not taking for granted the addressee's compliance.

The analysis showed that the intonation patterns form a continuous spectrum between two pools, labelled in what follows as "begging" and "requesting". The pools are distinguished by the amount of vowel prolongation and the resulting distribution of the pitch fall along the utterance. In utterances showing considerable amounts of vowel prolongation the pitch drop was more continuous throughout the length of utterance. These utterances articulated a highly imploring attitude of the speaker, stressing the importance of the compliance with the directive for the speaker, and expressing deference by signalling that the compliance was not taken for granted. In the other pool, there were utterances which showed an early sharp pitch drop and no vowel prolongation, and which expressed polite casual requests.

The intonation contour of several utterances displaying requestive and begging intonation was analysed using the Praat speech processing system[116], and contrasted with exemplary directive utterances produced in a matter-of-course manner, and directive utterances assumed to express an a reproachful and critical attitude (connected at the same time with the assumption of high legitimacy). The latter show a characteristic utterance-initial rise-fall pitch pattern. Briefly, the properties that can be proposed as distinguishers of "requesting/begging intonation" were: if there is no starter realised in a separate tone group, such as a verb of sensation or a vocative, there occurs a continually falling intonation with pitch drops between consecutive syllables below 30 Hz; if a starter occurs, it is uttered at a lower pitch than the onset of the head act tone group, so that a pitch rise occurs in the first syllable of the head act tone group; pitch difference of between one and two octaves occurs between the start and the end of the head act tone group; and there is a sharp pitch fall, including an octave jump[117] completed within two consecutive stressed syllables, between the onset or the end of one vowel and the end of this or one of the following vowels.

The classification of utterances into "begging/requesting", "reproachful" and "neutral" was tested by means of an evaluation task conducted with seven native speakers of Polish. The informants were presented with six utterances whose pitch contours, according to my judgement, were representing a begging or politely requesting intonation, four "neutral" directives, and four utterances expressing a critical and reproachful attitude. The informants were told that to classify the utterances into expressions of a reproachful, neutral, and beseeching attitude of the speaker. All or all but one of the seven informants agreed on the classification of nine of the utterances listed below. Utterances (6) and (7) elicited mixed responses: they were classified either as reproachful or as begging. Other utterances which elicited mixed responses are not included. All imperatives in the quotations are in 2nd person singular.

BEGGING/REQUESTING

> (1)   P3.   F cho:dź tato tutaj
> *come daddy here*

---

[116] www.praat.org
[117] The data contained also similar utterances in the imperative with a pitch drop of two octaves, independent of gender, within two stressed syllables; they were, however, addressed at a pet animal, and seemed to express a benevolent and nurturing attitude of the speaker.

```
(2)     P3.     F Mi:sia:
                Misia-VOCATIVE-term of endearment
(3)     P3.     F przesta:ń
                stop that
(4)     P3.     M daj pomaluję cię
                let me do your make up
(5)     P3.     F Ruda # nie idź
                Ruda-NICKNAME # don't go
```

MIXED EVALUATIONS (BEGGING/REPROACHFUL)

```
(6)     P3.     F Paweł # weź sobie to krzesło i go wypuść
                Pawel # take this chair for yourself and let him out
(7)     P3.     M pro:szę cię
                I am asking you
```

REPROACHFUL

```
(8)     P3.     F przesta:ń
                stop that                           (SAME SPEAKER AS IN 3)
(9)     P3.     F i rzuć te fajki wreszcie
                and finally throw these fags
```

NEUTRAL

```
(10)    P3.     F chodź do środka # bo: mała ma problemy
                let's get in # cause the little-girl-COLLOQUIAL is having problems
(11)    P3.     M to chodź coś zjesz
                then come eat something
```

In (5), there is a head act-initial pitch rise as in cases of reproach, but it is enforced by the use of a term of address of a middle pitch pre-posed to the head act. The respondents seem to have disregarded the prosody of this pre-posed vocative in their evaluations. The same utterance-initial rise of pitch as a result of accommodating a pre-posed term of address led, however, to a mixed judgement in the case of item (6). Three respondents classified as being reproachful and four respondents deemed begging. (7) deviates from a clear pattern of requesting in that there was a light utterance-initial pitch rise as in reproachful directives, and, accordingly, three respondents termed it as being reproachful and four respondents called it begging.

The same test was conducted with twelve native speakers of German. The utterances were translated to the respondents prior to the evaluation task. The results showed that for the eight items for which the Poles agreed among themselves, not including the potentially troublesome item 5, the recognition of the attitude expressed in the prosodic characteristics of the signal was above chance (i.e., significantly above 33%) for German respondents, who agreed with the Polish respondents in 60% of the cases[118]. The result confirmed both the existence and the weakness of correct cross-linguistic intuitions, and a highly language-specific character of prosody as a clue to the speaker's intentions.

By means of insistence and marking the dependence of S on H's good will, "begging intonation" offers no easy way out of compliance. This seems to invalidate the usual definition of negative politeness as a minimisation of a negative face threat. In an alternative approach, an illocutionary force maximising devices that stress the dependence of S on H's compliance would count as positive politeness, based on the hearers' positive face want to be "desirable to at least some others" (Brown and Levinson 1978). As I have defined the presupposition of consensus as the most essential property of positive politeness, I regard the fusion of the two conflicting principles – emphasizing the speaker's need and the missing presupposition of consensus – in requestive intonation as a manifestation of negative politeness. This is consistent with treating lexical illocutionary force indicating devices *please, bitte* and *proszę cię* as negatively polite modifiers.

---

[118] The hypothesis that this was a chance result was refuted at $p=0.02$ using the test-theoretical procedure. I am indebted to Professor Wolfgang Hackenbroch from the University of Regensburg for performing the calculations.

BEGGING

(1) **Diagram 19**

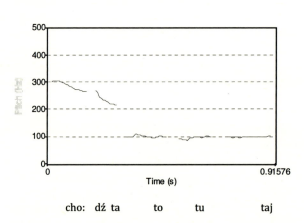

cho: dź ta   to   tu   taj

(2) **Diagram 20**

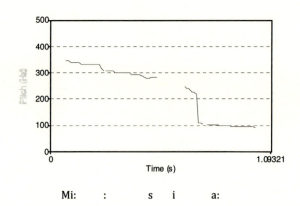

Mi: :   s   i   a:

(3) **Diagram 21**

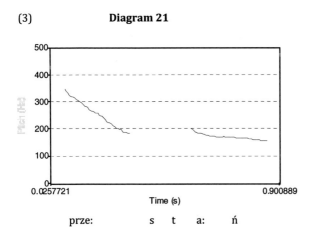

prze: s t a: ń

REQUESTING

(4) **Diagram 22**

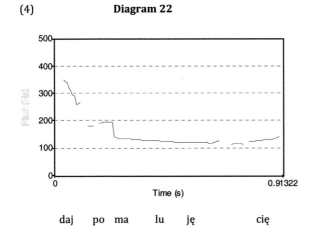

daj po ma lu ję cię

(5)   **Diagram 23**. Term of address + Head Act.

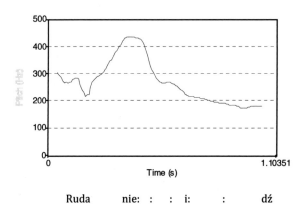

Ruda   nie: : : i: :   dź

MIXED EVALUATIONS (BEGGING/REPROACHFUL)

(6)   **Diagram 24**. Term of address + Head Act.

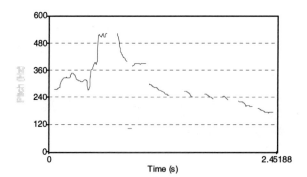

Paweł weź so bie to krzes ło i go wy puść

(7)   **Diagram 25**

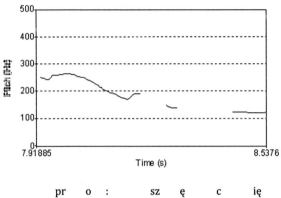

             pr   o   :   sz   ę   c   ię

REPROACHFUL

(8)   **Diagram 26**

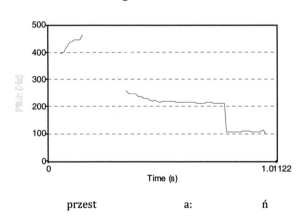

        przest   a: ń

(9)   **Diagram 27**

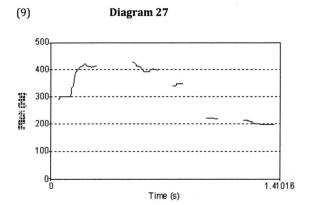

    i rzuć   te faj   ki wre sz cie

NEUTRAL

(10)   **Diagram 28**

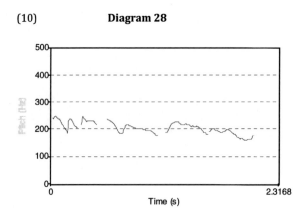

    chodź do śród ka   bo: mała ma problemy

(11) **Diagram 29**

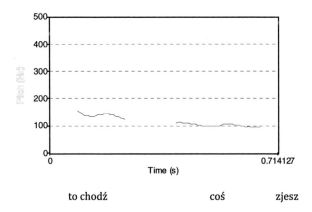

to chodź   coś   zjesz

Depending on the syntactic format of the head act, the high pitch can be located on:
- the stressed syllable of the verb of action predicating the future action of the hearer,
- the stressed syllable of the performative (IFID) verb *proszę/prosimy* ("I/we ask-beg"),
- utterance-initial negation particle *nie* in imperative inhibitive requests,
- the auxiliary element in periphrastic forms of the imperative, including an auxiliary verb (*weź/cie, chodź/cie, daj/cie*) in the imperative or the hortative particle *niech*.

Other types of utterances showing similar intonation patterns are emphatic apologies and comforters. The former is self-explanatory in view of the fact that an apology is a plea for forgiveness. The accompanying prolongation of the stressed vowel illustrated with the following data seems to be (nearly) obligatory with apologies.

The primary function of this intonation seems to mark the asking of a favour; however, it can also be extended to polite mitigation in teaching instructions or advice, making them sound less categorical, while at the same time, involvement is expressed by implication that the speaker is asking for something beneficial also to herself. Generally, signals of a speaker's dependence on the addressee's goodwill can be used to declare personal engagement in directives that are not requests for favours. The conversation below illustrates this use of the modifier "please" in English:

```
78-E3.
1 F1 I might leave
2 F2 what
3 F1 I might leave
4 F2 why
5 F1 because # . of # ohm # because of familiar reasons
6 F2 Anita # please tell me you're joking
...
7 F2 Anita # you are not fucking leaving # . you've got into this house
from hundred and fifty thousand people
8 F1 it's not me # though # . and I'm just … like tonight # . everyone
gets on really well # I have enjoyed it # . but # . I don't know # I just
. I just don't think I can make it
9 F2 oh you can # please don't think that
```

F2 is expressing involvement by using "please" as the illocutionary force indicating a device for marking the illocutionary force of request. In advising H, the speaker is at the same time making a request, showing that she treats H's problem as her own affair and wants her to stay in the house. The interjection *oh* and IFID *please* are used to express engagement and make the utterance sound like a request rather than a piece of advice. S implies that she wishes to further enjoy H's company and would treat H's exit as a personal loss. The following exchange from P3 is analogous in that the speaker is begging the addressee to stay in the house in the same context of the addressee who had just declared his intention of leaving. The role of *please* has been overtaken by begging intonation in the vocative appeal. Engagement is expressed by construing the speaker as the beneficiary of the directive and its means is an intonation pattern characteristic of solemn, emphatic favour asking:

```
98-P3. Several housemates are sitting in the living room.
1 M a: # nudzi mi się # _ idę do domu (stands up)
eh # I am bored # I go home
2 F Jaras # ^przesta:ń                              EXAMPLE (3) ABOVE
FIRST NAME-AUGMENTATIVE # stop that
```

The following exchange is a part of a longer interaction in which F1 (instructor) is issuing a series of imperative utterances to F2 (instructee); a rise-fall "begging" intonation modifies the directive and prevents the impression of an authoritarian tone which might arise otherwise. It marks the speaker's personal engagement construing the a predicated action as being in the interest of the speaker herself. The intonation mitigates the instruction, performed in the imperative, and implies that it is not only in the interest of F2 but also in the personal interest of F1, the instructor, that F2 performs well in the task. It also suggests that F1 might feel the need to sound apologetic because of having corrected F2's performance several times before.

99-P3. F1 teaches F2 karate and instructs her how to kick.
F1 wypro-# . rzu:ć tą nogę # ^wypro:stuj ją
str- # throw(kick?) this leg # stretch it

Requestive intonation is to some extent equivalent to *please* and *bitte*, because it signalises that the fulfilment of the request is not taken for granted, and that the speaker is dependent on the hearer. A crucial difference between lexical IFIDs such as *proszę, please* and *bitte*, and prosodic means of expressing insistence and prospective debt is that the latter are gradable. Supra-segmental features enable the speaker to mark emotional engagement and express dependence on the hearer's good will to a varying extent, stretching from "begging" through "requesting" to null. Using the analogy of a "digital versus analogue" transmission of information, lexical items are digital – they are either there or not. Prosodic devices, such as pitch rise-fall and vowel prolongation, are gradable additives which can be put into utterances in variable amounts.

Exploiting differences of relative pitch and other supra-segmental properties of the utterance, intonation can endow an utterance with multiple ambiguities with respect to its illocutionary force, the speaker's intention, her evaluation of the relationship between herself and the hearer, her assumptions concerning the status of a given interaction, and the implications of the utterance for the interaction. To sum up, using prosody rather than lexicon for encoding IFIDs seems to contribute to the property of communication characterised by a high degree of context-sensitivity, dependence on the "mutually known"[119], and an occurrence of messages open to multiple interpretation, labelled as "implicitness" in contrastive pragmalinguistics (House 1996), and as "high context" as well as

[119] A piece of background information x is "mutually known" to S and H if S knows that: 1) H knows that x, 2) H knows that S knows that x, and vice versa.

"high tolerance to ambiguity" by contrastive anthropology and social psychology (Hall and Hall 1989, Novy and Schroll-Machl 2003). A clear case of begging intonation, involving a deep fall in pitch in a request for the speaker's benefit, or a benefit of S's ingroup member, is not open to any other interpretation but as a strong signal of the hearer's dependence on the speaker's good will. However, less definite cases are also possible.

About four per cent of all requests in the Polish data are modified by requestive or begging intonation. This adds up with other means of a negative modification slightly changing the profile of modification in Polish, where requests were previously claimed to contain negatively polite modification in as few as 14% of the cases. However, even after the inclusion of this prosodic device of negatively politeness the amount of negatively polite modification in Polish requests still remains lower than in German and English (about 39% and 25%, respectively).

The skill of identifying the function of "requestive" and "begging" intonation, and encoding it, is decisive for the success of a foreign learner of Polish in social interaction. Since the use of intonation as a cue in interpreting the speaker's intention can be consequential in cross-cultural communication, training in the passive and active use of prosody needs to be integrated into curricula of foreign language teaching at an early stage.

6.4.3. LEXICAL HEDGES AND LEXICAL DIMINUTIVES

As much as 25% of all requestives were accompanied by lexical hedges in German, compared with 10% in English and 7% in Polish. The following lexical hedges and their combinations appeared in the function of internal modifiers:

German: hedging the predicate/verb: *mal*[120] (93x), *mal kurz, einmal, erst mal, gerne, gerne mal, ja gerne, einfach, doch, bisschen, lieber, einfach nur, ruhig (doch) einfach, ruhig mal, in dem Sinne, irgendwie, auch;*

English: hedging the predicate/verb: *just* (54x), *kind of, like, a little bit, better,* minimising the object: *little (little chat, little lay down);* modifying a supportive move: *just*

Polish: hedging the predicate/verb: *w ogóle* ("generally"), *sobie* ("yourself"), *chociaż* ("at least"), *jakby* ("as though"), *po prostu* ("simply"), *trochę* (3x) ("a bit"), *troszeczkę* (diminutive of *trochę*), substituting the whole predicate: *"ten"* (demonstr. pronoun masc. sing.), hedging a supportive move: *w końcu* ("at last"), time-related: *kiedyś* ("at some time"), *zaraz* ("at once"),

---

[120] The semantics and functions of the German "pragmatic particles" *mal, doch, auch, halt,* and *einfach* has been described in detail in Thurmair (1989).

chwilę ("a while"), *na chwilkę* ("for a while"-diminutive), *tam* ("there"), *taka jakaś* ("such some").

The Poles did not show preference for any lexical item; rather, morphological diminutive was repeatedly used, while the frequency of occurrence of the sum of morphological diminutive, lexical diminutive, and other forms of hedging expressions was significantly lower in Polish than in the other two languages. In both German and English, one particular lexical item was used with noticeable frequency.

About 80% of all lexical hedges in German were occurrences of *mal*, which accompanied every fifth requestive in the pool, alone or in combination with other particles and adverbials. According to Helbig (1988: 175), *mal* modifies the illocution from an order to a polite request; Hentschel (1991: 141) explains this function of *mal* ("minimisation strategy") as a derivative of its lexical meaning, related to *einmal* (once): "Its function is to stress that the act required need only be performed 'once' or 'for a short time'". In the data under analysis, it co-occurs with all sentence types and semantic dimensions, most frequently in the imperative. Approximately every fourth imperative is modified by *mal*, alone or in combination with other particles. That the lexical meaning has completely evaporated can be seen in its co-occurrence with the semantically contradictory item *immer* ("always"):

```
20-G4.
F und denkt mal immer daran # nach dem Pipi ist der Schei immer sauber zu
machen
```
and think HEDGE always about it # after peeing the dreck needs to be cleaned

In English, the mitigator *just* amounted to about 85% of all lexical hedges (including lexical diminutives) in English. Its frequency of occurrence was much lower than *mal* in German; it accompanied about 9% of all requestives. *Just* typically minimises the predicate (verb) in the head act:

```
79-E3. F2 is about to leave Big Brother house.
F1 to F2: will you just say hello to my mum from me
```

It was also used to modify supportive moves:

81-E3.

M guys # can I **just** ask # please don't treat me any differently # just cause I've been nominated again

or complex hedges in the form of subjectivity markers:

82-E3.

M I **just** think that # . for us to survive in here # . and . and . stay friends # we need to make sure # we clean up

In all three languages, lexical diminutives were used to minimise the object of request or supportive moves. In the following call for remedial action, the speaker prevents the addressees' objection to his idea by minimising the object of criticism. The minimisation is contained in the grounder prefacing the actual proposal:

83-E3. M has called the group to gather on the sofas to talk about order and hygiene, and delivers a little speech.

M right # the idea of this # at the moment is # . we can talk about what's been going on this week because obviously we . for example things like the shopping # we might have made a **little bit of a mistake** because we are sort of on rations and things like that # obviously as well . the kitchen # I know we all go= # not the `kitchen # the ^bathroom # we all go to the bathroom every day # well . most of us do anyway # . and it is getting **a little bit dirty** in there# and as you can see where the little lip is # . maybe it should be like a non-shoe area

In the next two data, the lexical diminutive is used to refer to intimate talks between friends:

84-E3.

F1 (embracing F2) let's go and have **a little lie down** in the bed
(F1 and F2 run to the bedroom and chat about men.)

The same form recurs in another invitation to cherish an intimate relationship:

```
85-E3. LITTLE CHAT
```
M1 has just revealed to M2 that he is going to voluntarily leave the Big Brother house.
```
1 M2 oh please stay # Ronny # please stay
2 M1 well # I'll speak to them again in the morning # but-
...
3 M1 I don't see why I should be putting myself through and other people
in the house being put through the fact that # . e . you know # . I am
being forced into: . this scenario # . because there is nowhere for me to
go # . you know what I mean #
4 M2 you can always put a chair there # I'll put a chair here # and we
can have a little chat
```

The intuitions of British native informants concerning the modifying function of diminutives are less clear than those concerning other types of modification. Why they may minimise the object of the request or proposal and, thus, express disinclination to impose, they also function as confidence-creating devices as in both data above, where they carry the connotation of secrecy (implying that it is desirable to keep the discussion out of the other person's view, hence, "little"), and create for the speaker and the addressee an intimate space of things done together while unobserved.

On the other hand, similarly as in Greek (Sifianou 1992a), morphological diminutives are frequently used in Polish in requests directed at strangers, where the message they carry is that of minimising the imposition by minimising the object of the request.

I decided to avoid a language-specific adjustment of classification criteria and classified all their occurrences among negatively polite modifiers, apart from one case in German where the infantile form of a noun, "Bettchen", *bed-DIM.* was used for a humorous purpose. This classification was consistent with the methodological postulate pursued here of minimising rather than maximising the intercultural difference in controversial cases (the Poles used more positively polite modification and less negatively polite modification, but more diminutives than the other two groups).

6.4.4. MORPHOLOGICAL DIMINUTIVE

The morphological diminutive has been placed among the devices of negatively polite modification because it plays a similar role as with hedging expressions – it symbolises care for the addressee's negative face wants and minimises imposition by symbolically minimising the object of request. The minimisation applies to the size of the objects involved, the time needed for performing an action, and the amount of action. While the use of the diminutive can be semantically motivated by the small size of the object, by choosing an infantilised, diminutive form from the available alternatives the speaker is at the same time characterising herself as a person showing positive properties associated with children: innocent, viewing the world as benevolent and unlikely to effectively impose things on others. Due to limitations on the construction of the morphological diminutive in English, these types of items did not occur in the English material. The Poles used the morphological diminutive in about 3% of the requestives, and the speakers of German just three times in the quantitatively analysed data.

In Polish, the euphemistic character of the diminutive where it attaches to concrete nouns (unless they are actually small in size), adverbs and adjectives (the latter two did not appear among the data) makes it a suitable tool for demoting a face threat in situations that have a relatively high potential of damage to the addressee's negative face wants, as illustrated in the following dialogue:

```
103-P3. LEGS-DIM
```
F is lying; M is sitting next to her on the sofa..
(F places a pillow and her head on M1's knees)
M (reproachfully) Barbi!
F prze:stań # ale złóż nóżki trochę
stop that # but close your legs-DIM a bit

In line 2, M objects to F putting her head on his knees by a reproachful exclamation of F's name (M is married, and his wife is likely to watch the action in the Big Brother house on TV). F insists by means of the imperative prze:stań ("stop that"), with emphasis added by a vowel prolongation. She asks M to put his legs together to make her position more comfortable, mitigating her heavy neglect of M's explicitly expressed desire to be left alone by means of an infantilising and desexualising diminutive.

The tendency to use diminutives in referring to the addressee's body is amply illustrated in the following piece of an instructional dialogue, in which F1 is teaching F2 karate.

```
104-P3. KICK TRAINING
```
F2 holds a plastic bottle for F1 to kick.

```
1 F1 ręce # _ łapki sobie # paluszkami sobie trzymaj
```
hands # your flippers-DIM # hold it with fingers-DIM

(F1 manipulates F2's hands holding the bottle)

...

(F1 holds a bottle for F2 to kick)

(F2 kicks the bottle)

```
2 F2 tak?
```
like that?

(F1 nods)

```
3 F1 ten łokiec bliżej Madziu # . tak żebyś mogła chować brzuszek #
wiesz?
```
this elbow closer FIRST NAME-DIM # so that you can hide the belly-DIM # you know?

The repeated use of the diminutive, both in the name of the addressee and the references to her body, expresses friendliness and protects F2, who is continually receiving commands from F1 in the course of several minutes, from the impression of being pushed around.

Nine out of 27 references to the addressee's body (legs, abdomen, hands, and fingers) in directives in the Polish data involve diminutive forms. All were produced by, or addressed at women.

6.4.5. CONSULTATIVE INTERACTION MARKER: QUESTION TAG

The following items appeared in the function of tag questions (rising intonation is marked by a question mark):

POLISH

- *tak?*   standard affirmative response particle
- *nie?*   standard negative response and negation particle,
               colloquial when used as a question tag
- *prawda* ?   ("truth") : noun
- *okay?*   Anglicism, colloquial
- *w porządku?* ("in order") prepositional phrase
- *dobra?*   ("good"-COLLOQUIAL) adverbial particle
- *co?*   ("what") impersonal interrogative pronoun

257

GERMAN

- *ja ?* — standard affirmative response particle
- *ne?* — colloquial negative response particle
- *oder?* — ("or") coordinating conjunction
- *oder was* — ("or what") coordinating conjuction + impersonal interrogative pronoun
- *okay?* — anglicism, colloquial

ENGLISH

- *shouldn't we* — question tag
- *can't you* — question tag
- *isn't it* — question tag
- *shall we* — question tag
- *okay?* — adverbial particle
- *yeah?* — colloquial affirmative response particle

Tag questions were characterised by:

- the occurrence of colloquialisms, including colloquial anglicisms, in question tags in German (*okay?, ne?*) and Polish (*okay?, nie?*), giving the tag question a double orientation in politeness (colloquialism being a means of maintaining informality and, hence, positive politeness),
- the syntactic complexity of the English question tag, compared to mostly mono-lexemic routines which appeared in Polish and German,
- the functional and sequential diversity of the English tag question within the utterance, where it is attached not only to a head act but also to supportive moves such as steers and grounders (e.g. *isn't it*),
- the interlingual lexical correspondence between some question tag routines: the agreement particle (*okay*) and the negative and positive response particles - *ja, ne* in German, *tak, nie* in Polish, *yeah* in English. (The German negative response particle, however, is a colloquialism and has a standard equivalent *nein*, whereas Polish *nie* is a standard negative response particle and acquires the character of a colloquialism only when used in the tag function).

Wierzbicka (1985) claims that a language works out a number of conversational routines for the strategies of interaction which are most frequently used in this language, so that the diversity of the syntactic-lexical forms in English tag routines points towards the popularity of the consultative strategy, whilst in Polish this strategy does not have much conversational value and interrogative forms have not developed syntactic and lexical complexity for that very reason. The claim is based on the premise of the functional grammar that a language grammaticalises the functions that are used most. From this, an expectation follows that the grammaticalised consultative devices tagged to the head acts of directive utterances in English should be more frequent in English than in Polish or German, languages which have not developed complex grammaticalised tag questions, but use single lexical items to fulfill the same function. The lack of grammaticalised tag questions would suggest a lower value of consultative strategy in these languages, confirmed also by the lower use of conventionally polite interrogatives in requests.

In fact, question tags occurred in requestives in all three languages with nearly the same frequency (about 3%) and failed to show the expected effect. The thesis about the relationship between the existence of a grammaticalised device for performing a particular function and the presumed social value of this function, associated with its frequency of use, failed to find support in the data under study. Moreover, the number of different forms of tag questions in the function of modifiers of requestive utterances was about the same in all three languages (five to seven forms). This result does not only counter this particular claim of Wierzbicka's, but also warns against bridging between cultural values and grammatical devices not based on quantified data in general.

6.4.6. CONSULTATIVE SUPPORTIVE MOVES

The following section concerns the functioning of consultative devices in English, as well as their interaction with aspects of positive politeness. It illustrates the relative complexity of the rhetorical means used in realising directive intentions which seems to be a distinctive characteristic in particular of English proposals. In the statistical counts, this complexity was displayed by the more frequent use of negatively polite supportive moves than in German and Polish.

Consultative supportive moves are a diversified rhetorical species, including routine formulas ("Can you do me a favour and" + VP), formal devices (paraphrasing the same propositional contents in the interrogative and the imperative or the declarative mood) and unique non-routine propositions. To start with, simple cases of interrogative prefacing supportive moves are routine formulas such as those exemplified by the following exchanges:

```
86-E3. PICKING CARROTS
```
F and M are picking carrots in the garden.
```
1 F yeah # that's enough
2 M 'what # ^five ^carrots
3 F no # there's # there's a couple more in there
4 M so we get a couple more
5 F are you sure? that's enough
```

Here, the categorical statement *"that's enough"* constituting a terminating directive is prefaced by a supportive move representing the consultative strategy.

```
87-E3. WASHING DISHES
```
F is standing at the kitchen sink and shouting to the people behind her.
```
F can I just say one thing # . I think that when you wash up # you should
really wash up properly # . because so far # we had to rinse everything
we used # ---
```

F1 is mixing two devices of the negatively polite strategy, such as an interrogative preface in the form of a "fake" permission request and a complex hedge ("subjectivity marker", "-committer[121]") "I think", with positively polite devices such as a deontic declarative and the lexical emphasiser "really".

A distinct type of prefacing supportive moves are those that express the same propositional contents as the following impositive formulations, and are subsumable under the notion of Multiple Heads. The concept of Multiple Head Acts (or Multiple Heads) was introduced by Blum-Kulka et al. (1987). Multiple Heads are defined as two or more chained propositions each of which alone realises the communicative intention of making a directive, that is, would count as constituting a directive also if the other one were absent. The interrogative syntax of their first constituent was a property shared by all the occurrences of Multiple Head Acts. Because of their rare occurrence, in the statistical analysis these interrogative components of multiple head acts have been counted as negatively polite modifiers (preparators) for the following positively polite head acts. This seemed to be the most meaningful way of incorporating them into the data while avoiding an excessive multiplication of categories, and at the same time ensuring a consistent basis for the calculations.

---

[121] Kasper and House (1981).

In the following episodes, a switch from negative to positive politeness is realised within one turn:

88-E3. A group of housemates, including S, are heading for the yard; the addressee of the utterance is sitting on a sofa.
F are you coming in? come in the air pool with us

89-E3. The housemates have been asked by Big Brother to pack their suitcases in the bedrooms. M1 is helping F1 to close her suitcase. Other suitcases are standing around, closed and prepared.
M2 have we got to bring them out? # bring them out

In these utterances, both steps have the same propositional contents. They only differ in the formal realisation by the different orientation in politeness of the syntactic routines applied: interrogative vs. imperative.

The first "head" of each utterance might have reflected the process of "thinking aloud" and expressed an actual uncertainty on the part of the speaker as to her directive intention. In this case, the second "head" would reflect the resolution of this doubt by the speaker himself. Another possibility is that prefacing an impositive requestive with a consultative move is a strategy of politeness and a pragmatic convention of English in the given context. The latter alternative is supported by the following example, in which a consultation of the addressee's preferences prefaces a definite statement of the speaker's opinion:

9-E4.
F does everybody want champagne? everybody should have a little drink

In the following two examples, the propositional content of the utterances realising requestive speech acts is more complex and is gradually expanded in several moves. In 90-E3, M1 reintroduces the proposal of camping in the yard of the Big Brother House, tests the consent of his two interlocutors and proposes the timing of a joint action.

90-E3.
1 M1 so are we going to set up a little camp # Camp David like
2 F1 definitely
3 M1 can we sort it out # then # [with the fucking mattresses]

261

```
4 M2 [yeah # but . I'm fucking=] # .well # I'm knackered # but I'm still
up with it
5 M1 so can we do it tomorrow # or we can do it tonight as well # _ I'm
up for it tonight # I am
```

The exchange starts with M1's series of requestives formulated in the interrogative and thus realising the considerateness strategy of optionality and non-insistence. In turn 1, the topic is re-opened in the form of a realisation interrogative, offering a choice to the speakers. In turn 5 by M1, where M1 is referring to the timing of the joint action, the switch from a negatively polite interrogative to positive politeness takes place:

```
M so can we do it tomorrow # or we can do it tonight # _ I'm up for it
tonight # I am
```

The utterance contains three head acts expressed in different forms. The competence interrogative of the first move is followed by a competence declarative, which is in turn followed by a declarative straightforwardly stating the preferences of the speaker. The intention of the speaker is realised in four steps developing gradually from the negative to positive orientation in politeness:

STEP 1 – consultative (neg. pol.)	so can we do it tomorrow
STEP 2 – suggestive (neg. pol.)	or we can do it tonight
STEP 3 – affirmative (pos. pol.)	I'm up for it tonight
STEP 4 – emphatic (pos. pol.)	I am

The speaker develops his thoughts while speaking and speaks while thinking. At the same time, he changes his strategic choice in favour of positive politeness, more adequate to the the peer group set-up promoting integrative strategies; positive head politeness was applied in 70% of English proposals.

In the following episode, the housemates have been given a task to fulfil, which is answering several quiz questions and writing the answers on a board. M proposes a division of labour in which the other housemates will answer the questions and he will write the answers down on the board.

91-E3.

```
M do you want me to write it # now guys # it's going to be on TV and
films # and all that # isn't it # . and I'm not the best # so I'll write
it
```

The forceful statement of the speaker's decision "I'll write it" is preceded by a negatively polite consultative device, in the conventionalised form of a question referring to the hearers' preferences. Devices of positive and negative politeness are interlaced in several steps:

STEP 1 - consultative (neg. pol.)	`do you want me to write it`
STEP 2 - appellative (pos. pol.)	`now guys`
STEP 3 - argumentative (grounder)	`it's going to be on TV and films #` `and all that`
STEP 4 - consultative (neg. pol.)	`isn't it`
STEP 5 - argumentative (grounder)	`and I'm not the best`
STEP 6 - affirmative (pos. pol.)	`so I'll write it`

A common feature of the constructions listed above is the use of the interrogative in combination with other basic syntactic patterns. This use of the interrogative is reminiscent of a question tag, but the strategic, syntactic and semantic complexity by far exceeds the complexity of the tag routine. Its repeated occurrence suggests that applying the interrogative as a preface to a more categorically formulated directive might be a pragmatic convention of English in the social configuration under study. It can not always be concluded from the data alone, though, whether this is a communicative strategy, a change of communicative intention (inquiry versus directive), or the result of the indecisiveness of S about the type of politeness which is appropriate in the context given. Each act of using a particular style does not only express the current status of a relationship but also contributes towards defining this relationship and pushing it towards less distance and more involvement, or towards more deference (in Lakoff's sense) and considerateness. That is to say, the ambivalence might concern the stylistic means adequate to the speaker's perception of the current status of the relationship and her conception of its future. Its roots may be searched for in the interplay between negative polite orientation frequently attested to the British culture "in general", and the current situational context that minimises distance, promotes ingroupness and fosters integrative strategies of communication. Such situations are, however, not unique to the experimental set-up but are a recurring experience of members of young peer groups, e.g. in flat-sharing.

The above-quoted utterances manifest a rhetorical complexity in combining positively polite strategies with negatively polite consultative devices. This property recurs in a more sophisticated mode in the following episode, in which a proposal is made to act in favour of the whole group, including the hearer and the speaker, and where the consultative strategy is used as the a means of leaving a margin of uncertainty regarding the illocutionary force of an off-record directive. What starts as a technical consultation (that is, an inquiry about the way to perform the action in question) is reinterpreted by the speaker in the course of further interaction as an "availability check" constitutive of a directive per se. This is done by means of interpreting the positive response of the hearer to the technical consultation as the compliance with its (non-obvious) directive intention. The speaker tests his assumption that the addressee accepted the proposal indirectly, by providing a comment which the addressee may take up. The presupposition of a consensus of a joint action is expressed first, but it is accompanied by consultative devices and the speaker denies that he has ever presupposed consensus as soon as it becomes manifest that it is actually missing.

92-E3. GREAT DAY OF COOKING

F is still in bed; M enters the women's bedroom and sits down on F's bed. The episode is preceded by a large delivery of food, which the housemates have to store safely for a longer period of time.

1 M can you:: # can we # can you cook a chicken and refreeze it # . we can cook mince and refreeze it # but I can't really cook _ chicken
2 F yeah # if you make it into a kind of [sauce] or something like that
3 M [dish]
4 F a dish # we've got to cook all that meat and could may be make
5 M **so # so we gonna have to do all that today # aren't we # that's going to be a big day of cooking # isn't it?**
6 F well # actually less the we # . because I have made a soup for lunch yesterday as well
7 M I mean # we as a team #
8 F right # . well # other people they haven't been doing anything and they should # . you know? _ you should just relax and chill out and let somebody else do it as well
9 M I know # but just need to make sure that it gets done # that sort of thing

In turn 1, M tests the consensus about preparing a chicken dish for refreezing. The proposal is expressed as a consultation: S tests whether the action is technically possible in H's opinion. The switch towards the "we" plural self-reference after the initial "you" in this turn seems to follow from the a need to disambiguate "you" as the indefinite generic pronoun rather than a personal reference to F. A further utterance in this turn which includes a personal reference to M (but I can't really cook _ chicken) is, however, ambiguous regarding the illocutionary function of the whole utterance. M may be explaining reasons why he is asking the question, but he may also be asking for assistance in performing the proposed action.

In turn 2, F responds with a technical evaluation using "you" as a generic impersonal pronoun, and switches to "we" later on in turn 4. M picks up on the "we", using it in a statement of necessity followed by a question tag in turn 5, and continues with a remark concerning the a "great day of cooking".

While availability checks (included in the category of negatively polite steers in the statistical analysis) are counted as devices of negative politeness, I argued when classifying the possessive dimension of interrogative among positively polite strategies that availability checks can be applied consciously as directives, rather than as prefaces to directives are positively polite (e.g. P-3: *Macie nożyczki?* "do you have scissors?"). Used in this way, they express the presupposition that the availability (possession, technical possibility) of the object to the addressee is the only precondition which must be met for the request to be granted. In other words, they presuppose the addressee's willingness to cooperate: it is taken for granted that he or she will comply if they are technically capable of complying. Although M seemed to be using "we" in turn 1 to disambiguate his use of "you" as generic rather than specific, he interprets F's similar use of "we" in turn 4, in which she confirms that a chicken dish could be made, as a self-reference and as an indicator of her acceptance of the proposal to cook the chicken together, possibly together with other housemates (the multiple referential potential of "we" precludes the definite interpretation). In turn 5, M mildly validates the directive intention behind the inquiry. The utterance suggests that he takes it for granted that F will comply after she confirmed the technical possibility he had inquired about. Thus, M takes a step towards presupposing consensus and co-operation. That this "taking for granted" might be a conscious strategy rather than a matter of fact is suggested that it is put to a test in the vague illocution in turn 5. The sequential organisation of this utterance creates a focus on the final comment it is going to be a great day of cooking, to which the final question tag refers, giving the addressee an opportunity to take up the subject. At the same time, F's consent to the premise of the comment, we gonna have to do all this today, is being put to a test. The vagueness is the function of the specific syntactic and semantic structure of the utterance:

STEP 1 - premise	`we gonna to have to do it all today`
STEP 2 - question tag of the premise	`aren't we`
STEP 3 - comment	`it's going to be a great day of cooking`
STEP 4 - question tag of the comment	`isn't it?`

Responding to the second question tag, i.e. commenting on the view that cooking a chicken dish would involve a lot of work, F would validate its presupposition, namely, that she is going to participate in "doing it all today". Instead, she questions the presupposition itself.

The following course of events shows that F's use of "we" in turn 4 is to be interpreted as being self-exclusive. Such use signals the identification attitude towards the group, in which the individual contribution of the speaker or the addressee is not necessarily at stake when the first person plural is used. (The same phenomenon is illustrated in the episode P3. PACKING SUITCASE, discussed earlier, from the Polish series, where the speaker offers the beneficiary assistance on the part of the group using the personal pronoun *my* "we" while showing no intention of participating in giving help.)

In turn 6 of E3. GREAT DAY OF COOKING, F makes clear that she interpreted M's "we" in turn 5 as including herself, rather than being similar to her own use of "we" in turn 4. She explicitly rejects the proposal by questioning the use of the personal pronoun, interpreted as including herself. In turn 7, M rejects F's interpretation of the pronoun in turn 6, justifying his use of the plural as a reference to "the team" (in a way that it was used by F in turn 4). F does not take this declaration at face value; advising M to `relax and chill out and let somebody else do it as well`, F implies that this is what she is going to do, and implicitly restates her rejection of the proposal. In response, M makes an assertion which avoids any specific personal reference (`just need to make sure that it gets done`). Similarly to the Polish adverbial *trzeba* (one should, one need), it underspecifies the illocutionary role of the utterance -- it may be interpreted as a justification of M's earlier act, or a restatement of the proposal.

A vagueness of illocutionary intention is used in this episode as a means of directive persuasion, and the positively polite presupposition of consensus on joint action is combined with the use of consultative devices that make it possible for the speaker to deny both the presupposition and the directive intention itself.

CONCLUSION: CONSULTATIVE SUPPORTIVE MOVES

The data at hand confirms the high value of consultative strategies based on the interrogative as a device typical for British English securing social acceptability of directive activities; at the same time, it shows that in a peer group context, consultative strategies tend to co-occur with positively polite, consensus-presupposing devices. The relationship between the two strategies varies. In some situations, consensus is actually presupposed and a negatively polite interrogative is used merely as a (negatively) polite signal of the speaker's unwillingness to impose on the addressee. In other cases, mixing both kinds of strategies (positively and negatively polite) takes the form of vagueness of communicative intention, and the presupposition of the addressee's action is expressed and disclaimed within a short stretch of interaction. These characteristics might relate to "uncertainty avoidance" as a basic descriptor of cultures in social psychology (Hofstede 1980); it might lead to confusion in cultures in which consultative and consensus-presupposing stances function as alternatives.

6.4.7. OVERPOLITENESS AS A STRATEGY OF DISTANCING

Routine formulae of conventional politesse can be applied in an inflated way to signal distancing as a means of hurting the hearer's positive face wants by accentuating negative face wants. The data below illustrate the respective uses of overpoliteness strategy in all three languages.

```
5-E1.
1 F Ron # can I just have a word with you please # if you don't mind
2 M yeah
3 F can I just tell you something # or just inform you # that # . when it
gets to the stage where its one o'clock in the afternoon # I don't have
to be quiet for anybody # yeah?
```

The utterance in turn 1 and the preface in turn 2 contain a series of negatively polite devices. Next to lexical devices such as the negatively polite IFID please and the minimiser just, lexical and syntactic devices are used to make the communication of the message contingent upon the addressee's preferences, such as the conditional (if you don't mind) and the repeated use of competence interrogative (can I just have a word with you/can I just tell you something). The unusual accumulation of devices of negative politeness signal social distancing amounting to the withdrawal of intimacy, and emphasises the negative face wants of the speaker expressed in the predicative content of the utterance by an apparent appeal to the negative face wants of the addressee.

The next data from G2 is a an excerpt from a longer dispute following F1's refusal to answer M1's question about the number of her past relationships, and her criticism of the inquiry as an act of excessive curiosity. Before, on the first day of the show, M1 tried to find out about the sexual orientation of other housemates and their current involvements.

47-G2.

6 F ja # aber das war schon am ersten Tag # wo wir uns angeguckt haben # wer- # wer ist hier gerade in einer Beziehung # und wer ist irgendwie . der Schwul # machst du das in deinem Privatleben auch? also ich mache es nicht so # . ich gehe nicht raus und sage nicht du # pass mal auf # bist du jetzt schwul

yes # but it was already on the first day # when we were looking at each other # who- # who is in a relationship at the moment # and who is like # the gay # do you do that in your private life too? # well I don't do it like that # I don't go out saying you # listen # are you gay

7 M genau # und dass meine ich damit # [du bist intolerant]#

exactly # this is what I mean # you are intolerant

8 F [nein # das ist unsensibel]

no # that is insensitive

9 M # du erzählst mir den ganzen Tag # wie du es machst

all day long you tell me # how you do things

10 F # nein # das ist unsensibel was du machst # . und das stößt [auch-]

 # no # it is insensitive what you are doing # and this strikes also-

11 M könntest du das auch zulassen # dass Leute auch eine andere Art haben zu leben als du?

could you also accept # that other people live a different way than you

12 F [abso- # absolut]

abso- # absolutely

13 M [wäre das möglich?]

would that be possible

F criticises M for transgressing the personal territory of others by asking indiscreet questions. In turns 7 and 9, M responds to F's reproach pointing to his negative face want of being able to act freely without being subjected to criticism, and accuses her of self-centredness and intolerance. In turn 10, F perpetuates the criticism of M, and M once more articulates his need and right to act freely, without being imposed upon by F in turns 11 and 13. The message is in accordance with the exaggerated attention paid to F's negative face wants. This is achieved by means of cumulated devices of negative politeness stressing that the addressee's compliance is not taken for granted, such as: a competence interrogative in turn 11, an epistemic modal expression in turn 13, and the repeated use of the subjunctive mood (Konjunktiv 2) in turns 11 and 13. At the same time, the general reference to "people" rather than himself in turn 11 expresses the assumption that F's behaviour represents a constant trait of her character rather than just a stance with respect to this particular incident involving M, and supports his earlier reproach of intolerance. The consultative formulation in turn 13 carries a sarcastic overtone. While introducing epistemic modality that is conventionally applied to express polite uncertainty about the addressee's will to comply with a directive, the utterance in (13) is also interpretable as alluding to the speaker's doubt about F's ability to comply. In other words, M puts in doubt F's ability to let others act in their own way, suggesting (rather than directly stating) that intolerance is a trait of F's personality. The accumulation of conventional devices of negative politeness correlates with the message concerning the speaker's own negative face wants. At the same time, it marks the speaker's sarcastic and critical attitude towards the addressee's lack of social competence in avoiding imposition, which is the principle of negative politeness.

In Polish, where a competence interrogative is used very rarely, its application becomes spectacular in the following interaction:

105-P3. F1, F2, F3, M1 and M2 are lying on their mattresses; the light is off.
(F1 and F2 crawl over to M1 and start caressing him, taking the quilt off of him.)
1 M1 Wiesior nie zaciskaj mi na moich udach # swojej-
FIRST NAME-MASCULINE-AUGMENTATIVE do not squeeze my thighs # with your-
(F1 stops caressing M1 and returns to her mattress)
2 M1 a możesz mnie nakryć kołdrą?
and can you cover me with the quilt?
(F1 covers M1 with the quilt; M1 does not move)
3 M1 ale porządnie
but properly
(F1 properly covers M1 with the quilt)

F1 and F2 initiate the interaction by a playful turn-on in which they play the role of women eager to fulfil M1's supposed sexual fantasies. M1, who is known as a man constantly in search of erotic adventures, strictly refuses to co-operate on the tease in turn 1. The refusal is addressed at F1 and enmity is expressed by the use of the augmentative and gender-switching, masculine form of the addressee's first name (*Wiesia->Wiesior;* the latter is not a really existing name). This "defemalising" device deranges F1's "feminine" behaviour, displayed in the caressing of M1, by disclaiming her female attractiveness. A further means applied to emphasise the speaker's negative face wants are the possessive pronouns *swojej* (your) and *moich* (my) in references to F1's and M1's bodies, that are used here to contrast M1 and F1. The exceptionality of this form cannot be rendered in English or German, where, other than in Polish, possessive pronouns are normally included in references to parts of the addressee's body. After F1 withdraws herself, in turn 2 M1 demands that F1 herself restores his initial state (F1 should put the quilt back over him), further emphasising an unwillingness to be in any way affected by F1's behaviour. The display of the speaker's negative face wants in the propositional content is accompanied by a negatively polite form of request unmodified by any means of positive politeness, very rare in the Polish data.

The exchanges above show that verbal expressions of negative politeness in the form of consultative devices in the interrogative are used as a signal of social distancing in all three languages. Negative politeness with respect to the addressee is used to signal the speaker's own negative face wants. The signal is adapted to the general preferences in interaction strategies of a given speech community by the number and the quality of negatively polite devices; that is, the use of negatively polite forms of expression is enhanced relative to their standard use.

7. SOCIAL AND INTERACTIVE ASPECTS OF DIRECTIVE ACTIVITIES: THE GROUP IN FOCUS

The following chapter focuses upon the group-oriented aspects of directive activities in the Big Brother houses, the interlingual similarities and interlingual contrasts in this respect. The interlingual comparison in this domain touches upon the relative values of individualisation and group bonds, and on the related topic of considerateness and involvement as strategies of verbal interaction in directive activities observable in the German, Polish and British Big Brother houses. Requestive utterances are analysed with a view to their implications for the notion of proper behaviour as displayed by different nationals in the Big Brother houses. The available material is approached from perspectives offered by interpretative sociolinguistics, spoken language analysis, ethnography of communication, and social psychology.

The analysis is based on all the available material, including the entire E3, P3 and G4 editions and some episodes from E1, E2 and G1 editions. Taking into account a full edition of the program in each language provides a broad perspective, showing the absence, occurrence, and recurrence of some types of verbal and non-verbal behaviour, and suggesting conclusions about their culture-specificity or otherwise.

The I/C issue is important in this discussion. My claim is that impositiveness and tentativeness in directives in the context analysed is related to I/C of the respective societies, in such a way that higher impositiveness corresponds to a stronger attachment to the collectivist perception. The claim relies on the premise that the preference for collectivism is higher among the Poles, as indicated by research in comparative social psychology (cf. chpt. 4.2). The premise was supported by indicators of I/C attitudes within the program itself, which will be pointed out prior to the discussion of directive activities. These indicators, which are related to the perception and maintenance of interpersonal distance, group solidarity, and group-orientation, include:

- aspects of program design,
- aspects of verbal and non-verbal behaviour of the housemates in particular houses,
- voices of people outside the Big Brother houses, such as the audience, the presenters, and the housemates' relatives.

Finally, some episodes containing directive activities will themselves provide an illustration of inter-cultural difference in I/C attitudes. At the same time, other episodes selected will

271

substantiate the link between impositiveness and group-orientation of directives in all three cultures under study.

7.1. THE PROGRAM DESIGN

I assume that just as the events which took place in the Big Brother house are expressions of national cultures, so are the conceptions of the various Big Brother Houses. I also assume that the "for sale" character of the program, in which evictions of unpopular participants by votes by all the housemates and the TV audience were applied to uphold the viewers' interest, amplified the distinctive features of the three cultures under consideration. In short, the commercial aspect promoted a design which offered good prospects of being rewarded, the reward for the designers being high viewing figures for the program, and the reward for particular housemates being their high personal acceptance by other housemates and the audience. It promoted a design, and behaviour resulting from this design, which were in line with the cultural logic of a given society, that is, which were in one way or another admissible, understandable and commendable within the frame of a given culture and subculture.

7.1.1. THE EXPOSURE OF FAMILIES AND FRIENDS

The different conceptions of the program in the three countries involved different degrees of exposure of the social backgrounds of the participants. While interviews with families and friends were frequently used in the Polish and German versions of the program, there were very few of them in the British version. The Polish and German housemates were shown against the background of their family ties and other social relationships, which were thus visibly conceived as being relevant information for the public. This aspect of the program's design can be interpreted either as confirming the high value of discretion and privacy in British society, or as reflecting a view of an individual which stresses personality and observable behaviour rather than social bonds as the central defining characteristics of a person.

Notwithstanding this, it should be noted that the family background of the housemates in E4 was sketched in short portraits of the housemates which were presented in the beginning of the program.

A childless single person was the preferred type of housemate in the German and English series, which made the program attractive to teenagers and unmarried adolescents by the potential it provided for sexual idolisation. In Poland, the ratio of married housemates and parents was notably higher than in the other two countries. The housemates were portrayed in their roles as children, mothers and fathers, competing for better futures for themselves and their relatives. As a result, unlike the other two countries, the audience of the Polish series was not confined to teenagers and adolescents. According to my observations, the series attracted viewers from all generations; and spectators of different ages, including persons two generations older than the housemates themselves, were interviewed by the TV team in the editorial part of the program.

7.1.2. BIG BROTHER BATTLE – GROUP STABILITY

The Polish and the third British series of Big Brother, as well as the fourth German series, were based on the concept of the "Big Brother Battle", distributed by the Dutch company Endemol B.V. This concept replaced the earlier, less eventful design. It introduced a contest for living standards as a new element into the game in order to increase the attraction of the spectacle, which had become rather monotonous and repetitive.

By the end of 2003, four series of Big Brother had been broadcast in the United Kingdom, four in Germany and three in Poland. The third Polish and the fourth German series of the program were created in line with the outline owned by Endemol B.V. In accordance with this outline, two teams, red and blue, fought "battles" against each other; and the individual performance of each team member on a task contributed to the fate of the whole group who were subsequently moved to the "poor" or the "rich" living area, depending on the success in combat, for the following several days or hours. This created an awareness of interdependence promoting the development of responsibility for others and mutual reliance. While competing individually for the final victory, the housemates are at the same time fighting daily for the group's sake. They are rewarded for their good performance by the group's gratitude and the perception of "their" group enjoying a certain collective well-being; and they risk punishment in the form of the group's disappointment for having performing badly on competitive tasks. The common fate is crucial to the emergence of identification (Reykowski 1994). Experiments in social psychology showed that mere assignment of people to antagonistic groups performing competitive tasks were sufficient to induce group solidarity within particular groups; these effects were enhanced when distinctive names and clothing were assigned to the competing groups (Brown 2000).

A comparison of the course of interaction in Polish editions P1 and P3, as well as German editions G2 and G4, suggests that the difference in design exerts an influence upon the perception of mutual responsibility of the housemates towards each other. Instances of assuming responsibility for the team or group in the "battle" editions in the context of directive activities will be discussed in sections 7.1.3. SOLIDARITY AND CONFLICTS OF CONSCIENCE, and 7.4.5. DIRECTIVES IN DECLARATIONS AND SYMBOLIC DISPLAYS OF SOLIDARITY.

Contrary to the original concept by Endemol B.V., there were no teams in the third British series. The weekly "combat" between the housemates for their standard of living (being on the losers' "poor side" or the winners' "rich side") was exclusively individual. Each person could become a member of the "rich side" as a result of his or her own performance on a task. The design prevented the formation of feelings of solidarity within each group of current winners and current losers because the configuration of both groups changed from one week to another, which minimised the opportunities for forming stable multilateral bonds. While the design does not prove anything about the strength of the interpersonal bonds in the British Big Brother house, these bonds were more based on choice and less group-oriented than in the other two groups: each housemate chose the persons with whom to interrelate. As mentioned before, though, the choice of the design does not reveal much about the program editors' evaluations concerning the preferences of their viewers, because it is likely to have been influenced by the occurrence of group combat in another reality TV series, "Survivor", broadcast at about the same time. For that reason, a meaningful comparison between the details of the respective "battle" designs can be made for Polish group P3 and German group G4 only.

In these two series, the "battles" were realised in slightly different ways, reflecting the production team's expectations concerning the audience's tastes and preferences. In both of them, there were two stable teams. However, in the German "battle" group, a re-shuffling of groups by moving one or two members from one team to the other was relatively frequent and occurred several times when a temporary lack of balance in the gender structure and the size of the groups occurred. In the Polish edition, it only happened once because there were only four participants left. The program's designers chose to find ways to adapt the combat to the unbalanced group structure, rather than stick to the balance at the cost of shifting loyalties. Presumably the popularity of the program would have suffered had a different policy been adopted. After the initial period, in which the groups were growing together, the constancy of the teams as "basic units" of action was taken for granted by viewers and housemates, and was strictly observed by the program's creators. In the German version, the teams were temporary: yesterday's allies were sometimes today's enemies. This promoted the perception of mutual support involved in the team combat as a matter of individual strategy for survival, in which each person profits individually by membership in a collective performance. The introduction of team mixing in G4 accorded with the attitude of the housemates in G4 towards the team identities, in particular seen in the reaction of team members in G4 in the fifth week of the competition to the news that they needed to, for the first time in the program, appoint one of their male team members to join the other team. Instrumental rather than integrative factors are named as a reason for dissatisfaction with this arrangement. Rather than express regret because of the bonds of friendship that had grown in the team, the team captain reacted by commenting that this was going to be a loss because both candidates are strong, capable players who contribute a lot to the team's success in the sporting competition. Hofstede (1980) found a correlation between his individualism score and the view of collective actions as a means to an end rather than an end in themselves. Similarly, Triandis (1988) views individual benefit as the engine of co-operation in individualist societies, whereas co-operation tends to be based on the ingroup's benefit and mutual duty in collectivist ones. In the German scheme, where loyalties change from one day to the next, striving for a group victory is about a pursuit of co-directional individual goals rather than about the team as a "basic unit of survival". At the same time, this scheme promotes the bonds within the greater ingroup consisting of all housemates that are not related to the competitive tasks. The design highlights the playful aspect of the competition and reduces the participants' emotional identification with just one of the two teams. There where the teams are not mixed, as in the Polish version, initial loyalties – even if they result from a configuration of the teams which from the perspective of the housemates are due to "mere chance" – are constant and promote stronger emotional bonds within the smaller ingroup. The housemates felt safe to profile their emotional bonds in accordance with this design, and verbalise them without running the risk of appearing superficial or two-faced when the next piece of luck forced them to join "the enemy's" formation.

To sum up, the German Big Brother Battle design, which included moving individuals from one side to the other, promoted the awareness that the participants constituted one group and that division into teams with antagonistic aims was purely accidental. Hence, both team bonds and the antagonism between the two teams are to be viewed as instrumental and temporary: the housemates must work hard in whatever team they happen to be a part of in order to reach their aims, shared by other members of their team. The attitude promoted in the participants by the Polish design is to make strong emotional associations with people with whom they have been united by coincidence, to develop strong feelings of team solidarity and loyalty, and to show themselves off by displaying these emotions: "feel with others and talk about it".

7.1.3. COLLECTIVISM AND CONFLICTS OF CONSCIENCE

An instance of the interaction of the program's design with I/C tendencies of the cultures under consideration is the emergence of conflicts of conscience. The program formula of Big Brother places its participants concurrently within two schemes which are out of step with each other: competition and developing interpersonal bonds. The manifestations of the competitive scheme are the different living conditions of the two teams in design B and C (editions P3, G4, E3), and the task faced by each housemate of eliminating other persons from the game by a weekly vote in spite of the reality and sincerity of the interpersonal bonds which arise in the Big Brother house. The three national groups manifest diverging attitudes towards both aspects of interpersonal combat.

The nominations in which one of the participants is being voted out of the house become at times a heavy burden for the housemates. While explicit confessions about the difficulty of nominating other housemates as potential candidates for leaving the house were missing in the British edition, a female housemate reacted emotionally to the pressure, weeping before she made her nomination. For the Polish housemates, this situation occasionally gives rise to the loyalty question, in which the rules of the program and the principles of friendship are viewed as divergent and necessitate a personal decision of which set to follow.

A facet of team bonds is the loyalty towards one's team members and its authenticity transgressing the frame of the program design. This is visible in particular in situations where this loyalty clashes with the loyalty and obedience owed by the housemates to the program's editors, in view of their voluntary agreement to respect the rules of the game and a written contract. An illustration of such a clash is the following scene from P3:

- After several weeks, one of the teams is given the task of nominating two members of their own team for eviction from the house by public vote, while the other team is allowed to vote for any two persons (members of one team or the other). This causes an "uprising" in which F1 and M (from the first team) declare that they are not going to vote against their friends, break the rules of the play and are themselves nominated for eviction. The program's editors must have realised the commercial value of the immense popularity which these two persons won among the public by the display of emotional bonding with their team; without actually specifying the reasons, they quickly gave the viewers an option to vote out a different person, which the viewers actually did.

In the scene, the program's editors utilised the integrative needs of team members in order to maximize the excitement by forcing them into an ethically repelling situation, and putting them under pressure that was only as exciting for the viewers as it was authentic for the housemates themselves. The scene illustrates how the display of collectivist predilections of the Polish participants was promoted by the team design. It also exemplifies Reykowski's (1999: 33) contention that in ingroups within collectivist cultures, "harmony within the group rather than effectivity on a task is the main criterion for structuring mutual relationships ... This is particularly significant with respect to tasks whose recipients are others ... It can lead to a situation where a "collective of suppliers" promotes harmony and good relationships among themselves at the cost of the clients, patients, pupils etc." (transl. HP). Rejecting competitive activity within the closest ingroup, the housemates rejected the obligations towards their employer Endemol-Neovision which they had accepted earlier. Miller and Bersoff (cited in Reykowski 1999: 27), comparing how conflicts between the norms of justice and personal bonds were solved by the Hindus and Americans, showed that the Hindus preferred loyalty to the norm resulting from personal relationships to the norm of justice. The results show that members of collectivist cultures (India favours collectivism, in contrast with the USA) manifest a much stronger tendency to define themselves in terms of group membership, and to define the group as "we" – a network of bonds; at the same time, the obligations towards their own group have for them a higher status than the obligations towards impersonal norms of justice. Within the ingroup, which can be based on bonds of family, culture (nationality, language, religion), region and friendship, the greatest importance is associated with internal harmony and support, and not with task fulfilment.

The scene illustrates the principle of the priority given to the ingroup loyalties over any tasks and obligations from outside the group, and demonstrates the collectivism of the Poles in the erception of social norms. It also shows that the team is viewed as an ingroup by the housemates involved. Asked to give reasons of her refusal to play by the rules, one of the rebellious housemates emotionally explains that the nomination would be a betrayal of "her" people. When Big Brother points out that the participants consented to play by the rules when subscribing to the game, the other rebel explains that he no longer likes the game because the game has become "unhealthy" (morbid): to się zrobiła niezdrowa zabawa. He explicitly uses the notion "solidarity", making a reproachful comment about the program's creators: oni nie wiedzą co to jest solidarność # komuna ich jeszcze nie nauczyła chyba ("they do not know what solidarity is # the commune did not teach them in its time")[122]. The word *komuna*, "commune", is a derogatory name of the communist regime which collapsed in 1989 when the speaker was about twenty years old. The comment refers not so much to brotherhood as the value proclaimed by the communist system, as to the solidarity which developed in reaction to the hardships of living in a totalitarian state, and which gave the name to the workers' union Solidarity, a major force in the abolition of the old regime. The relatives (mother, father, and wife) of the two "rebellious" housemates interviewed by the host of the program were asked whether they were proud of the decision made by their respective relative. The very fact that this question was asked shows that the reasoning behind the rule-breaking was perceived as rational by the program's editors, too, because "communication requires that speakers should base their interactions on validity claims that are acceptable to their fellows" (Agozino 2003: 104).

The rebels' parents interpreted the decision as a manifestation of loyalty to friends, group solidarity and high moral standards. Votes and interviews showed that the decision also gained audience approval and generated popularity for the "rebellious" housemates. In the same edition, another female housemate (F2) refused to nominate anybody explaining that she could not nominate friends, and that this was a decision of conscience. F2's mother, commenting on this event in an interview explained approvingly that her daughter "didn't want to nominate anybody because she regarded them as her nearest and dearest" (nie chciała nikogo nominować # ponieważ uważała że to są jej bliscy). In the final stage of the competition, two other housemates conspired and refused to vote, possibly believing that they would increase their popularity among the audience by such a display of solidarity and friendship. After they were "broken" by Big Brother and withdrew their decision, they both lost to the third candidate in the final audience vote.

This contrasts with the German cultural standard, described in the following way by social psychologist Sylvia Schroll-Machl (2003: 78-79):

> [Die] Verlässlichkeit wird nun nicht vorrangig dadurch erreicht, dass es Instanzen gibt, die von außen kontrollieren, sondern dass jeder an seinem Platz von sich aus das tut, was von ihm erwartet wird. »Deutsche machen vieles ohne ersichtlichen Zwang dazu«, sagen nichtdeutsche Beobachter. Der Handelnde hat nämlich gar nicht mehr das Gefühl, dass er Erwartungen anderer erfüllt, sondern es ist ihm selbstverständlich, das zu tun. Er hat sich im Prozess der Planung, der Strukturierung oder als er die Stelle antrat, damit bereits

---

[122] The translation of "jeszcze" as "in its time" follows the assumption that the line of thought was "we have been taught solidarity as early as by the commune, and they have not". The translation of "jeszcze" as "yet" would be absurd as it would presuppose that the "commune" still existed as the utterance was produced.

identifiziert. Das ist mit »internalisierter Kontrolle« gemeint: Durch Einsicht in die »Notwendigkeit« oder Optimalität bestimmter Regeln oder Verfahrensweisen kontrolliert sich ein Individuum weitgehend selbst. Es hält sich dabei entweder an vorgegebene Normen oder an selbst erstellte Pläne. Eine Person erlebt von innen gesehen diese Selbststeuerung weithin als persönliche Autonomie und Selbstbestimmung ... Weil hier Strukturen, Normen, »Objektives« internalisiert werden, besteht auch die deutsche Zuverlässigkeit gegenüber der Sache ... Die Beziehungen, die zu den beteiligten Personen existieren, beeinträchtigen oder fördern die gezeigte Gewissenhaftigkeit wenig ... man hat die Aufgabe zu erledigen. Und man will das auch, denn man findet die Sache im Prinzip gut, sonst wäre man nicht an dieser Stelle und nicht in diesem Job. Das Pflichtbewusstsein gilt somit in erster Linie den konkreten Vorgaben, die Loyalität der Firma, bei der man (gerade) arbeitet. Die Pflicht ist - zumindest beruflich - wichtiger als das Vergnügen: Ob jemand Lust hat oder nicht, ob er gerade von Problemen heimgesucht ist ... ob es ihm sehr viel Mühe abverlangt oder ... Spaß macht, spielt eine untergeordnete Rolle: Er hat die Selbstdisziplin aufzubringen, sein Bestes zugeben. Denn er hat Ja gesagt zu dieser Vereinbarung oder dieser Stelle und nun steht er in Pflicht und Verantwortung.[123]

Another potential ground for conflict of conscience is the different standards of living of the housemates in the "battle" set-up. The following scene from P3 showing the conflict of conscience faced by the "winners" in the battle concept is quoted here for two related reasons. Firstly, it shows the collectivist predilections of at least some Polish group members, in accordance with Reykowski's (1999) contention, discussed before, about

---

[123] "The reliability is achieved in the first place not through the existence of control from outside, but by everybody doing at their positions what is expected of them. >>The Germans do a lot without visible pressure<<, non-German observers say. The agent no longer has the impression of acting because of the expectations of others; rather, it is obvious to do what needs to be done. In the process of planning and structuring or already at the moment of entering a given position, he identified himself with it. This is meant with an >>internalised control<<: a person controls himself through understanding the >>necessity<< or optimality of certain rules or procedures. He orients himself after pre-existent rules or self-made plans. He experiences this from inside as personal autonomy and self-governance ... The internalisation of structures, norms, "objectives" constitutes the German reliability with respect to the thing ... The relationships towards persons involved do little to disturb or aid the reliability ... one has a task to fulfill. And one wants to do it, too, because one finds the thing good in principle, otherwise one would not be in this position and doing this job. The sense of duty is oriented first of all towards the task, loyalty towards the company for which one is currently working. The task is – at least in work-related contexts – more important than pleasure: whether one likes it or not, whether one has personal problems, whether it requires much effort or is fun is of secondary importance: one is to bring enough self-discipline to do one's best. Because one has said Yes to this agreement or this position and now one is bound to duty and responsibility." (transl. HP)

279

collectivists favouring unwritten obligations towards the current group at the expense of formal obligations (in this case, a written contract with the producer). Secondly, it shows plainly the link between social attitudes and the occurrence of directives, and contradicts the instrumental view of directives by showing how they emerge in response to the conceptualisation of the situation induced by the particular cultural logic of the interactants, in this case dictating to the winners a bad conscience towards the underprivileged.

106-P3. SHARING FOOD

M2, M3 and F1: winning team; M1, F2, F3 and F4: losing team. After the victory in the very first contest between the two teams, team blue are rewarded with a hot luxurious supper. The losing team, red, serve the food to the winning team, but are not allowed to join in.

1 M1 prosimy bardzo
help yourselves please
(simultaneous group speech)
2 F1 czerwoni # e # - boli was to bardzo?
team red # ei # is this very painful for you?
3 M1, F2 nie:
no
4 F3 nie absolutnie # jedzcie
not at all # eat-IMP-plural
5 F1 no to
well then
6 F4 [jedzcie]
eat-IMP-pl.
7 M1 [o czym ty mówisz w ogóle]
what are you talking about (conversational formula meaning: don't talk nonsense)
8 F3 <start laughing><ale jedzcie>
do eat-IMP-pl.
9 F1 <start laughing><jeszcze siłę mają>
they are strong in spite of it
(The following moves take place against a noisy background of simultaneous group speech. M1 and M2, both from the winning team, are sitting at the table next to each other together with the rest of their team.)
10 M3 to M2: --- co się buntujesz
why are you rioting

11 M2 to M3: nie to nie chodzi o bunt # tylko o jakiś moralny- # wiesz
no this is not about a riot # but something like a moral- # you know

12 F1 jedz # zjadaj normalnie jedz
eat-IMP-sing. # eat-IMP-sing. it off normally eat-IMP-sing.

13 M3 to M2: [bicie] żeś poczuł # no [---] to jest inna lekcja
you have sensed the beating # and this is a different lesson

...

14 M2 to M3:[---] ja tego dobrze nie przeczytałem [---] podpisałem [---]
I have not read through that exactly # I have signed it

...

15 M3 (decides to strike the fork into the food) a zresztą kurwa mać
well after all CURSE

16 F2 to M2: wsuwaj Bartek i nie marudź
eat-COLLOQUIAL FIRST NAME and don't grumble

17 M3 Bartas jedz
FIRST NAME eat

18 M1 (stops the gesture of striking the fork into the food) no Bartek # no nie: wiem # weź się bo się będziemy co pięć minut- # . to się dzielimy # grupa się dzieli
well FIRST NAME # well I don't know # now every five minutes we are going to- # well then we share # the group is going to share

In line 2, F1 from the winning team makes accepting the privilege of the luxurious supper contingent upon the emotions of the members of the losing team, who are reduced to watching the winners enjoying their meal:

2 F1 czerwoni # e # - boli was to bardzo?
red team # hey # is this very painful for you?

In the turns 4, 6, 7 and 8 members of the losing team insist politely that the winners should eat their meal; by implication, they see it as viable that the winners might feel bad about the situation and refrain from eating out of consideration for the losers. In the lines 10-13, M1 and M2 talk about M2's bad conscience and in line 14, M2 speaks about the rules of the contract with the producers of Big Brother, admitting that he has not read through them. The utterance implies that that M2 did not know or was not fully aware of what might be expected of him in the Big Brother house, and was taken by surprise by so much hardship.

While members of both teams try to persuade M2 to eat (turns 16 and 17), M2 inflicts his own bad conscience upon M1. Finally, under M2's pressure, M1 proposes that the winning team should make a group decision concerning whether the program's rules should be violated and the food shared with the "poor" team (turn 18).

Two Polish viewers who watched the scene were divided in their opinions: while one thought that M2 was sincere and found it difficult to eat a luxurious meal under the other team's jealous eyes, the other viewer thought that he may have been conscious of the popularity he would gain among the audience by a display of solidarity and moral uprightness. Both interpretations point towards a positive social evaluation of putting solidarity with peers above playing by the rules of the game.

Shortly after that, M1 was interviewed by Big Brother, who referred to the fact that M1 decided to eat the food rather than follow the other option, and required an explanation for the reasoning behind this. M1 explained that because he was ill and had been excluded from the competition for this reason, he decided to eat the food so that he could recover and become a useful member of his team. Even if it is legitimate to doubt the genuineness of this post-factum justification, the point is made: M1 finds it necessary to justify his "playing by the rules" of Big Brother by highlighting his allegiance to the team, and to play loyalty and "bad conscience" towards his team against loyalty and bad conscience towards the whole group.

In German "battle" edition G4, the sense of guilt and doubts about the propriety of the rules is explicitly expressed by two members of the team on the rich side. A male housemate does it repeatedly while reporting his emotions to Big Brother and the viewers in his daily "confessions", and while talking to his team members; among other things, he expresses regret for his achievement in a boxing match saying ich bin traurig, weil ich einen Freund geschlagen habe ("I am sad because I have beaten a friend"). A female housemate admits that it was extremely unpleasant to her to join in the luxurious meals while watching the other team having their poor supper. Both housemates who admitted remorse were non-native speakers of German and had migrated to Germany from the former Yugoslavia and the Ukraine as teenagers or young adults[124]. They think in a similar way as Polish housemates in the above-quoted scene. The same male housemate proposed not to take part in a combat in a discipline which he was good at, arguing that the other team, with its temporarily higher proportion of female contestants, had lost the sporting contest several times in a row and the

---

[124] According to Reykowski (1994), quoting Smolenska and Wieczorkowska (1990), different measures of collectivism and individualism in different nationals appear early in personal development; there was a strong difference between German and Polish subjects for the population aged 14-16.

chances should be balanced. The proposal met with a firm objection from several German members of his team, who commented on it among themselves as being outrageously unreasonable. They also attempted to change their Yugoslavian teammate's stance, pointing out in individual conversations that the rules were just and justified. Incidentally, the decision not to take part in the contest on exactly the same grounds was taken and, in absence of protests from any but one female housemate, was put into action by the strongest member of one of the teams in P3.

Another manifestation protest of solidarity with the underprivileged in G4 came from a Hungarian female housemate, who, while on the winning team, proposed repeatedly that her team should beg Big Brother to arrange a celebration of a birthday of a housemate on the "poor" side, which was rejected by her team members: they thought that it was not their business, and that Big Brother could not be influenced anyway.

While it does not share the Slavic background of Poland, Ukraine, and Yugoslavia, Hungary shares their recent membership of the East European block.

While the few scenes quoted above have in themselves only an anecdotal value, and cannot serve as a basis for any generalisations, Reykowski (1994, 1999) claims that the collectivist stance regarding some aspects of social life in Poland was associated with the state ideology, and that a shift from collective to more individualist attitudes took place after 1980, the year which marked the beginning of the decline of communism in Poland. Song Mei Lee-Wong (2000) concluded in her study that impositive formulations of directives had a higher social acceptability in PRC than among the speakers of Chinese in Singapore. She hypothesises that it might be due on the one hand to the Anglo-Saxon cultural influence on the social and linguistic perception of Singapore subjects, and on the other to the communist ethos of the PRC which might have played a considerable role in the formation or perseverance of linguistic habits and underlying social perceptions.

Rather than looking for the roots of collectivist attitudes in the ideology of the protective and totalitarian state, I propose to divorce the attitude towards the state and anonymous society at large from the attitude resulting from identification with the current group. Hofstede (1990) argues that collectivism is inversely correlated with national wealth; this suggests that it might not be the state communist ideology in itself but rather its oppressive methods and meagre economic results that, by making survival dependent on co-operation rather than compatible with competition, promoted the need for nurturing and collectivist attitudes.

7.2. ENTERING THE BIG BROTHER HOUSE

While watching the initial scenes from various versions of the program, my attention was attracted by differences in the behaviour of various nationals when they first met. I assume that they reflect culturally rooted assumptions about the level of intimacy appropriate between young people who meet for the very first time, knowing that they are going to have intensive contacts with each other enforced by living together. The entrance scenes available for comparison were those from series 1, 2 and 3 in German; series 3 and 4 in English; series 3 in Polish, and a short fragment of the entrance scenes from P1 showing the entrance of the first and the last couple out of six. I am highly indebted to Endemol Germany and Endemol-Neovision Poland for providing videotaped material.

The following brief presentation of the verbal and other indicators of the ease of the first contact and the strategies of approaching each other suggests how different stances on I/C may contribute to different shapes of these encounters, and provides a background for the following discussion of directive utterances which occurred in this context.

In order to avoid both presenting my subjective judgements as facts and a lenghty and meticulous description of what happened, I discussed the scenes with six respondents, one per gender and country[125]. A spontaneous comment was provided by each respondent after watching each scene, and after watching all scenes twice they had an opportunity to make comparative comments. After that they were asked specific comparative questions concerning openness, togetherness and nervous tension[126].

Asked a specific question regarding how they evaluate the extent to which the participants acted together as a group, all the viewers apart from the British male respondent agreed that the Poles in P3 behaved most like a group, in that they acted together and greeted the newcomers together as a group. The British male respondent selected both the British group in E3 and the Poles in P3 as showing most coordinated action. He pointed to the team spirit that developed among the male housemates in E3 already before the women's arrival, shown in the fact that several men performed consecutively the same action of walking to the top of the stair and carrying a woman's suitcase downstairs. All the respondents paid attention to the fact that the Poles greeted newcomers together doing the same things at the same time, and all but the German male respondent paid attention to the

---

[125] A much more detailed discussion of the outcomes of these interviews can be found in Pulaczewska 2006.
[126] P1 has not been included in this procedure because only a short fragment of the entrance sequence was broadcast and made available for analysis.

fact that they entered the house simultaneously as a group only after the last person arrived. The German female respondent used the notion of a "welcoming committee", which I had applied myself when describing the scene in my notes, to characterise the line built in the yard facing the newcomers and acting jointly to greet them by singing and cheering. Asked a specific question about the group consolidation, she said that the Polish group was the only one where there was definitely a group action, while the greetings exchanged in the other groups were on an individual point-to-point basis, even if the participants stood at times in a circle or a line as in G1, E3 and E4.

While in both Polish and British groups, all persons who had already entered the house are present during the entrance of every new housemate and focus their attention upon the newcomers, the German groups show a markedly different approach. Greetings and handshakes frequently took place in pairs or threes. All the German series shared a pattern of forming groups of two or three persons engaged in conversations, who temporarily didn't interfere with each other. The quick building of smaller subgroups in all the German scenes, observed by several respondents, suggested that the German participants might have found it easier to communicate with fewer numbers of individuals than with the group as a whole.

All but the German male respondent characterised the Poles as being most open and the British as being between the Poles and the German. The German male respondent redefined openness as having a real interest in each other and thought it was displayed in G1 and sporadically in the initial stages of the English entrance scenes in small group conversations (before they were joined by a larger number of newcomers arriving one by one), while superficial masks dominated most of the time everywhere else; in the Polish group, individuals hid behind the group ("*sie verstecken sich alle hinter der Gruppe*"), which was the opposite of showing one's real self.

While the German male respondent thought that it is natural to build small groups in order to really get to know one's interlocutors and it shows an authentic interest in each other, the male British respondent interpreted "splitting into groups" as a sign of tension and reserve and juxtaposed it with "*interacting with each other straight away*"; while the Polish male viewer commented approvingly that the Poles did not isolate themselves by launching into conversations as the German housemates did ("*nie było tak że ktoś się izoluje i sobie rozmawia*"). The German female respondent commented that she probably once viewed forming small subgroups as the most natural thing to do in similar circumstances but could not continue to hold this view because of her long-term experience of going out with a group of British friends and colleagues who managed to have conversations "with the whole table" rather than form conversations among two or three people.

As confirmed by the respondents' comments, all the German entry scenes were characterised by spatial dispersion, the building of small groups, and especially the immediate engagement in a conversation with people around, while not paying attention to those who were currently entering the building. In the remaining three groups, the focus of the encounter was upon the welcoming of the newcomers and the verbal interaction with the persons present was temporarily suppressed when a newcomer entered; this led to some amount of coordinated action in all these groups, while they differed on its amount and the speed of its development. My impression from the German scenes of the first encounter was that the scheme of a social encounter activated in all of them was such in which the care and interest shown to one's current interlocutor precludes the simultaneous display of the same care and interest to others. This relates to the issue of group-oriented interaction, because a group action makes it possible to simultaneously attend to many persons in a differentiated way: as those who are currently at the centre of attention, and as those who share an interest in the current "centre of attention" and cooperate in its display. The difference pertains also to a further differentiator of cultures proposed by Hall and Hall (1989) known as "monochronic" versus "polychronic" time. The notion concerns the approach to the chronological arrangement of activities acquired in the process of social maturation: while the monochronic time concept tends to promote successive attention and action, polychronic time promotes a split of attention and piece-by-piece completion of many simultaneous activities, in particular during social encounters involving several interlocutors, without perceiving them as being in conflict with each other. The German first encounter was organised on a person-to-person basis, and the interest in other group members was shown in a consecutive way, suggestive of the monochronic time concept observable as a norm of social behaviour in many everyday situations in the German social context, where diverging behaviour may cause irritation and be interpreted as a deficit in social skills. Conversely, the monochronic characteristics of the German first encounter were viewed as impolite and earned a pejorative comment by the polychronic Polish viewers, while the British respondents did not reveal judgements in their comments even if they noted the facts. Conceptually and geographically, monochronic time roughly correlates with high individualism (cf. Hall and Hall 1989 and Hofstede 1983), while Hall and Hall (1989) place the German culture on the upper extreme of the scale in monochronic time.

Another concept applicable in analysing the differentiated structure and perception of the encounters is Brown's (2000: 9) notion of the distinction between an interpersonal and a group encounter. In the former, people meet as unique individuals and in the latter, they act towards each other as representatives of a group towards members of the same or the other group or groups. An indicator of group behaviour is the uniformity of behaviour of group members, which "suggests that the participants appear to be interacting in terms of their group membership rather than their distinctive personal characteristics" (while one needs to remember that "the interpersonal/group distinction is based on a continuous dimension and is not an either/or dichotomy", ibid.).

The behaviour of the German housemates, coupled with the commentaries provided by the German observers, suggest that they tended to view encounters between peers in interpersonal rather than group terms to a higher degree than the other two groups. The building of smaller subgroups or pairs during the entrance scenes in all the German series, suggesting that they felt less at ease interacting with larger groups, points in the same direction as the higher degree of negative politeness displayed by the German speakers in directives addressed at multiple addressees compared to directives at individuals, as noted in the statistical analysis. It supports the assumption that the statistical difference was systematic, rather than being just a casual property of the sample.

The picture that emerges is that in the German groups, the level of intimacy and the tone of the interaction proper for a given social occasion depends crucially on the degree of personal acquaintance which determines how much common background is assumed. This hypothesis is supported by a decrease of negative politeness in favour-asking by the German speakers in the middle part of the program compared to its initial stage, which was not observed in the other groups. The communicative behaviour of the British and the Poles and the comments by native respondents seem to indicate a conception of common background in which it is to a larger extent co-constituted by the awareness of a shared past and future experience than by the duration of the acquaintance alone.

7.3. IDENTIFYING INTERDEPENDENCE AND AUTONOMY IN VERBAL INTERACTION

I assume that the tendency of Big Brother participants to manifest "high on involvement" or "high on considerateness" (Tannen 1984) interaction styles in general, and in directive activities in particular, is a function of their perception and interpretation of social relationships in the given situational context. This perception is influenced by the subjects' cultural background. The assumption to be defended in what follows is that a crucial factor in this influence is the degree of collectivism or individualism promoted by the interactants' culture-dependent social experience.

The following list enumerates some properties of interaction which I propose to regard as manifestations of the "high on involvement" interaction style with respect to directive activities in (in)group interaction, that is, most generally, devices reducing interpersonal distance[127] and maximising familiarity. In the context analysed, most facets of this interaction style are related to the group-orientation of the interactants' social attitudes. This reflects the fact that the reduction of distance between members of a small group takes place for a large part in the form of group integration rather than cultivation of separate dyadic, interpersonal relationships.

High frequency of directive activities. A mutual nurturing attitude of the ingroup members; the view that they are mutually responsible for acting toward the benefit of each other; the high legitimacy of requests to act in favour of other ingroup members; the expectation that advice and instructions will be accepted, and the promotion of group activities all result in a high frequency of directives.

Family metaphor in legitimating directive activities. In high-on-involvement and group-oriented interaction style, the ingroup can be metaphorically conceptualised as a family. The conceptualisation legitimises certain types of directive activities, in particular of a corrective and nurturing type with respect to other group members.

Blurred boundaries between advice and instruction. High-on-involvement style corresponds to nurturing attitudes between the ingroup members. As in other nurturing relationships, this results in many instructional directives being produced.

Blurred boundaries between request, demand and advice. In involvement situations, the boundary between actions that are in the interest of the addressee and those which are in the interest of the speaker becomes less clear; speakers treat the addressee's worries as their own, and solutions to the addressee's problems as solutions to problems affecting the speaker herself. Verbal insistence is used to change the addressee's temporary preferences. The distinction between the advice, request and demand, in the non-technical sense of these words, is blurred and the predicated action is implicitly or explicitly presented as beneficial to both the addressee(s) and the speaker.

Impositiveness of form. Directives are perceived as obviously legitimate by the speaker and are correspondingly realised by impositive head acts, such as imperatives and realisation declaratives, mitigated by positively polite modifiers.

Creativity in naming practices. Creating nicknames and derived (distorted) names corresponds to the perception of the right of in-group members to mutually influence each

---

[127] Or, to use another spatial metaphor conceptualising social experience in terms of physical experience, "lowering interpersonal boundaries" between people involved.

other, including influence on the name as a person's icon, and creates an insider language that reflects the possession of common ingroup history.

Frequent use of plural forms of address and plural self-reference. The addressees of directives are frequently groups; speakers conceive themselves as benefiting from the proposed action together with others and formulate the directives accordingly.

Directives for another group member's benefit. The nurturing and protective attitude of the ingroup members towards each other is accompanied by a high legitimacy of requests made in favour of other ingroup members.

Appeals for the display of bonds. Interpersonal bonds may be displayed by a symbolic joint action that must be called for and arranged.

Demands for personal information. In a high-on-considerateness context, the insistence on receiving personal information is viewed as being boorish; ingroup members feel free to emphasise explicitly their and everybody else's right to keep personal information private, and to openly articulate the opinion that certain interpersonal boundaries should not be transgressed. In contrast to this, in high-on-involvement contexts, group members expect to obtain personal information about each other and feel entitled to demand it.

Well-meant abuse. Offensive and critical behaviour can be used to express the desire to sustain and deepen the relationship with the addressee, and as a means to persuade the addressee to abandon actions reducing her bond with the group.

Requests for action against the recipient's will. Extreme manifestations of involvement and the assumption of joint responsibility for other group members are calls to act in ways viewed as being beneficial to the recipients of the action while opposed to their temporary preferences.

Joking directives. Directives that are not meant to be followed are used as humorous socialisers and "general interaction modifiers". In social psychology and interpretative sociolinguistics, humour is predominantly regarded as a means of expressing and enhancing group integration. Joking directives are based on the assumption of having a common background, that is, the assumption that the audience and the addressee will be able to recognise the lack of an actual directive intention although it is signalled by the utterance's syntactic form and propositional contents.

Teasing and practical jokes. A reduction of distance corresponds to a tolerance and the expectation of tolerance of humorous abuse; teasing and practical jokes are typically collective activities in which the actors collaborate against a single "victim".

Fake directives. The habit of verbal impositiveness, acquired in interactions abundant in impositively formulated directives, may give rise to (non-joking) utterances that resemble directives in that they are realised in imperative sentences, but are not really meant to result in the addressee's performance of an action, and are in fact comments on the current situation or declarations of intention.

Politeness as mainly a matter of non-verbal supportiveness. The main component of politeness in high-on-considerateness encounters is verbal mitigation; strong impositiveness is viewed as being boorish. In a high-on-involvement approach, a lesser significance is attached to verbal non-imposition and higher significance to being helpful.

Primacy of concern for group integrity over individual relationships. If a conflict occurs between group integrity and point-to-point relationships, the group may insist on individuals subordinating some aspects of their bilateral bonds to the interests of the whole group.

Gender-based subcategorisations. Gender-based use of "we", "you-PLURAL", and gender stereotyping corresponds to the focus upon group aspects of the social encounter, rather than its interpersonal aspects.

Joint performance of directives. Directives can be performed collectively, in a consecutive way (through repetition, paraphrase, completion) or simultaneously (choir chanting).

The observation that the high-on-involvement style, with its impositive verbal form of directives, occurs in all groups in situations particularly relevant to the maintenance of group ties lends support to the claim that group-orientation and the involvement attitude are closely related.

In what follows, I will examine selected occurrences of these elements in the data and indicate the properties of the context which promote their occurrence.

7.4. INTERACTIVE AND RHETORICAL CONTRIBUTIONS OF DIRECTIVE ACTIVITIES TO FORMING AND EXPRESSING SOCIAL RELATIONSHIPS

7.4.1. FIRST ENCOUNTER – FIRST DIRECTIVES

The following description of the very first directives uttered in each of the Big Brother houses during the entrance scenes, or immediately following exchanges, should be read against the background of the description of these scenes in the preceding section 7.2. Just as the first encounter in general exposes differences in social expectations, first directives reflect the spirit of the encounter and capture some characteristics of later interaction.

G1, G2 and G4. Two of the respondents in the interviews mentioned in the previous section noted that focusing interest upon the shared material environment was used as a strategy for initiating interaction specific to German first encounters. The following three scenes present the first directives uttered in the German series.

5-G1. Immediately after introducing themselves upon entering the house, F1, F2, F3 and F4 are on their way to the women's bedroom.

1 F1 to F2: guck mal # der Garten # ist doch total lustig # es sind die Hühner drin

look # the garden # it is quite funny # there are hens in it

2 F2 (laughs)

3 M <starts shouting from a distance>< --- >

4 F3 to M: <starts shouting from a distance><ja # du kannst auch mitkommen>

yes # you can come along too

48-G2. F1 and F2 are walking along the hallway after their brief introductions upon entering the house.

1 F1 Küche # schau # schau # schau

the kitchen # look # look # look

2 F1 guck ma

let's have a look

3 F2 genau

exactly

4 F1 ganz ruhig # wir nehmen das super relaxed

quite calm # we stay quite-COLLOQUIAL calm now

5 F2 das ist das Badezimmer

this is the bathroom

6 F1 das ist doch groß # ne?

but it is large # isn't it?

7 F2 sag mal # diese Dusche # wo ist das jetzt

say MITIGATING PARTICLE # this shower # now where is it

(F2 enters the shower and lets water run)

8 F1 Dusche ge:ht

the shower works

9 F2 ein Mikro unter der Dusche

a microphone-COLLOQUIAL under the shower

10 F1 ein Mikro # sie müssen es heiß machen

a microphone-COLLOQUIAL # they will make it hot

11 F2 wie geht die Tür zu

how does the door close

12 F1 (closing the shower door) na geht doch # guck mal

it does work # look MITIGATING PARTICLE

21-G4. The first pair enters the house. Prior to the start of the program, the press reported that the house was going to be divided into the "rich" living area and the "poor" area with straw beds.

1 F cool # (laughs) # . so # jetzt müssen wir gleich zum Stroh

right # now we must walk straight to the straw

2 M Klasse

great

3 F (moving along the floor) <start whisper><komm # guck mal>

come # look MITIGATING PARTICLE

4 M müssen wir gleich zum Stroh? wow # du weißt schon mehr . mehr als ich wohl

must-we walk straight to the straw? # wow # you seem to know more than I

5 F (pointing to a wardrobe with towels) hei # guck # wir müssen keine ^Handtücher mitbringen

hey # look # we don't need to bring any towels

(F and M walk through the house to the straw beds)

- In turns 5-G1/1, 48-G2/1, and 21-G4/1 comments on the material environment are being produced, and a personal relationship is introduced by an invitation to share an interest about an aspect of the surroundings. The speakers create a common background in a one-to-one encounter by offering comments about the current situation and the environment, and by inviting each other to share attitudes (turns 48-G2/4, 21-G4/1) and recognitions related to the environment (turns 48-G2/1, 48-G2/6, 48-G2/12, 48-G2/2, 21-G4/5) by means of imperatives of verbs of sensation and speech. The utterance in 5-G1/1 is morpho-syntactically marked as being directed to a single person even if the current group which is spatially close together consists of four persons. All three scenes realise a pattern of one-to-one interaction even when it is not enforced by the situation itself.
- In turn 5-G1/2, a joking directive not meant to be followed is being produced, which reduces distance by means of a teasing tone which will recur in the German

interaction. Even if M's utterance which provoked F3's response was not identifiable, two German respondents agreed that the response could not be meant seriously; they based their judgement on the incompatibility of the propositional contents with the actual situation (male and female speakers were expected to sleep separately) and the cultural acceptability of exchanging teases between men and women in informal encounters between young peers. The utterance is notable in so far as teasing practices, including fake directives meant to be interpreted as such, contribute considerably to the ice-breaking activities in the initial stages of the German editions.

P3 and P4. The characteristic features of the conversational style which will be perpetuated in Polish edition P3 are displayed within the first minute of their contact. The housemates arrive sliding down a slide dressed up in helmets and boxing-gloves which turn the mutual embraces into a somewhat clumsy action. The female housemate F, approached and hugged on her arrival down the slide by a male housemate, reacts by uttering a request:

107-P3. EMBRACE
F dajcie nam się porozbierać z tego
let-IMP-pl. us take this off

While uttering these words, the speaker is on her way towards embracing the addressee and embraces him immediately after that.
Several properties peculiar to a group-oriented and high-on-involvement style are displayed in this initiation.

- The interaction is initiated by producing a directive utterance. It anticipates the ease and high frequency with which directives will be produced in the Polish group.
- Its linguistic form is the imperative. It displays a tendency towards impositiveness in directives.
- As shown by the accompanying action, it is not meant to be followed but is produced as a mere socialiser, and a comment on an aspect of the situation.
- It is marked as being directed at a plural addressee by the use of 2nd plural, in a direct reaction to the behaviour of one of the addressees (the intended embrace), displaying the speaker's tendency to see herself as confronted by a group rather than by individuals, and to attribute actions by individuals to groups.

- The 1st plural personal pronoun is used in self-reference. This signalises that the speaker is speaking on behalf of the speaker and the person following her, assuming that what she says represents also her follower's wish and is in her follower's interest. It shows the speaker's tendency to view herself as facing her environment together with somebody else who shares her perceptions and attitudes. Pluralisation of the beneficiary constitutes a group-oriented politeness strategy which neutralises what otherwise could be interpreted as the speaker's hint at her negative face want (the desire not to be impeded), and a selfish rejection of a friendly gesture (the embrace). The "we" and the plural "you" are being construed on the spot.

The sequence concludes with a group-oriented proposal and the carrying out of the predicated action by the group:

108-P3.
1 (simultaneous speech)
2 F1 Jezus jak zimno # chodźmy do środka
Jesus it's terribly cold # let's get inside
3 (simultaneous speech)
3/1 F1 (to F2 who is the only person who still has the fancy gown on, and starts taking it off) chodź
come
3/2 F1 (takes F2 by the arm) # . chodź się tam przebierz # . tam
come change clothes there # over there
4 (simultaneous speech)
5 M1 wszyscy jesteśmy?
are we all there
6 (simultaneous speech)
(the group enters the building)

In turn 2, F1 expresses the expectation of a coordinated action: she expects all the participants to enter the building as a group. Since F2 is still busy undressing, F1 persuades her to postpone the individual action until the completion of the group action, and allows her no choice by physically interfering with her attempt to undress. M1 makes sure that nobody was left out, and the group enters the house.

Further directive activities occurring as functions of consolidating the group and breaking the ice follow immediately after the first encounter. The second scene, which directly follows the entrance scene, shows the female housemates gathered in the living room.

109-P3. F1, F2, F3, F4, F5, and F6 are sitting or standing in a circle in the living room.
1 F1 chce-my-jeść! [chce-my-jeść!]
we-want-to-eat
2 F2, F3 [chce-my-jeść!]
we-want-to-eat
3 F1, F2, F3 [chce-my-jeść! chce-my-jeść!]
we-want-to-eat # we-want-to-eat
4 F4 na jedzenie trzeba sobie zasłużyć
one must earn one's food
5 [(simultaneous speech)]
6 F3 ta:k
yes
7 [simultaneous speech]
8 F5 [będziemy ganiać]
we will be made to sweat (literally: we will run-IMPERFECT)
9 [(simultaneous speech)]
10 F2 właśnie
exactly
11 F3 zawody # no
contest # yes
12 F1 (clapps her hands) no to drogie panie # poruszamy tutaj jakieś takie
tema:ty fa:jne # trzeba się poznać
well dear ladies # we start talking about like cool themes # one-must get to know each other

In turn 1, F1 attempts to animate the current group to join in a collective performance of the demand addressed to the program production team, in the form of the routine formula chce-my-jeść whose formulaic properties include a chanting intonation and a group performance. Jointly chanting demands to a third party is a powerful means of creating group spirit. The attempt is partially successful since two or possibly three of the five group members present choose to join in. In turns 4 through 11, the participants refer to their shared future experience, anticipating that they will be forced to take part in a sporting competition before they get food. In turn 12, F1 proposes in factual terms (realisation declarative in present tense) a round of talk about "cool themes". F1 is evidently referring to the type of conversation known to the participants from the preceding two series of the program, where the housemates were made to discuss themes related mainly to ethical questions and interpersonal relationships. Clapping hands prior to uttering the directive is typical of teacher-pupil and parent-child contacts, and can only be interpreted here as a humorous "as-if" – a fake sign of F1 assuming authority. F addresses all persons present at the same time, and faces them as a group, acting as a teacher in a teacher-class interaction. This contextualisation cue marks the proposal as not being meant seriously. It is not intended to be followed but is meant to create a common background by pointing to the shared knowledge about the conventions of the program, and by anticipating a shared experience: it is not expected that the women will start having serious discussions out of the blue. At the same time, F1 refers to the current situation and speaks of the necessity to get to know each other using a deontic predicate. It is a recurring feature of the early stages of the Polish edition that the participants expect a general readiness to talk about intimate themes, and that they speak about getting to know each other in terms of a social obligation.

7-P1. The housemates, including M1, M2 and M3, have gathered in the living room shortly after the arrival of the last couple. M2 is walking through the room.
1 (simultaneous speech)
2 M1 to M2: ^daj jakąś zapalniczkę # bo on chce palić   BEGGING INTONATION
bring a lighter # because he wants to smoke

M1 utilises the integrative function of requests made for the sake of another group member, triggering a small favour paid by M2 to the beneficiary M3. He attends simultaneously to M3 as the beneficiary of the predicated action, and to M2 as its actor, and construes a situation in which the needs of a group member are responded to by a co-operative action of two people. At the same time, using begging intonation as a mitigating device, M1 construes himself and M3 as a unit whose needs M2 is expected to respond to. M1 construes a group plane of interaction by placing himself at the intersection of two (dyadic) units, i.e., people expressing a need and people responding to the need of the other. In what follows, I will refer to directives of this type as "diagonal".

E3 and E4. In E4 and E3, no directives occurred in the greeting sequence. The large amount of simultaneous speech occurring in the early stage of the encounter did not allow me to idenfity with certainty the occurrence of the first directive speech acts in E4; the exchange in 10-E4 below refers to one of the earliest intelligible ones.

296

93-E3. The interaction takes place immediately after greeting the last newcomer. The speaker is male, and the addressees are all the female housemates. In turn 4, the speaker, M2, points to the door of the less comfortable of two unlabelled bedrooms. M2 and other male participants are aware of the differences between the two bedrooms.

1 (simultaneous speech)
2 M1 shall we show you around?
3 (simultaneous speech)
(the group walk towards the bedrooms, M2 points to the door of the "poor" bedroom)
4 M2 this is the girls' bedroom # this is the number two
5 (simultaneous speech)
(the women walk into "poor" bedroom 2)

Further consequences of the scene will be discussed in the following section. Here, it is sufficient to remark that it anticipates several recurrent properties of interaction in the British programs:

- A proposal is being made, anticipating a high frequency with which proposals will be made in this and both British groups in the early part of the program.
- It is put into a tentative formulation that makes it dependent on the addressee's acceptance.
- The female and male subgroups are being distinguished as points of reference by the use of "we" and "you" in turn 2, as well as by the trick itself.
- A practical joke is being played which paves the way towards reducing interpersonal distance.

The reference to the distinction between the male and female sub-groups also occurs early (after the first half-hour of the encounter) in E4:

10-E4. Men and women are having an argument about whether the toilet seat should be left up or down.
1 M let's have a national debate # right now # the toilet seat stays where it is
(simultaneous talk)
2 M please pay attention to the men's rules

In turn 1, M makes a joking proposal referring to the debate among the housemates as a "national debate", thus placing the interaction in the Big Brother house on a larger group plane, as an event representing the entire British nation. The debate itself is built around a piece of gender stereotyping (different toilet habits of men and women). In turn 2, M makes a request directed at the female part of the population on behalf of the male part, for whom he is (jokingly) speaking as a representative.

According to Brown (2000), gender stereotyping is a typical component of group encounters, where people conceive themselves as representatives of groups, rather than interpersonal ones. The uniformity of behaviour, discussed earlier as an indicator of a group-oriented concept of a social situation, may take the form of social stereotyping, gender stereotyping being one of its current forms:

> Take, for instance, an interaction between just two people who happen to belong to different social categories (e.g. a man and a woman). Is this encounter an interpersonal one because just two people are involved or is it a group-based interaction because of the category difference? ... what would be needed before we could characterize this situation would be a close study of the content of the interaction between them. If it appeared by word and gesture that the participants were orientating towards each other in a relatively predictable and sex-stereotypic fashion then this would indicate an instance of group behaviour. In the absence of this, the idiosyncratic nature of the interaction would suggest a more interpersonal encounter ... (Brown 2000: 9).

While gender stereotyping indicates self-concept of the interaction participants as members of different groups, I assume that it does not preclude the possibility that the participants perceive themselves at the same time as members of the same superordinate group. On the contrary, the group-oriented perspective on self and other promotes the "identification" attitude in general. Taking a group-oriented perspective on the current interaction facilitates sub-grouping of the participants by differentiated roles or status difference. In other words, the conception of a group as a "we" encourages rather than precludes the perception of self and others as participants in further "we"-formations, as it encourages viewing people in terms of their social similarities rather than their unique characteristics. I propose to view gender stereotyping in a group context as a facet of group-orientation, and a contribution to the perception of its participants as a group – composed of gender subgroups – rather than an aggregate of persons. Thus, it plays an integrative role not only internally for each of the two gender camps but also for the larger group as a whole. Gender stereotyping fosters group integration not only because it facilitates the adoption of an identification perspective ("we"-think) in general, but also because it is based on gender-sensitive rules of conduct we acquire when growing up, regulating some aspects of interaction between men and women. The evidence of sharing the knowledge of these rules confirms the common background of the people involved in the interaction. It also gives each participant a ready-made recipe of how to behave towards others in a socially appropriate way, and promotes social closeness by diminishing the "unknown" component of interaction, that is, the necessity to get to know other people personally in their idiosyncrasies in order to be able to interact with them in adequate ways. As with any stereotyping, gender stereotyping increases the feeling of safety of interaction. In contrast, however, to some other, phobic kinds of stereotyping, gender stereotypes are mutually known, free of serious antipathies and largely agreed upon, so that in the context given they help group members to overcome the initial distance, and promote a fast development of social closeness.

To sum up, the ice-breaking role of directives could be observed in all three languages but the observation suggests that particular strategies were culture-specific. Among the Germans, directives occurred mainly in calls for interpersonal sharing of perceptions of the environment. Humorous gender grouping and stereotyping formed the context in which they occurred among the British[128]. The Poles produced directives which involved many people at the same time (as actors and beneficiaries), and presented the speaker as having needs shared with others. Of these three strategies, the first one is more strongly affiliated with the interpersonal dimension of the interaction and the latter two with its group dimension.

7.4.2. HOW TO CLAIM A BED IN THE BIG BROTHER HOUSE

The following scenes have been selected as illustrations of conversational styles occurring in particular language groups because they take place in very similar situational contexts. At the same time, secondary contextual differences provide coverage of issues such as group construal, gender bonds, responsibility towards external beneficiaries and the influence of these social constructs upon both the occurrence and the linguistic form of directives.

The scenes transcribed below take place in slightly different set-ups:

G1. ENTERING THE WOMEN'S BEDROOM, E4. ENTERING THE WOMEN'S BEDROOM, G1. ENTERING THE MEN'S BEDROOM and E4. ENTERING THE MEN'S BEDROOM – the female and male subgroups sleep in separate bedrooms which have been assigned to them in advance.

---

[128] Humorous gender stereotyping may be present in 5-G1, involving cross-gender teasing; the amount of stereotyping cannot be assessed because of the difficulty interpreting the male participant's speech..

E3. ENTERING BEDROOMS – the male and female subgroups are also going to share separate bedrooms, but the two bedrooms have not been assigned to the groups in advance, a condition that paves the way for group negotiation.

P3. ENTERING THE RICH BEDROOM 1 and P3. ENTERING THE RICH BEDROOM 2 – mixed groups consisting of both male and female housemates are going to share bedrooms appointed to them.

P3. ENTERING THE POOR BEDROOM 1, P3. ENTERING THE POOR BEDROOM 2, P3. ENTERING THE POOR BEDROOM 3 and G4. ENTERING THE POOR BEDROOM – groups of male and female housemates enter unfurnished rooms where they are going to sleep on the floor or on straw.

G4. TALKING ABOUT THE RICH BEDROOM does not take place in the bedroom but in another room, and the arrangement is only verbally negotiated, without corresponding action.

P3. OFFERING NEIGHBOURHOOD 1, P3. OFFERING NEIGHBOURHOOD 2, G4. OFFERING NEIGHBOURHOOD and E3. OFFERING NEIGHBOURHOOD – one of the housemates suggests to another that he or she should occupy a bed or place next to his or her own bed.

7.4.2.1. CONSIDERATENESS: THE OTHER AND I

6-G1. ENTERING THE WOMEN'S BEDROOM

F1, F2, F3, and F4 enter the bedroom. F1 walks a few steps and puts her bag on a bed. F2 who follows her was just about to put her bag on the same bed.

1 F2 bleibst du da?

are you taking this spot here?

2 F1 ist egal

all the same

3 F2 mir ist auch egal

it is all the same to me too

4 F1 ich gehe auch dahin # ich gehe da # okay?

I will also go over there # I am going over there # okay?

(F1 moves her bag to another bed)

5 F1 ich gehe da # okay # ist ganz gut

I am going over there # okay # it is fine

6 (F3 and F4 laugh)

7 F1 ist alles gut
it is all right
8 F2 wir können immer tauschen (smiling)
we can always swap
9 F1 kein Problem
no problem

The scene takes place a short time after the interlocutor's first encounter. The exchange results from the conflicting preferences of F1 and F2 for the same bed. F2 has been surprised by F1 who put her bag on the bed of F2's choice. In turn 1, F2 declares her preference for the same bed in a negatively polite manner by a mild hint, inquiring about F1's intention which has been unambiguously manifested a second before by F1's action. In the situational context given, F2's utterance implies that she is interested in occupying the same bed; it is the most plausible and situationally relevant interpretation, and this is how the utterance is actually interpreted by F1. In turn 2, F1 disclaims her preference for the bed, and F2 withdraws her indirect request in turn 3. Rather than taking this response at face value, F1 enhances the plausibility of her earlier declaration by proclaiming, in a realisation declarative, her readiness to move to a different bed, followed by a question tag, a signal of consultative strategy:

4 F2 ich gehe auch dahin # ich gehe da # okay?
I will also go over there # I am going over there # okay?

Having met with no objection, F2 carries out the declared action and comments on it reassuringly, saying:

5 F1 ich gehe da # okay # ist ganz gut
I am going there # okay # it is fine

In uttering (5), F1 is making it clear that she has not interpreted the situation as harmful to her in any way, be it by material disadvantage or by suffering a face threat. The group contributes to releasing any potential tension by laughter. In turn 6, F1 again reassures F2 that everything is fine and that there are no ill feelings. F2 offers to swap beds in the future in a competence declarative, leaving it open and up to F1 as to whether the switch will actually take place:

9 F2 wir können immer tauschen (smiling)
we can always swap

F2 reacts to it with a conversational formula kein Problem, offered also in response to apologies and thanks. Thus, she is both re-iterating her satisfaction with the solution and recognising F1's offer as an appreciative response to her own behaviour. Consideration is shown on both sides for the preferences of the interlocutor, visible in the appearance of disclaimers of own preferences and redressive action, behavioural and verbal, by both parties. Both F1 and F2 show unwilling to impose upon their interlocutor and to carry out their initial intentions. On-record directives do not occur.

7-G1. ENTERING THE MEN'S BEDROOM
M1, M2, M3 and M4 move into the men's bedroom.
1 M1 gibt es besondere Wünsche # wo jemand schlafen will?
are there any special wishes # where someone wants to sleep?
2 M2 ja # Bettnässer schläft ganz oben # ne?
yes # bed-wetter sleeps on the top # right?
3 M3 meinst du?
do you think so?
4 M4 hehehe
hehehe
5 M3 aber
but
6 M1 (stretches his hand to M3) Thomas
FIRST NAME
(M1 and M4 shake hands)
7 M4 nimmt es mir bitte nicht übel # ich muss öfter mal nachfragen
don't blame me please # I need to go quite often
8 Mx ^ja ja
yes yes
9 M3 ja ich auch
yes me too
(M3 leaves; M1, M2 and M4 stay in the room)
10 M1 habt ihr etwas dagegen wenn ich- (points to a bed)
to you mind if I-

11 M2 haben nichts dagegen
we don't mind

The considerateness strategy is shown at the very beginning by by M1's polite inquiry about the addressee's preferences concerning the sleeping arrangement. M2 reacts in a positively polite manner producing a paradoxical joke in a realisation declarative, referring to an imaginary "Bettnässer" and proposing an unreasonable solution with a potentially catastrophic outcome. M3 receives the joke po-faced, and M4 shows appreciative through laughter. M4 takes up the theme introduced jokingly by M1 by a polite apology for his future "bad habits" which could be_disturbing to the addresses. Mx (not identifiable) reacts by an affirmative particle that functions as an acceptance of apology; the repetition functions as emphasis and assures M4 that his misbehaviour is not only excusable but also something likely to occur, and as such not to be criticised. M3 further excuses M4 by declaring that he, too, suffers from the same problem. In turn 10, M1 reintroduces the subject of sleeping arrangements and declares his preference non-verbally by pointing to the bed of his choice, while inquiring in a negatively polite manner whether this is going to clash with the others' preferences. M1 declares his specific preference in turn 10 only after he has made sure, by means of his earlier interrogation in turn 1, that nobody else has declared interest in the same bed. M2 responds on behalf of the group, displaying a sign of the interdependence-based approach to the situation.

In this exchange, too, negative politeness and the consideration for the others' territory are predominant. Anything which might provide a potential for conflict is disarmed. On-record directives do not occur. The final claim for a particular bed by M1, amounting to a request for the others making a different choice, is realised indirectly by means of interrogation, making sure that no clashes of interest exist or might result from this act.

11-E4. ENTERING THE MEN'S BEDROOM
M1, M2, M3 and M4 enter the men's bedroom.
1 M1 it's not bad # eh
2 M2 this is swish # boys
3 M3 you want that one # do you
4 M4 ah ah I'll have # is everybody happy if I take this one?

The same strategy is applied by M3 and M4 as in the preceding scenes, G1. ENTERING THE WOMEN'S BEDROOM and G1. ENTERING THE MEN'S BEDROOM. While a joint background is created by comments in turns 1 and 2, where the speakers are sharing their impressions with the rest of the group, expressions of preference for one or another bed are framed into interrogation about the interlocutor' preferences in the following two turns. On-record directives do not occur.

A contrary strategy is exemplified by turn 2 in the following interaction in E4, which takes place within the female group of five on entering a bedroom where there is one double bed and four single ones.

12-E4. ENTERING THE WOMEN'S BEDROOM FEMALE
F1, F2, F3, F4 and F5 enter the women's bedroom.
1 F1 oh my God
2 F2 I'm having the big one
3 F3 (looking round the room) oh # I like this (referring to the room not a bed)
4 F4 I'm not fast # I will have a small one
5 F5 I take it # this one is mine then (sits on the remaining vacant bed)

The reaction of F4 in turn 4 is a comment upon F2 directly claiming the best bed in the turn 2, and has an accusatory overtone: F4 agrees to have a smaller bed while she suggests that it is an act of resignation and that she would also like to have the big bed, but was too slow in claiming it for herself. F4's reaction shows that the immediacy and directness with which F2 claimed the privilege of the big bed for herself in the same gender group was prominent enough to be worth a comment. Later in the series, one of the female housemates nominated F2 for eviction from the house on the grounds of her having claimed the big bed for herself. F2, a minority native speaker of English, was also simultaneously nominated for eviction on first impression by all the other housemates, who believed she did not fit in with the group because of her outspoken and uninhibited style of interaction.

All four scenes above involve an individual negotiation of the sleeping arrangement. In all but the (consequential) last one, the individual negotiation finds a correlation in negative politeness strategy, based on attentiveness directed towards non-interference with the other's wishes and intentions. A very different stance is taken by the interlocutors in the following scenes from British edition B3 and Polish edition P3.

7.4.2.2. IMPOSITIVENESS: THEM AND US – CLAIMING RIGHTS IN MIXED GENDER GROUPS

The scene discussed below comes from the beginning of the third British series and is a continuation of E3. FIRST DIRECTIVE quoted in section 7.4.1. The negotiation is framed into the separation of the negotiating parties into two gender camps, pre-established by the program's creators. Group negotiation replaces individual negotiation; the local "Schicksalgemeinschaft" within two gender groups changes claims for one's own benefit into claims for the benefit of the whole group, including the speaker. In this scene, the female housemates, led by a minority native speaker, F1, claim a more comfortable sleeping room in ways that are on par with the directness of the Polish women in the Polish scene that will be discussed later. The forms chosen contrast sharply with preferences shown in asking for one's individual benefit above, where the negatively polite interrogative was the preferred form and unmodified impositives were exceptions.

94-E3. ENTERING BEDROOMS

The last female housemate has entered and finished shaking hands with the rest of the group in the central area. It is known to the housemates that there are separate bedrooms for men and women. The men arrived before the women, and had some time to look around. The suitcases of all the housemates are standing in the central area.

1 M1 to F1, F2, F3, F5 and F5: shall we show you around?

2 (simultaneous speech)

(The group walks towards the bedroom doors. M2 points to the door of the "poor" bedroom.)

3 M2 this is the girls' bedroom # this is the number two

4 (simultaneous speech)

(The women walk into the "poor" bedroom. The women talk simultaneously entering the bedroom while M1, M2 and M3 stay silent behind the door. M3 laughs silently and appreciatively pats M2 on the back, unobserved by the women. After the women disappeared behind the bedroom door, the men laugh silently and M1 moves his arms in a sprinter-like manner in a gesture expressing suppressed joy. The men run away from the door.)

(F1 leaves the "poor" bedroom, approaches M1)

5 (simultaneous speech of women in the "poor" bedroom)

6 F1 to M1: (smiling) where are you sleeping? # _ where are you sleeping?

7 (simultaneous speech)

editorial cut

(M3 and M4 enter the "rich" bedroom and occupy two beds)

8 M3 ---

(M5, M1 and M2 enter)

9 M5 oh that's nice # they've been told that this is the lads' room

10 M3, M4 (laugh)

```
11 M5 I think we've got to wait # surely they will tell us or the girls
will
```
(F1 and F2 enter the "rich" bedroom)
```
12 (simultaneous speech)
13 F2 oh # no # why
14 F1 that's too much # I'm having not bad bed # . oh I don't care # what
anyone says right # I'm having no arguments (F1 lies down on the double bed)
15 (simultaneous speech)
16 F2 [Big Brother # this is our room # .. this is our room]
```
(F3 and F2 place themselves on the beds next to F1)
```
17 F3 [---] haven't sorted their room yet # ha ha ha
18 M5 what do you reckon lads
19 M2 yeah # we are getting thrown out
21 M3 yeah
22 F1 to M2, M3 and M5: go there # you should be all right with that
23 F2 this is our room
```
(F2 gets upon a bed and jumps several times, laughing)
```
24 F3 to F1: our room is so much better than theirs
```
(M2 approaches F1)
(F1 smiles, looking at M2, and clings to her bed as though she were afraid that he wants to claim it)
```
25 (simultaneous speech)
```
(all housemates walk out of the "rich" bedroom)
```
26 F2 who's taking the double bed
```

The construction of the gender-based grouping already takes place in the first line of this interaction, where M1 construes the plural "you" and the "we" along the gender boundary by the corresponding use of the pronouns:

```
1 M1 to F1, F2, F3, F5 and F5: shall we show you around?
```

By their use of the personal pronouns "you" and "we", and their treatment as obvious and self-explanatory, M1 maintains male and female "sub-group" identities that have already been introduced by the conditions set by the program's creators, who let all male housemates enter the house prior to the female ones. The use of the pronouns is based on the fact that it is the male members of the group who now have "expertise" of the house and may serve as guides to the female housemates.

Typical for the spirit of the British programs, a practical joke is being played here, immediately following the first meeting of the housemates. The female housemates are deceived into occupying the poorer of the two bedrooms. Male solidarity is displayed in a joking collaboration against the women, and generates non-verbal gestures of solidarity such as M2 patting M1 on the back as a sign of appreciation for the successful deception. That the men treat it as a joke (possibly with the exception of M5, as suggested by his utterance in turn 11), and anticipate that things may not end up that way, is visible in the fact that they do not take their suitcases with them into the "good" bedroom but leave them outside in the hall.

The women react by claiming their traditional privilege of comfort. The reaction is modified by non-verbal signs of non-aggression such as smiles and laughter, but on the verbal plane the attack upon the women's privileges is taken and fought back seriously, leading to the production of requestive speech acts. In demanding that the men move to the other room, F1 and F2 use a speaker-centred strong hint and the imperative:

14 F1 that's too much # I'm having not bad bed # . oh I don't care # what anyone says right # I'm having no arguments

17 F3 --- haven't sorted their room yet # ha ha ha

22 F1 to M2, M3 and M5: go there # you should be all right with that
23 F2 this is our room

In turn 17, F3 "drops a remark" based on the presupposition that the "rich" bedroom belongs to the women. The utterance functions as a "strong hint" in which F3 presupposes an arrangement she prefers, that is, presents the possession of the better room as unquestionable, and implies the men should leave. The directive intention and the intentionality of letting the men "overhear" the remark are signalled by emphatic laughter, whose intentionality is contextualised by the rhythmical and over-articulated production of laugh particles in absence of genuine laughing. The sarcasm of the remark functions as a positively polite modifier; it is intended that the men recognise the remark as an intentional "shameless joke", "witzige Unverschämtheit" (Kotthoff 1998).

The gender difference puts in force its own rules, based on the rules of social conduct which prescribe chivalrous behaviour for men and legitimise the claims of the women. The scene shows how the awareness of membership in a group is reflected in the verbal behaviour in directives, pushing the form towards more impositiveness in situations where claims are being made on behalf of a group including oneself rather than for individual benefits. I interpret this as a sign that the impositive style in directives reflects not just nationality per se but, more essentially, the degree to which the claims are perceived as legitimised by the rules of social conduct, referring not to individuals alone, but to the frame of socially and situationally rooted bonds and alliances, such as the gender bond. The highly impositive style of the above quoted utterances seems to reflect an awareness of a group right; by claiming comfort for herself, each woman is also claiming it for other female housemates. The scene displays male and female ingroup solidarities, as well as a presupposition of consensus about the values and standards of behaviour, in the impositive directives directed towards the men by the female group. Four native speakers who watched the scenes judged it utterly unlikely that any of the women involved would claim a better room for herself only, that is, if the rooms were single and each of them individually were the only beneficiary involved, using an impositive verbal form like in the scene above. Significantly, in turn 26, F2 switches to a negatively polite interrogative ("giving options") when introducing the topic of bed distribution in the "rich" room within the female group (who's taking the double bed). The utterance in 26 shows that F2 regarded the preceding negotiation between men and women as a collective act whereby an individual occupying one or another bed (the double bed was occupied by F1) didn't mean making a claim for this particular bed. Rather, F2 viewed the negotiations as a means to the collective end, and assumed that after this end was achieved, the situation could be or needed to be renegotiated among the women on an individual basis.

Three native speakers, one male and two females, interviewed about this scene thought that although the men were prepared to leave and not be bothered by it, they might have kept the room if they had not been made to leave; the fourth female viewer thought that they would have given the room up in any case. The male respondent thought that if the women did not realise at once that they were occupying a worse room, the men would have told them anyway. All respondents thought that men would not have insisted on staying in the better room as soon as it was claimed by the women, and all confirmed that the event was a practical joke. For the two female and two male German respondents it seemed obvious that the men really intended to stay in the better room. The third male respondent took the spontaneous affirmative answer back on reflection and thought that the men would eventually propose a more democratic solution, such as throwing a coin or turn-taking, of their own will. The same respondent failed to realise that the utterances in 18-21 signalled the women were successful in getting the men to leave, and did not know who was going to sleep in the better room after it was vacated by both the men and women[129], which indicates that he did not take the actual outcome of the negotiation for granted. The other male German respondent thought that after a couple of days the men might become more prepared to reject the women's claim, while they were probably more polite and prone to make concessions at the start when the interpersonal distance was greater. He found it interesting to see that the women managed to push their claim through ("*es ist interessant, dass die Mädchen es schaffen, dort zu bleiben*"). All the German respondents thought that the outcome of the negotiation was uncertain, as the men could as well have insisted on staying in the better room, while one of them reckoned that that the men did not really mind leaving the better room because they could more easily put up with less comfortable leaving conditions, and because they were already satisfied by the successful joke which was actually more important than successfully claiming the better room. All the German observers and two of the British respondents thought that a different group of women might have put up with the situation and stayed in the worse room; the reaction depended on their personalities. The remaining two British respondents thought that it was quite unlikely that the women would have stayed in the worse room knowing that it was worse. The four Polish respondents thought that the behaviour of the male housemates was meant as a joke, that the men would have left the better room anyway, that any serious attempt by them to stay there would be a breech of social norms, and that no group of women would put up with occupying the worse room. The difference between the German and the Polish respondents in answers to questions about the men's actual intention to stay in the better room, the possibility of a different outcome of the negotiation, and the possibility that a group of women would not have made the demand for the better room were statistically significant[130]. To sum up, while the German respondents tended to experience the directive activities of women in this scene as framed in a real clash of goals, most remaining respondents, including all the Poles, experienced it as merely fulfilling the inevitable based

---

[129] This could not be due to deficient acoustic reception or semantic interpretation of the verbal clues as the transcript was read to all non-native speakers to ensure understanding. All non-native respondents were highly proficient students of English or used English as their only language in long-term intimate relationships.

[130] Question 1: df=1, chi^2 = 4.8; p<0.05; question 2: df=1, chi^2 = 8.0; p<0.005; question 3: df=1, chi^2 = 8.0; p<0.005.

on a cultural script. This suggests a lesser degree of gender stereotyping in the perception of this scene among the German viewers and a more interpersonal conception of the situation.

7.4.2.3. INVOLVEMENT: BE FRIENDLY AND IMPOSE – THE CASE OF THE POLISH

The following interaction shows a mixture of the contextual features of the preceding scenes. On the one hand, the negotiation of sleeping arrangements takes place individually. On the other, the group consists of men and women, so that the gender aspect may influence individual behaviour by differentiated, gender-based legitimizations of claims, offers, and proposals made within the scene. Like the preceding ones, the scene takes place on the first day of the program. In the transcript below, two parallel conversations are distinguished by separate turn counts and by moving one of them to the right hand column.

110-P3.ENTERING THE RICH BEDROOM 1

The team that has just won the competition enters the luxurious bedroom, as ordained by Big Brother. M2, M3 and M4 won a boxing match against the other team who will have to sleep in the "poor" bedroom. The walls of the rich bedroom are padded with pink fabric.

1A M1 to M4: to ty to zrobiłeś # popatrz
it's you who did it # look

> (F1 enters the room and walks up to a bed)
> 1B F1 ja chcę to
> *I want this one*

2A M1 to M4: dzisiaj zrobiłeś demolkę # [chodź zobacz jak] tu jest
today you have given a beating # come and see what it is like in here

> 2B F2 [gdzie śpimy]
> *where do we sleep*
> 3B M2 ale bajera
> *wow*
> 4B F1 [albo nie # ja chcę to] (turns to the other bed and picks up a cushy pillow)
> *or no # I want this one*

3A M3 [przecież to jest pokój] dla Mariolek
but this is plainly a room for Mariolas-FEMALE FIRST NAME PLURAL
4A (simultaneous speech)

5B F1 albo nie # ja chcę to (turns back to the bed she chose before and throws the pillow back to the bed she picked it from)
or no # I want this one
6B F3 [ja od ściany] # bo ja się-
I'm next to the wall # because I-
7B M3 no to [ja chcę to] (sits down on the bed vacated by F1)
then I want this one
8B F3 ja się się gdzieś muszę przytulić # o # proszę bardzo (walks to a bed in the corner)
I must nestle against something # o # here you are

5A M1 wiecie co wam powiem #
you know what I will tell you
6A (simultaneous speech)

9B F2 ja tu # . ty tu? (to F1, pointing to a bed next to hers)
me here # you here ?
10B F1 no (nods)
yeah
11B M2 to M3: no wskakuj między laski # [bożeś kawaler] # no
well jump between the girls # as you are a bachelor # yeah

7A M1 e # chłopaki # ... słuchajcie # ja myślę od razu taka jedna rzecz
eh # boys # listen # I am immediately thinking about one thing
8A M2: no
yeah

12B F1 to M3: albo nie ja tu chcę # (picks up a cushy pillow lying on the bed on which M3 is sitting)
mogę ja tu?
or no # I want here # can I be here?

9A M1 że jak oni będą na przykład spać w gorszych warunkach # to my
pójdziemy --- # a dziewczyny przyjdą tu
that when they for example will sleep in worse conditions # then we will go --- # and the girls will come here

311

13B M3 no ^dobra # no (stands up from the bed he is sitting on and turns to sit down on the bed vacated by F1)
well okay # good
14B F2 to ja chcę tu (points to the bed vacated by F1 and occupied now by M3)
then I want to be here
(M3 walks to another bed)

10A M4 nie wolno
it is not allowed
11A F3 nie pozwolą #[proponowaliśmy już]
they will not allow that # we have proposed that already
12A M4 [nie ma takiego ---]
there is no such ---

Tannen (1984: 110) makes a point about "the strategy of involvement" saying:

> Throughout the Thanksgiving dinner, our conversational behaviour shows that Peter and Steve and I operate on the assumptions that if someone wants to say something, s/he will find the time to say it. By this system, the burden of the speaker is not to make room for others to speak nor to ascertain whether others want to hear one's comments. Rather, the conversationalist's burden is to maintain a show of rapport by offering comments. (87) ...The "high-involvement strategists" showed a high tolerance for noise and diffuse topics as opposed to silence. All these devices operated to give the conversation its 'frenetic' tone, and to establish among us a sense of a rapport and successful communication (95) ... Peter verbalised one aspect of the high-involvement strategy that has been discussed: the expectation that, having something to say, speakers will say it. It is not the burden of the interlocutor to make it comfortable and convenient for others to express their ideas, but rather to be free and spontaneous with reactions.

While Tannen's observations refer to "conversations" in the classical sense, her remarks can be generalised to apply to the field of directive activities. Conversationalists applying a high-on-involvement style seem to "care about themselves" rather than offer room for others' contributions, led by the assumption that everybody will be able to fulfil his or her needs by pursuing the same strategy. In the same vain, preferences are expressed forcefully when it comes to making directives within an ingroup in the high-on-involvement

312

style, and the resulting frenetic tone of the interaction establishes a sense of rapport and successful co-operation.

All three female housemates execute their right to choose first by making lively and direct claims for a bed of their choice. F1 changes her mind several times and contributes significantly to the "frenetic" tone of the scene. Her indecision can be interpreted as an expression of enthusiasm about the luxurious standards in the "rich" bedroom: by claiming one bed after another, F1 is also showing that she likes them all and is appreciative about being able to choose among several tempting alternatives. In turn 12B, she makes M1 get up and vacate a bed which she allowed him to have after a period of indecision. As this is the third time that F1 causes M1 to move, and involves him being physically removed from the place he is occupying, the situation poses a relatively high face threat to M1, and she pays tribute to his negative face wants by reformulating her initial impositive utterance as a request for permission:

12B F1 to M3: albo nie ja tu chcę # mogę ja tu?
or no I want here # can I be here?

M3's permission amounts to his fulfilling the request by moving to another bed, from which he is banned again by F2 in turn 14B. M3 responds to the negative politeness of F1's utterance in 12B by saying no ^dobra # no ("well okay # good") with a distinguished high rise-fall intonation. In making assents, this intonation pattern is a carrier of a precisely identifiable recurrent "meaning" in the relationship space. It expresses not only the a lack of objections to a proposition (or assertion), but also communicates that insistence, be it begging or impositive, is pointless because the current speaker has absolutely no intention of refusing.

Previously, M3 adopted the plain assertive tone introduced by the women in turn 7B by claiming a particular bed after F1 had vacated it:

7B M3 no to [ja chcę to] (sits down on the bed vacated by F1)
then I want this one

but is far from actually showing any preferences and eventually takes what F1 and F2 left for him, illustrating the the workings of a premise analogical to Tannen's (1984: 87) description of the attitude underlying the conversationalist involvement strategy: "My message in conversation is the excitement and exuberance ... It is not my intention to hog the floor. I fully expect that others will talk over me."

While all three female group members in the scene above exercise their customary right to choose first, the male group members assert themselves in other ways. M1 commands M3 to "jump between the girls" (occupy the bed between F1 and F2), explaining that M3 is a bachelor and implying that it is proper for a bachelor to sleep between women while it might not be appropriate for the rest of the men (including himself), who are married:

11B M2 to M3: no wskakuj między laski # bożeś kawaler # no
well jump between the girls-colloquial # as you are a bachelor # yeah

In commanding M3, M2 seems to be anticipating what M3 might like doing, and acts and acts in such a way as to facilitate M3's decision to carry this out. The attentiveness of M2 is directed not towards non-interference with the others' territory, but, rather, towards an active facilitation of the addressee's decision by guessing his preferences and imposing on him to act to his own advantage. At the same time, M1 proposes to the male group members to give up their privileges to the women from the other group:

9A M1 [że jak oni będą] na przykład spać w gorszych warunkach # to my pójdziemy --- # a dziewczyny przyjdą tu
that when they for example will sleep in worse conditions # then we will go --- # and the girls will come here

Involvement and positive politeness, that is, the presupposition of consensus, are central to the linguistic behaviour in this scene. Claims for a particular bed are made in a self-assertive and emphatic tone, even where there is no intention of insisting on the choice declared (as shown in 7B). Besides, directives are being produced which are directed towards the benefit of either the addressee himself (11B), or an external beneficiary (7A), and are articulated in an impositive verbal form.

These properties of interaction, including its linguistic form, recur in the next scene, which shows the other team moving into the rich bedroom two days later.

111-P3. ENTERING THE RICH BEDROOM 2.
M1, M2, F1, F2, F3 and F4 enter the "rich" bedroom.

1 M1 no już czuję że się zaraz stąd będziemy stąd wynosili # w sumie ładnie # . dobra to już widzę # . swoje wyrko

well I already feel that we will march out of here after a short while # pretty in general # well I see it already # my bed-COLLOQUIAL

(M1 walks up to a bed in the corner)

(F1 sits on the bed of her choice)

(F2 sits on the bed of her choice)

(M3 enters)

(F2 sits on the bed of her choice)

(F3 goes up to the bed next to F4)

(M2 picks up a pillow from a free bed)

2 M3 (to M1 who is situated next to the bed of his choice in the other corner of the room): Pablo (points to a bed situated a distance away from M1 and close to himself)

Pablo-CREATIVE DISTORTION[131]

3 M1 to M3: tam?

there?

4 M1 (to F1, F3, F4; F1 and F4 are occupying the beds next to the bed of his choice, and F3 is standing close to him) chcecie Mirki?

do you girls-COLLOQUIAL want?

5 F3 ´no

yeah

6 M3 (to F4, who cuddled with him last night and is sitting on a bed next to the one he chose) --- spać tu w środku tutaj

--- sleep-INF in the middle here

(M1 walks towards M3)

In turn 1, M1 declares a preference for a particular bed by saying "już widzę swoje łóżko", "I see my bed already". A declaration of possession of an object can be a joking way to claim this object for oneself, and not only in Polish, as shown by its occurrence in a British episode:

2-E2. F1, F2 and M are unpacking a gift of cosmetics from Big Brother.

(M looks into the basket of presents)

---

[131] The Italian version of the Polish *Paweł*.

M non-strip bronzer? that I think is mine

Clearly, such emphatic possessive declarations communicate satisfaction and strong appreciation of the object in one's possession.

During the following couple of seconds, other housemates enter and place themselves on the beds of their choice. M3 ignores M1's declaration of preference in turn 1, assuming, quite in accordance with the involvement strategy described above, that declarations of intention are not to be taken too seriously as they can be overridden by an equally vigorous declaration of contrary intention by another speaker. M3 wants M1 to occupy a bed next to him. He produces a directive by addressing M1 in a creatively distorted Spanish version of his name and by pointing to the bed that he wants M1 to occupy. The term of address accompanying the directive gesture expresses intimacy and closeness. The appeal to M1 to occupy a bed close to his own is a declaration of togetherness, in which M3 takes it for granted that M1 wants the same as M3, that is, to tighten the bonds to M3 by sleeping next to him. M1 responds with an interrogative tam? ("there?"), showing consensus with M3 concerning M3's right to make a choice for him. At the same time, M1 notices that F1 and F4 occupy the beds next to the bed of his choice, and that F3 is standing close to him, possibly aspiring to the same bed. Rather than ask F3, who is the only one who has not yet placed herself on any bed, whether she would like to have "his" bed, he produces an interrogative in the plural. He directs the check of preferences to all three women in his vicinity, that is, as well as to F3, to F1 and F4, who are already sitting on their beds. M1 believes that the three women might want to sleep next to each other, and articulates his perception of the interaction in terms of the encounter of two gender "camps". F4 (rather than F3) confirms this and M1 starts walking towards M3. In the meantime, M3 seems to have produced a directive to F2, with whom he was cuddling the night before, concerning which bed she should, or might want to, sleep on – unfortunately, the actual form of his utterance is not recognisable.

The scene reflects a spirit of involvement and group-orientation, reflected both in the housemates' impositive claims making plain their own preferences and in the construction of "we" and plural "you". M1 firmly assumes that nobody else will aspire to the bed of his choice and declares it to be his, making a strong claim which expresses his satisfaction with the present arrangement. M3 overrides M1's declaration and presupposes that M3 has the same preferences as he does, taking it for granted that M1 is willing to sleep next to him, and that it will be more important to him than adhering to his first choice. M1 perceives a group of three female housemates as the proper addressee for his offer to vacate a bed in the form of a preference check, in a situation where a different, more interpersonal logic of social encounter might dictate that he address only one of the persons present (F3), because the other two have already chosen their beds.

During this scene, the action taking place in the other "poor" room is partly audible to the TV audience. The utterances which could be transcribed are those of one housemate only (M4). His female interlocutor's (or interlocutors') responses were hardly audible and their wording could not be identified.

```
112-P3. ENTERING THE POOR BEDROOM 1
```
Voices over (coming from the other, "poor" bedroom)
```
1 M4 kobiety śpią od y: drzwi
```
women sleep at the e:rm next to the door
```
2 Fx ---
3 M4 nie
```
no
```
4 Fx ---
5 M4 nie mieszaj porządku
```
don't mix up the order
```
6 Fx ---
7 M4 Biedronka no nie możesz tam spać # nie możesz tu
```
Ladybird-NICKNAME you can't sleep there # you can't here
```
8 F1 ---
9 M4 ^nie mo:żesz          BEGGING INTONATION
```
you can't

Even if the female part of the exchange is missing, the general traits of the impositive conversational style can be clearly observed in M4's verbal behaviour. He attempts to impose a particular sleeping arrangement upon other team members, turning it into a rule that the women should sleep next to each other on one side of the room. His proposal apparently meets with objections on the part of at least one female interlocutor, and M4 appeals to her not to "mix up the order" in a bare imperative:

```
5 M4 nie mieszaj porządku
```
don't mix up the order

M4 is married and, knowing his wife will be watching the TV show, does not want her to get jealous. Two days before, he referred to the relationship between the sleeping arrangement and the people's marital status when his group were locating themselves in the "rich" bedroom:

```
110-P3. ENTERING THE RICH BEDROOM 1
10B M2 to M3: no wskakuj między laski # [bożeś kawaler # no]
```
well jump between the girls # as you are a bachelor # yeah

Another situation in which M1 produces directive utterances which are motivated by thoughts of his wife's sense of decency is described in section 6.2.4. In view of this repeated behaviour, M4 appears here to be acting as a guardian of proper group conduct rather than insisting on his own preferences.

While M4's initial "matter of fact" declarative

```
1 M4 kobiety śpią od y: drzwi
```
women sleep at the e:rm next to the door

presupposes consensus and compliance of the addressees, the responses of the addressees (or one of them) show that there is a clash of preferences. In what follows, M1 declares, obviously in response to a noncompliant behaviour by one of the female housemates, that she cannot sleep in the spot she had chosen:

```
7 M4 Biedronka # no nie możesz tam spać # nie możesz tu
```
Ladybird EMPHATIC PARTICLE you can't sleep there # you can't here

The repetition of the inhibitive in turn 9, following a not identifiable response made by F1, is mitigated by the begging intonation that makes it obvious that M4 is not trying to exert authority but, rather, appealing to his interlocutor's goodwill. This is the only negatively polite aspect which occurred in M1's contribution to the exchange, and it occurred only after his interlocutor's repeated objection (be it verbal or behavioural) showed a conflict of preferences between him and the former. Besides, a non-impositive positively polite modification was used in the appeal, the nickname "Ladybird" with which the speaker signalled intimacy, confidence, and lack of bad feelings towards the non-compliant addressee.

7.4.2.4. DE-GENDERING OF NEGOTIATION: GROUP VERSUS INTERPERSONAL PERSPECTIVE

The following exchange comes from German edition G4, realised in design B ("Big Brother battle"), as was the Polish exchange above. The interlocutors are members of one team who have won a competition and are about to move into the "rich" bedroom.

22-G4. TALKING ABOUT THE RICH BEDROOM
M1, F1 and F2 are in the bathroom to the "rich" bedroom, talking about the different kinds of beds: a pair of double beds and a pair of single beds.
1 F1 Jungs wo wollt ihr denn
boys where do you want to be
2 M1 ihr dürft die großen haben # ist ja selbstverständlich
you may have the large ones # it is EMPHATIC-PARTICLE obvious
3 F1 ne # mir ist es wurscht # kann auch auf dem kleinen # wer bedeckt sich dann viel
no # I don't care # I can also have a small one # who covers themselves a lot
4 F2 ich
me

M1 is the only male housemate present. In turn 1, F1 refers to male and female sub-group identities, addressing the single addressee (M1) through the use of a term of address in the plural, Jungs "boys", followed by an interrogative with a verb in 2nd plural. While talking to a single addressee, F1 makes it plain that she addresses him as a representative of his gender group, and implicitly suggests that the sleeping arrangement should be established according to gender-based groupings. F1's form of address implies that she takes it for granted that the two men will sleep next to each other as will the two women. In negotiating the sleeping arrangement with M1 as a representative of "the boys" rather than with F2, F1 presupposes that F2 will sleep next to her. At the same time, she applies the considerateness strategy in dealing with the addressee as a representative of "you-plural", and starts the negotiations by means of a preference check. This is an approach contrary to the involvement strategy in which "everybody cares for himself", counting firmly on everybody else doing the same within the limits set by common rules of conduct. This scene contrasts with the behaviour of female housemates in the Polish group in the analogous situation, where the excitement about and the satisfaction with the luxurious living conditions are expressed by explicit and forceful claims being made for the bed of one's choice.

M1, who is Swiss, seems to interpret F1's initial contribution as an indirect claim for the more comfortable pair of beds on behalf of herself and F2. M1 reacts to F1's gender-based subcategorisation by referring to gender-stereotyped rules of conduct as the underlying source of his offer. He perpetuates F1's gender-based use of the pronoun ihr (you-plural), and offers the female group more comfortable beds in a negatively polite competence declarative, continuing F1's strategy of non-imposition and offering a choice. The use of the modal "dürfen" marks it as permission, and does not contain any impositive element. Instead, it signalises the offering of an option, which the addressees may make a use of according to their own preference:

2 M1 ihr dürft die großen haben # ist ja selbstverständlich
you may have the large ones # it is PARTICLE obvious

In reaction to M1's offer, F1 distances herself from the gendered group perspective which she has herself introduced through her earlier reference. In turn 3, in which she declares that she has no preference, the togetherness of F1 and F2 (membership in a gender group) is not evoked, and any self-evident privileges are denied. F1 proposes to replace the gender-based principle (women sleep on large beds and men on narrower ones) by an individual one: big beds should be occupied by people who need a lot of space while sleeping, independent of gender. This is implied through F1's interrogation of the addressees' sleeping habits. This time, F1's formulation includes F2 as an addressee, rather than a person represented by F1:

3 F1 ne # mir ist es wurscht # kann auch auf dem kleinen # wer bedeckt sich dann viel
no # I don't care # I can also be on the small one # who covers themselves a lot

In turn 4, F2, a minority native speaker of German, reacts in a self-assertive way, admitting the habit of "covering herself a lot", and, by implication, claiming a wide bed for herself.

Although the concept of the team naturally falling apart into two sub-groups along the boundary of gender is clearly invoked, it is rejected again by one of the potential beneficiaries when she receives a signal that this might have been interpreted as claiming a group privilege of comfort, and an individual, gender-free difference is pushed into the foreground instead. F1 occupies a narrow bed and one of her male housemates has a larger one. In the English and Polish scenes quoted earlier, negotiations of group benefit and the more or less explicit appeals to the male obligation of courteous behaviour correlate with the occurrence and impositive style of women's directives. In the exchange currently under discussion, the eventual refutation of the principle of group benefit legitimizing a privilege through gender finds a correlation in considerateness being the main strategy applied in turns 1 and 3.

7.4.2.5. OFFERING CLOSENESS: THE STRATEGIES

The scene quoted above, P3. ENTERING THE RICH BEDROOM 2, involves a sequence in which a male housemate appoints his male mate a bed next to his by means of non-verbal communication, seeking spatial and social closeness to the addressee, signalling that he perceives their relationship as being intimate, and presupposing co-directionality of the addressee's desires and preferences with his own. The scenes below further illustrate two different interaction strategies available to the speakers when they declare interest in tightening social bonds with the addressee by means of proposing a "neighbourhood" in the bedroom.

G3. ENTERING THE POOR BEDROOM

M1 and M2's team just lost a contest and were moved to the "poor" bedroom, whose floor is covered with smelly straw to sleep on.

1 M1 so eine Scheiße ei # .. o:h # .. fuck
such shit ei # o:h # fuck
(M1 throws a knapsack upon one of the mattresses lying on the floor)
2 M2 es ist aber echt # ich finde es hat aber was # hihi # . bist du
hier? (points to a mattress) ich schlafe hier (points to the neighbouring mattress)
it is really # but I find this is somehow good # hihi # are you taking this spot? I will sleep here
3 M1 ist mir scheißegal # hier liegt überall Scheiße # glaube ich
I don't care # here there is shit lying everywhere # I think

M1 is applying a high-on-involvement strategy producing a strongly-emotionalised expression of opinion intensified by cursing and interjections. After M1's pejorative comment on the living conditions in the poor area in turn 1, in turn 2, M2 seems to be indirectly suggesting that M2 might occupy a place next to his. M1 does not respond to what might be a mild hint that M2 would like to tighten his bond with M1; instead, he continues to comment expressively on the situation and to express his dissatisfaction. The hint turned out to be too mild to catch on (since M1 and M2 are applying incompatible rhetoric).

An offer of closeness occurs in E3, in a scene where F1 proposes to F2 to occupy a bed next to hers:

95-E3. OFFERING NEIGHBOURHOOD
F1, F2 and M1 enter the bedroom.
(F1 sits down on a bed)
1 F1 to F2: Joan # you can go here (pointing to a bed next to hers)

F1 does not leave any doubt about her directive intention, and F2 complies. Although the utterance expresses the intention clearly, it is realised by a means of conventional indirectness; F1 expresses her belief that F2 might want to sleep next to her, but signals politely that she does not take it for granted and shows her respect for F2's freedom of choice. This strategy contrasts strongly with the gestural-vocative directive used by M1 in turn 2 of scene 111-P3 which was discussed above.

7.4.2.6. CHOOSING BEDS: A SUMMARY

To sum up, the following tendencies occurred in particular languages, providing a potential guideline for the analysis of inter-cultural difference:

In German, negatively polite strategies are used in negotiations both in mixed and homogenous gender groups; a gendered, i.e. group perspective is offered in a mixed group, but it is eventually withdrawn and replaced by the interpersonal perspective.

In English, the gendered perspective is offered in negotiations involving male and female groups, and co-occurs with the use of positively polite formulations of directives. Negative politeness occurs in negotiations within the same gender group; the user of impositive forms receives a negative social evaluation and is perceived as a trespasser of the rules of proper conduct.

In Polish, in mixed groups negotiations take a gendered character; men and women are perceived as groups. Forceful claims are being produced, independent from the producer's gender; their impositive linguistic form substantiates their perception as highly legitimate by the producers. People tend to guide actions of others "for their own good", "for mutual benefit" or as guardians of proper conduct.

Most generally, gendered negotiations correspond to the tendency to use positively polite forms of directives and non-gendered (interpersonal) negotiations correspond to the tendency to use negatively polite ones. This substantiates the relationship between the speakers' group-based perspective and their estimation of the legitimacy of claims and expectations.

7.4.3. PACKING THE SUITCASE: DIFFERENT CULTURES, DIFFERENT SPEECH ACTS?

The discussion below is concerned with some culture-specific courses of interaction including, or centred on, "altruistic" requests, where the only beneficiary is neither the speaker nor the hearer, and demonstrates some intercultural contrasts as well as similarities. The scenes have been selected so as to involve similar themes and analogous contexts; a full commensurability of themes and contexts could not be achieved or expected in natural interaction.

The following two interactions result alike from the announcement of a group member's eviction from the Big Brother house. Some of the remaining housemates offer to help the evicted persons pack their belongings.

In the Polish scene, which takes place on the third day of the program, F3 (the evicted) has just taken part in a contest and is wearing wet clothes. She is given five minutes to leave the Big Brother house. The housemates have been together for two days. For the sake of brevity, some passages have been omitted.

115-P3.

1 BB ...[i przygotuj się do wyjścia] # _ masz pięć minut na opuszczenie domu Wielkiego Brata
and prepare to leave # you have got five minutes to leave the Big Brother house

2 [simultaneous speech]

(F3 goes to the bedroom)

3 M1 Wielki Bracie # to dopiero pierwszy raz # do trze- do dwóch razy sztuka
Big Brother # this was just for the first time # all good things are thr- are twos (meaning: let the limit be two times)

323

(7 seconds)

4 F1 pomóżemy jej się spakować # nie?
we will help her pack # right?

5 BB decyzja Wielkiego Brata jest nieodwołalna
Big Brother's decision is final

6 F1 możemy pomóc Weronice?
can we help Weronika?

7 F2 (in the bedroom, speaking from far away) nie # ja sobie poradzę
no # I will manage myself

(2 second)

8 F2 możemy # nic nie mówi
we may # he doesn't say anything

(F1 and F2 walk towards the bedroom)

... (8 seconds)

9 F1 to F3: chodź pomożemy ci
come on we are going to help you

(F1, F2 and F3 go up to F3's suitcase)

10 F3 nie # poczekajcie ja tylko # <[wiecie co # nie]
no # wait a moment # you know what # no

11 F2 [gdzie jest twoja torba]
where is your bag

12 F1 [_ szybko --- . ty znoś rzeczy]> # a my ci pakujemy #
quick # you carry-IMP-sing. the things in and we are packing # carry-IMP-sing. the things in

13 F2 my ci pakujemy
we are packing for you

(F3 draws her suitcase to the middle of the doorway, F1 starts opening it)

14 F1 [znoś rzeczy]
bring-IMP-sing. the things

15 F1 [otwórzcie ją] # . ale ja mam tylko to
open-IMP-pl. it # but I only have this

(F3 puts a handful of things into the case)

16 F3 [---]

17 F1 [klapki] sobie ubierz # buty ci przyniosę
put the slippers on # I will get your shoes for you

... (about 13 seconds during which the remaining housemates walk from the living room to the hall)

18 F2 (loudly to the group): dajcie jej klapki # tutaj # te

give-IMP-2nd pl. her slippers # here # these ones

19 F4 te?

these ones?

20 F3 --- dżinsowe

--- denim

21 F2 (loudly, to everybody): gdzie są jej dżinsowe klapki

where are her denim slippers

... (8 seconds during which the issue of the slippers has been settled, and everyone in the group has gone to the doorway; the rest of the group are now standing around while F1 and F2 are packing F3's suitcase)

22 F3 (running to the bathroom): ja mam spodnie mokre # wszystko # dajcie mi tą walizkę tu

my trousers are wet # and all # bring-IMP-2nd pl. me this case over there

23 M2 dajcie jej się przebrać # _ przebieraj się # a my ci wiesz # . pomożemy

let-IMP-2nd pl. her change her clothes # change-IMP-sing. your clothes # and we will you know # help you

24 (simultaneous speech)

25 F4 Weronika # wykąp się

Weronika # take a bath

(M2 picks up a bottle of water from the floor and walks slowly away from the bathroom, while F2 pulls F3's suitcase to the bathroom; F3 changes her clothes in the shower)

26 (simultaneous speech)

27 BB Weronika # masz trzy minuty na opuszczenie domu wielkiego brata

Weronika you have got three minutes to leave the Big Brother house

28 M2 ile ma?

how many?

29 M3 [---]

30 F4 [trzy minuty] ma na opuszczenie domu

three minutes to leave the house

31 (simultaneous speech, F3 walks towards the bathroom)

32 F5 to F3: ty się nawet nie kąp przecież

you don't-IMP even take a shower

33 F3 tam gdzieś została moja kurtka ze skóry przynieście mi ją

there is my leather jacket somewhere over there # bring-IMP-2nd pl. it to me

... (8 seconds)

(F4 comes in with a jacket)

34 F4 Weronika # czy to jest twoja kurtka?
Weronika # is this your jacket?

35 F3 nie: # taka brązowa
no # it is like brown

36 F1 Weronika # czy to twoje buty?
Weronika # are these your shoes?

(editorial cut)

37 F3 mordę muszę sobie umyć
I must wash my face-AUGM

(runs to the sink and starts washing her face)

38 F2 to F5: dawaj wsadzaj (putting clothes into A's suitcase)
come on put it in

39 F4 zo.staw # lepiej idź # . karę ci dadzą czy coś […]
leave that # you better go-IMP-sing. # they will give you a punishment or something

40 (simultaneous speech)

(F1, F2 and F4 search for F3's jacket in the background. F3 walks to the doorway, puts her overcoat on and runs back to the sink, while F6 pulls her suitcase to the door)

41 BB Weronika # . masz dwie minuty # na opuszczenie domu
Weronika # . you have got two minutes # to leave the Big Brother house

42 F3 pozwól mi się chociaż umyć
at least let me wash my face

43 F2 chodź tu # Weronika
Weronika come here

44 F3 czekaj umyję się tylko (running back to the sink)
wait-IMP-sing. I only will wash up

The tone of this scene is dictated by the short time given to F3 to leave the house. Under these circumstances, the remaining housemates create an atmosphere of rushed confusion. The proposal to help F3 pack her belongings, addressed towards the remaining housemates, is uttered by F1 in turn 4 in the form of a realisation declarative predicating the future action of the speaker and the multiple addressees:

4 F1 pomo^żemy jej się spakować # nie?
we will help her pack # right?

The intonation pattern of this utterance, with a rise-fall in the middle, expresses both the expectation of F1 that the proposal will be accepted and her uncertainty whether the others also take it for granted. This is iconised as a rise typical of questions followed by a fall typical of declaratives. The intonation pattern fulfils a function similar to the following question tag. Both the intonation pattern and the following question tag are devices of negative politeness in which the consensus is yet to be negotiated. This is the only occurrence of negative politeness within the scene.

After permission was requested of Big Brother and the absence of a reply is interpreted as a positive answer by F2, F1 and F2 proceed to pack F3's suitcase. Although F3 reacted to F1's earlier utterance (addressed at the group) shouting from outside that she would be able to pack her things herself, F1 and F2 fail to react to this announcement. F1 produces an offer directed towards F3 in the form of a realisation declarative predicating the future action she and F2 will take:

9 F1 to F3: chodź pomożemy ci
come on we are going to help you

The declarative is prefaced by the auxiliary imperative chodź (come) which endows the offer with a directive force. It declares that the offer requires F3's active cooperation, which is taken for granted. This type of construction has been discussed in section 6.1.3., dealing with the functions of the imperative-declarative (periphrastic imperative), containing grammaticalised imperative auxiliary verbs ("chodź", "daj", and "weź").

After declaring that she plans to help F3, F1 assumes the role of the instructor in a joint activity and proceeds to tell F3 how to contribute to the joint action, ignoring completely F3's verbal behaviour. F3, who is busy getting her suitcase, seems to be mildly protesting against the plan being put into operation by F1 and F2 since she produces a negative particle twice, and an inhibitive requestive (czekaj "wait-IMP-sing"), but it is not clear what she is referring to; she fails to make a point and seamlessly engages in the joint action. It seems that for F3, packing is less of a problem than finding her things scattered all over the house. F3 accepts help and addresses imperative requests in the plural to her helpers in turns 15 (open the suitcase), 22 (carry the suitcase to the bathroom) and 33 (search for and get her leather jacket). F1 tells F3 to put on her slippers in turn 17, which leads to F2 going to look for F3's slippers. In turns 18 and 21, F2 passes on the task of getting them to the whole group.

Subsequently, contrary to advice given to F3 by different persons, who variously tell her to take a bath and then not to in lines 25 and 32, respectively, in the unmitigated imperative. A piece of advice and another directive, both in the imperative, to F3 follow in turns 39 and 43.

In the meantime, M2 admonishes the helpers to let F3 change her clothes, and promises her that they will take care of the rest, speaking in the first person plural ("change your clothes # and we will you know # . help you"). No action of that sort by M2 actually follows; M2 walks away in a relaxed manner and F3's suitcase is brought to the bathroom by F2 and F4. None of the men and all but one of the women participated in packing and collecting F3's belongings and carrying her suitcase.

Several types of participant structures appear in the directives contained in this interaction: from the beneficiary to the actors (request) in turns 15, 22 and 33; from a helper to other helpers (request) in turns 18 and 21; from a helper to beneficiary as a co-actor (offer and instruction) in turns 9, 12 and 14; from a helper to the beneficiary as actor (advice/nurturing command) in turns 17, 25, 32 and 39; from a spectator (M2) to the helpers on behalf of the beneficiary (request) in turn 23; and from a spectator (M2) as a representative of the helpers to the beneficiary (offer and advice/nurturing command) in turn 23. The syntactic patterns used are the imperative, the imperative-declarative and the realisation declarative.

The attitudes of involvement and interdependence are displayed throughout the scene:

- the speaker F1 assumes initially that some others will join her in performing an action beneficial to EXT, and expresses her proposal in the positively polite form of a realisation declarative while expressing attention to the interlocutors' negative face wants by means of partially interrogative intonation and a question tag;
- the other speaker, F2, assumes that the group are willing or obliged to join, asking them to provide help by means of a plain imperative (turns 18 and 21);
- it is presupposed of the beneficiary that she will accept help and cooperate in receiving it;
- numerous pieces of advice are given to the beneficiary in a categorical tone, presupposing her compliance;
- an offer of help is made by M2 on behalf of the group as a whole, although M2 himself does not engage in helping the beneficiary;
- the beneficiary submits to the actions and commands of the others;
- the beneficiary presupposes the cooperation of other persons by requesting in an impositive form that her jacket be brought to her, and her case carried to the bathroom;
- the beneficiary formulates all her requests in the plural, without specifying the actor.

The amount of attention the interlocutors offer to the negative face in both form and content of the interaction is minimal. Nearly all the face work is directed towards the positive face needs of all the addressees and stresses ingroup responsibility. The speakers manifest a nursing and patronising attitude towards the beneficiary, and feel entitled to act for her benefit through straightforward demands, both initiating and inhibitive, directed at the other group members. The actions of the individuals are viewed as actions by the group.

The following is a piece of interaction following the announcement of M1's eviction from the Big Brother house in E3. F1 and M1 (the evicted person) are bound by an intimate relationship; despite M1's declaration that they are just "mates", in the days preceding the eviction they exchanged hugs and engaged in intimate conversations. M1 is given one hour to pack his belongings and say his goodbyes. The housemates have been in the Big Brother house for about three weeks.

B3.

F1, F2 and M1, are sitting at the table, M2 standing close to them. M2 was a candidate for eviction along with M1 but M1 is the one who has been voted out by the public. After the result was announced, M1 and M2 hugged each other.

```
1 F1 do you want help packing
(M1 starts walking towards the bedroom)
2 M1 if you want
3 F1 oh # I won't then # I'll be sitting here
4/1 F2 to F1: (standing up) yeah # . come on with me
(M2 moves to join F1 and F2)
4/2 F2 # . let's go baby (clapping M2 on his back)
(F1, F2 and M2 move to the bedroom)
5 M1 I'm wicked # . I don't- # no change in what I'm feeling
6 F1 sure?
7 M2 are you sure (pats M1 on his shoulder)
8 M1 I'm wicked # honestly
9 F2 [what are you wearing # can you show me what you] are wearing
please?
10 M1 yeah # ---
11 M2 [I'm so- # I'm so-] # . God # [I was so sure it was going to be me]
12 F1 he is just happy # he's going out
(F1 walks to M1 to hug him)
```

(M1 embraces F1 and pats her on her back)
```
13 F1 what # that's not a hug
```
(M1 and F2 hug; F1 and M1 hug)
```
14 M2 ---
15 M2 to F1: are you all right
16 F1 yes?
17 M2 are you sure
18 F1 yeah?
19 F1 ---
20 M2 (patting M1 on his shoulder) you're sure # you're all right # yeah?
```
(F2 hugs M2)
```
21 M1 totally
22 F1 Tom # you've got two shoes over here mate
23 M1 like you said # I have experience # I've done it # I've done it
24 M2 do you want a hand to pack # do you want to give him a hand to pack
25 M1 ehm # I'll pack # I'll pack # if you want to hang by you can do but
I'll pack
```

Compared to the scene from P3 discussed above, M1 is given enough time to complete packing his belongings, which is reflected in the slower tempo of interaction, and in the major part of the conversation (turns 5-8, 10-21) concentrating on issues unrelated to packing, such as the participants' impressions and emotions. Still, a comparison is made possible by the fact that, as in the previous scene, help is being offered and directives are produced in the course of putting the offer into action. In turn 1, F1 offers help by asking M1 whether he desires help. Rather than accepting enthusiastically, M1 makes F1's action dependent on her own decision. It seems less than F1 expected; as a result, she feels offended and takes back her offer. F2 interferes with the developing ill-feeling by producing an affirmative particle, standing up and commanding F1 and possibly M2, who is also present, to come with her to the bedroom where the packing of M1's suitcase is to take place. In the same turn, F2 issues an imperative addressed to M2 who declared an inclination to join in by moving in the same direction (towards the bedroom), and modifies it positively by signals of intimacy such as clapping his back and a pet name. In the bedroom, the conversation focuses on the feelings of the persons involved, while F1 tries to be helpful and reminds M1 to think about his appearance during the studio interview he is going to give immediately after leaving the house; the reminder has the form of polite interrogation mitigated by please (turn 9). In turn 24, M2 returns to the subject of packing; he offers help to M1 and asks the remaining housemates present (F1 and F2) to join him in helping M1. A native-speaking respondent suggested that the directive utterance (do you want to give him a hand to pack) in turn 24 was in fact directed at M1 and meant to be "overheard" by him. Through the complex structure of this turn, consisting of an offer of help directed at M1 (do you want a hand to pack) followed by a directive in the form of a preference check directed at other potential helpers, a differentiation was introduced between the person offering help (M1 only) and other people present. Contrary to an offer made in the first person plural, this differentiation made it possible for M1 to react to the offer selectively, for example by accepting M2's help and rejecting the other housemates' participation. Rather than viewing the action as a joint action by the group, a perspective was offered that differentiated between the potential actors and made selective reactions by the beneficiary possible. In turn 25, M1 objects to being actually helped while he agrees that the others can watch him pack, provided that this is what they want.

The following characteristics highlight the contrast to the preceding scene, constituted by the degree to which the speaker verbally signals attention to the addressee's negative face wants:

- F1's offer of help is declared in the form of a check of the beneficiary's preference (turn 1), and the beneficiary's response is taken seriously;
- the beneficiary accepts the offer provisionally making it dependent on the preference of the person offering help (turn 2);
- the conventionally indirect (negatively polite) interrogative form is used in a reminder on changing clothes (turn 9);
- M2 makes an offer by asking about the beneficiary's preference (turn 24);
- M2 asks other persons to join in helping M1 by asking about their preferences (turn 24);
- producing two speech acts in turn 24, M2 differentiates between his and other potential helpers' actions;
- M1 permits the others to assist him passively during his action, making it dependent on their preference (turn 25).

The hearer-centred interrogative or conditional including the verb "want" appears five times in this scene, for instance, in M2's act of asking other housemates to help M1 (turn 6), and an imperative is used twice. The verbal considerateness strategy, in which the speakers express their respect for negative face wants and refer clearly to the preferences of the hearers as preconditions for any actions, predominates. At the same time, the opposite or

331

complementary strategy of a positive face address is by no means absent. First of all, it is present in the area unrelated to the issue of packing, offering help and directive utterances, namely, questions and responses expressing mutual concern by showing interest for other persons' emotional states (turns 7, 8, 16, 18, 21). On the action-oriented plane, attention to the beneficiary's positive face wants is first expressed in the proposal to help M1 and a step is taken towards realising it, in the form of following M1 to the bedroom. It is also visible in numerous details of form and contents of verbal interaction:

- F1's taking offence at M1 making her help contingent on her own preference rather than affirming his need for help (turn 3). F1 signals that she expected an answer appealing to her positive face needs, and that these needs were not met by M1's distancing reaction;
- F2's decision to help M1 although he did not ask for it (turn 4/1);
- F2's impositive appeal to M2 to join her in helping M1, positively modified by a pat and an intimate vocative (turn 4/2);
- M2's appeal to other team members to join in helping M1 (turn 24).

These two sequences illustrate how the strategies of involvement and considerateness intermingle in the British patterns of interaction, and how impositiveness is used as a predominant means of expressing care and involvement in the Polish group, without any attention given to the beneficiary's and only minimal attention given to other group members' negative face wants. While British housemates F1, F2 and M2 signal "giving options" to both the beneficiary and other potential helpers, Polish housemate F1 judges for herself that F3 is in need of help, that this help is to be granted by the group, and takes it for granted that F3 will be willing to accept help and the role of the instructee during this joint action, overriding the beneficiary's innocuous attempts to manage the course of action. Polish beneficiary F1 submits to this role. In contrast with this, M1 in the British scene adheres to his negative face wants and defends his personal territory by rejecting help, which in this case involves a manipulation of his personal belongings by the others: obviously, his choice does not need any justification, since no justification is offered. At the same time, concern is expressed by talking about emotions, and the interest shown by particular housemates concerning the emotional states of their interlocutors.

The group-orientation of the Polish scene is expressed by the beneficiary formulating her requests in the plural, which signals her perception of the helpers as a group rather than as individuals who have to be addressed separately in directives. The helpers themselves also treat actions by any members of the group as an action of the group, and they mutually take the participation of other persons for granted. In the British group, speakers make offers on their behalf, and expressions of involvement tend to be based on one-to-one interpersonal bonds.

7.4.4. EXTERNAL BENEFICIARY

7.4.4.1. INTERLINGUAL COMPARISON: POLISH AND ENGLISH

The statistics showed that the Poles tended to produce considerably more directives for the benefit of a third person or persons ("external beneficiary", EXT) than the British; the difference was impressive (every 11 minutes of interaction, compared to every 58 minutes in the case of the British, or 11% versus 4% of all requestives). Initiating (i.e. non-inhibitive) requestives were the preferred type (about 73% in each language).

The following two sets of data demonstrate the intercultural contrast concerning the presupposition (or its absence) of the beneficiary's consent, and the effects of the underlying attitudes – group-orientation and interpersonal orientation, with their links to interdependence-involvement versus autonomy-considerateness preference – upon the types of directives produced. In particular, they show how this contrast contributes to the above-mentioned quantitative difference. A proposal on the (putative) beneficiary's behalf is produced in the one case, and a P-offer at the beneficiary (non-requestive, i.e. not included in the statistically analysed data) in the other. The context of the directives is in both cases the arrival of a new housemate in the Big Brother house.

116-P3. WALK GIRL AROUND
Week 5. F1 has just arrived in the Big Brother house. M1. M2, M3, F2 and F3 have been waiting for her in the yard.
1 M1 może ją oprowadzimy
maybe we will show her around
(simultaneous speech)
2 F2 to M1, M2: weźcie się zajmijcie dziewczyną # no
AUX-IMP-2nd pl. take-IMP-2nd pl. care of the girl # yeah

Consider now the analogous situation in which a new female housemate, E3, is offered a walk round the house with the speaker:

96-E3. WALK GIRL AROUND
Week 3. F1 has just arrived in the Big Brother house.

```
1 F1 to F2: do you want to see the house
2 F2 to F1: yeah # go on then
```

Offering to show F2 the house, F1 makes the predicated action dependent on F2's preference. As shown in the reaction of F2, and confirmed in the native respondents' judgements, she makes the offer in her own name. This contrasts with P3. WALK GIRL AROUND where the predication in turn 1 is based on the speaker's own judgement that the action will be beneficial to the beneficiary, whose compliance is taken for granted and whose opinion is not being consulted. The utterance in turn 1 of P3. WALK GIRL AROUND is a proposal directed at the other team members. This scene is reminiscent of the entrance scene in which the Poles reacted to the newcomers collectively, by means of a coordinated action. It is one of the hearers, F2, and not the beneficiary, who reacts to M1's tentatively formulated proposal on the (putative) beneficiary's behalf. She strongly supports the idea in an imperative utterance addressed to the previous speaker and his addressees. It should increase the probability that the action will be performed; at the same point, by producing a diagonal request F2 shows that she has interpreted the proposal as addressed to the male part of the group only, and that she assumes it to be their gentlemanly duty to take care of the female newcomer. In this move, F1 introduces gender role stereotyping, emphasising the group-based rather than interpersonal component of the encounter, and offers attention at the same time to F1 as a beneficiary and other team members as actors. A verbal negotiation and action concerning an external beneficiary expresses and confirms the consolidation of the existing group, who collectively deal with the recipient of the favour.

One should not have the impression that the "benevolent incapacitation" is a matter of gender perception by the Polish speakers. The scheduling of activities for guests and newcomers as a Polish cultural script has been documented by Boski (2003: 121), using the "cultural standard" method and reporting on the cultural shock of a male German visitor to a Polish host family: "... er wurde als kostbares, zerbrechliches Objekt behandelt, ja genau, als Objekt, nicht als Subjekt, das eigenständig Entscheidungen treffen konnte. Er wurde nicht einmal nach seinen eigenen Wünschen gefragt."[132]

In Polish and English alike, the prevailing majority of requests for the sake of an external beneficiary are realised using impositive head act forms. Hardly any cultural contrast could be assessed by means of form analysis alone. The cultural difference pertains

---

[132] "He was treated as a valuable brittle object, yes, exactly, as an object, not as a subject who could make decisions on his own. He was not even asked about his own wishes."

in the first place to tendencies in choosing the speech act to be performed in response to a given situation (see diagram 2, chpt. 1). These tendencies are constitutive of differences in "interaction styles" characterised by a stronger or weaker presence of directive activities. They are distinct from directly observable differences in "communication styles" characterised by a stronger or weaker impositiveness of actually produced directives. Briefly, taking only the form aspect of interlingual contrasts into account would obscure rather than expose the degree of interlingual and intercultural difference.

7.4.4.2. INTERLINGUAL COMPARISON: GERMAN AND POLISH

The quantitative analysis revealed that in German, half the requestives produced on behalf of an external beneficiary was of the inhibitive type, in contrast with Polish where their ratio was under 30%. Only the initiating sort occurred with considerably higher frequency in Polish than in German (8% versus 4% of all requestives, about every 13 versus every 51 minutes of recorded interaction, respectively).

A closer look at the data reveals that directives in favour of EXT (non-speaker, non-addressee) form a spectrum of activities from such that aim at initiating an action beneficial to EXT, to such that are directly critical of the undesirable behaviour of the addressee:

- reprimands: they are corrective, and can be therefore interpreted as meta-comments on the rules of proper conduct;
- admonitions: result from S's belief that H would not pursue a rule of politeness if not told otherwise, rather than comment directly on H's improper behaviour which has occurred before; they are only mildly critical by implying an anticipation of a trespass;
- attention organisers: do not imply criticism but make H attentive to aspects of the situation that make H's current behaviour undesirable;
- triggers: directives aiming at triggering action advantageous to EXT, referring in no way to any actual or anticipated trespass.

As shown in the following examples, reprimands are prevailingly although not necessarily inhibitive. Admonitions and triggers cannot be reliably distinguished alone on the basis of their syntactic and lexical form and the context; the prosodic characteristics of the utterance, such as the occurrence of reproachful intonation, may need to be taken into account.

TRIGGER

23-G4. F is preparing to leave the Big Brother house.

F ich will auf jeden Fall einen Kuchen haben # ja?

I want to have a cake in any case # right?

M1 to M2: schneide schnell ein grosses Stück für die Khadra ab

quickly cut a big piece for Sandra

REPRIMAND

24-G4.

1 M to F1: Carmen

Carmen-FIRST NAME

2 F2 warte # sie unterhält sich doch gerade # warte # nicht dazwischen

wait # she is EMPHATIC PARTICLE having a conversation right now # wait # not in between (meaning: don't interrupt)

49-G2.

1 M1 to M2: und wie viele Frauen hattest du schon so?

and like how many women have you already had?

2 F to M1: [oh komm # Stefa:n] # [e:cht]

oh come on # Stefa:n # really

ADMONITION

117-P3.

A new female housemate descends a ladder to the yard.

1 F1 to M1, M2: ^idźcie po dziewczynę   REPROACHFUL INTONATION

go-IMP-2nd pl. pick up the girl

2 F2 ^no idźcie   REPROACHFUL INTONATION

EMPH-PARTICLE go-IMP-2nd pl.

ATTENTION ORGANISER

118-P3.
M mogę wam coś powiedzieć? to jest tak # do wszystkich # drużyno
czerwonych # poproszę o chwilkę ciszy # [i do drużyny czerwonych]
may I tell you something? it is like that # everybody # team red # I am asking for a moment of silence # so
team red
F [e # posłuchajcie na chwilkę]
e # listen for a while

Abstracting from the ethically neutral case of attention organisers, the speakers of
German frequently decided to react correctively to improper behaviour, while the Poles
showed a preference for triggers; admonitions were rare in Polish. In the German scenes
quoted above, the breach of the norm which elicits a corrective comment on behalf of an
external beneficiary is a transgression by the impostor of the personal territory of the other,
e.g. by demanding confidential information (24-G4) or an interruption in a conversation (49-
G2). The sanctioning of tactless or verbally aggressive behaviour is undertaken by a group
member who is not directly affected by the trespass. Such diagonal reprimands hardly
occurred in Polish.

A clear illustration of the social sanctionability of a group member's failure to perform a
small favour to EXT suggested by the situation in Polish is provided in episode P3. MUSIC
BOX below.

119-P3. MUSIC BOX
F, M1 and M2 are sitting at the table, the music box in front of M1; M2 moves to reach for the music box
1 F to M1: patrz patrz patrz # ojciec po magnetofon sięga
look-sing. look-sing. look-sing. # Father reaches out for the tape recorder
(M1 pushes the music box to M2)
2 F zamiast zakręcić sam # to wziął mu popchnął
instead of winding it up himself # he just pushed it to him
3 F (laughs) (points at M1 with her finger)
(M2 winds up the music box)
4 M1 [nie- # no ale- # ja-]
no # but- # I-
5 F [(laughs)]

337

F ridicules M1 for having failed to pre-empt M2's intention of winding up the music box, which could have been expected of him because it was standing on the table in front of M1. M1 reacted falsely to F's attentive reference to M2's intention to reach for the music box in turn 1. The reaction F expected of M2 was to wind up the box for M1 (M1 obviously wanted to listen to the music). F humorously distances herself from M2 by pointing at him, which is a conventional way of punishment through ridicule for misbehaviour – among children and, jokingly, among intimates. At the same time, F depersonalises M1, talking about him in the third person, in contrast with her previous utterance in which M1 was explicitly marked as an addressee by the imperative patrz ("look"). The utterance is not directed to M2 who, like M1, is referred to in the third person, but marked by F as an "inner monologue" commenting on the situation and meant to be "overheard" by M1. This device has a punitive function: M1 is temporarily deprived of the status of the interlocutor. Laughter signals that the "punishment" staged by F1 is not seriously intended, and turns it into friendly criticism. However, in order to be meaningful, and to be capable of being "disarmed" by laughter, a criticism of this kind must be expected to have validity for others. F expects her interlocutors to share her understanding of social co-operation.

High acceptability of demands for information on self among the Poles, and the near non-occurrence of reprimands for verbal transgressions of personal territory, suggest that the issue of such transgressions is non-central to the Polish concept of proper interpersonal conduct. At the same time, the data suggest that it constitutes an important component of this concept in the German groups. The number of situations is small and not sufficient for a definite generalisation but the constellation, including the case of non-directive criticism in P3. MUSIC BOX, suggests that for the Poles an important aspect of impolite behaviour is non-verbal – a failure to perform a small favour required or made possible by the situation. These two perspectives correspond respectively to the cultural focus on freedom from imposition, characteristic of individualist societies, and on interdependence, characteristic of collective societies. At the same time, members of both the German and the Polish groups display the tendency to regulate the conduct of other group members with respect to each other (and, in a few cases, also towards outgroup members), which is an element of interdependence attitude.

7.4.5. DIRECTIVES IN DECLARATIONS AND SYMBOLIC DISPLAYS OF SOLIDARITY

Discussing the occurrences of strongly impositive formulations of requests for personal favours, I suggested that the impositive form was part and parcel of directives whose predicative content depended on the assumption of closeness and intimacy, and which could hardly occur outside an intimate relationship. The following discussion offers a more detailed look at directives of the integrative type, in which the message itself expresses the aspiration to bond with others and the expectation of its reciprocation. The data in all three languages include actions symbolic of group ties, which need to be called for and arranged. The following exchanges from E3, E4, G4 and P3 make visible the relation between group ties and the degree of impositiveness perceived as appropriate in issuing directives.

9-E4.

1/1 **F1 does everybody want champagne? everybody should have a little drink**

1/2 F1 (pouring champagne into wine glasses) **no one drink anything yet # no one drink anything yet** # no one is to drink anything # okay?

2 F1 Ron (extending her hand, holding a glass of wine)

M1 (takes the glass)

3 F1 to M1: **don't drink it yet # don't drink it yet**

4 F2 please sir # can we have some more?

5 F1 **we have to wait for Pablo**

6 **F1 Pablo!**

7 F1 (to M1, M2, M3, M4, F2, F3, F4 and F5): **okay # wait # now we'll drink # because we've got quite a bit left # I thought # I'll let you know** (pours champagne into the glasses kept by M1 and F2)

A strongly impositive inhibitive requestive whose directive force is enhanced by repetition is being directed at the group in turn 1/1-1/2. F1 activates the phatic function of raising toasts and joint drinking, and appeals to the group members not to drink until everybody else is prepared to join the toast. The requestive is legitimised by the integrative goal rooted in social ritual. Uttering it, F1 appeals to the housemates to perform an integrative symbolic gesture and invokes a group spirit. Impositives in the form of the imperative and the deontic declarative occur in turns 3 and 5. In turn 7, F1 uses the strongly impositive form of realisation declarative leaving no doubt about the addressee's compliance (although it is mitigated by the negatively polite past tense in the following supportive move).

The type of situation that strongly promoted integrative directive behaviour was the departure of a participant from the Big Brother house. Directive speech acts produced in this context frequently serve as declarations of friendship and solidarity, foster team spirit and highlight concern for the integrity of the group. An emphatically impositive form is used in the next scene in the context of appealing to the group for a collective performance of a symbolic enactment of togetherness by means of a "group hug", in reaction to the group integrity being threatened by F1's sudden decision to leave.

97-E3 . F1 has told M1, M2, M3 and F2 that she has decided to leave the house, and discusses it with them.
(F1 stands up, embraces M2)
(M1 stands up)
1 M1 I tell you what we need # . we need a group hug #
2 M3 [hehehe]
3 M4 [I've never done one # ---]
4 (simultaneous speech)
5 M1 come on # group hug
(M1 makes a hand movement in the direction of F2, M2 and M3 as though he was collecting them in front of him, and stretches his hand out to M2 and F2)
6 (simultaneous speech)
7 M1 we have all seen group hugs before
8 F2 (approaching M1, F1, M2 and M3) group hug
9 (simultaneous speech)
10 F1 to F2: you are going in the middle

The scene shows the close ties between impositiveness and ingroup bonding. The head act of the proposal in turn 1 has the form of a deontic declarative stating the performance of the proposed joint action as a necessity, and is introduced by a positively polite modifier in the form of a speaker-centred preparatory, a strong statement of a speaker's opinion ("+committer" in Kasper and House 1981). Compared to a bare deontic declarative, the additional reference to the speaker as the source of the directive (I tell you what we need) by means of a performative speech act verb expresses an even higher degree of the speaker's self-assurance. The directive is repeated in turn 5 in the elliptical form whose illocutionary force is enhanced by the utterance-initial imperative.

By symbolically enclosing F1 in a group embrace, group unity and the status of F1 as a group member are displayed and emphasised. The highly impositive form is legitimised by the propositional contents, because the directive dramatises unity and group solidarity itself. Indirect strategies, signalising the recognition that the individual group members are free

340

not to participate, and that consensus is perceived as optional and putative, to be created rather than already in existence, would carry pragmatic implications contrary to the function (cf. *"would you like to do a group hug?"*).

In Polish, where impositive forms are strongly preferred in all contexts, the use of the imperative cannot substantiate the relationship between impositiveness and symbolic manifestations of group integrity. As discussed elsewhere, the realisation declarative, which is used frequently and inconspicuously in proposals (especially in Polish and German), is more impositive than the imperative in requests, and is only used in them in exceptional circumstances. As it is the only direct form of request which is remarkable as regards impositiveness, in the following exchange this form is selected in the realisation of an appeal for a symbolic display of group solidarity.

120-P3. SAD TUNE
M1, F1, F2 and F3 are talking of M2's exit from the Big Brother house; a music box is playing a nostalgic melody. F1 comes from the same team as M1 and M2; and F2 and F3 are from the other team.
(F1 starts weeping)
1 F2 nie płacz_ # nie płacz mała
don't cry # don't cry little one
2 F3 to F1: mamuśka
mum-DIM
3 F2 ty i Ojciec zgasicie tu światła
you and Father will turn the lights off here
4 F3 mamuśka nie płacz # --- pozytywka gra
mum-DIM don't cry # the music box is playing
5 F2 ostatni stąd wyniesie tą pozytywkę i da Bartkowi
the last one will take this music box and give it to Bartek
6 F1 mhm

F2 interprets F1's tears as a sign of nostalgia with which she responds to the gradual diminution of the ingroup, prompted directly by M2's exit and the tune playing on the music box. In turn 5, F2 pins it down by reference to M2 and implies that he remains part of the group. She predicates a future action of the last person to leave, symbolic of group bonds. She uses the realisation declarative in the future tense to demand an action on behalf of the group (taking the music box with him or her and giving it to M2) from whoever happens to stay longest. During her departure from the house several days later, F2 reminds the remaining housemates about the music box by saying zabierzcie pudełko ("take-IMP-pl. the box out"). In fact, the winner in the game took the music box with him when he left the Big Brother house.

The following set of data comes from the German series, G4, carried out in the battle design. The initial period of distance reflecting the awareness of diverging team goals, in which the housemates tended not to include the members of rival teams in the definition of their ingroup, was followed by a period in which the competitive goals were no longer viewed as an obstacle to group-wide integration, and relationships were formed regardless of which team the individuals were members. The following scene comes from day 28 of the program.

25-G4. RON'S DEPARTURE
1 HOST: also # Ron oder Sandra # wer muss heute das Haus verlassen # ich mache es kurz und schmerzlos # ...# und zwar wird das . Ron sein
so # Ron or Sandra # I will make it quick and painless # ... # it will be Ron
2 F1 ^Scheiße
shit
3 HOST: Ron verabschiede dich bitte # und . atme tief durch # wir freuen uns auf dich # . bis gleich
Ron say your good byes please # and take a deep breath # we are waiting for you # see you soon
4 M1 komm lass uns alle zusammen --- # ehrlich
come let us all --- together # honestly
(M2 hugs M3)
5 M1 to M3: hol die Zigarre
fetch the cigar
6 M3 (hugs SANDRA-F3) <starts to whisper><--->
(M2 hugs F3)
(F3 hugs F2)
(M2 hugs M4)
7 M1 Ron # komm # hei lass dich feiern # ganz ehrlich # (hugs M2) #_ Scheiß
Ron # come # hey celebrate # honestly # shit
8 M1 irgendwie Scheiß
somehow shit
9 M5 (hugs M2) <starts to whisper> <--->

10 M2 (hugs F4) kleiner --- # **trinkt im Team auf mein Glück # okay?**

little --- # drink-IMP-pl. as a team to my good luck # okay?

11 F4 ja (laughs)

yes

12 M2 to M3, F2, M2: **hier wird geraucht auf mich**

one will–IMPERS. smoke for me here

13 M6 sogar ich rauche ne Zigarre (hugs M2) # _ in zwei Wochen drüben # definitiv

even I will smoke a cigar # in two weeks over there # definitely

14 F5 hei Ron # fahr rein (hugs M2)

hey Ron # drive in

15 SANDRA-F3 (sobs)

16 M2 Sandra nicht # ist ja okay # Sandra # . ist völlig okay # Quatsch (embraces weeping F3) # <starts to whisper><Quatsch Quatsch Quatsch # . es ist okay # Baby es ist okay # es ist völlig okay # Bonbon # wir sehen uns draußen # wir sehen uns draußen # . wir sehen uns draußen # okay? # . --- Zeit zu genießen # --- # es ist absolut kein Thema (kisses F3) # mach dir bloß keinen Vorwurf # hörst was ich gesagt # _ okay?>

Sandra no # it is all right # Sandra # it is quite all right # rubbish # rubbish rubbish rubbish # it is all right # baby it is all right # it is quite all right # sweetie # we will see each other outside # we will see each other outside # we will see each other outside # okay? # --- time to enjoy # --- # it is no problem # do not blame yourself in any case # you hear what I said # okay?

(M2 stops hugging F3)

17 F3 (sighs)

18 M2 (sighs) # <starts to whisper><Scheiße ist es # . mai>

shit this is # gee

(M2 embraces F1)

19 M2 <starts to whisper> <nicht weinen # nicht weinen # --- # nicht weinen # du machst es auch ohne mich>

don't cry # don't cry # don't cry # --- # don't cry # you will make it even without me

(F5 hugs SANDRA-F3)

(M2 stops hugging F1)

20 M2 <starts to whisper> <**kriege noch ein Stück Torte vor dem Scheiß Ding**>

I will have a piece of cake before this shitty thing

(F4 puts a piece of cake on a plate and gives it to M2)

(F1 hugs F3)

(M3 eats cake)

(M4 comes up to M2 and gives him a cigar)

21 M3 ah # Danke # . soll ich jetzt
ah # thanks # should I now

22 M1 ja
yes

23 M2 okay
okay

(M3 gives M2 a light)

(M2 starts smoking the cigar)

(M1 hugs F3, M6 is standing next to them)

24 M1 Ron # ich passe auf die Naddel auf
Ron # I will take care of Naddel-NICKNAME

25 M6 ne # . Ron # . ich bin verheiratet # ich passe auf
ne # Ron # I am married # I will take care

26 F3 er ist auch verheiratet
he is married too

27 M2 passt alle auf sie auf
everybody take care of her

28 M1 aber --- # (laughs)
but

(F3 hugs M6)

29 M2 soll ich euch was sagen? # . es war für mich hier # _ die schönste
Zeit meines Lebens bei euch # . echt # . bleibt so wie ihr seid # ehrlich
ist absolut geil # . ihr seid eine super Truppe # . ne? # bei den
Battles Gegner ist okay # . bei- # **wenn ihr euch hier in die Haare kriegt
. ich komme hier rein # versohle jedem einzelnen von euch den Arsch**
*can I tell you something? for me this here was # the most beautiful time of my life with you # really # stay as
you are # honestly # it is absolutely great # you are a great team # right? # it's okay to be an opponent in the
battles # if you start being at loggerheads in here # I will come in here # spank the ass of every single one of
you*

30 F4, M3 (laugh)

31 M3 gut
good

(F3 embraces M2)

32 M2 <starts to whisper> <nicht weinen # so ist das # nicht weinen # Mäuschen>

don't cry # don't cry # mousy-DIM

33 M5 ich warte auf das was jetzt passiert

I'm waiting for what will happen next

(F3 and M2 kiss)

34 F1 <starts to whisper> <ei # zum Kotzen # ei>

hey # this is puking bad # hey

(M2 stops embracing F3, shows the cigar he is holding to M3; M3 walks over to him and takes the cigar)

(M2 embraces M1)

35 M1 wir sehen uns # ich will dich sehen # wenn ich da rauskomme will ich dich dort stehen sehen

we will see each other # I want to see you # when I get out of here I want to see you standing there

(M3 embraces M1 and M2 who are embracing each other)

36 M2 auf jeden Fall

definitely

37 M1 es wird wahrscheinlich nächste Woche sein (laughs)

that will probably be next week

(M1 stops embracing M2)

(M2 and M3 walk up to the exit; M3 is embracing M2)

38 M3 und wenn du mal wieder kotzst # ist alles weg # . ruf mich an

and if you puke again # it will all be gone # give me a call

(F1, F2, F3, F4, M3, M4, M5 and M6 follow M2 and M3)

39/1 M2 (nods) <starts talking extra loud> **und ich will je:den Ta:g beim Statement meinen Namen hören** <end extra loud>

and I want to hear my name in the statement every day

39/2 M2 <start whisper> <shit # verdammte # ei # Scheiße # _ Nadinchen # komm mal # meine Süße> (M2 hugs F1)

and I want to hear my name every day in the statement # shit # damn # ei # shit # Nadin-DIM # come # my sweetie

40 M1 komm # lass uns --- Friedenspfeife ziehen # .wir werden dann --- # und bei Aufräumen wir sagen was (M1 gives a cigar to M3)

come # let us --- smoke a pipe of peace # we will then --- # and when we're clearing up we will say something

(M6 embraces F3)

(M1 gives the cigar to M4)

41 M4 (takes the cigar from M1) ich habe noch nie geraucht
I have never smoked
42 M1 egal
it doesn't matter
43 M4 heute
today
(M2 hugs F1)
44 M2 unterstützt mein Captain weiter # ne? .. Team Red
keep supporting my captain # will you? team red
45 F1 hol mich nächste Woche ab # ja? hast du gehört? hol mich nächste Woche ab

The strongly emotional tone of this exchange is visible on the extra-verbal plane as the housemates seek physical closeness to each other, in sobbing and sighing, and the phonetic characteristics in particular of the vocal performance of M2, who whispers as though he does not want his voice to give away his becoming emotional. On the verbal plane, directives oriented towards positive face wants are produced frequently and without redress to a negative face. The sequence of turns 4 through 43 (interaction between housemates) contains a record number, for any of the German series, of 15 requestive utterances within five minutes of interaction, and four further imperatives in consolations. In turn 10, M2 produces an imperative predicating the team drinking to his luck, presupposing positive affection on the part of the remaining housemates and their willingness to perform its symbolic display in a ritual joint action. The predicative content of the message is strongly oriented towards everybody's positive face wants, and so is its linguistic form. In turn 12, M2 addresses members of the rival "loser" team, who are not allowed to drink alcohol: they should smoke to his luck instead. Again, M2 displays his trust in their positive affection. M2 uses a realisation declarative in the passive voice, a strong form of impositiveness[133] anticipating no argument. The utterance carries a humorous overtone as there is a clash between the expectation of the addressees' concern expressed by the predicative content, and the depersonalised form of reference – the passive voice. In turn 20, M2 demands a piece of cake, choosing a form of the impositively modified impositive head act. The head act has the form of a definite statement of a future event: kriege noch ein Stück Torte vor dem Scheiß Ding *(I will have a piece of cake before this shitty thing),* meant as a request for cake, and centred upon the speaker's want without specifying the actors of the implied

[133] In requests; it is moderately impositive in proposals.

action. Through choosing the impositive form not accompanied by means of negative modification, M2 expresses the presupposition that his claim is viewed as highly legitimate by the remaining group members, and that they are willing to respond to his needs.

The topic of remembrance and tribute to M2 during his absence is reassumed in 39/1, where M2 declares that he wants the remaining housemates to mention him in their daily reviews ("statements") in the diary room, which were intended to depict the insiders' perception of current events and were broadcast regularly on television. The utterance in turn 39/1 is realised as a strong statement of the speaker's will, in impositive linguistic form and without mitigation by any modifiers of the "intimacy" type. This substantiates the point that impositiveness alone (contrary to the background assumption in Blum-Kulka's 1990 study of parent-child interaction) can function as an adequate vehicle for expressing and addressing positive face wants. The same strategy of unmitigated impositiveness characterises the utterance in 35, a strong statement of the speaker's will uttered by another housemate, M1, and addressed to M2. M1 expects M2 to wait for him when he himself leaves the house. The compliance with the request might possibly involve an extreme "cost" to the addressee, who lives in a different part of Germany. The request is a declaration of friendship and presupposes the reciprocation of positive affection on the part of M2. The declaration of concern constitutes in itself a compensation of the extreme cost involved in compliance with the directive. The integrative character of the request is based on the assumption that asking M2 to do a favour to the speaker will give him an opportunity to prove his affection towards the speaker, and benefits M2 as well as M1. Rather than maximise the need for redress to the negative face, the high cost in association with the presupposition of benefit to both sides via the bond of friendship makes an impositive linguistic form the only viable choice for the speaker. Two native speakers of German were asked to imagine the same request formulated in a negatively polite linguistic form (competence interrogative): one found it inappropriate, although he could not find an explanation for this impression. The other interviewee commented that if he had used a tentative formulation, M1 would fail to communicate how important it was to him to have M2 by his side when he left the house, which was an integral part of the intended message and the justification of the directive.

In turn 29, M2 expresses his concern for group harmony, threatening humorously that he would come in and punish the remaining housemates if they quarrelled and stopped being friends in the future course of events. Although leaving the house, M1 declares himself to be responsible for the group's conduct, implicitly claiming the status of a group member despite his physical absence from the house. This is a powerful proclamation of ingroupness and solidarity. The inhibitive directive is preceded by another explicit reference to being a group, in the form of a compliment addressed to everybody present for being a "great team" (ihr seid eine super Truppe). The impositive form of the directive corresponds to the communicated intention to support group solidarity and to claim continued group membership. The form and the communicated intention show that the speaker perceives the addressees as his ingroup rather than just a temporary "community of interest".

I have argued elsewhere that one aspect of group orientation is the production of diagonal directives to ingroup members, i.e. directives whose beneficiaries are persons other than either the speaker or the hearer, in particular other ingroup members. Such directives certify the speaker's belief that he or she is entitled to interfere with the behaviour of the addressee towards others. A diagonal directive occurs in turn 5, in which M1 asks M3 to fetch a cigar for M2 to smoke. M1 is here appropriating the role of a stage director for M2's exit, and by issuing a directive to another group member, he turns it into a group enterprise rather than an issue between himself and M2. After M4 turns up with the cigar, M2 signals that he consents to the role of being a participant in a cooperative enterprise by interrogation whether or not he is expected to smoke the cigar right now. M2 therefore recognises the right of other group members to decide on his actions, confirming his perception of the event as a joint enterprise. M1 persists in shaping the course of events by an unmitigated confirmation in turn 22. Between turns 34 and 35, M2 shows the cigar to M1 who comes up and takes it from him freeing M2 for another embrace. It has been argued elsewhere that non-aggressive communication through gesture alone is a powerful display of shared background, as it implies empathic "understanding without words".

In turn 40, M1 proposes that the group should smoke the cigar together as a ritual display of group friendship. In turn 41, after the suggestion was made by M1, M4 stresses how exceptional his participation is in the ritual by revealing that he had never smoked before. M1 responds with egal "all the same", responding to the possible illocutionary force of M4's utterance as an objection to smoking in general. M1 strongly imposes on M4 by stating that M4's preferences and principles do not count in the present situation, implying that M2's departure is far more important than M4's general inclinations. Thus, M2 takes it upon himself to decide on the hierarchy of values which he sees as binding for M4. This is a facet of the collectivist attitude towards social relationships, where social control is regarded as good (cf. Triandis and Vassiliou 1972). Gender stereotyping occurs (only men are expected to smoke the cigar), which is an aspect of a group-oriented, rather than an interpersonally-oriented, concept of the situation.

The episode concludes with M2's directive addressed to the members of his "team red" to support the group captain, F1, in turn 44. By producing the directive, and by using the

348

possessive pronoun when calling F1 "my captain", M2 not only expresses positive affection towards F1 but also emphasises his continued membership in the group.

The scene shows that although it has taken the German housemates longer than the Poles, because the housemates presupposed less intimacy among themselves in the beginning, high group integrity was in fact achieved in the "battle" edition, G4.

For comparison, the following scene from P3 contains a recorded monologue of a former male housemate broadcast to the house after he had voluntarily left the house.

121-P3. MONOLOGUE FROM TAPE. The scene takes place shortly after M1's unexpected exit from the house after three weeks of the program.

1 BIG BROTHER: (loudspeaker) uwaga # Big Brother zaprasza drużynę czerwonych i drużynę niebieskich na sofy

attention # Big Brother invites everybody to the sofas

(M1's voice comes from the loudspeaker)

(shouts, laughter)

2 M1 (voice over) przepraszam że w tej chwili nie będę dżentelmenem #

excuse me for not being a gentleman at the moment

3 chciałbym w tej chwili uderzyć do chłopaków #

I would like to appeal to the boys at the moment

4 ty Mario I ty Harnasiu a i ty również Chemiku #

you Mario[134] and you Mountaineer-NICKNAME[135] and also you Chemist-NICKNAME

5 mam nadzieję że przejmiecie moje obowiązki # znaczy # m:: #

I hope that you will take over my duties # I mean # m::

6 przejmiecie # _ y:: # rolę # . moją jaką # _ tam pełniłem w domu Wielkiego Brata #

take over # y:: # the role # . mine that I # played there in the Big Brother house

7 podzielicie się tym i będzie sprawiedliwie #

you will divide it among yourselves and it will be just

8 ty Maras z Harnasiem # sądzę że będziecie tutaj twardzi i _ mocni do końca #

you-sing. Maras[136] with the Mountaineer # I believe that you will be strong here and tough till the end

---

[134] The first name of the addressee playfully distorted by the use of its Italian version.

[135] "Harnaś: ringleader of a band of robbers in the Tatra mountains". *The Great Polish-English Dictionary.* Edited by Jan Stanislawski, Warszawa 1989. The addressee comes from the Tatra Mountains..

[136] A playfully distorted version of the addressee's first name.

9 _ róbcie wszystko po prostu tak jak robiliście do tej pory #
do everything just like you have done before
10 mam nadzieję że będzie wszystko grało # <u>wam</u> powierzam pole bitwy # na
zewnątrz #
I hope that everything will go well # to <u>you</u> I turn over the battlefield # outside
11 _ a ty Chemik # bądź podporą przede wszystkim dla naszych dziewczyn #.
czyli dla Stasi która myślę że zrozumie to co zrobiłem # to co się
wydarzyło w dniu dzisiejszym w domu
and you Chemist # give support first of all to our girls # . that is to Stasia who I think will understand what I
have done # what has happened today in the house
12 F1 czekaj tam na mnie i nie marudź!
wait there for me and don't grumble
13 M1 też sobie myślę że będziesz podporą dla pani kapitan
I think you also will support Ms. Captain
(F1, F2, Mx and Mxx laugh)
14 M1 a resztę dopowiedzcie sobie sami
and the rest fill-IMP-2nd pl. in yourselves
15 i jest wszystko w porządku # mam nadzieję że nie będzie wam . ciężko
po tej . rozmowie którą w tej chwili .. skierowałem do was # trzymam za
was kciuki # trochę będę nadal z wami # na- nadal będę walczył # tylko że
(laughs) troszeczkę w innych warunkach # trochę gorszych
and everything is all right # I hope you will not be grieving after this talk which I have given to you # I cross
my fingers for you # I will still be with you a bit # I will sti- still be fighting # but in slightly different (laughs)
conditions # a bit worse
16 także co # _ trzymajcie się i za każdym za każdym razem kiedy będzie
ktokolwiek z was wychodził # pamiętajcie o tym że ja tam jestem i będę za
wami czekał obojętnie na to co by się nie wydarzyło
and what else # take care and every time when anyone of you goes out # remember that I am there and will be
waiting for you no matter what happens

The manifestations of the high-on-involvement style of interaction pertaining to
directive activities included, next to the frequent use of directives, the impositive linguistic
forms: the imperative and the future realisation declarative; frequent use of nicknames and
playful treatment of first names (Maras vel Mario, Stasia, Chemik "Chemist", Harnaś
"Mountineer", pani kapitan "lady captain"), zero use of regular forms of the first names; the

use of the imperative as a socialiser in performing a speech act other than a directive (promise in turn 16: pamiętajcie o tym że… *remember that…)*; directives based on the feeling of shared responsibility for others, including directives reflecting the assumption of the need of female housemates for care and support and gender-based responsibility of male housemates for the female ones; and "blurring" of advice with a categorical demand. Another element of form suggestive of a collectivist perception of the situation was the occurrence of a formal indeterminacy between plural and singular address (ty Maras z Harnasiem, *sing-you Maras with Harnaś*).

Common aspects of 121-P3. MONOLOGUE FROM TAPE and the previously cited episode, G4. RON'S DEPARTURE include:

- gender stereotyping and gender sorting; next to "we" including both male and female participants, a secondary gender-based "we" was introduced by addressing a directive to male hearers by a male speaker,
- taking for granted the positive affection of the hearers,
- the frequent use of directives,
- their impositive form,
- the occurrence of directives as an expression of responsibility for the group,
- the occurrence of directives as vehicles of self-aggrandisement, based on the speaker's awareness of being an important group member.

The latter facet of both interactions illustrates a point made by Hofstede (1980, 1983, 1991) that ego enhancement (masculinity) and interdependence (collectivism) are not contrary values. Significantly, in both cases the housemate parting company from the ingroup produces a number of directives formulated in an impositive linguistic form as a means to express the desire to be viewed as a group member even after departing from the Big Brother house.

To summarise, the presupposition of consensus entrenched in the impositive linguistic form seems to be part and parcel of directive activities oriented towards confirming and strengthening group bonds and initiating the realisation of joint acts symbolic of team spirit; this could be observed in all three languages.

7.4.6. ADVISORY DEMANDS

In the chapter on method, I argued that in view of existing social relationships and the complementarity or co-directionality of interacting agents' aims and perspectives, the boundaries between advice and request are not at all as clear as have been postulated in classifications undertaken from the perspectives of the speech act theory. The next set of data, consisting of three successive scenes separated by editorial cuts, illustrates the function of impositiveness as an expression of responsibility for, and the resulting nurturing attitude towards, the addressees-beneficiaries. The blurring of boundaries between advice, instruction and demand in the context of group activities comes clearly into play.

98-E3. CAMPING IN THE YARD 1

F1 and M1 are talking about the plan to sleep in a tent.

1 M1 I did warn you # are you camping with us?

2 F1 yeah

3 M1 we are setting up camp at the moment # have you got a fleece for yourself

4 F1 no (turns and starts walking towards the bedroom)

5 M1 put some trousers on # put some trousers on

(F1 leaves)

98-E3. CAMPING IN THE YARD 2

F1, F2, M1, M2 and M3 prepare to leave the living room and sleep outside. F2 is the youngest housemate; M1 is two years older.

(M2 and M3 are talking to each other)

(M1 enters the room)

1 M1 to F2: --- # _ you haven't got any T-shirt on you

2 F2 no

(M1 walks up to F2 and puts his hands crossed over his breast)

3 M1 go and get them then # . off you go (makes a head gesture)

4 F2 why are you patronising me

5 M1 I'm not patronising `you # . I am telling you # . so that you'll keep warm!

6 F2 <starts singing><nanana>

7 M2 what? what is she saying

(F2 sips some champagne, puts her glass down and leaves)

8 M3 to M1: have I got to get my mattress and covers?

9 M1 I don't know # . it would be best if you did but # . but . PJ's at the moment trying to make a canopy

(F2 comes in with a sweater)

98-E3. CAMPING IN THE YARD 3
1 M1 you want thin layers # girls # lots of thin layers
(F1 nods)
2 (simultaneous speech)
3 M2 short or long
4 M1 I'd put on a long T-shirt # and then a T-shirt and a fleece # and
you can't go wrong
5 (simultaneous speech)
6 M1 to F1: you should definitely put socks on # and you should
definitely put another T-shirt on # . between that one and your other one
7 F1 [these socks are=]
8 M1 to F2: [Jane # I'm not] telling you again # it's up to you what you
want to do
9 F2 to M1: all right # what's the matter with you # . why are you being
rude to me
10 M1 because I've told you ten times # and you are still not doing it
11 F1 Trevis # . are these socks suitable camping socks
12 M1 oh come on # camping supervisor # [no they're not] # _ wear proper
socks and thin layers
13 F1 [can I wear them and that]

M1's taking command of the group is shown by the amount of directive activity on his part in turns 5/-1, 1/-2, 3/-2, 9/-2, 1/-3, 4/-3, 6/-3, and 11/-3. His directive behaviour has a gendered profile. In E3. CAMPING IN THE YARD 1, M1 signals the inclination to assume the position of authority by the use of the verb "warn", presupposing his knowledge of what happens if F1 does not comply with his directive. A strong hint is offered in turn 3, and F1 signals compliance by setting off, apparently in order to get some warm cloths. An imperative intensified by repetition follows in turn 5. Another strong hint referring to the missing warm clothes is directed at F2 in E3. CAMPING IN THE YARD 2; as the addressee, F2, does not react in the expected way, an imperative and the strongly impositive routine formula "off you go" follow. F2 does not accept M1's self-appointment as a person in charge entitled to display a paternal attitude towards her, and reacts defensively to the offence against her negative face wants. In turn 8 M3 asks M1 for instructions, which can be read as an indirect comment on the earlier exchange between M1 and F2, showing that, contrary to F2, M3 accepts M1 as an expert and a supervisor of the joint undertaking, supports him in this role and does not find his impositive behaviour illegitimate. M1 limits his claim of expertise and signals deference by admitting uncertainty and giving no definite answer. E3. CAMPING IN THE YARD 3 starts with M1 directing further instructions at "the girls". M2 joins the position appointed by M1 to the "girls", that is, the role of a non-expert dependent on M1's instruction, asking for instructions in turn 3. M1 shows that he is unwilling to impose on M2 in the same way. Rather than use an impositive form, he uses a deferent form of advice based on the conditional in his response in turn 4. He continues the instruction in a deontic declarative intensified by the lexical emphasiser "definitely" when addressing the women in turn 6. In turn 8, while speaking to F2, M1 produces a resignative routine formula recognised by the native speakers as being characteristic of parents talking to unsubordinated children, implying that he has lost patience with F2, who interprets it as being highly offensive. Another routine formula I have told you ten times typical for the same context of parent-child interaction follows in turn 10. F1 re-directs M1's attention and ostentatiously confirms his role as a supervisor by asking for instructions in turns 11 and 13; in doing that, she appeals to his positive face want "that his wants be desirable to (at least some) others" (Brown and Levinson 1978: 67). While commenting with apparent dissatisfaction about his role of "camping supervisor" in turn 12, M1 in fact sticks to the role, giving a blunt and definite answer: no they're not # wear proper socks and thin layers. The three scenes include four turns in which other housemates confirm their acceptance of M1 in the leader's role by consulting him on matters of proper preparation.

M1 shows concern for the needs and comfort of the group during the joint undertaking, takes the responsibility for the group and, in doing that, leaves the concern for F2's negative face wants aside, going so far as to provoke a reproach of being patronising. Speaking of parental instruction, Blum-Kulka (1990) commented that the signs of involvement can be threats to the other's individuality, and, "as stated by one of our Israeli informants, conveying involvement with no threat to individual space can be difficult; one needs 'to find a proper balance between involvement and interference'". As involvement means basically that you are treating other people's affairs as your own, a massive amount of involvement wipes away the distinction between advice and demand and may lead to a neglect of negative face wants displayed in selecting highly impositive ways of expression. Whether we may still talk of "positive politeness" here is controversial; clearly, F2 interpreted the utterance as not polite at all, while assuming an impositive, parental attitude by one's interlocutor can also be experienced as pleasant and reassuring, in particular by members of a culture that puts more emphasis on supportiveness than on the need to stay unimpeded[137]. A test of correlation between collectivism-individualism measured by Hui's (1988) INDCOL Scale and psychological needs as measured by Edwards Personal Preference Schedule (EPPS) showed that collectivist orientation correlates highly with the need of succorrance and nurturance (Hui and Villareal 1989)[138].

Three native speakers who watched the scenes – E3. CAMPING IN THE YARD 2 and E3. CAMPING IN THE YARD 3 – agreed that M1 was quite rude and patronising, while two of them, a male and a female respondent, thought that it was justified by the benevolent intention: it expressed how seriously M1 took his volunteered function. The female respondent confirmed that M1 was quite rude but at the same time thought that he was "being nice" to F2. The fourth, a female respondent, thought that the directive utterance in E3. CAMPING IN THE YARD 2 was produced within the joking frame of a parent-child role play and, therefore, was not improper or impolite (translated in the language of politeness research, it displayed "positive politeness"), while he was rude in the following scene, E3. CAMPING IN THE YARD 3.

Of five German respondents, four agreed on the evaluation of M1's interference with F2's freedom of action in E3. CAMPING IN THE YARD 2 as highly inappropriate, as F2 was an adult and could decide for herself, and one of them thought that M1 must have suffered as a result of F1's having caught a cold and becoming a burden to him in the past. The remaining German respondent judged the behaviour of M1 in E3. CAMPING IN THE YARD 2 as quite improper because of his body language only. All five German interviewees found that M1 behaved in a way that was impolite and improper, interfering heavily with F2's freedom of action in E3. CAMPING IN THE YARD 3, and they found her reaction proper and reasonable.

Of four Polish respondents, one also noted the impoliteness of M1's head gesture and bodily posture in E3. CAMPING IN THE YARD 2, and thought that it was the non-verbal component which triggered the self-defensive reaction by F2 rather than his verbal action. Two respondents failed to observe any rudeness, and one registered a verbal imposition but thought that it was justified by the benevolent intention. The three Polish respondents who did not find M1's behaviour impolite or improper described the scene as M1 giving a piece of

---

[137] Cross-cultural misunderstandings continue to occur even after a long exposure of one of the interlocutors to the other's native culture. Anecdotally, a close German friend of mine, having issued an impositive directive that prevented me from trodding on scattered shards of glass, interpreted my sincere thanks as ironic and apologised for the patronising tone of the advice.
[138] One might object, though, that the whole idea of making such measurement is circular in its results and premises; it presupposes that the high need of concern and nurture is separate from the collectivist stance rather than included in its definition (see also Reykowski 1999).

advice to F2. All Polish respondents found that F1 showed an exaggerated reaction. Three Polish respondents thought that M2's impositive behaviour was justified by the benevolent intention even if not particularly polite in E3. CAMPING IN THE YARD 3, too, and that F2 overreacted in turn 9. The remaining female respondent evaluated M2's behaviour as being excessively teacher-like and inappropriate, motivated probably by an aspiration to self-aggrandisement rather than actually caring for F2, and found F2's reaction appropriate.

On the whole, the German respondents showed themselves least sympathetic to any impositive verbal behaviour based on assuming a father-child relationship between the speaker and the addressee that restricted the addressee's freedom of action "for her own good", while the other respondents regarded it as at least partly justified. Because the answers to the questions posed were of a complex nature rather than "yes" or "no", no attempt will be undertaken to translate them into statistical significances. What could be shown was that well-meant impositiveness "for the beneficiary's own good" within the peer group has some amount of social acceptability in both Poland and Great Britain, and that the benevolent intention may override the impositiveness of form in the perception of social acceptability of an impositive directive at least for some observers, and at least for constellations involving male speakers and female addressees-beneficiaries. It seems to be least acceptable in the German cultural context.

The following scene where male speakers are giving categorical advice to a female housemate comes from P3. The speakers assume that the supportive intention offered legitimises the heavy impositiveness of the advice, and formulate it as a categorical demand. As in the preceding exchange, the scene shows that advice and requestives formulated in categorical, strongly impositive terms are not exclusive categories in the ingroup context. While the hearer is meant to be the main beneficiary of the advice, the speakers insist heavily that the advice should be followed – for her own good, and for the good of the group. The advice is offered by collaborating group members rather than by a single person.

The two essential features of the interdependence stance are mutual supportiveness directed towards positive face needs and group-oriented pressure directed against the negative face wants. The latter is visible when group members insist on an individual following a piece of advice, because his or her problems or inadequacies are being regarded as problems affecting the group and as inadequacies of the group. The following scene illustrates the social acceptability of the stance that personal problems should be shared with the group. The distinction between request and advice is neutralised by M1's explicit expression of the view that the hearer is obliged to reveal personal problems to the group, since group integration can only be achieved by intimate mutual knowledge. The speakers

M1 and M2 insist that if she keeps her personal problem to herself, the addressee F1 has little chance of regaining emotional stability and also threatens the group integration. The interaction takes place on the second day of the program.

122-P3. PERSONAL PROBLEM
Conversation in a circle including M1, M2, F1, F2 and F3.

1 M1 to F1: to co masz w sercu to jest napewno bardzo cen[ne] #
what you have in your heart is certainly very valuable

2 M2 [ta:]
yeah

3 M1 ja to czuję # _ **ale musisz się troszeczkę do nas otworzyć # jak mamy taki jakiś kontakt złapać**
I feel this # but you must open yourself up a little bit-DIM towards us # if we are to make some sort of contact

4 M2 ta:
yeah

... (editorial cut)

5 F1 natomiast # ja miałam ostatnio związek który miał się skończyć ´mał`żeń´stwem # (sighs)
and # I had a relationship lately which should have ended in marriage

6 M2 <start fast speech rate><nie musisz o tym mówić>
you don't need to talk about that

(F1 starts to cry)

7 M1 (sighs) ojejku: # oh oh
INTERJECTION # INTERJECTION

(silence 3 seconds)

8 F2 to nic złego # _ emocji się nie ukrywa
it's not a bad thing # emotions are not to be hidden

9 M2 to jest Marta dobre jak się wyładujesz tutaj # wiesz? bo: . ja widzę że ty się męczysz od samego początku # **musisz się tak właśnie- # . wywa:lić z siebie**
it is good Marta when you let yourself go here # you know? as I see that you're aching from the very beginning # you must just so- # . throw it out of yourself

10 M1 a my ci w tym pomożemy
and we will help you

11 M2 my ci pomożemy # po prostu
and we will help you # simply

12 M1 [przegadaj się i tyle]
talk yourself out

13 F2 [każdy ma swoje słabości] # każdy jakoś cierpi na swój sposób # każdy z nas coś przeszedł i musiał przez to przejść # bo inaczej byśmy się tu nie znaleźli # bo to . o to chodzi # szoł szołem a ludzkie uczucia są ludzkimi uczuciami # nie?
everybody has a weakness # everybody suffers in one way or another # everybody has gone through something and had to go through # otherwise we would not be here now # as this . it is all about that # a show is a show and human feelings are human feelings # right?

14 M1 nikt ci nie będzie miał za złe że ci coś nie wyszło # traktuj to normalnie jako rozmowę # taką towarzyską # bo w sumie wiesz no # dobrze że tak się ´dzieje # człowiek musi czasem wywalić z siebie coś # Marta
nobody is going to hold it against you that you have had a bad outcome # treat this simply as a conversation # a collegial one # because all in all you know # good that this happens # one has to spit certain things out of oneself # Marta

After gratifying F1's positive face wants by a complement regarding her personality in turn 1, in turn 3 M1 appeals to F1 to open herself up to the group. He formulates it in terms which imply that he is talking as the representative of the whole group, and presupposes the group's consent. He articulates the view that F1 should do something for herself and by doing so she will do something for the group, namely, integrate into the group – "open up" so that the group members can "make some sort of contact" to each other. In his appeal to F1's positive face, M1 expresses his personal appreciation for F1's feelings (turns 1 and 3); but this is the group ("us") which she should "open up" to (turn 3). M1 presupposes the shared perception of the individuals involved as an ingroup already in the beginning of the program. The reference to "us" exposes the view that "being in it together" is sufficient for treating the participants as a unit, whose interests he can voice. Good personal acquaintance (which is not yet there on the second day of the program) is not necessary for that. Group integration and openness among group members are seen as values in themselves, and the implication is that individual members should feel obliged to contribute to this integration by self-disclosure. The request-advice in turn 3 is formulated in direct terms using a deontic declarative mitigated by a lexical hedge in the diminutive: musisz się otworzyć do nas troszeczkę "you must open yourself up a bit-DIM towards us". M1 receives support from M2 in turns 2 and 4.

F1 shows that she perceives the directive as legitimate by her unsuccessful attempt to be co-operative and comply in turn 5. M2 shows consideration by granting F1 the right not to speak of her experiences. F2 attempts to make F1 feel relaxed about her emotional reaction declaring that an open display of emotions is a social norm, and M2 concludes that an opening in the form of a disclosure of an intimate experience will be good for F1, and uses a deontic declarative in a request-advice directed at F1, who "must throw everything out of herself" (musisz się tak właśnie- # wywa:lić z siebie). The focus of attention is now shifted towards the benefit of the addressee herself: opening herself to the group will do F1 good because it will relieve her suffering. In turns 6 and 7, M1 and M2 offer of help in strong declarative terms: my ci w tym pomożemy/my ci pomożemy po prostu, "we will help you on that/we will simply help you", unmitigated by means of conditional or interrogative expressions, presupposing the supposed beneficiary's compliance with the preceding advice, as well as the consensus on the part of the rest of the group on whose behalf the offer is made. Three native speakers who watched the scene thought that in using the plural personal pronoun "we", M1 and M2 are acting as representatives of the group, presupposing the group's consensus for their intention. The fourth respondent thought that in using the form "we", M1 and M2 were referring to each other rather than the group as a whole, on the basis of their recognition that they represented the same point of view.

Contrary to Lakoff's politeness maxim "give options", F1 is told that she must comply with the advice because it is good for her, and she is told that she will be helped, rather than given an offer in a form signalling that she is free to comply.

The scene displayed several features characteristic of the interdependence stance:

- The speaker M1 marks his utterance as made on behalf of the group by the use of the personal pronoun in the first person plural (turn 1).
- Keeping a personal problem to oneself is regarded as bad for the addressee and sharing the problem with the group is regarded as good for the addressee.
- Keeping a personal problem to oneself is regarded as bad for the group and sharing the problem with the group is regarded as good for the group.
- It is implied that the addressee is obliged to do what is good for the group.
- Little distinction is made between what is good for the addressee and what is good for the group.
- The value of mutual understanding is emphasised.

- The addressee legitimises the speaker's point of view by making an initial effort to comply with the directive.
- An offer of help is articulated in the verbal form presupposing acceptance rather than inquiring about the addressee's need of help.
- The offer is made on behalf of a group, minimally involving the speaker and at least one other; the group's consensus regarding co-operation in helping the addressee is presupposed.
- The consensus is confirmed by another speaker producing an utterance that repeats the previous speaker's formulation (turn 11), thus emphasising that he is of one mind with the previous speaker.

Three Polish respondents asked to evaluate the scene reacted to it as an attempt by the group to support a group member through a difficult time, while the fourth respondent thought that M1 was insensitive in particular at the beginning of the scene, talking in too casual a tone about a grave personal problem. All the respondents denied that the interlocutors were exerting pressure (Polish: "wywierali nacisk") on F1, and did not think that she may have experienced it as an illegitimate intrusion into her personal sphere. The occurrence of the scene as well as the respondent's reactions suggests that a strong impositiveness has a high legitimacy in the Polish cultural context if a supportive intention is declared, and in particular when issues related to group integration, viewed as advantageous to all group members, are at stake.

A high status of group integration relatively not only to individual but also to interpersonal goals and perspectives is confirmed by another episode from this series, not included here for the sake of brevity, in which three team members criticise the open display of bilateral bonds existing within their team (a male friendship and a heterosexual relationship) as drawbacks to team integrity. The broadcast part of the response to the criticism comes from the female housemate involved: she apologises and promises improvement. This confirms her perception of the directive as legitimate rather than an unwarranted intrusion into her and her friend's private affairs.

7.4.7. OVERPOWERING THE BENEFICIARY: WITHDRAWALS FROM THE BIG BROTHER HOUSE

The strongest form of a directive intervention is issuing directives that oppose the current preferences of the putative beneficiary. A situational context recurring in various series of the program is the confrontation of the group with a group member who turns her back upon joint activities, or decides to leave the Big Brother house altogether. This forces the remaining housemates to respond to the act itself, and the potential threat it poses to their sense of group integrity. The directive activities emerging as a part of the behavioural and verbal responses to this situation form the content of this chapter. The following scene comes from Polish edition P3.

123-P3. F1 climbs up onto the roof, obviously intending to escape from the Big Brother house.

1 F2 to F1: Kaśka chodź tutaj

Baśka-FEMALE-FIRST NAME-TRUNCATED-AUGM come here

2 F3 Kaśka wariatko

Baśka you're nuts

3 F2 Baśka weź ją! weź ją!

Baśka take her # take her

(M1 runs towards F climbing up the wall)

(M1 supports M2 who starts climbing up the wall in the direction of F1, who reached the roof and is walking on it towards the exit)

4 F3 Basia schodź # .. prosiłam cię żebyś dwa razy przemyślała zanim coś zrobisz

Basia-FEMALE FIRST NAME TRUNCATED get down # I asked you to think twice before doing something

5 F4 to M1: ty # zostaw Pabla # zostaw Pabla # nie

you # leave Pablo-MALE FIRST NAME CREATIVE DISTORTION # leave Pablo # no

6 M1 to M2: ściąg ją stamtąd # a bo jeszcze ty zjedziesz # nie nie nie

pull her down # oh lest you slide down yourself # no no no

7 F5 Pawulo nie wychodź

Pawulo-MALE FIRST NAME CREATIVE DISTORTION don't get up

8 M1 nie # nie # nie # bo jeszcze ty będziesz miał

no # no # no # lest you will have (implied: problems)

The housemates remaining in the yard produce a cross-fire series of imperative directives of two types. On the one hand, there are directives addressed to the beneficiaries themselves: to F1 to stay in the house (turns 1 and 4), and to M2 to abandon his intention of stopping F1 because he might harm himself, by getting physically hurt or by being punished for breaking the rules (turns 6, 7 and 8). On the other hand, there are directives in which the speaker appeals to the potential actor to act in favour of EXT in ways contrary to the latter's current choice. M2 is asked to hinder F1's escape (turns 3 and 6), and M1 (who helps M2 climb the wall) is asked to abandon the support potentially harmful to M2 (turn 5). Benevolence is expressed by countering the beneficiaries' (F1's and M2's) observable intentions, i.e., displaying "benevolent incapacitation", which was discussed before as a cultural script of Polish and a facet of the interdependence stance.

Significantly, when a voluntary departure occurs in the third British series, it is similarly accompanied by impositive directives as a device of showing care, accompanied by a joint verbal action symbolic of team bonding and fostering camaraderie. In the following scene, M2, who had proclaimed before that he was going to leave the house of his own will, unexpectedly leaves the group while they are watching television, and is preparing to escape from the house by climbing onto the roof.

99-E3. M2 goes out to the yard and starts climbing the wall. Other housemates are watching televison in the living room. M1 is on the "rich" side of the yard and M2 on the "poor" side of the yard; the rules of the program do not allow the housemates to cross the dividing line.

```
1  F1 Sammy!
2  M1 no:::!
3  M1 don't let him # don't let him go # [do= # do= # don't let him go]
4  F2    [is he doing this]
5  M1 # cause he'll hurt himself # don't let him go
6  M3 is he being ^serious
7  F2 no: # Sammy
8  R F3 Sammy!
```
(the group leave the house and run to the yard)
```
9  F4 go # go Sammy
10 F3 Sammy go
11 F2 <starts singing><[go:: # Sammy # go] ><ends singing>
15 M4 [you're having a laugh]
12 F3 <starts singing>   <[ go # go]
13 F4                    [ go # go # go]>    <ends singing>
14 F3 <starts singing>   <[[go:: # Sammy # go]
15 F2                    [go go]
16 F4                    [go go go]>         <ends singing>
17 M1                    [Sammy be care]]ful! Sammy be careful!
18 F3 Sammy be careful!
19 (loud cheers)
```

When M2 starts climbing the roof, the group is confronted by the necessity to react to this rather than leave him alone and leave his spectacular act without an audience. The display of bonds with M2 consists of two phases. In turn 3, M1 starts displaying an "ingroup identity" by appealing to the responsibility of other housemates for M2 in imperative form, signalling the intensity of the intention and the assumption of its high legitimacy. The multiple repetitions in turn 3 and 5 intensify the directive and forcefully express insistence. In these imperatives, M1 demands that the addressees stop M2, i.e. act against his will, which is a powerful expression of preference for interdependence rather than autonomy. In turns 6 and 7, M1 finds support in F1 and F2 who verbalise their care for M2 as an attempt to interfere with his intention. Then, in turn 8, F4 expresses concern for M1 by an affirmative verbal act, consistent with the autonomy perspective, which is then immediately taken up by F3 and also by F2, who had previously joined M1 in his protest. F2 joins in, "discovers" the melody of the popular funk song "Go Sally" as a means of articulation of encouragement for M5, and is joined by F3 and F4, who sing the chorus part. F2, F3 and F4 engage in a collective performance of verbal action. At the same time, two housemates from the "poor side", F2 and M3, break the rules of the Big Brother game through stepping over the fence dividing them from the "rich" part of the yard (from which M2 is climbing to the roof), and join the group on the rich side in applauding M2. The rest of the current "poor" group stay behind the fence. In this crossing of the symbolic barrier, the two group members symbolically break out from the staged reality of Big Brother in order to manifest the authenticity of their feelings for M2. While M2 is physically leaving the territory of the Big Brother House, F2 and M3 are enacting the same move by transgressing the conventional border, and at the same time the conventional order. Thus, for a moment they turn the symbolic territory of the Big Brother house – a stage with its symbolic "boundary" – into a "normal" territory, stressing that they are acting as their true selves and not as a part of the game. This violation of the rules is a manifestation of the authenticity of their feelings and an act of solidarity with M2. Asked by Big Brother for the reasons for this transgression, F2 explains: I just wanted to show that I respect him. M3 responds to Big Brother's requirement that he think over the breaking of the rules, and his ability to live by them, by asking Is Sammy okay?, clearly juxtaposing the concern for the ex-housemate with concern for the rules and implying that the former matters more to him. These comments contextualise the transgression as a symbolic display of concern and authenticity, which confirms the high emotional load present in the escape scene.

Although the initial directive addressed by M1 to the group for the sake of external beneficiary in turn 3 runs counter to what happens next (the group starts encouraging M2 instead of stopping him), it shows that in the dramatic moments relevant to group integration, such as a housemate's departure, the responsibility of the group for a group member is being emphasised, and the means of this emphasis can be categorical demands. The strongly impositive linguistic form (imperative and multiple repetitions) on the formal side is accompanied by a dominance of values characteristic of interdependence: the responsibility of a group for particular group members, and the view that it is legitimate to act against a group member's own will if this is perceived as beneficial to him or her. Wierzbicka (1985: 167) states: "If our view of what is good for another person does not coincide with his/her own, Anglo-Saxon culture requires that one should rather respect the other person's wishes (i.e., his/her autonomy) than to do what *we* think is good for him/her; Polish culture tends to resolve the dilemma in the opposite way". Here, we see the dictum attributed by Wierzbicka to the Anglo-Saxon culture being violated in a group-oriented directive promoting interdependence values.

The following two sets of data also provide support for the claim that a factor which triggers an interaction style contesting the principle of non-imposition, independent of nationality, are circumstances that threaten group integrity by putting it into doubt, such as a housemate's decision to leave the Big Brother house voluntarily or such as refusing to participate in group activities.

100-E3. The housemates are bobbing for apples. M1 is the next contestant. F2, a high-ranking professional, refused to participate in some group activities, especially some that might be viewed as uncultivated. On this occasion, again, she chose not to participate.

1 M2 hey # you're not even playing # so leave him alone (laughs)
2 F1 (laughs)
3 F2 I threw the dice man # I threw the dice
4 M2 (laughs)

While I initially interrpreted the directive as purely a joke because of the laughter, two native speakers evaluated the laughter as a lubricant and the directive as an expression of irritation at F2's refusal to participate in a joint activity. In the following scene, M1 comments on the offensive strategy he had applied towards F1. The notation preserves the identities of the housemates in the previous data.

101-E3. UNDERCONFIDENT
1 F1 I've decided to leave the house # _ tomorrow

2 M2 to[morrow] !

3 M1 [---]

4 F1 yeah

(M2 hugs and kisses F1)

6 M1 [---] a bit more

7 M3 I'm not surprised

8 F1 hehe

9 M1 I'm just a bit e:= # .you know # this is= # this is your= # this is=
this is something different # you know # you're= # we are twelve people
that have been given the opportunity to do this # you know #. because
I've met people before that are a little bit timid you know

10 F1 I'm so not timid!

11 M1 [not timid # . not timid #. you know # but --- underconfident ---]

12 F1 [I'm so not timid # I'm not underconfident ---]

(editorial cut)

13 M1 and now I've given you a hard time about it # because [---]

14 F1 [but mate # you know what I mean]

15 M1 but that's what I said to my mom # --- my mom --- computers # and I
know that she can't work the telephone # or the radio # and I always said
to her # you can't do it # . you can't work the computer

16 F2 (laughs)

17 F1 [---]

18 M1 [---] listen # the way that my mom is # if I tell her you can do
something # with her # she's all well # . I can't do it # it's too
complicated #. but if I tell her # you can't do it # . she's all # hm #
I'm gonna show him # . and she has # and I can't believe my mum has done
so well # [she's got her first]

19 F1 [---]

20 M1 computer this week # you know

In turns 13-15 and 18, M1 justifies his earlier attacks on F1's self-esteem by revealing that it has been both intentional and well-meant. M1 interprets F1's conduct as lack of confidence, and explains the psychological mechanism he intended to spark off: he has been using an offensive strategy as an instrument to provoke F1 into doing the opposite, for her own benefit. At the same time, from M1's perspective, a group benefit was at stake, as shown by his comment regarding F1 in an explanation given to Big Brother: the reason why we nominate people # is that they are not a part of the group. In M1's eyes, group integration suffers from F1's unwillingness to join in; the use of the plural in the personal pronoun emphasises the aspiration towards group consolidation. A face threat seems to be a justified and legitimate means of persuasion because it can benefit both the addressee and the group.

The offensive strategy referred to by M1 in the explanation of his motives appears in the contributions of German speakers M2 and M3 in the following scene. The offensive strategy initiated by M3 is taken up by M2 and is developed in a joint action of the two speakers.

50-G2. BE A MAN

The conversation takes place among M1, M2, M3 and M4. Because of some clashes with some members of the house, M1 previously declared that he was going to leave voluntarily. He has just proposed in a circle of his supporters to play a trick on those housemates who are happy about his decision. The trick would be to proclaim, contrary to his actual intention, that he has changed his mind and is going to stay in the Big Brother house. The topic is continued in the following sequence.

1 M1 aber so Spaßes halber könnte man das durchziehen # oder? wenn ich heute Abend ins Bettchen ´gehe
but just for fun one could carry it out # right? when I go to bed-DIM. tonight

2 M2 wieso Spaßes halber # mach's doch einfach
why for fun # just do it

3 M1 ne # nur um die blöden Fressen zu sehen
no # just to see these bloody mugs

4 M2 Chrischi
FIRST NAME-distorted

5 M1 ihr müsst dann voll mit darauf einsteigen # ihr müsst dann aber nicht so:-
you must fully play along with it # but you mustn't then like-

6 M2 Chris # du bist hier in einem Spiel # das hast du nie wieder # du hast nichts zu verlieren # wenn du jetzt rauskommst-
FIRST NAME-truncated # you are here in a game # you'll never get to do it again # you have nothing to lose # if you get out now-

7 M3 Mann du hast doch mindestens uns
man you at least have us

...

8 M1 hei # soll # sollen wir es mal spaßeshalber durchziehen?

hey # should we carry it out just for fun?

9 M3 welche Spaßes halber # mach's Mann # <u>mach's! ich meine das</u> `ernst #
habe dir schon im Zimmer mal gesagt # ich finde es cool wenn du bleibst #
du hast hier kein Grund zu gehen

what fun # do it man # do it! I mean it seriously # have told you in the room already # I find it cool if you stay
 # you have no reason to leave

10 M2 ich wusste dass er das nicht packt # --- # ich wusste dass er
seinen Schwanz einzieht und haut ab

I knew that he wouldn't manage to do it # --- # I knew that he would chicken out and run away

11 M3 --- Wette?

bet?

12 M1 hei Penner # soll ich euch mal den Schwanz lang ziehen?

INTERJECTION you beggars # should I pull your cocks?

13 M2 komm ran

come up

14 M3 da musst du erst mal die Eier haben um hier zu bleiben dann kannst
du erst mit mir reden # --- wie wir

first you need the balls to stay here and only then you can talk to me # --- like we

15 M2 erst mal musst du Mann sein # um mal einfach durchziehen

first you must be a man # to just get through it

16 M3 und du # kaum wird es dünn um dich # ode:r . bissche Glatteis-

and you # as soon as you are on shaky ground # or things get slippery-

17 M1 dünn? Glatteis? seid ihr blöd?

shaky ? slippery? are you stupid?

Turns 4 and 6 include the use of a creatively transformed and a non-standard truncated form of the addressee's first name (Christian), which is relatively rare in the German material and shows a high involvement of the speakers. In turn 7, M3 speaks for the whole group present referring to it as "we" (acc. uns) and declaring loyalty to M1 on everybody's behalf. When warm positively polite persuasion in turns 2, 4, 6, 7 and 9 does not seem to work, the speakers take recourse to offence. In turns 10, 14, 15 and 16 the male virtues of M1 are put in doubt by M2 and M3, and he is declared faint-hearted and lacks confidence. In turn 10, M2 uses a provocative strategy of claiming that M1's decision was predictable because it resulted from weakness which is an essential trait of the addressee's personality, which M2 is familiar with.

By apparently offending F1 and M1 (violating their need for free choice and non-impingement on their positive image of themselves), the speakers in both episodes are attempting to make them join in or stay in the house, and thus expressing the wish to continue and intensify the relationship with the addressees. In this context, pressure on the addressee may take impositive and offensive forms which attack the addressee's self-esteem and threaten his or her negative face. As a desire for the hearer to stay in the house amounts to a declaration of positive feelings towards him or her, the violation of negative face needs and personal territory is legitimised through emotional involvement and "meaning well" for the addressee. As Tannen (1986) notes, "everything said as a sign of involvement can be in itself a threat to the other's individuality". In the exchanges above, a face threat is consciously used as a device of the involvement strategy which provides its legitimation. When others join in and collaborative persuasion results, as in G3. BE A MAN, the group-oriented character of the act is made explicit.

7.4.8. MODESTY

While the preceding sections emphasise the role of impositive directive strategies in minimising distance and fostering group integration, the observations of the occurrence of interactional modesty point to alternative options applied in this function. The term "interactional modesty" is used here to denote the principle of minimising self-praise and maximising self-criticism, included by Leech (1983) in his Politeness Principle under the heading of Modesty Maxim. While it does not involve any degree of impositiveness, it does not belong to the repertoire of negative politeness, either, and is applied in directive activities as a "third choice" constitutive of a distance-diminishing strategy of a non-impositive sort. English was the only language in which it occurred (and repeatedly so) as a modifying device in directives within the analysed data.

An admittance of one's own weakness may function as a confirmation of a fraternising disposition by indicating openness and trust. It hints at the speaker's view of the others as benevolent persons with whom he may talk openly about his weakness as they will not use it against him, and his relationship with them as being not loaded with a face threat requiring constant attention to his own positive image.

In the following scene 91-E3, the housemates have been given a task of answering several quiz questions and writing the answers on a board. M proposes that the other housemates should answer the questions and he will write the answers down on a board.

```
91-E3.
M do you want me to write it # now guys # it's going to be on TV and
films # and all that # isn't it # . and I'm not the best # so I'll write
it
```

Here, M's comment on himself implies that he does not feel the need to pay much attention to working on his image as a capable person without any flaws because he feels at ease with his companions and takes their benevolence for granted.

This interaction strategy relates to the "honesty and openness" emphasised by a native British respondent commenting on the first encounter as a specific property of the British interaction style (*it is typically British to be completely honest and open with emotions*), an attribution that apparently reversed Schmid's (2003) comment referring to the "typically British" constraint on showing intense emotions (anger, joy and impatience were used as examples). The source of the apparent controversy is revealed by the broader context of the respondent's comment: according to the respondent, Germans would not admit to nervous tension because it could be interpreted as a sign of weakness, while the British applied it as a device for breaking the ice and a means by which common ground was created. The British speakers reduced distance offering comments on their undesirable emotions, as well as their minor flaws. Gonzáles Bermúdes (2005), who analysed Spanish and British directives using the questionnaire method, observed that in asking for a pen from a mate during a university lecture young British respondents usually offered self-derogatory comments referring to their lack of organisation skills.

Interactional modesty as a politeness device has been emphasised by Marcjanik (1997) as being characteristic of the Polish style of politeness, conceived in terms of a "verbal play". Marcjanik referred to ritualised forms of outgroup interaction, though. I didn't note any occurrences of polite modesty in the Polish data.

7.4.9. THE CONSTRUAL OF THE BIG BROTHER HOUSE AS A FAMILY

One of the indicators of perceiving the joint presence in the Big Brother house as producing strong and not just voluntary bonds and mutual obligations is when the group are metaphorically referred to as a family. The two scenes below, both from P3, show how the family metaphor reflects the self-perception of the group, and illustrate the role which this perception plays in legitimising directives. In both scenes, the scope of the family metaphor is the whole group, consisting of members of the "red" and "blue" teams.

124-P3. RHINOCEROS
On the third day of their stay in the Big Brother house, M1 criticises M2 for abusing F2, and is supported by F1 who claims the group is a family.
(M2 enters)
1 M1 to M2: --- facet # żeby to zrobił z wiewiórą # to musi być tak jak. nosorożec
a man # who does it with a squirrel-AUGM # must be like a rhinoceros
2 M2 jak to z wiewiórą # ---
what do you mean by a squirrel-AUGM
3 M1 bez . bez uczuć # bez- # bez- # no . ta:k # jak nosorożec
without feelings # without # without # well just so # like a rhinoceros
4 M2 bez ^uczuć
without feelings
5 M1 bez ^uczuć jak nosorożec #
without feelings like a rhinoceros
6 F2 co ma wiewióra do seksu # przepraszam bo nie rozumiem
what does a squirrel have to do with sex # excuse me because I do not understand
7 F1 no ja też nie wiem # w ogóle
yeah I don't know either # at all
8 F2 sam nie wie o czym mówi
he himself doesn't know what he is talking about
9 M2 Bartek # o co ci chodzi (laughs)
Bartek # what is this about
10 M2 wiesz zrób to dobrze # . żebym- # ja potem-
do it well though # so that I- # afterwards I do not-
11 F3 nie # no ta: k # on ma rację
no # well yes # he is right
12 M2 ale przecież ty nie będziesz świecił za mnie oczami
but this is obviously not like you will have to be ashamed of me

13 M3 żeby on nie musiał poprawiać
so that he will not have to amend this
14 F3 nie no # słuchaj # jesteśmy rodziną
well no # listen # we are a family
15 M1 mnie chodzi o to żebyś-
what I am after is that you should-
16 F2 proszę bardzo # jeżeli któryś z moich przyjaciół to ogląda # proszę
mi to nagrać
please # if a friend of mine is watching this # please record it
17 F1 (laughs)
18 M1 mnie chodzi o to żebyś jej nie zawiódł bo ona- . # zranisz jej
uczucia po prostu
what I am after is that you don't disappoint her because she- # you will hurt her feelings simply

In this interaction, M1 is trying to intervene in the sexual relationship between F1 and M2, whom he accuses of having no true feelings for F1, amounting in his eyes to animal and insensitive behaviour. "With a squirrel", an expression for having sex without any emotional bonding, is unknown to other group members, who react towards his performance without understanding (turns 6 and 7), requiring additional comment. Upon understanding M1's intention, F3 in turn 11 declares that he is correct. In turn 12, M2 expresses his hypothesis about the intention behind M1's preceding unfinished utterance (turn 10): he interprets M1's intervention as hinting that he is afraid of being made responsible for M2's actions and having to be ashamed of them. In turn 14, F2 uses the family metaphor as a justification of M1's behaviour and as support for his involvement. In her eyes, M1 is acting correctly because like family members, the housemates have the right and duty to control the behaviour of other group members towards each other. The scene takes place on the third day of the program; the conception of the group as a family and F2's claim is not legitimised by the housemates' intimate knowledge of each other and mature friendship, but by the fact that they are taking part in the show together. Polish respondents interpreted the use of the family metaphor alternatively as pointing out that the advice is meant well for the addressee (*radzimy ci jak rodzina*, "we advise you like your family"); pointing out that M2's behaviour is putting the group's image at risk and the "good reputation" of the group; or pointing out the right and duty of group members to interfere with actions which put one member of the group at a disadvantage. All interpretations legitimise interference by rendering M1's behaviour towards F1 as an aspect of collective conduct.

In the following interaction which comes from the fourth week of the program, the family metaphor also occurs in the context of moral persuasion. F1 persuades F2 and M1 to stop quarrelling, arguing that it is the Easter holidays and they are her only family present.

125-P3.

1 BB uwaga # Wielki Brat prosi o chwilę skupienia # __ zbliżają się .
święta . Wielkiej Nocy # _ niech w domu Wielkiego Brata zapanuje zgoda #
attention # Big Brother is asking for a moment of concentration # Easter is coming # let peace rule in the Big Brother house

2 M2 o # . tak samo mówię
hear hear # this is exactly what I say

3 BB kto się kłócił # . niech wyciągnie do siebie ręce
who was quarrelling # extend your hands to each other

4 F1 w tej chwili?
right now?

5 (several housemates applaud)
(F1 and M1 join hands, approach each other, then embrace)
(some other housemates embrace in pairs, are reconciled)
...

6 M3 jakby-
like

7 F1 jakby czuję lekki niedosyt
I feel like not quite having got enough

8 M3 no # tak
right # yes

9 M4 ja tak samo
the same about me

10 F1 to M1, F2: jest jakaś szansa żebyście się pogodzili? _ to są święta
słuchajcie # w tej chwili wy jesteście moją rodziną
is there any chance that you will put an end to your clash? it's Easter # listen-IMP-pl. # at this moment you are my family

11 M2 dokładnie
exactly

12 M4 no to podnieść tyłki # . i # . podać sobie ręce
then lift-INFINITIVE your bottoms # and give-INFINITIVE each other your hands
(simultaneous talk)
13 M3 do wtorku
till Tuesday
14 F1 chociaż do wtorku (laughs)# naprawdę # w tej chwili jesteście moją rodziną # nie mam nikogo innego ---
at least till Tuesday # really # at the moment you are my family # I have nobody else

In turns 10 and 14, F1 insists upon reconciliation between F2 and M1 grounding the requestive in the metaphorical conceptualisation of the group as her family. The grounder at the same time explains why F1 puts a high value upon peace within the group, especially during the Easter holidays (lasting till the following Tuesday) which are celebrated as an important family feast in Poland. F1 gives F2 and M1 an additional incentive to comply by pointing out their obligation to care for F1's well-being as a member of their family. The Polish logic of the interaction encourages overt references to ingroupness, and there is little restriction on emphasis in their verbal realisation.

Another marker of the conceptualisation of the Big Brother communities along these lines is the emergence of Mum and Dad figures. In P3, the group assigns these roles to two housemates through giving them appropriate nicknames. They are from different teams and play their respective roles for the whole of the house. The roles of the Mother and the Father are assigned to the oldest man and one of the oldest women in the house, who are also parents several times over in their life outside the Big Brother house. This stereotyping is exhibited by repeatedly addressing them as "Mum" (*mamuśka*), "Mother" (*Matka*), "Father" (*Ojciec*) and "Dad" (*tato*), as well as the occasional longer stretches of interaction involving a verbal play on the parental role, such as the following:

126-P3. F1, F2, F3 and F4 are sitting in the yard; M1 and M2 are playing volleyball; M3 is standing nearby
(M1 throws the ball)
1 M3 stłuczą szybę a ja będę płacił za to
they're going to break the window and I'll have to pay for that
2 F1 ^chodź tato tutaj
come here daddy
3 M3 to M1, M2: _ a ja będę za was płacił!
and I'll have to pay for you!

4 F2 ^cho:dź tato lato # tato la:to   BEGGING INTONATION
come daddy maeddy (a nonsense rhyme)
5 F1 ^chodź tato tutaj # do dzieci adoptowanych się nie przyznawaj # ---
znam taki kawał
come here daddy # don't admit adopted children # --- # I know a joke that goes like that

In turn 1, M3 comments humorously on M1's action (who is of approximately the same age as M3) by producing a stereotypical complaint of a parent afraid that his or her children's play might cause damage which s/he will have to pay for. M3 is here verbally enacting the parental role attributed to him by the housemates.

Scenes in which older housemates behave in ways which could be interpreted as involving a parental attitude are also present in the German program. In a later stage of G4, after the housemates had spent two months together, a female group "captain", a mother in "real life", displayed an authoritarian attitude towards a male housemate's order of food he delivered by phone to Big Brother, arguing that he is not really going to need as much as that, and actually cancelling some of the order in her call to Big Brother. This behaviour was interpreted as "maternal" by the host of the show, who commented on it as being typical of mothers who deny unreasonable demands by their children. While his role as a father figure was not overtly referred to in the material available to me, the oldest male housemate in G2, a father of six, displayed a style of interaction which was suggestive of a parental attitude towards the younger housemates, as in the following scene where he adopts an authoritarian attitude predicating the interlocutor's compliance with a directive as a matter of fact:

51-G2. ROPE
M1, M2 and F1 are in the yard, M1 is preparing a loop on a rope, while M2 is close to him, and F1 is watching from a distance.
1 M1 ich werde es einmal ganz ausrollen # _ jetzt wirst du mir mal helfen
I will just uncoil all of it # now you are going to help me
(M2 approaches M1)
2 M2 wie ist das Thema?
what's the topic?
3 M1 Knoten # jetzt wirst du hier machen einen Knoten
a knot # now you will make a knot here
(M2 makes a knot on the rope)

```
4 M1 zieh
```
pull
(M2 pulls the rope)

The same German speaker also imposes in a parent-like manner on another younger housemate in the scene 50-G2. BE A MAN, discussed earlier in 7.4.7. This impression, however, which I shared with all three Polish viewers who watched these and other scenes featuring M1, was not confirmed by the native German respondents. While all the Polish viewers claimed that age difference might have contributed to both the occurrence and the impositive form of the directives produced by M1, all five German viewers perceived his impositive behaviour in terms of a dominant personality and rank co-determined by bodily posture, and did not note the age factor. None of the Poles, including two male respondents, noted M1's bodily posture as a potential source of his high self-assurance. The difference was statistically significant[139]. Two out of four British respondents also claimed that the age difference might have played a role in M1's verbal behaviour.

In the third British series, a potential candidate for the father figure because of his age was a childless bachelor, who on the second day of the program signalled an inclination to take over the responsibility for the group of younger inmates by suggesting to his female equivalent, the oldest woman in the group, that she cooperate with him for the sake of the group – by cooking something to prevent the food from decaying. F not only rejected the implicit suggestion but also was critical of M because of what she saw as excessive involvement. A verbal construal of family bonds in E3 was restricted to one case of nicknaming using a family term, where M is called "uncle" rather than "father". The non-explicit metaphorisation of the group into a family-type of ingroup is present, however, in the nickname "baba" given to the youngest female group member, and the paternal attitude displayed towards her by some group members. In E4, the family metaphor was once used jokingly by a male speaker who was the oldest person in the group and about 14 years older than the addressee:

15-E4. M is reading in the garden and F enters.
```
M sit down # sit down son # tell your old man a story
```

To sum up, the conceptualisation of the Big Brother house as a family found explicit expression within the analysed material only in P3, where the family metaphor was

---

[139] df=1; chi^2 = 7; p<0.01

repeatedly used to legitimise directive acts. While some elements in the German and English editions suggest that this perspective was compatible with at least some insiders' perception of the group, the absence of explicit predications of the metaphor precludes definite conclusions.

7.4.10. PLURAL REFERENCES: "WE" AND "YOU-PLURAL"

It has been noted before that the form of directive utterances can contribute to the verbal construction of others as groups, oneself as a group member, and individual actions as actions by the group. This section deals with a small range of linguistic devices which help articulate such a perception and construction of relationships in current interaction.While the linguistic construal of a group as interaction and discourse participant occurs in the data involving all three languages under analysis, different cultures and languages are likely to facilitate such a perception in different degrees.

In several Polish scenes, the perception of "the other" as a group rather than a number of individuals was manifested in underspecifying the actor while making requests by means of a plural form of address. On the other hand, the perception of self as sharing attitudes and goals with the others was reflected by the speaker using the first person plural for self-reference. The speakers "spoke for the group" (including at least the speaker and one other person) on the assumption that they were articulating the group's feelings and attitudes. This is to be distinguished from the hearer-inclusive "solidarity plural".

7.4.10.1. SOLIDARITY PLURAL

The best-known application of the use of the first person plural in directives referring to the action by the addressee in the 1st person singular is the so-called "Krankenschwesterplural", used in hierarchical set-ups in role-based communication in instructions by a person in authority towards a patient, pupil, child, etc. In peer-to-peer communication, the we-plural is used in a different way, in order to promote rapport by an appeal to a background common to the speaker and hearer (in the form of having to obey the same rules, or wanting the same thing, etc.), or by a re-casting of the action by the hearer as the joint action of the speaker and the hearer. Consider the following examples of solidarity plural:

```
52-G2.
M1 wollen wir es machen oder?
```
do we want to do it or?

This form is a routine formula of German, by which a "joint volition" of M1 and M2 is created; the speaker symbolically signals that he is inquiring about the "joint preference" of himself and the addressee, implying that he will treat the addressee's preference as his own, sharing it in advance. A semantically analogous construction appears in the English data:

```
103-E3.
F1 to M1: are we ready to do this outside # because it's getting hot in
here
```

In the following exchange in Polish, M1 is using the plural to minimise the face threat posed by a corrective directive addressed at M2 by stating it as a general rule applying to everybody, including M1 and himself:

```
33-P3.
M1 to M2: nie puszczamy bąków dobra?
```
we don't fart # okay?

The re-casting of the predicated action of the hearer as a joint action is visible in the following two sets of data:

127-P3. F1 has been talking into her microphone for the last couple of minutes, begging the sound technicians to play her favourite song for her.

```
F2 dajmy dźwiękowcom żyć
```
let's let the sound people live (meaning: let's leave them in peace)

```
104-E3.
M let's just end all conversation about it
```

In 104-E3, M directs his utterance to a group of housemates engaged in a discussion. M is free not to participate in the conversation, and his own participation is not at issue here. What he is in fact doing by means of this utterance is not issuing a proposal of doing (or not doing) something together, but a request to the other participants that they stop talking about a subject that he finds not worth talking about. While I do not share the view represented by Aijmer (1996) that all apparent proposals are in fact camouflaged requests, I believe that in some cases the use of a plural self-reference is an act of re-casting a request into a form typical for proposals for reasons of promoting rapport and solidarity.

Besides the routine formula "wollen wir x" in German, the use of the solidarity plural is sporadic, and qualitatively similar in all three groups. The data does not provide any structured insight into the differences between the interaction strategies at this point between the three groups. It was to be expected because the use of the solidarity plural does not imply the existence and significance of a group as the a background to the interaction between the speaker and the addressee, and can be analysed within the interpersonal dyadic model of speaker-hearer communication.

7.4.10.2. SINGULAR SPEAKER, PLURAL SELF-REFERENCE

I have selected the following scene as an illustration of the plural "you" in addressing others and the plural "we" in self-reference:

128-P3. SLEEPING IN THE CORNER

The members of the winning team – F1, F2 and M1 – enter the "rich" bedroom after the losing team have had to move out. F1 and F2 are the only women in the team, which also includes M1, M2 and M3.

1 F1 nie no # my z Barbi idziemy spać tam w kąt # (to M1:)a wy tu

no # Barbi and (literally: we with Barbi)[140] I go sleeping there in the corner # (to M1:) and you-pl. here

---

[140] The functionality of the personal pronoun "we" in Polish exemplified in turn 1 above contrasts with the two other languages under study. The literal translation into English is:

we with Barbi go-1st pl. to sleep there in the corner

"We with Barbi" is the standard construction in the Polish language that corresponds to the English "Barbi and I" and the German "Barbi und ich", which results in numerous cases of communicative disturbances due to its transfer by Polish learners into German and English. Self-reference can also be made in the singular as in English and German, for example:

Idę	z kolegą	do kina.
I'm going	*with a friend*	*to the cinema.*

This form is infrequently used and carries different social connotations; it individuates the speaker, and focuses on the speaker rather than the action itself. In contrast, forms of expression with a self-reference in the singular – *Barbi and I, Barbi und ich* – are standard ways of predicating the state of affairs in English as

(F1 points to two beds in the corner)

```
2 F2-BARBI a czemu?
```
and why?

```
3 F1 tak # bo tu poprzestawiali # i dobrze
```
yes # because they have moved the furniture around # and this is good

(M2, M3 come in)

```
4 F1 ej # . wy śpicie teraz tu (points to a place)
```
hey # you sleep here now

```
5 M1 dlaczego?
```
why?

```
6 F1 ^bardzo prosimy          BEGGING INTONATION
```
we ask-please very much

```
7 F2 to M1 dajcie nam tutaj # weź mi tą # . walizkę # _ daj mi tą walizkę
```
give-IMP-pl. us # bring-IMP-sing. me the # the suitcase # give-IMP-sing. me that suitcase

In this scene, the plural is used three times in the contexts where a different form could also be applied but would carry a different social value:

---

well as in German. The use of addressee-exclusive "we" requires specification of the referents in an attached nominal phrase:

We go to the cinema today, Jaś and myself.
Wir gehen heute ins Kino, Jaś und ich.

If Wierzbicka (1985, 1986) were right in arguing that each language grammaticalises forms of expressions corresponding to the values and attitudes of its members, this plural form of reference unique to Polish could reflect the preference for a relationship-oriented perception of self. The issue of the link between syntactic structures and the perceptions of reality, social reality included, in a given culture counts as one of the most controversial issues in functional grammar. It concerns, for example, such widely divergent phenomena as subjectless sentences in Slavic and other languages, or the obligatory use of the third person honorifics in Japanese. The opponents of easy-made back-tracing of grammaticalisation phenomena to underlying social perceptions and construals of reality argue that language is a historically grown phenomenon which has an evolution behind it, influenced by a complex network including factors such as social change, language contact and historical incident; and that any attempt to explain grammatical structures by reference to culture-dependent conceptual structure is deemed to be overly simplistic and speculative. Currently, any systematic model is missing for the link of grammaticalisation phenomena to sociocultural characteristics of a language community. I assume that a massive amount of detailed studies of synchronic contrastive studies and diachronic studies of particular languages is needed before such a model can be postulated, or before the viability of any such model can be rejected in principle.

Singular speaker – plural subject

- In turn 6, F1 uses "we" referring to herself and the other female housemate, F2, when declaring that they are begging the male group members for their consent to the proposal, without actually having checked whether F2 accepts the proposal. She does it even if at first F2 does not understand the reason for F1's proposal, as shown by her question in turn 2 (a czemu? "and why"?)
- In turn 7, F2 confirms the perception of the team as consisting of "we" (a female subgroup) and "you" (a male subgroup), as introduced by F1 in turn 1, when she asks two male housemates to carry her suitcase into the room. She uses the dative of the personal pronoun 1st. plural nam ("us") rather than the 1st. singular in the indirect object, referring to herself and F1 as beneficiaries (recipients). Later in the same turn, she narrows the reference down and specifies herself as the recipient (beneficiary) by the use of the pronoun mi (me-dative) as the indirect object.

7.4.10.3. SINGULAR ACTOR, PLURAL ADDRESSEE: SPEAKING TO THE GROUP

I observed in the statistical analysis that the high frequency with which requests are directed to a plural addressee in Polish can be partly due to the frequent use of the plural in directives at an indefinite singular actor or a particular single person. The following exchange illustrates the use of 1st and 2nd person plural in this function.

129-P3. A cat enters the house. M1, M2 and F2 are sitting as F1 approaches the cat.

1 M1 usiądźmy # usiądźmy słuchajcie # bo się będzie bał i będzie w szoku
sit-IMP-1st pl. down # sit-IMP-1st pl. down listen # otherwise it will be afraid and will be in shock

...

(F1 picks the cat up)

2 M1 zostawcie go # . połóż go # on się musi oswoić
leave-IMP-2nd pl. it # put-IMP-2nd sing. it down # it must get used to everything

(F1 walks around with the cat)

3 M1 puść go Basia
let it go Basia

4 F2 puść go Basiu # niech on się oswoi # _ on niech sobie pobiega
let it go Basia # it should get used to everything # it should run around a bit

(F1 lets the cat go and follows it)

5 M1 to nie chodźmy za nim

so not follow-IMP-1ˢᵗ pl. it

6 M2 nie chodźmy za nim # siedźcie

not follow-IMP-1ˢᵗ pl. it # sit-IMP-2ⁿᵈ pl.

In turn 1, M1 reacts to F1's undesirable action (lifting the cat) by means of an inhibitive directive in 2ⁿᵈ plural in the initial part: zostawcie go ("leave-IMP-2ⁿᵈ pl. it"), and narrows down the scope of address in the following phrase połóż go ("put-IMP-sing. it down"). The use of the plural (in the first and second person) in turns 5 and 6 of the exchange above may be interpreted as a means of polite modification of a terminating request directed at F1. The directive loses some of its critical force directed against F1's behaviour when formulated by the speaker as directed to a group, and as self-inclusive (nie chodźmy za nim, "NEG follow- IMP-1ˢᵗ pl. it"). In the end of turn 6 the speaker switches to 2nd plural (siedźcie "sit-IMP-2ⁿᵈ pl."), directed to all the persons present rather than to F1, who was the only person to follow the cat and is the only person not seated. Both uses of the plural – in 1ˢᵗ and 2ⁿᵈ person – show the tendency to refer to an action of particular group members as an action by the group, and blunt the critical edge of the corrective directives by defocalising the actual trespasser.

I propose to interpret the tendency to address inhibitive requestives to groups when the actors performing undesirable activities are single persons as symptomatic of a collective perspective taken by speakers when attributing trespasses and distributing blame. The following exchange does not contain requestive utterances relevant to this subject but is quoted here as support for this interpretation.

130-P3. RED HAIR

F is dyeing M1's hair.

(M2 comes up to M1 and points at his head)

1 M2 a tu nie ma w ogóle tego?

and here there is no stuff at all?

2 F nie # jest # wszędzie jest dużo farby

but yes # there is # there is a lot of dye everywhere

(M2 walks away, leaving M1 and F alone)

3 M mój tata patrzy i mówi # co ten debil robi

my dad is watching and saying # what is this idiot doing

4 F czy ty możesz uklęknąć # cokolwiek zrobić # tak żebyś nie musiał na razie patrzeć # w lustro?
can you-EMPHATIC kneel down # do anything # so that you do not have to look right now # into the mirror?
5 M głowę nawet mam czerwoną # przecież skórę # . ej mam czerwoną nawet skórę # zafarbowaliście mi skórę # zobacz # że mi zafarbowaliście skórę
but even my head is red # the skin # ei I have red skin # you-PLURAL have dyed my skin # look-SINGULAR # that you-PLURAL have dyed my skin

There is only one person involved in dyeing M1's hair. Some other members of the group function as passive observers at some stage and later have left the scene. However, in turn 5, even though only the actual actor is present, M1 blames the outcome on the group, using the plural form of the pronoun "you".

Selected examples of directives formally addressed to a plural addressee while predicating an action that can be performed by one person only listed below. In all of them, the speaker removes the focus from individuals, expressing his or her perception of the situation as him- or herself dealing with a group rather than with individuals, and implying that the predicated action is a collective enterprise of the addressees.

131-P3. F1, F2, F3 are dining at the table.
F1 weźcie podajcie mi sól
take-IMP-2nd pl. pass-IMP-2nd pl. me the salt

115-P3. F is preparing to leave the Big Brother House.
F tam gdzieś została moja kurtka ze skóry # przynieście mi ją
my leather jacket is lying around somewhere # bring-IMP-2nd pl. it to me

132-P3. F approaches a group in which one person is smoking a cigarette.
F dajcie mi fajkę # bo ja nie wiem gdzie są # bo schowałam # . ale znajdę
give-IMP 2ndpl. me a cigarette # because I don't know where mine are # because I've hidden them # . but I'll find them

133-P3. The housemates enact a talk-show; the interviewee, F1, goes back to her place. Previously, the group had confiscated her sunglasses in an effort to watch her facial expression.
F2 okulary oddajcie
the glasses give-IMP-2nd pl. back

134-P3. F2 enters the room.

F2 to M1, M2: dajcie na moment zapalniczkę
give-IMP-2ndpl.for a moment the lighter

The strategy of referring to the plural when directing a request to a singular referent (typically indefinite in initiating, and identifiable on the basis of the situational context in inhibitive directives), observable in Polish, cannot be observed in English on the basis of spoken data alone because the plural and singular forms of the imperative are not differentiated. In German, the two forms are differentiated in informal relationships, where the T-address is used. The underspecification of the addressee by using the second person plural imperative while the predicated action can only be performed by one person, or when a specific referent was meant, did not occur in the German data.

To realise underspecification of the addressee (actor) of an imperative request, Polish, German and English have developed the imperative form VP- IMP-2nd sing. + INDEFINITE PERSONAL PRONOUN, as in:

German: komm mal einer her
            komm mal jemand her
            come someone here

English: come here # anybody

Polish: chodź/chodźcie no tu   który/która
            come-IMP-2nd sing./pl. here   *someone-sing.masc./-sing. fem.*

Alternatively, it is possible to formulate a request using a hortative particle and an indefinite personal pronoun in the singular:

niech mi ktoś poda sól
HORTATIVE-PARTICLE me someone give-sing. the salt

The above quoted exchanges in Polish manifest a preference for using the plural address rather than any of the available forms quoted above of an underspecified address using the indefinite singular personal pronouns *który, która, ktoś* ("someone-male", "someone-female", "someone"), which hardly ever occurred in the data. In English, speaker-centred formulations were used in some contexts where the plural occurred in Polish:

```
16-E4.
M can I get some butter?
```

```
17-E4.
M could I have the sugar and milk # please?
```
Alternatively, an indefinite personal pronoun was used:

```
18-E4.
M can anyone pass me the milk?
```

The imperative in the 2nd person plural seems to be functionally equivalent to such constructions in Polish in the peer ingroup context. This function-form correspondence is reflected in the repertoire of choices offered by the grammar. As indicated before, the following construction is grammatical in colloquial Polish:

chodźcie no tu   który/która (masc./fem.)
come-IMP-2nd pl. here   *someone-sing.*

The plural form of the imperative is used while the singular pronoun indicates that only one person is meant to perform the predicated action and the speaker relies on a single volunteer's reaction.

7.4.11. COLLABORATIVE PERFORMANCE OF DIRECTIVES

Trying to analyse natural data using the conceptual equipment developed in the analysis of (dyadic) role plays and questionnaires, the analyst will soon be irritated by the fact that instead of making it easy by supplying neatly distinct occurrences of spontaneous, original Head Acts and Supportive Moves, people frequently repeat, paraphrase, and complete each other's directives. The status of an utterance supporting, repeating, or completing somebody else's directive is controversial: it may be classified either as a minimal unit (head act), a supportive move for another speaker's earlier move, or else a second head act within a multi-head collaborative speech act. Sometimes, speakers collaborate on performing long speech events consisting of many turns, together constituting a piece of instruction or a plea. The most powerful articulation of the collective performance of directives is choir chanting, in which the group is profiled as being in unity by its simultaneous realisation.

A "collaborative performance" of a directive speech act occurs when two or more persons collaborate in performing a speech act. This can be realised by the speakers

- jointly chanting a demand or request,
- completing fragments of each other's utterances in such a way that only the combination of turns by more than one person constitutes a directive speech act or a sequential directive speech event, or
- supporting each other's utterances through paraphrase or repetition.

In what follows, choir chanting, remarkable for being a simultaneous rather than sequential realisation of a collective speech act, is examined in more detail. Then sequential collaborative directive speech is discussed, utilising linguistic devices such as paraphrase, repetition, and collaborative topic development.

7.4.11.1. SIMULTANEOUS COLLABORATIVE DIRECTIVE SPEECH ACTS: CHANTING

Chanting a text is a directive routine where the routine feature is prosody in itself. The lexical content of chanting may undergo lexicalisation yielding a chanting "formula" which is applicable in particular recurrent situational contexts. Specific metrics is the basic element of ritualisation, necessary for giving the formula their illocutionary force.

Choir chanting is a means of articulating requests by a group of people sharing a need or attitude. As a directive, which does not exhaust all of its conventionalised applications, it is used to

- express group support for somebody; includes applauding in a competition,
- articulate a group's request directed at a person or persons in power,
- articulate a group's request whose content is the addressee's public performance,
- perform other directives showing some "family resemblance" with the basic usages listed above.

In Big Brother, choir chanting appears in all three basic functions:

- directed to group members as a way of supporting them in a competition or in performing a task (Polish, German)
  form: imperative, vocative

- directed to group members as requests for a public performance

  form: imperative (Polish), vocative (Polish, German)
- directed to Big Brother (the production team)

  form: declarative need statement

EXAMPLES:

53-G2. All the housemates are gathered on the sofas in the living room

1 GROUP: Da-vid-Da-vid-Da-vid (GROUP: clap their hands)

(F1 pulls M1 by the hand, forcing him to stand up)

2 (applause)

3 M2 Emma auf den Bullen!

Emma on the bull

4 F1 Emma auf den Bullen

Emma on the bull

5 M3 Emma geht auf den Bullen

Emma is getting on the bull

(simultaneous speech)

(M1 starts acting out Emma's bull ride which took place earlier)

6 (applause, laughter)

135-P3.

GROUP: chce-my-jeść! chce-my-jeść! chce-my-jeść!

we want food – we want food – we want food

In these types of directives, the primary function of choir chanting is not to improve the audibility of the request but to articulate group solidarity and group power which are already in existence, or to create group solidarity and collective identity by stimulating individuals to join in a group activity in the form of a physically powerful expression of collective will. Chanting organises individuals into a group, individual requests to group requests, and individual support into group support. The articulation of solidarity by chanting a text formula has two directions: inward – by providing the feeling of solidarity, belonging and joint action to the group members involved; and outward – by the articulation of group power before the group's interlocutor. In cases when the chanting is directed at a group member, the addressee is temporarily excluded from the group and transformed into the group's interlocutor. By yielding to pressure, she or he rejoins the group and releases the tension created by the temporary suspension of membership.

Other cases of joint vocalisation of ritualised texts that create and enhance group identity and confirm the group membership of the participants include declamation of prayers, singing political hymns, and football chants. In P3, the ritual function of simultaneous speech acts is also utilised by one of the competing teams (Team Red) by an appropriation of a melodic football chant comprising four lines each with eight syllables of text, appropriately adapted. The necessity of having a team chant was referred to on the very first evening after the first team defeat. After that, the chant was half-sung, half-shouted at the beginning of each competition. The number of group members who joined the singing increased with time. Persons who seemed rather reserved at the beginning, probably in view of the low cultural connotation of the text and the whole song, later lost their reserve, possibly recognising the consolidating effect on their own team, as well as the intimidating effect on the other team.

7.4.11.2. REPETITION AND PARAPHRASE

Expressing affirmation and support for a directive proposition can be articulated by numerous means, for example the use of affirmative particles, statements of agreement, or naming additional grounds for performing the directive by the predicated actor(s). What is peculiar about a paraphrastic or repetitive utterance is its redundancy of the propositional contents in the "content space" of the discourse. The speaker apparently "ignores" the earlier utterance's propositional contribution to the content space; the resulting message in the "rhetorical space" is that of being fully of one mind with the earlier speaker, not merely affirming but actually thinking the same thoughts and enacting the same piece of interaction.

Repetition is one of the simplest ways of expressing support. In the following sequence, turn 2 merely copies a part of the preceding turn:

136-P3. M1 is trying on a vest; M2 is helping M1 as M3 watches.

1 M3 dobra jest # ściągaj

okay # take it off

2 M2 ściągaj

take it off

The following scene from G2 involves a uniform and strongly impositive collective verbal action in a situation where an ethical norm, breaking a promise, is involved. M1 is a member of a religious and ethnic minority from a conservative family background, and is the only male housemate who wears underwear when he is in the shower. After a great deal of comment on his stance by the group, M1 reveals to a group of female housemates that he is considering breaking the promise given to his mother. The group reacts collaboratively by a vivid disagreement. Emotional involvement and the uniformity of the speakers' opinion is expressed by producing utterances expressing the same propositional contents, involving repetition and paraphrase in turns 2, 3, 4, 5, 9 and 10.

1-G2. NUDE IN THE SHOWER

M has just declared that he is going to take a shower undressed, contrary to what he had promised his mother.

1 M   ja # vielleicht überlege ich mir das mal # aber-
yeah # maybe I will give it some more thought # but-

2 F1   hör auf # tu's deiner Mami nicht an # [wenn du es versprochen hast?][141]
stop that # don't do this to your Mum # if you promised?

3 F2   [nein # du hast es versprochen]
no # you promised

4 F3   [versprochen ist versprochen]
a promise is a promise

5 F4   [du hast es versprochen]
you promised

6 F1   komm # also # . wir wollen kein Gruppenzwang # das finde ich . blöd
come on # well # we do not want a group pressure # I think that's stupid

7 M1   ja # wenn das sich nicht ändert # werde ich: . das aber-
yeah # if this does not change # I will anyway-

8 M2   wieso dann? [---]
but why?

9 F1   [du machst] dir hier # [. völlig unnütz Gedanken]
you are worrying about nothing

10 F2 [das ist völlig in Ordnung]
that is quite all right

Although each of the women produces the directive just once, repeating the same proposition in partly the same wording in turns 2 through 5, they accumulate in their effect,

---

[141] Square brackets indicate simultaneous speech. Hashes indicate tone group boundaries.

resulting in heavy impositiveness. Gender solidarity with M's mother might be playing a considerable part in this discussion. The performance of the directive becomes strongly impositive not only because it is realised in an impositive verbal form, but also because it involves a collective action by several speakers repeating and paraphrasing contributions of their precedents.

7.4.11.3. COOPERATIVE PRODUCTION OF DIRECTIVES IN VERBAL PLAY

Co-operation with others and being a part of a group is not only a way to achieve task-oriented and survival-oriented goals but also an opportunity for playing. It evokes Huizinga's notion of "homo ludens", the conception that a human being is primarily a socially-oriented creature and playing is a basic way of self-expression by entering into and cultivating bonds with others. For "homo ludens", play is an activity basic to life rather than being second-rate and inferior to task-and-survival-oriented activities. The following exchanges show how the fun function of directive activities is triggered and furthered by their collaborative execution.

In the following collective joke, containing a long act of group persuasion, the sense of co-ordinated action among the speakers is created by simultaneous vocalisation and interactive, multi-vocal repetition, paraphrase, topic development, and prosodic similarity between consecutive utterances.

```
105-E3. NAKED WOMEN
F1, F2, and F3 are in the hot tub together; M1 is nearby taking a shower outside.
(shouting)
1 F1 slave boy # . come and lick my eyes!
2 F2 slave boy # . come and lick my ass!
3 F1 slave boy # . come and lick my feet!
4 F3 come hither now # slave boy!
5 F1,F2,F3 slave boy!
(silence 4 seconds)
6 F1 we've got to be really seductive and try and lure him # our aim is
to lure him into the hot tub
...
7 F2 we'll show you our bits honestly # we promise # come on Tom!
8 F1 we want to play with you!
9 F2 yes Tom # we want to play with you
10 F3 we want to do things to you that haven't been done for ages
```

11 F1 three naked women # when has that ever happened to you in the hot
tub
12 F1 this is your wildest dream what you've been thinking about every
night with your gin screaming hard on
13 F2 Tom
14 F3 it's an offer that won't come back in a hurry
15 F1 we're slipping off each other
16 F2 we need your help
17 F1 we're waiting for you
18 F3 we can't keep still
19 F1,F3 Tom!
20 F2 we can't stop thinking about you
21 F2,F3 To:::::m!

Consecutive speakers repeat the utterance of the preceding speaker as in turns 8 and 9, develop the theme by repeating the beginning of the utterance and alternating the final element, as in turns 1, 2, 3 and 13, 14, 25, 16, 18, or produce the same text simultaneously, as in turns 5, 19 and 21. The 1st person plural pronoun is used throughout. The groups of utterances in turns 1-3 and 10-18 have the same intonation pattern, and form a rhythmical consecutive chant. The joint objective is explicitly stated in turn 6:

6 F1 we've got to be really seductive and try and lure him # our aim is
to lure him into the hot tub

It is formulated as a deontic declarative and followed by a factual statement defining "our aim", in which the group consensus about the joint goal is taken for granted.

In the next set of data, coming from the German data, a collective is formed by a group of females by means of repetition, partial repetition, mimetic code mixing and the statement of will formulated in the 1st plural:

54-G2. A group of male and female housemates practise riding a mechanical bull one by one in a self-appointed order which is yet to be negotiated. The utterances below are produced by a subgroup of female housemates who are sitting in the stands awaiting the next performance.
1 F1 der Mister Großkotz # einmal die Sieben # [wir wollen unbedingt-]
mister boaster (literally: Big Puke) # the seven once # we definitely want-

2 F2 [wir wollen ---] # wir wollen Bigmause
we want --- # we want Big Mouse
3 F1 [Mister Bigmaus # genau]
mister Big Mouse # exactly
4 F3 [wir wollen ihn fliegen sehen]
we want to see him fly
5 F2 ja # wir wollen ihn fliegen sehen
yes # we want to see him fly
6 F1 Mister Bigkotz
mister Big Puke
7 F3 sieben!
seven
8 F2 sieben! einmal die Sieben fährt
seven ! the seven rides once
9 F1 Walter
Walter-FIRST NAME
10 F2 little Walter

The elliptical (bare vocative) formulation of F1's directive in turns 1 and 3 consists in the identification of the next contestant by his starting number, which is then repeated by F3 and F2 in turns 6 and 7. As well as being identified by the starting number, the addressee is identified by the use of a humorously abusive, colloquial term of reference "Großkotz", meaning "boaster", and the derived ad-hoc nickname *Bigkotz*, "Big Puke". Code mixing is introduced by the formal English term of address *mister* and adding the English adjective *big* to the augmentative German root *kotz* ("puke") in a neologism which has the form of a compound noun. The procedure of code mixing introduced by F1 is taken up by F2 in another nominal compound in turn 2, *Bigmaus*, and in another English adjective, *little*, in turn 10. The first name *Walter* in turn 8 is pronounced as in English in turn 9 by F1, and recurs in turn 10 by F2 using the same pronunciation. The collaborative authorship of the directive is signalled by F1 in turn 1 in the explicit declaration of a joint preference (1st person plural), and confirmed in its repetitions by F3 in turn 4 and F2 in turn 5. The male housemates present in the audience do not join in.

Both scenes above, as well as the previously quoted scene 93-E3. ENTERING BEDROOMS, involving a practical joke illustrate the fact that collective fun is frequently gendered in mixed gender groups, that is, co-operation takes place within one gender group and is directed against a member or members of the other gender.

The last scene above belongs to the category of speech events known as "teasing" in English and "frotzeln" in German (cf. Günther 2000). In Polish, it can be roughly translated as either "kpiny" or "przekomarzanki"[142]. Teasing is a non-serious mode of discourse implying the a division of roles into its temporarily superior performers and the inferior victim of their criticism which is not quite intended to be serious. The scenes 105-E3. NAKED WOMEN displays a central characteristic of teasing, i.e. collective fun at the cost of the "victim"; at the same time, it misses the humorously critical element typical of teasing (cf. Günther 2000). Directives have a central role to play in teasing, where the addressee is frequently being non-seriously persuaded to do something which she or he does not wish, which makes no sense, or which gives the performers the opportunity to continue the tease. Teasing in the Big Brother house occurs in all three languages, and nearly always involves a group of speakers collaborating against an individual victim and the corresponding self-reference in plural, "we" (cf. also Pulaczewska 2006: 483-504).

---

[142] These notions that are close to each other but not synonymous;"przekomarzanki" involve the expectation of self-defense by the initial victim, leading to a balance of roles, a point-scoring game of equal partners; "kpiny" may seriously offend the victim's negative face wants.

8. SUMMARY AND CONCLUSIONS

In this study of patters of verbal interaction, a link was created between the production and the form of directives and interaction patterns embedded in social and situational contexts. The study encompassed both the referential and formal aspects of directives, and their cultural significance. One part of it included an analysis of verbal patterns: grammatical, lexical, semantic, interactive and prosodic devices used in particular languages. Beyond this, the following aspects were discussed and supported by empirical evidence:

- The function of the aforementioned devices and procedures is tightly bound to the interactive context of their occurrence and the development of interaction. Only a corpus-based approach to language use which analyses forms of verbal expression in contextually embedded interaction can assess the contextual factors that influence their verbal form.

- The occurrence and form of directive utterances cannot be accounted for within the instrumental treatment of politeness in directives, focused on reaching a goal prior to, and independent from given interaction; directives carry social implications extending beyond instrumentality, as they perform phatic and relationship-oriented, and not just transactional functions.

- Observations on non-verbal aspects of group-related and interpersonal behaviour provide insights into cross-cultural contrasts that render the analysis of its verbal aspects socially relevant.

- The sociocultural differences in interaction styles between particular speech communities occur in the first place in the preferred choices of the response to the actual context, such as the speech act to be performed.

- Some recurrent properties of the utterance goal (type of action to be performed, actor, beneficiary, embedding in pre-planned vs. spontaneous activities) can be used to categorise directives, which makes possible a quantitative analysis of the relationship between the form and the context when working on corpus data. However, the choice of relevant contextual parameters should not be made a priori before any qualitative analysis of some corpus data. The analysis demonstrated relevance of contextual parameters that did not occur in earlier studies on directives, based on role-plays and questionnaires. This shows the limitations of any preconceptions on what is relevant.

- The use of particular devices in particular interactive contexts can prevailingly be analysed in terms of tendencies and relative frequencies, and graded, i.e. socially defined acceptability. However, there also exist determinist links between recurrent aspects of the context of an utterance and its form. Some of them have not been treated as facts of grammar before (e.g. the fact that the infinitive in the directive function is confined to plural addressees in informal contexts in Polish). The determinism of the link between the context and the form is limited, though, because the interaction participants can take recourse to fictionalisation, indicated by applying contextual cues, such as code switching or socially inappropriate forms of address.
- As shown by interviews with native and non-native respondents, the evaluations of social appropriateness of the occurrence and the form of directive speech acts show cross-cultural variance.
- Directives are an important vehicle of establishing and maintaining interpersonal relationships and group bonds. They have a vital role to play in group interaction as they promote group integration through initiating group activities, indicating the speaker's trust in the acceptability of attempted influence on others, and expressing the assumption of shared responsibility for other group members. Directives promoting or expressing group integration were realised in impositive and strongly impositive forms in all languages, indicating a link between group-orientation and an impositive communication style.
- Peer groups representing different cultures differ in the amounts of directives produced and their kinds, defined in terms of their interactive structure (types of action and participants). The significantly higher collectivism of the Poles compared to the other two groups seemed to be reflected in the higher frequency of directives representing non-dyadic encounters, while the frequency of dyadic encounters was similar for the Poles and speakers of other languages.
- Cross-linguistic differences occurred in the degree of preference for positively polite forms of expression, which was strongest in Polish. At the same time, positively polite forms were preferred in all peer groups and for all types of directives, apart from requests for personal favour by the British speakers. The latter showed an exceptionally high ratio of negatively polite formulation, explicating the prevailing view of English as a language of negative politeness in directives.

- Different factors influenced the choices of politeness strategies in particular languages. The speakers of German proved to be more deferential – i.e., to use more negative politeness – when addressing requests and proposals at groups, than in speaking with single persons. The Polish and the British, on the other hand, proved to be sensitive to the type of beneficiary, as they produced more negative politeness if the beneficiary was the speaker alone than in utterances where the beneficiary included further persons. However, these differences did not outbalance the general tendency to use positive politeness in the peer context group in all three languages, with the notable exception of requests for personal favours in English.
- Interlingual differences and similarities occurred in the use of formal and content-related means to express deference, distance-diminishing procedures and group-integrative procedures as shown in the following overview:

English:

DEFERENTIAL
- frequent use of negatively polite modification
- frequent use of conventional indirectness in requests for personal favours
- occurrence of vagueness of communicative intention

DISTANCE-DIMINISHING
- occurrence of interactional modesty (minimising self-praise)
- frequent use of impositives

GROUP-INTEGRATIVE
- frequent occurrence of proposals of joint action
- strong differentiation between strategies of politeness used in asking for personal favours and strategies of politeness used in asking for action concerning groups
- calls for symbolic displays of group integrity
- collective performance of joking directive speech acts
- gender-based use of "we" and "you"

Polish:

DEFERENTIAL
- no considerable occurrence

DISTANCE-DIMINISHING
- the use of impositives and positively polite modification, little use of negatively polite modification
- positively polite forms of address and impositive modifiers as outstanding forms of modification
- fictionalisation: frequent joking directives, occurrence of joking self-stylisation and formal forms of address

GROUP-INTEGRATIVE
- asking for favours to others as the main form of group-oriented social control
- imposing upon individuals to identify with group goals as a form of social control
- frequent occurrence of participants constellations other than singular speaker-singular addressee
- the frequent use of "we" and plural "you" in defining the authorship and the addressees of the directives
- calls for symbolic displays of group integrity
- referential use of positively polite forms of address
- gender-based use of "we" and "you"

German:

DEFERENTIAL
- frequent use of negatively polite modification, in particular lexical hedges

DISTANCE-DIMINISHING
- the occurrence of teasing and humour
- the use of impositives and positively polite modification
- fictionalisation: frequent joking directives, occurrence of joking self-stylisation

GROUP-INTEGRATIVE
- calls for consideration to others as the main form of group-oriented social control
- collective performance of teasing
- calls for symbolic displays of group integrity
- gender-based use of "we" and "you"

The study demonstrates the analytical potential of integrating the quantitative and interpretative approach to linguistic data. Moreover, owing to the use of natural data, the quantitative analysis could also be applied to the occurrence of directive activities, rather than merely the correlations between pre-selected aspects of context and form.

The study touches upon areas that may provide socially relevant recognitions, applicable in language learning and practical instruction in intercultural communication. A drawback is the relatively small number of native speakers whose intuitions were exploited as a source of verification for the hypothesis won out of the corpus data. I opted for making suggestions which were made reasonable by the data at hand, which can serve as a point of entry for further study, rather than an immediate verification through a broad application of interviews as an ethnomethodological tool. Practical limitations made it impossible to strictly verify all of the suggestions proposed. The focus of this work is the unification of the quantitative and qualitative methods of analysis, and the systematic adoption of a single well-understood parameter suggested by comparative social psychology as an explanatory basis for explaining interlingual contrasts. Of the two research strategies possible, the possibly exact verification of conclusions drawn from a small-scope data and a broad identification of possible lines for future research, the latter was predominantly preferred.

The study situates itself within a stream of interpretative sociolinguistics, and this means that it does not limit the analysis to how context affects the performance of directives. It also pursues the question of the role of directive activities in creating social contexts. This was not a theoretical postulate prior to the analysis of data. Rather, it followed from the recognition growing at every step of the analysis that the description of the forms of directive activities, their interpretation and evaluation of their social significance can be made meaningful only through frequent reference to social attitudes and extra-verbal behaviour. This transgresses the traditional limits of linguistics as the discipline dealing with the verbal, and in particular formal aspects of communication. The influence of social context on the form of verbal action, and the contribution of verbal action to the construction of social context proved to be inseparable faces of the coin. The study indicates the realism of the postulates stated in Hornscheidt's (1993) call for a cross-disciplinary approach to communication and cross-cultural issues, and illustrates Holden's (1993: 1796) contention:

> All these new questions are being raised in the context of a disciplinary structure that is no longer very well suited to them. The social science disciplines were defined a century ago and despite the rash of multidisciplinary centres and programs in academia, departments are still divided along those traditional lines. [...] it's still true that the safest way to carve out an academic career is to publish in the traditional mainline concerns of your disciplines. Trouble is, traditional disciplinary boundaries are nowadays being blurred and

bent almost out of recognition to accommodate torrents of new knowledge, to respond to the demand for socially relevant research by funding agencies, and to reflect the fact that the problems of greatest moment today have to be tackled by multiple approaches.

While the question of what constitutes the context of an utterance has preoccupied the students of language use for the last four decades, it is now visible that social sciences can provide relevant descriptive categories because they are well-equipped to assess how social contexts, and social attitudes alongside, can be described and cross-culturally compared in socially relevant ways. Social psychology provides notions such as individuation, identification, group, ingroup and group integration, and contrastive social psychology provides dimensions of contrast such as Individualism/Collectivism or sensitivity to power distance; cultural anthropology provides still other dimensions (such as the notion of monochronic and polychronic time, or low vs. high context) in terms of which cultures can be described as manifestations of one or another "parameter setting". This book demonstrates the fruitfulness of such an approach, and I see it as confirmed by the results.

It is seductive but frequently also speculative to provide "cultural" explanations of language use by linking it directly to aspects of a nation's ideology, history, or world view. Lee-Wong (2000) shows that it can be done productively in some cases (in her case, the comparison was made possible by the existence of two Chinese states that share a bulk of historical experience and were separated in the recent past). And yet, such interpretations sometimes seem far-fetched. A commonly occurring phenomena can be interpreted in this vain as a unique characteristics of a culture, resulting from its specific national outlook or ideology. Here count, for example, Wierzbicka's (1992) attempt to trace the proliferation of subjectless structures in Russian back to the fatalist world view, or Blum-Kulka's (1990) hint at the Zionist social and political program as a source of directness in family discourse. History as the ultimate source of culture is too far away from both grammar and language use, too susceptible to myth-making, and too episodic to be acceptable as the basic explanatory hypothesis for linguistic routines. Proposing a direct link between a speech community's history and ideology on the one hand, and its grammar and language use on the other, can be a very subjective and creative move. Socio-metric measures worked out by contrastive social psychology and cultural anthropology can be applied fruitfully as a "missing link" between history and language. They measure difference and similarity between cultures without diving into historical detail, and generalise over societies with completely different historical backgrounds.

A more particularised perspective focused on nation-specific norms is also occasionally deployed in this study in references to the culture standard method of comparative social psychology. However, the availability of pan-cultural socio-metric descriptions reduces the appeal of historical, nation-specific accounts of links between grammar and language use on the one hand, and other aspects of culture on the other.

The first part of this book analyses the trends in language use in peer groups translating them into figures. While it shows that the more collectivist Poles are at the same time more prone to use positively polite and in particular impositive means of expression, which by definition presuppose co-operation of the addressees with the performer of a directive speech act, it does not in itself prove causality. As the study only covers three languages, the figures themselves do not provide sufficient support for the hypothesis that it is natural for these two aspects of cultures to correlate with each other in the context given (young peer groups). It is the qualitative part dealing with group-related aspects of directives that shows how it works: what type of situations induce positive politeness and make it a preferred choice in directives, and which social attitudes facilitate its occurrence; in short, it indicates the links of positive politeness to group integration and group-orientation of a given exchange, suggesting at the same time how this fits into the respective culture's profile.

The focus on collectivism-individualism as differentiators of cultures, and on group-integrative directive activities helped channel the discussion and select the material, providing a principle of organisation for heterogeneous data. It also helped me to take a step towards doing in linguistics what Brown (2000) set off to realise in social psychology, that is, outbalancing the predominance of inter-personalism predominant in current studies of politeness and directives, with their heritage from the speech act theory. At the same time, the discussion indicated clearly that other socially relevant foci were possible and could provide meaningful results, such as, for example, negotiations of leadership and hierarchies within the groups, or gender roles, which repeatedly provided legitimation for both demands and succouring attitudes.

Bibliography

Agozino, Biko. *Counter-Colonial Criminology. A Critique of Imperialist Reason.* London: Pluto, 2003.

Aijmer, Karin. "Sort of and Kind of in English Conversation." *Studia Linguistica*, 38:2 (1984), 118-128.

Aijmer, Karin. *Conversational Routines in English.* London: Longman, 1996.

Asante, Molefi Kete; Newmark, Eileen and Blake, Cecil A. (eds.). *Handbook of Intercultural Communication.* Beverly Hills: Sage, 1979.

Attardo, Salvatore. *Linguistic Theories of Humor.* Berlin: de Gruyter, 1994.

Bach, Kent and Harnish, Robert M. *Linguistic Communication and Speech Acts.* Cambridge, MA: MIT, 1982.

Barbe, Johanna Katherina. *Irony in Conversational German. A Linguistic Approach.* UMI Dissertation Services, 1989.

Bateson, Gregory. "The Position of Humor in Human Communication." 1-47. Von Forster, H. (ed.). *Cybernetics. Ninth Conference.* New York: Josiah Macy Jr. Foundation, 1953.

Bateson, Gregory. "A Theory of Play and Phantasy." 177-93. Bateson, Gregory (ed.). *Steps to an Ecology of Mind.* San Francisco: Chandler, 1972 [1954].

Bardovi-Harling, Kathleen and Hartford, Beverly S. "Refining the DCT: Comparing Open Questionnaires and Dialogue Completion Tasks." *Pragmatics and Language Learning Monograph Series*, 4 (1993), 143-165.

Bauman, Richard and Shener, Joel (eds.). *Case Studies in the Ethnography of Speaking.* Austin: SEDL, 1984.

Béal, Christine. "Keeping the Peace: A Cross-Cultural Comparison of Questions and Requests in Australian English and French." *Multilingua*, 13:1-2 (1994), 35-58.

Beebe, Leslie M. *Speech Act Performance: A Function of the Data Collection Procedure?* Paper presented at the Sixth Annual TESOL and Sociolinguistics Colloquium at the International TESOL Convention New York, 1985.

Beebe, Leslie M. and Cunnings, M. C. "Natural Speech Act Data versus Questionnaire Data: How Data Collection Method Affects Speech Performance." 65-86. Gass and Neu, 1995.

Bellah, Robert Neelly. *Habits of the Heart: Individualism and Commitment in American Life.* Berkeley: University of California Press, 1985.

Berman, John J. and Jahoda, Gustav (eds.). *Cross-Cultural Perspectives. Nebraska Symposium on Motivation 1989.* Lincoln: University of Nebraska, 1990.

Berry, John W. "On Cross-Cultural Comparability." *International Journal of Psychology*, 4 (1969), 119-128.

Biber, Douglas. *Variation Across Speech and Writing.* Cambridge: CUP, 1988.

Bierbrauer, Günter; Meyer, Heike and Wolfradt, Uwe. "Measurment of Normative and Evaluative Aspects in Individualistic and Collectivist Orientations: The Cultural Orientation Scale (COS)." 189-199. Kim et al., 1994.

Bjørge A. K., "Power distance in English lingua franca email communication." *International Journal of Applied Linguistics*, 17.1 (2007), 60-80.

Blum-Kulka, Shoshana. "Indirectness and Politeness in Requests: Same or Different?" *Journal of Pragmatics*, 11:1 (1987), 141-146.

Blum-Kulka, Shoshana. "You Don't Touch Lettuce with Your Fingers: Parental Politeness in Family Discourse." *Journal of Pragmatics*, 14:2 (1990), 259-288.

Blum-Kulka, Shoshana. "Playing It Safe: The Role of Conventionality in Indirectness." 37-70. Blum-Kulka, Shoshana; House, Juliane and Kasper, Gabriele (eds.). *Cross-Cultural Pragmatics: Requests and Apologies.* Norwood, NJ: Ablex, 1989.

Blum-Kulka, Shoshana and House Juliane (eds.). *Interlingual and Intercultural Communication*. Tübingen: Narr, 1986.

Blum-Kulka, Shoshana; House, Juliane and Kasper, Gabriele (eds.). *Cross-Cultural Pragmatics: Requests and Apologies*. Norwood: Ablex, 1989.

Blum-Kulka, Shoshana and Katriel, Tamar. "Nicknaming Practices in Families." 58-78. Ting- Toomey and Korzenny, 1991.

Blum-Kulka, Shoshana and Olshtain, Elite. "Requests and Apologies: A Cross-Cultural Study of Speech Act Realization Patterns." *Applied Linguistics*, 5:3 (1984), 196-213.

Bodman, Jean and Eisenstein, Miriam. "May God Increase Your Bounty: The Expression of Gratitude in English by Native and Non- Native Speakers." *Cross-Currents*, 15:1 (1988), 1-21.

Bogardus, Emory S. *Play Attitudes, Myrthful Attitudes. Fundamentals of Social Psychology*. New York: Appleton, 1942.

Boski, Paweł. "Polen." 120-134. Thomas et al., 2003.

Boxer, Diana. *Complaining and Comiserating*. New York: Peter Lang, 1993.

Brown, Roger and Gilman, Albert. "The Pronouns of Power and Solidarity." 253-276. Sebeok, Thomas (ed.). *Style in Language*. Cambridge, MA: MIT, 1960.

Brown, Penelope and Levinson, Stephen C. "Universals in Language Use: Politeness Phenomena." 56-289. Goody, 1978.

Brown, Penelope and Levinson, Stephen C. *Politeness. Some Universals in Language Use*. Cambridge: CUP, 1999.

Brown, Rupert. *Group processes*. Bodmin: Blackwell, 2000.

Brown, R.J. and Turner, J.C. "The criss-cross categorization effect in intergroup discrimination." *British Journal of Social and Clinical Psychology* 18 (1981), 371-83.

Campbell, D. T. "Fate, similarity, and other indices of the status of aggregates of persons as social entities." *Behavioural Science* 3 (1958), 14-25.

Campbell, D.T. "The Two Distinct Routes Beyond Kin Selection to Ultra-Sociality: Implications for the Humanities and Social Sciences." Bridgman, D. (ed.). *The Nature of Prosocial Development: Theories and Strategies*, 11-41. New York: Academic Press, 1983.

Cialdini, Robert B.; Wosinska, Wilhelmina; Barret, Daniel W.; Butner, Jonathan and Górnik-Durose, Małgorzata. "Compliance With a Requests in Two Cultures: The Differential Influence of Social Proof and Comittment/Consistency on Collectivists and Individualists." *Personality and Social Psychology Bulletin*, 25:10 (1999), 1242-53.

Cole, Peter and Morgan, Jerry L. (eds.). *Syntax and Semantics, vol. 3: Speech Acts*. New York: Academic Press, 1975.

Conley, John M.; O'Barr, William M. and Lind, E. Allan. "The Power of Language: Presentational Style in the Courtroom." *Duke Law Journal*, (1978), 1375-99.

Coser, Rose Laub. "Laughter in the Ward," 84-89. *Life in the Ward*. East Lansing: Michigan State University Press, 1962.

Coulmas, Florian. "On the Sociolinguistic Relevance of Routine Formulae." *Journal of Pragmatics*, 4 (1979), 249-66.

Coulmas, Florian. "Diskursive Routine im Fremdsprachenunterricht." 3-45. Eppender, Ralf (ed.). *Routinen im Sprachenerwerb*. München: Goethe Institut, 1986.

Coulmas, Florian (ed.). *Conversational Routine*. The Hague: de Gruyter, 1981.

Cucchi, Constanza. "Vague Expressions in the European Parliament: A Marker of Cultural Identity?" In Garzone, G. and Archibald, J. (eds.) *Discourse, Identity and Roles in Specialized Communication*. Bern: Peter Lang, 2010. 85-107.

Cunita, Alexandra. "Multiple Levels of Comparison in Comparative Analysis." *Revue-Roumaine-de-Linguistique*, 42:4 (1987), 241-246.

Dąbrowska, Marta. "Women, Language and Politeness." Mazur, Zygmunt and Teresa Bela (eds.). *New Developments in English and American Studies. Proceedings of the Seventh International Conference on English and American Literature and Language, Kraków, March 27-29, 1996.* Kraków: Jagiellonian University, 1997. 511-522.

Davies, Eirlys E. "A Contrastive Approach to the Analysis of Politeness Formulas." *Applied Linguistics*, 8:1 (1987), 75-88.

Dekker, D. M.; Rutte, C. G.; Van den Berg, P. "Cultural differences in the perception of critical interaction behaviors in global virtual teams." *International Journal of Intercultural Relations* 32 (2008), 441-452.

Delin, Judy. "Plans but No Scripts: Planning, Discourse, and Interpretation in the Step Aerobics Workout." 199-222. Ventola, Eija (ed.). *Discourse and Community: Doing Functional Linguistics.* Tübingen: Narr, 2000.

Deregowski, J.B.; Dziurawiec, S.; and Annis, R.C. (eds.). *Expiscations in Cross-Cultural Psychology. Selected Papers from the 6th Internat. Cong. of Internat. Assn. for Cross-Cultural Psych.* Lisse: Swets and Zeitlinger, 1983.

Dittmar, Norbert and Schlobinski, Peter (eds.). *The Sociolinguistics of Urban Vernaculars.* Berlin: de Gruyter, 1988.

Dolnik, Juraj. *Werthaltung und Modalität.* Modality in Slavonic Languages. 25-37. Hansen, Björn und Karlik, Petr (eds.). München: Sagner, 2005.

Doumanis, Mariella. *Mothering in Greece: From Collectivism to Individualism.* New York: Academic Press, 1983.

Drew, Paul. "Po-Face Receipts of Teases." *Linguistics*, 25:1 (1987), 219-253.

Dreyfus, Jeff. *Traffic is Pretty Heavy, huh?* University of Michigan, 1975.

Edmondson, Willis J. *Spoken Discourse. A Model for Analysis.* London: Longman, 1981.

Edmondson, Willis J. and House, Juliane. *Let's Talk and Talk About it: A Pedagogic Interactional Grammar of English.* München: Urban and Schwarzenberg, 1981.

Edwards, A. L. *Edwards Personal Reference Schedule.* New York: Psychological Corporation, 1959.

Eppender, Ralph (ed.). *Routinen im Spracherwerb.* München: Goethe Institut, 1986.

Escandell-Vidal, Victoria. "Towards a Cognitive Approach to Politeness." *Language Sciences*, 18:3-4 (1996), 629-50.

Ervin-Tripp, Susan. "How to Make and Understand a Request." 195-209. Parret et al., 1981.

Erwin-Tripp, Susan. "Is Sybil There? The Structure of Some American English Directives." *Language in Society*, 5 (1976), 25-66.

Fillmore, Charles J. "Remarks on Contrastive Pragmatics." 144-164. Fisiak, 1980.

Fisiak, Jacek (ed.). *Contrastive Linguistics.* Berlin: de Gruyter, 1980.

Fraser, Bruce. "Perspectives on Politeness." *Journal of Pragmatics*, 14:2 (1990), 219-236.

Fukushima, Saeko. "A Cross-Cultural Study of Requests: The Case of British and Japanese Undergrates." 671-688. Jaszczołt and Turner, 2003.

Fukushima, Saeko. "Request Strategies in British English and Japanese." *Language Sciences*, 18:3-4 (1996), 671-88.

García, Carmen. "Apologizing in English: Politeness Strategies Used by Native and Non-Native Speakers." *Multilingua*, 8:1 (1989), 3-20.

Gass, Susanne M. and Neu, Joyce (eds.). *Speech Acts Across Cultures. Challenges to Communication in the Second Language.* Berlin: de Gruyter, 1995.

Gawlikowski, Krzysztof; Jedlicki, Jerzy; Kochanowicz, Jacek; Kowalik, Tadeusz; Obuchowski, Kazimierz; Reykowski, Janusz; Szacki, Jerzy and Wesołowski, Włodzimierz. *Kolektywizm i Indywidualizm*. Warszawa: IfiS PAN, 1999.

Gebauer, Gunter. "Über Aufführung der Sprache." 224-247. Trabant, Jürgen (ed.). *Sprache denken. Positionen aktueller Sprachphilosophie*. Frankfurt: Fischer, 1995.

Geertz, Clifford. *The Interpretation of Cultures*. New York: Basic Books, 1973.

Geis, Michael L. and Harlow, Linda L. "Politeness Strategies in French and English." 129-153. Gass and Neu, 1993.

Georgas, James. "Changing Family Values in Greece. From Collectivist to Individualist." *Journal of Cross-Cultural Psychology*, 20:1 (1989), 80-91.

Goffman, Erving. *Interaction Ritual. Essays in Face-to-Face Behaviour*. Chicago: Adline Publishing Company, 1967.

Goldschmidt, Myra. "From the Addressee's Perspective: Imposition in Favor-Asking." 241-56. Gass and Neu, 1993.

Gonzáles Bermúdes, Patricia: *A Comparative Study of Requests and Refusals in Spanish and English: Positive and Negative Politeness*. Unpublished manuscript. Course "Contrastive Pragmatics", English Linguistics, University of Regensburg 2005.

Goodenough, Ward H. *Descriptions and Comparisons in Cultural Anthropology*. Cambridge: CUP, 1979.

Goodrich, A., J. Henry and Goodrich, D.W. Laughter in Psychiatric Staff Conferences: A Sociopsychiatric Analysis. *American Journal of Orthopsychiatry* 24 (1954), 175-184.

Goody, Esther. *Questions and Politeness: Strategies in Social Interaction*. Cambridge: CUP, 1978.

Gough, David H. "Some Problems for Politeness Theory: Deference and Directness in Xhosa Performative Requests." *South African Journal of African Languages*, 15:3 (1995), 123-125.

Graham, Elizabeth E.; Papa, Michael J. and Brooks, Gordon P. Functions of Humor in Conversation: Conceptualisation and Measurment." *Western Journal of Communication*, 56 (1992), 161-183.

Graham, E.E. and. Rubin R.B. *The Involvement of Humour in the Development of Social Relationships*. Paper presented at the Speech Communication Association, Boston, MA, 1987.

The Great Polish-English Dictionary. Edited by Jan Stanislawski. Warszawa: PWN, 1989.

Green, G. M. "How to Get People to Do Things with Words: The Whimperative Question." 107-141. Cole and Morgan, 1975.

Greenberg, Robert D. *The Appellative Expressions in the Balkan Slavic Languages*. UMI Dissertation Services, 1993.

Grice, Herbert Paul. "Logic and Conversation." 41-58. Cole and Morgan, 1975.

Gudykunst, William B. (ed.). *Intercultural Communication Theory: Current Perspectives*. Beverly Hills: Sage, 1983.

Gudykunst, William B. and Asante, Molefi Kete (eds.). *Handbook of International and Intercultural Communication*. Newbury Park: Sage, 1989.

Gudykunst, William B. and Nishida, Tsukasa. "Theoretical Perspectives for Studying Intercultural Communication." 17-46. Gudykunst and Asante, 1989.

Guillén-Nieto, V. "Crossing Disciplines in Intercultural Communication Research". In Guillén-Nieto, V.; Marimón Llorca, C.; Vargas-Sierra, C. (eds.) *Intercultural Business Communication and Simulation and Gaming Methodology*. Peter Lang: Bern, 2009. 29- 63.

Gülich, Elisabeth and Henke, Kathe. "Sprachliche Routine in der Alltagskommunikation: Überlegungen zu 'pragmatischen Idiomen' am Beispiel des Englischen und des Französischen." *Die Neueren Sprachen*, 79 (1980), 2-44.

Gumperz, John J. *Discourse Strategies. Studies in Interactional Sociolinguistics*. Cambridge: CUP, 1982.

Gumperz, John J. "Sociocultural Knowledge in Conversational Inference." 191-212. Saville-Troike, M. (ed.). *Georgetown University Round Table on Languages and Linguistics*. Washington: Georgetown University Press, 1977.

Günther, Susanne. *Vorwurfsaktivitäten in der Alltagsinteraktion*. Tübingen: Niemeyer, 2000.

Hakuta, Kenji. "Prefabricated Patterns and the Emergence of Structure in Second Language Acquisition." *Language Learning*, 24 (1974), 287-97.

Hall, Edward T. and Hall, Mildred Reed. *Understanding Cultural Differences*. Yarmouth, Me.: Intercultural Press, 1990.

Hansen, Maj-Britt Mosegaard. *The Function of Discourse Particles*. Amsterdam: Benjamins, 1998.

Hatipoğlu, Ç."Computer Mediated Language and Culture: Salutations and Closings in British and Turkish 'Call for Papers' Written in English." *Studies About Languages (Kalbų Studijos)* 8 (2006), 31-38.

Haverkate, Henk. "Toward a Typology of Politeness Strategies in Communicative Interaction." *Multilingua*, 7:4 (1988), 385-409.

Hazekamp, Jan L.; Meeus, Wim and te Poel, Yolanda (eds.). *European Contributions to Youth Research*. Amsterdam: Free University Press, 1987.

Helbig, Gerhard. *Lexikon deutscher Partikel*. Leipzig: Verlag Enzyklopädie, 1988.

Held, Gudrun. "On the Role of Maximization in Verbal Politeness." *Multilingua*, 8:2-3 (1989), 167-206.

Held, Gudrun. "Politeness in Linguistic Research," 131-53. Watts et al., 1992.

Held, Gudrun. *Verbale Höflichkeit. Studien zur empirischen Theoriebildung und empirischen Untersuchung zum Sprachverhalten französischer und italienischer Jugendlicher in Bitt- und Danksituationen*. Tübingen: Narr, 1995.

Hellinger, Marlis and Ammon, Ulrich (eds.). *Contrastive Sociolinguistics*. Berlin: de Gruyter, 1996.

Hentschel, Elke. *Funktion und Geschichte deutscher Partikel ja, doch, halt und eben*. Tübingen: Niemeyer, 1986.

Hill, Beverly; Ide, Sachiko; Ikuta, Shoko; Kawasaki, Akiko and Ogino, Tsunao. "Universals of Linguistic Politeness: Quantitative Evidence from Japanese and American English." *Journal of Pragmatics*, 10:3 (1986), 347-71.

Hindelang, Götz. *Auffordern. Die Untertypen des Aufforderns und ihre sprachlichen Realisierungsformen*. Göppingen: Kümmerle, 1978.

Hofstede, Geert. *Culture's Consequences. Comparing Values, Behaviors, Institutions and Organizations Across Nations*. Sage Publications, Thousand Oaks, 2001.

Hofstede, Geert. *Cultures and Organisations: Software of the Mind*. London: McGraw-Hill, 1991.

Hofstede, Geert. "Dimensions of National Cultures in Fifty Countries and Three Regions." 335-55. Deregowski et al., 1983.

Hofstede, Geert. *Culture's Consequences: International Differences in Work-Related Values*. Beverly Hills: Sage, 1980.

Hofstede, Geert; Hofstede Gert Jan and Minkov, Michael. *Cultures and Organizations: Software of the Mind*. 3rd Edition, McGraw-Hill USA, 2010.

Holden, C. "New life ahead for social sciences." *Science* 261 (1993), 1976-98.

Hosman, Lawrence. "The Evaluative Concequences of Hedges, Hesitations, and Intensifiers. Powerful and Powerless Speech Styles." *Human Communication Research*, 15:3 (1989), 383-406.

Hornscheidt, Antje. "Sprach(wissenschaft)liche Kulturen." 57-88 in http://www.*linguistik-online*.de/14_03/hornscheidt.pdf

House, Juliane. "Contrastive Discourse Analysis and Misunderstanding: The Case of German and English." 345-61. Hellinger and Ammon, 1996.

House, Juliane. "Some Methological Problems and Perspectives in Contrastive Discourse Analysis." *Applied Linguistics*, 5:3 (1984), 245-254.

House, Juliane and Kasper, Gabriele. "Politeness Markers in English and German." 157-85. Coulmas, 1981.

House, Juliane and Vollmer, Helmut J. „Sprechaktperformanz im Deutschen: Zur Realisierung der Sprechhandlungen BITTEN/AUFFORDERN und SICH ENTSCHULDIGEN." *Linguistische Berichte* (1988), 114-144.

Hübler, Axel. *Understatements and Hedges in English.* Amsterdam: Benjamins, 1983.

Hui, C. Harry. *Individualism–Collectivism: Theory, Measurement, and its Relationship to Reward Allocation.* Unpublished doctoral dissertation. University of Illinois, 1984.

Hui, C. Harry. "Measurment of Individualism – Collectivism." *Journal of Research in Personality*, 22 (1988), 17-36.

Hui, C. Harry and Villareal Marelo, J. "Individualism – Collectivism and Psychological Needs : Their Relationship in Two Cultures." *Journal of Cross-Cultural Psychology*, 20 (1989), 310-323.

Huizinga, Johan. *Homo ludens. Vom Ursprung der Kultur im Spiel.* Reinbek: Rowohlt, 2004 [1938].

Hymes, Dell H. "The Ethnography of Speaking." 99-138. Fishman, Joshua A. (ed.). *Readings in the Sociology of Language.* The Hague: de Gruyter, 1972.

Ide, Sachiko; Hill, Beverly; Carnes, Yukiko; Ogino, Tsunao and Kawasaki, Akiko. "The Concepts of Politeness: An Empirical Study of American English and Japanese." 281-97. Watts et al., 1992.

Institut für Deutsche Sprache, Forschungsstelle Freiburg. *Freiburger Corpus.* München: Institut für Deutsche Sprache, 1971.

Jahoda, Gustav. "The Cross-Cultural Emperor's Conceptual Clothes: The Emic - Etic Issue Re-Visited." 19-38. Deregowski et al., 1983.

Janney, Richard W. and Arndt, Horst. "Universality and Relativity in Cross-Cultural Politeness Research." *Multilingua*, 12:1 (1993), 13-50.

Jassem, Wiktor. *The Phonology of Modern English.* Warszawa: PWN, 1983.

Jaszczołt, K. M. and Turner, Ken (eds.). *Meaning Through Language Contrast, vol. 2.* Amsterdam: Benjamins, 2003.

Jones, Stanley E. "Integrating Etic and Emic Approaches in the Study of Intercultural Communication." 57-74. Asante et al., 1979.

Kachru, Yamuna. "Culture and Speech Acts: Evidence from Indian and Singaporean English." *Studies in the Linguistic Sciences*, 28:1 (1998), 79-98.

De Kadt, Elizabeth. "Requests as Speech Acts in Zulu." *South African Journal of African Languages*, 12:3 (1992), 101-106.

Kallmeyer, Werner. "Formulierungsweise, Kontextualisierung und soziale Identität. Dargestellt am Beispiel des formelhaften Sprechens." *Lili: Zeitschrift für Literaturwissenschaft und Linguistik*, 16:64 (1986), 98-126.

Kaplan, H.B. and Boyd I.H. "The Social Functions of Humor on an Open Psychiatric Ward." *Psychiatric Quarterly* 39 (1965), 502-15.

Kasanga, Luanga. "'I am Asking for a Pen': Framing of Requests in Black South African English." 213-35. Jaszczolt and Turner, 2003.

Kasper, Gabriele and Blum-Kulka, Shoshana (eds.). *Interlanguage Pragmatics.* New York: Oxford University Press, 1993.

Katan, D. *Translating Cultures: An Introduction for Translators, Interpreters and Mediators.* St. Jerome Publishing: Manchester, 2004.

Katan, D. "It's a Question of Life or Death: Cultural Differences in Advertising Private Pensions". In Vasta, N. (ed.) *Forms of Promotion Texts, Contexts and Cultures.* Pàtron Editore: Bologna, 2006. 55-80.

Keim, Inken. "Formelhaftes Sprechen als konstitutives Merkmal sozialen Stils." 318-344. Seltig and Sandig, 1997.

405

Keim, Inken and Schwitalla, Johannes. "Formen der Höfflichkeit – Merkmale sozialen Stils." 129-145. Janota, Johannes (ed.). *Vielfalt der kulturellen Systeme und Stile (=Kultureller Wandel und die Germanistik in der Bundesrepublik 1)*. Tübingen: Niemeyer, 1993.

Kim, Min-Sun; Hunter, John E.; Miyahara, Akira; Horvath, Ann-Marie; Bresnahan, Mary and Yoon, Hei-Jin. "Individual- vs. Culture-Level Dimensions of Individualism and Collectivism: Effects on Preferred Conversational Styles." *Communication Monographs*, 63:1 (1996), 29-49.

Kim, Uichol; Triandis, Harry C.; Kagitcibasi, Cigdem; Choi, Sang-Chin and Yoon, Gene (eds.). *Individualism and Collectivism*. Thousand Oaks: Sage, 1994.

Koeman, J. "Cultural values in commercials: Reaching and representing the multicultural market?" *Communications* 32 (2007), 223-253.

Kotthoff, Helga. Spaß versehen. Zur Pragmatik von konversationellem Humor. Tübingen: Niemeyer, 1998.

Kuiper, Koenraad and Haggo, Douglas. "Livestock Auctions, Oral Poetry, and Ordinary Language." *Language in Society*, 13:2 (1984), 205-34.

Krzeszowski, Tomasz P. *Contrasting Languages*. Berlin: de Gruyter, 1990.

Lakoff, George. "Hedges: A Study in Meaning Criteria and the Logic of Fuzzy Concepts." *Journal of Philosophical Logic*, 2 (1973), 458-508.

Lakoff, Robin. "The Logic of Politeness, or Minding your P's and Q's." *Proceedings of the Ninth Regional Meeting of the Chicago Linguistic Society*, 1973, 345-356.

Lange, Willi. *Aspekte der Höflichkeit*. Franfurt a. M.: Lang, 1984.

Leech, Geoffrey N. *Principles of Pragmatics*. London: Longman, 1983.

Lee-Wong, Song Mei. "Imperatives in Requests: Direct or Impolite – Observations from Chinese." *Pragmatics*, 4:4 (1994), 491-515.

Lee-Wong, Song Mei. *Politeness and Face in Chinese Culture*. Frankfurt/M.: Peter Lang, 2000.

Le Pair, Rob. "Spanish Requests Strategies: A Cross-Cultural Analysis from an Intercultural Perspective." *Language Sciences*, 18:3-4 (1996), 651-70.

Leung, Kwok and Bond, Michael Harris. "On the Empirical Identification of Dimensions for Cross-Cultural Comparisons." *Journal of Cross-Cultural Psychology*, 20:2 (1989), 133-151.

Levinson, Stephen. "Conceptual Problems in the Study of Regional and Cultural Style." 161-90. Dittmar and Schlobinski, 1988.

Levinson, Stephen C. "The Essential Inadequacies of Speech Act Models of Dialogue." 473-492. Parret et al., 1981.

Long, Debra L. and Graesser, Arthur C. "Wit and Humor in Discourse Processing." *Discourse Processes*, 11:1 (1988), 35-60.

Longman Dictionary of Contemporary English. Warszawa: PWN, 1989.

Loukianenko Wolfe, Maria. "Different cultures – different discourses? Rhetorical patterns of business letters by Russian and English speakers." *Contrastive Rhetorics: Reaching to intercultural rhetoric*. Connor, Ulla; Nagelhout, Ed; Rozycki, William (eds.). John Benjamins: Indianapolis and Las Vegas, 2010. 87-121.

Lundberg, Craig C. Person-Focused Joking: Pattern and Function. *Human Organisation*, 28 (1969), 22-28.

Lwanga-Lumu, Joy Christine. "Politeness and Indirectness Revisited." *South African Journal of African Languages*, 19:2 (1999), 83-92.

Manes, Joan and Wolfson, Nessa. "The Compliment Formula," 115-32. Coulmas, 1981.

Marcjanik, Małgorzata. *Polska grzeczność językowa*. Kielce: Wyższa Szkoła Pedagogiczna, 1997.

Marek, Bogusław. "Intonation of Imperative Sentences and Requests in Polish and English." *Papers and Studies in Contrastive Linguistics*, 2 (1973), 161-79.

Markiewicz, Aleksandra: *Der Imperativ im Deutschen und Polnischen*. Kraków: Universitas, 2000.

Markkanen, Raija. *Cross-Language Study in Pragmatics*. Jyväskylä: University of Jyväskylä, 1985.

Markus, Hazel R. and Kitayama, Shinobu. "Culture and Self: Implications for Cognition, Emotion, and Motivation." *Psychological Review*, 98 (1991), 224-253.

Márquez Reiter, Rosina. *Linguistic Politeness in Britain and Uruguay*. Amsterdam: Benjamins, 2000.

Meeuwesen, L.; van den Brink-Muinen, A. and Hofstede, G. 2009. "Can dimensions of national culture predict cross-national differences in medical communication?" *Patient Education and Counseling*, 75 (2009), 58-66.

Meier, A. J. "What's the Excuse? Image Repair in Austrian German." *Modern Language Journal*, 81:2 (1997), 197-208.

Miller, Joan G. "A Cultural Perspective on the Morality of Benefice and Interpersonal Responsibility." 11-27. Ting-Toomey and Korzenny, 1991.

Miller, J. G. and Bersoff, D. M. "Culture and Moral Judgements: How Are Conflicts Between Justice and Friendship Resolved." *Journal of Personality and Social Psychology*, 62 (1992), 541-554.

Mills, Margaret. "On Russian and English Pragmalinguistic Requestive Strategies." *Journal of Slavic Linguistics*, 1:1 (1993), 92-115.

Müller, Andreas P. "Inferiorität und Superiorität verbalen Verhaltens: Zu den 'Rollenstilen' von Vorgesetzten und Angestellten." 217-253. Selting und Sandig, 1997.

Müller, Klaus. "Partnerarbeit in Dialogen. Zur Kontaktfunktion inhaltlich redundanten Elemente in natürlicher Kommunikation." *Grazer Linguistische Studien*, 10 (1979), 183-216.

Naroll, R.; Michik, G. L. and Naroll, F. *Handbook of Cross-Cultural Psychology, vol. 2*, 1980.

Nattinger, James R. and de Carrico, Jeanette. *Lexical Phrases and Language Teaching*. Oxford: Oxford University Press, 1992.

Nekula, Marek. *System der Partikel im Deutschen und Tschechischen*. Tübingen: Niemeyer, 1996.

Novy, Ivan and Schroll-Machl, Sylvia. "Tschechien." 90-102. Thomas et al., 2003.

Odlin, Terence. *Language Transfer: Cross-Linguistic Influence in Language Learning*. Cambridge: CUP, 1989.

Ogiermann, Eva. Politeness and in-directness across cultures: A comparison of English, German, Polish and Russian requests. *Journal of Politeness Research* 5:2 (2009), 189-216.

Ogiermann, Eva. On Apologising in Negative and Positive Politeness Cultures. Amsterdam/ Philadelphia: John Benjamins, 2009.

Okabe, Roichi. "Cultural Assumptions of East and West: Japan and the United States." 21-44. Gudykunst, 1983.

Oleksy, Wieslaw (ed.). *Contrastive Pragmatics*. Amsterdam: Benjamins, 1989.

Palmer, Gary B. *Towards a Theory of Cultural Linguistics*. Austin: Univ. of Texas Press, 1996.

Paltridge, Brian. *Genre, Frames and Writing in Research Settings*. Amsterdam: Benjamins, 1997.

Parret, Herman; Sbisà, Marina and Verschueren, Jef (eds.). *Possibilities and Limitations of Pragmatics: Proceedings of the Conference on Pragmatics at Urbino, July 8-14 1979*. Amsterdam: Benjamins, 1981.

Pawley, Andrew and Syder, Frances H. "Two Puzzles for Linguistic Theory: Nativelike Selection and Nativelike Fluency." 191-226. Richards et al., 1983.

Pawluk, Cheryl J. "Social Construction of Teasing." *Journal for the Theory of Social Behaviour*, 19:2 (1989), 145-167.

Pike, Kenneth. *Language in Relation to a Unified Theory of the Structures of Human Behaviour*. The Hague: de Gruyter, 1954; rev. ed. 1967.

Pogrebin, Mark R. and Poole Eric D. "Humor in Briefing Room: A Study of the Strategic Uses of Humor Among Police." *Journal of Contemporary Ethnography*, 17 (1984), 183-210.

Pufal Bax, Ingrid. "How to Assign Work in an Office." *Journal of Pragmatics*, 10 (1986), 673-692.

407

Pułaczewska, Hanna. "Modality in Proposals." Hansen, B. and Karlik, P. (eds.) *Modality in Slavonic Languages. New Perspectives.* München: Sagner, 2005. 315-26.

Pułaczewska, Hanna. *Directives in Media Encounters. A Pragmalinguistic Study of British English, German and Polish.* Unpublished manuscript (Habilitationsschrift). Universität Regensburg, 2006.

Pułaczewska, Hanna. "Syntactic reduplication as an iconically-driven pragmatic principle in the spoken language." Lewandowska-Tomaszczyk, Barbara and Dziwirek, Katarzyna (eds.) *Cognitive Corpus Linguistics Studies.* Frankfurt/Main: Peter Lang, 2009. 111-128.

Quirk, Randolf; Greenbaum, Sidney; Leech, Geoffrey and Svartvik, Jan. *A Comprehensive Grammar of the English Language.* London: Longman, 1985.

Reykowski, Janusz. "Collectivism and Individualism as Dimension of Social Change." 276-292. Kim et al., 1994.

Reykowski, Janusz. „Kolektywizm i indywidualizm jako kategorie opisu zmian społecznych." 23-50. Gawlikowski et al., 1999.

Reynolds, Paul D. *A Primer in Theory Construction.* Indianapolis: Bobbs-Merrill, 1971.

Rhodes, Richard A. "'We are Going to Go There': Positive Politeness in Ojibwa." *Multilingua,* 8:2-3 (1989), 249-258.

Richards, Jack C. and Schmidt, Richard W. (eds.) *Language and Communication.* London: Longman, 1983.

Riley, Philip. "Towards a Contrastive Pragmalinguistics." *Papers and Studies in Contrastive Linguistics,* 10 (1979), 57-78.

Rinnert, Carol and Kobayashi, Hiroe. "Requestive Hints in Japanese and English." *Journal of Pragmatics,* 31:9 (1999), 1173-1201.

Roche, Reinhard. "Floskeln im Gegenwartsdeutsch." *Wirkendes Wort,* 15 (1965), 485-405.

Rose, Ken. "Japanese, American English, and Directness. More than Stereotypes." *JALT Journal,* 18 (1996), 67-80.

Roy, Alice Myers. "Irony in Conversation." *Dissertation Abstracts International,* 39 (1978).

Sandig, Barbara. *Stilistisch-rhetorische Diskursanalyse.* Tübingen: Narr, 1986.

Schmid, Stefan. "England." 53-71. Thomas et al., 2003.

Schneider, Klaus. *Small Talk. Analysing Phatic Discourse.* Marburg: Hitzeroth, 1988.

Schonpflug, U. and Jansen, X. "Self Concept and Coping With Developmental Demands in German and Polish Adolescents." *International Journal of Behavioral Development,* 18:3 (1995), 385-406.

Schourup, Lawrence. *Common Discourse Particles in English Conversation.* Columbus: Ohio State University, 1983.

Schroll-Machl, Sylvia. "Deutschland." 72-89. Thomas et al., 2003.

Scollon, Ron and Scollon, Susanne B. K. *Narrative, Literacy and Face in Interethnic Communication. Advances in Discourse Processes.* Norwood: Ablex, 1981.

Searle, John R. "A Classification of Illocutionary Acts." *Language in Society,* 5:1 (1976), 1-23.

Searle, John R. "Indirect Speech Acts." 59-82. Cole and Morgan, 1975.

Selting, Margret. "Interaktionale Stilistik: Methodologische Aspekte der Analyse von Sprechstilen." 9-44. Seltig and Sandig, 1997.

Selting, Margret and Sandig, Barbara. "Einleitung." 1-8. Seltig and Sandig, 1997.

Selting, Margret and Sandig, Barbara (eds.). *Sprech- und Gesprächsstile.* Berlin: de Gruyter, 1997.

Sifianou, Maria. "The Use of Diminutives in Expressing Politeness: Modern Greek versus English." *Journal of Pragmatics,* 17:2 (1992), 155-174. (a)

Sifianou, Maria. *Politeness Phenomena in England and Greece. A Cross-Cultural Perspective.* Clarendon Press: Oxford, 1992. (b)

Sinha, D. "Social Psychology in India: A Historical Perspective." *Psychological Studies,* 25:2 (1980), 157-163.

Sinha, D. "Cross-Cultural Psychology: A View from the Third World," 3-17. Deregowski et al., 1983.

Smith P. B.; Dugan, S.; Peterson, M. F.; Leung, K. "Individualism: collectivism and the handling of disagreement. A 23 country study." *International Journal of Intercultural Relations* 22.3 (1998), 351-367.

Smoleńska, Z. and Frączek, A. "Life Goals and Evaluative Standards Among Adolescents: A Cross-National Perspective." 131-143. Hazekamp et al., 1987.

Smoleńska, Z. and Wieczorkowska, G. *Changes in the Evaluative Processes Among Adolescents: A Cross-Cultural Perspective.* Warsaw: Polish Academy of Science, 1990.

Sorhus, H. B. "To Hear Ourselves – Implications for Teaching English as a Second Language." *English Language Teaching Journal*, 31:3 (1976), 211-21.

Sperber, Dan and Wilson, Deirdre. *Relevance. Communication and Cognition.* Oxford: Blackwell, 1986.

Statistisches Bundesamt: Bevölkerung mit Migrationshintergrund – Ergebnisse des Mikrozensus 2005.

Stenström, Anna-Brita. *An Introduction to Spoken Interaction.* London: Longman, 1996.

Earl Stevick, W. *Memory, Meaning and Method.* Rowley, MA: Newbury House Publishers, 1976.

Tannen, Deborah. *Conversational Style: Analysing Talks Among Friends.* Norwood: Ablex, 1984.

Tannen, Deborah. "Indirectness in Discourse: Ethnicity as Conversational Style." *Discourse Processes*, 4:3 (1981), 221-38.

Thomas, Alexander; Kammhuber, Stefan and Schroll-Machl, Sylvia (ed.). *Handbuch Interkulturelle Kommunikation und Kooperation.* Göttingen: Vandenhoeck & Ruprecht, 2003.

Thomas, Jenny. "Cross-Cultural Pragmatic Failure." *Finlance*, 2 (1982), 79-109.

Thomas, Jenny. "Cross-Cultural Pragmatics." *Applied Linguistics*, 4:1 (1984), 91-112.

Thomas, Jenny. "Cross-Cultural Discourse as 'Unequal Encounter': Towards a Pragmatic Analysis." *Applied Linguistics*, 5:3 (1984), 226-235.

Thurmair, Maria. *Modalpartikeln und ihre Kombinationen.* Tübingen: Niemayer, 1989.

Ting-Toomey, Stella and Korzenny, Felipe (eds.). *Cross-Cultural Interpersonal Communication. International and Intercultural Interaction Manual, vol. 15.* London: Sage, 1991.

Ting-Toomey, Stella. *Communication Across Cultures.* The Guilford Press, New York, 1999.

Triandis, Harry. "Collectivism v. Individualism: A Reconceptualisation of a Basic Concept in Cross-cultural Social Psychology." 60-95. Verma and Bagley, 1988.

Triandis, Harry. "Cross-Cultural Studies of Individualism and Collectivism." 41-134. Berman and Jahoda, 1990.

Triandis, Harry. *Individualism and Collectivism.* Boulder, CO: Westview, 1995.

Triandis, Harry. "The Measurment of the Etic Aspects of Individualism and Collectivism Across Cultures." *Australian Journal of Psychology*, 38:3 (1986), 257-267.

Triandis, Harry C. and Vassiliou, V. "An Analysis of Subjective Culture." Triandis, Harry C. (ed.). *The Analysis of Subjective Culture.* New York: Wiley, 1972.

Tsui, Amy B. *English Conversation.* Oxford: Oxford University Press, 1994.

Vandana, Shiva. *Stolen Harvest: The Hijacking of the Global Food Supply.* Cambridge, MA: South End Press, 2000.

Vassiliou, V. and Vassiliou, G. "The Implicative Meaning of the Greek Concept of Philotimo." *Journal of Cross-Cultural Psychology*, 4 (1973), 326-341.

Ventola, Eija (ed.). *Discourse and Community: Doing Functional Linguistics.* Tübingen: Narr, 2000.

Verma, Gajendra K. and Bagley, Christopher (eds.). *Cross-Cultural Studies of Personality, Attitudes and Cognition.* London: Macmillan, 1988.

Verschurren, Jeff. *Understanding Pragmatics.* London, 1999.

Vinton, K.L. "Humor in the Workplace: It is More Than Telling Jokes." *Small Group Behavior*, 20 (1989), 151-166.

Watts, Richard; Sachiko, Ide and Ehlich, Konrad (eds.). *Politeness in Language*. Berlin: de Gruyter, 1992.

Weasenforth, Donald and Biesenbach-Lucas, Sigrun. "Evidential Reliability in Pragmatics: A Comparison of Ethnographic and Elicitation Approaches." *LACUS Forum*, 28 (2002), 133-44.

Wierzbicka, Anna. "Contrastive Sociolinguistics and the Theory of 'Cultural Scripts': Chinese vs English." 313-344. Hellinger and Ammon, 1996.

Wierzbicka, Anna. *Cross-Cultural Pragmatics. The Semantics of Human Interaction*. Berlin: de Gruyter, 1991.

Wierzbicka, Anna. "Different Cultures, Different Languages, Different Speech Acts. Polish vs. English." *Journal of Pragmatics*, 9:2-3 (1985), 145-78.

Wierzbicka, Anna. "Does Language Reflect Culture? Evidence from Australian English." *Language in Society*, 15:3 (1986), 349-374.

Werlen, Iwan. "Vermeidungsritual und Höflichkeit. Zu einigen Formen konventionalisierter Sprechakte im Deutschen." *Deutsche Sprache*, 11 (1984), 194-218.

Wierzbicka, Anna. Moje podwójne życie: dwa języki, dwie kultury, dwa światy. *Teksty drugie* 4:45 (1997), 74-94.

Willer, Bernhard and Groeben, Norbert. "Sprachliche Hinweise auf Ironische Kooperation: Das Konzept der Ironiesignale unter Sprechakttheoretischer Perspektive Re-Konstruiert." *Zeitschrift für Germanische Linguistik*, 8:1 (1980), 291-313.

Yamada, H. "Talk-Distancing in Japanese Meetings." *Journal of Asian Pacific Communication*, 5 (1994), 19-36.

Yorio, Carlos A. "Conventionalized Language Forms and the Development of Communicative Competence." *TESOL-Quarterly*, 14 (1980), 433-442.

Zajdman, Anat. "Contextualization of Canned Jokes in Discourse." *HUMOR: International Journal of Humor Research*, 4:1 (1991), 23-40.

Zajdman, Anat. "The Transactional Implications of the Jewish Marriage Jokes," 143-161. Ziv, Avner and Zajdman Anat (eds.). *Semites and Stereotypes: Characteristics of Jewish Humor*. Westport, CT: Greenwood, 1993.

Zijderweld, Anton. "The Sociology of Humor and Laughter." *Current Sociology*, 31, 1983.

Appendix 1

Participant age: mean, minimum, maximum
P3: 28, 20, 41
P1: 29, 20, 47
E3: 26, 21, 43
E4: 26, 20, 32
G2: 26, 21, 40
G4: 27, 20, 35

Gender structure and professions of the participants:

G1 - *female*: schoolgirl, merchandiser, entrepreneur, skilled worker, stewardess, project manager, IT attendant; *male*: skilled worker (3), entrepreneur, student

G2 - *female*: student, office clerk (3), teacher, hair-dresser, paediatric nurse, medical doctor; *male*: sports teacher, skilled worker (3), hotel manager, unemployed, entrepreneur, student

G4 – *female:* student (2), banker, stripper, artist, stewardess, technical assistant, *male:* security guard, salesman, pool attendant, financial advisor (2), football trainer, video film producer, restaurant owner

E3 - *female*: DJ, cinema worker, secretary, IT attendant, student, clerk, barrister; *male*: model, gym coach, student, personal shopper, finance officer, ? , ?

E4 – *female*: student, shop assistant, clothes designer, clerk, shop manager, hair-dresser, ? ; *male*: cook, fish merchant, employed in a family restaurant, IT administrator, marketing manager, ?

Polish 1 - *female*: photographer, entrepreneur, student (2), shop assistant, manager; *male*: personal assistant, chemist, skilled worker, unemployed, lifeguard, advertisement specialist, soldier, farmer, student

Polish 3 - *female*: business consultant, schoolgirl, merchandiser, photographer, security guard, secretary (2), bartender, model; *male*: entrepreneur, student (2), merchandiser, manager, skilled worker, waiter, technician, security guard

I

Appendix 2. Types of modification with examples.

SUPPORTIVE MOVES	
NEGATIVELY POLITE	
apology	13-E3. F okay # can you come here # can you come closer # **sorry mate**
imposition minimiser	14-E3. F **if you wake up early enough** # can you help me to scrub off that tattoo on my back
object minimiser	15-E3. F could you not shout at me please # **that's all I ask**
concession	16-E3. M **and fair enough you can do it at your home** # but people here do not like the idea of peeing in the shower
preparator	17-E3. F **can I just say one thing** # . I think that when you wash up # you should really wash up properly # . because so far # we had to rinse everything we used # --- 10-G2 F **du könntest mir den Gefallen tun** und mein Handtuch schon mal- *you could do me a favour # and my towel already*
consultative device (non-tag)	18-E3. M **what do you think** # we may as well talk about it
POSITIVELY POLITE	
	ENHANCING IMPOSITIVENESS
emphasiser	19-E3. F1, F2, M1, M2, M3 arranged that they will go camping together. F1 is waiting for F2, M1, M2, M3 to come out. F1 well # I want to go camping # **I am all ready** 20-E3. F oi # everybody from the rich side # … # get your ass in the air # .because # . we've spend over a hundred pound more on shopping # and if we don't do it in the next fifteen minutes # we won't get no shopping # so get in the bedroom # _come on # _come on # **.quick** 21-E3. M shut up both of you # shut up both of you # listen to me # please # **oh come on guys** # please # guys 22-E3. F Alex go away with them # . **Alex I mean it** # go away
grounder	23-E3. **M you don't do it** # . and you now # fair enough you can do it in your own house # but **people don't like the idea here of a . of peeing in the shower** # because we have got no # we haven't cleaned them at all 24-E3 M okay # we should better start drinking that champagne # **because I . I'm not waiting for anybody** # _ **since I finished `mine** # . it's going

	25-E3. F don't even think about coming to me with your feet # **or I'll slap you** # silly
specifier (presupposing compliance)	11-G2. F **wir machen jetzt ein Spiel** # **wenn du jetzt den** **Roten ziehst** # **mach die Augen zu** # **dann gewinnst du**
preparator	26-E3. M I tell you what we need # . a group hug
steer	1-E4. M1 and F are sitting together; M2 is sitting alone while other housemates are involved in conversations. M1 to M2: **Bill # what are you doing over there** F Bill what are you doing # **come over here** 2-E4. F is standing at the edge of the swimming pool. F **I really want to go in # I'm not going in on my own #** **Tania wants to come in** # come on Tania # come on Tania
	ENHANCING CONFIDENCE/INFORMALITY
appreciation	12-P3. F is sitting in a chair in a night gown which opens showing a leg. M ka- ka- Karolcia # kontroluj kulaski # przykryj troche (F looks closely at her legs, tries to cover them with her gown) M **no no # no widzisz # ładnie** *ka ka Karolina-diminutive # control the legs-dialectal-diminutive # cover them a bit #* ***good good # now you see # now that's pretty***
disarmer	27-E3. M **I know you think I'm being funny** # but don't you think we should be careful with this money we're getting
compliment	13-P3. M ty # zrób chyba jeszcze jedną kanapkę # **bo takie** ci powiem **dobre** robisz *you # make perhaps one more sandwich # **because you know you make good ones***
steer (colloquial, humorous, intimate)	1-G4. F Jan # **ich habe niemanden der mich kuschelt #** machst du das? *Jan # I have nobody to cuddle with me # will you do this?*

Table 2. Types and examples of politeness-relevant supportive moves accompanying directive
speech acts.

NEUTRAL	
grounder	28-E3. F oi # everybody from the rich side # … # get your ass in the air # . **because # . we've spent over a hundred pound more on shopping # and if we don't do it in the next fifteen minutes # we won't get no shopping** # so get in the bedroom # _ come on # _ come on # . quick
steer incl. availability check	14-P3. F tam gdzieś została moja kurtka ze skóry # przynieście mi ją *my jacket is left somewhere over there # bring-pl. it to me* 29-E3. F you are going to get up early in the morning # ´right M I'm going to try to F will you wake me up as well # . if it's about quarter to nine
preparator	15-P3. M e # chłopaki # słuchajcie # **ja myśle od razu taką jedną rzecz** # że jak oni będą na przykład spać w gorszych warunkach # to my pójdziemy --- # a dziewczyny przyjdą tu *hey # boys # listen # I think one such thing at once # that if they for example sleep in worse conditions # then we will go there # and the girls will come here*
specifier	16-P3. M dobrze # wypro . może przeprowadźmy próbę # . **ja ci po- #. ja ci pokażę jak ja biegam#.a ty powiesz jak ty biegniesz # komisja to oceni** *well # maybe let's make a test # . I will sho- #. I will show you how I run # . and you will say how you run # a jury will evaluate this*

Table 3. Types and examples of supportive moves neutral in politeness.

IV

INTERACTION MARKERS		
NEGATIVELY POLITE		
request- IFID	30-E3. F can you let us in # **please**	
question tag	12-G2. M aber so Spaßes halber könnte man das durchziehen # **oder?**	
POSITIVELY POLITE		
	ENHANCING IMPOSITIVENESS	
STARTERS		
imperative (no verbs of sensation)	17-P3. M **dawaj** Pawulo walimy im po garbach i do domu	
	come on (name-based nickname) we beat their backs and go home	
	13-G2. M1, M2, M3 are in the hot tub.	
	M1 **komm** # wir machen eine Welle	
	come on # we make a wave	
	31-E3. M **come on** # group hug	
negation-based link/summons	32-E3. M **no** # don't try an escape # you'll hurt yourself	
	ENHANCING INFORMALITY/CONFIDENCE	
positively polite term of address	33-E3. F **girls** # let's work as a team	
interjection	14-G2. M **hei** # soll # sollen wir es mal spaßeshalber durchziehen?	
	hey # should we do it just for fun	
verb of knowing	18-P3. F **wiecie co::::?**	
	you know what?	
	M no	
	yeah	
	F potrzebuję co:ś	
	I need something	
	M o::	
	F pod głowę jeszcze:	
	to put under my head	
imperative of verb of sensation	19-P3. M **słuchajcie** # już dawno zamknęliśmy ten temat	
	listen-pl # we have already closed that theme	
NON-STARTERS		
term of address in non-starter function	pet names, terms of endearment	15-G2. F kommst du nicht # **Schatz?**
		are you coming # darling? (lexical meaning: "treasure")

	colloquial	20-P3. M chodź się **młody** wykąpiemy # bo dziewczyny chciały wejść do wiesz # do żakuski *come **youngster** we'll take a bath # as the girls wanted to get into you know # into the jacuzzi -DIMINUTIVE*
	humorous	34-E3. M let's go for entertainment # . **uncle**
	nicknames	22-P3. M chodź **Ken**[1] *come Ken*
	creative alterations of first names[2]	23-P3. M dawaj **Pawulo**[3] walimy im po garbach i do domu # bo nie ma
cajoler	expression based on verb of knowing in non-starter function	16-G2. M ei # du # wenn du die fünf Minuten nicht brauchst # sagst du bescheit # dann machen wir eine Reihe # _ **weißt du?** *ei # if you don't need the five minutes # you tell us # then we will queue # **you know***
cajoler	imperatives of verbs of sensation in non-starter function	24-P3. F nie róbmy sobie **słuchajcie** ciśnień *let's not put each other, **listen,** under pressure*
	strongly colloquial question tag	17-G2. M ja # Prost zusammen # **ne?** *well # cheers together # **QUESTION TAG***
	strongly colloquial link	25-P3. M **dobra** # dawaj dawaj ***LINK** # come on come on*
	strongly colloquial summons	26-P3. M **no to dobra** # to . przynoście wszystko co jest i na stół proszę ***SUMMONS** # then bring all what is there and on the table please* 18-G2. F **na** bleib doch ruhig ***SUMMONS** stay EMPHATIC PARTICLE quiet*
NEUTRALY POLITE		
link		35-E3. M **I know # but** just need to make sure that it gets done # that sort of thing
summon		36-E3. F **well** # I want to go camping # I am all ready
standard term of address – starter		37-E3. F **Daniel** # will you wake me up as well

---

[1] Ken is a good-looking man, named so after the male equivalent of the Barbie doll.
[2] Nicknames proper, humorist ad-hoc labels and first-name based forms different from the standard colloquial form of the first name are amalgamated together as "nickname/humour" in the statistical evaluation.
[3] Full first name form: Paweł. "Pawulo" is a non-standard ad-hoc creation, possibly by analogy with Pablo; ulo/-ula (masc./fem.) is also a rarely used productive morphological ending for creating sympathetic diminutives, e.g. dziad-dziadulo "poor filthy old man – poor dear little old man".

standard term of address – non-starter	38-E3. F come over here # **Ted**

Table 4. Types and examples of interaction markers accompanying requestive speech acts.

INTERNAL MODIFIERS	
NEGATIVELY POLITE	
depersonalisation (agent avoidance)	27-P3. M trzeba jeszcze zaśpiewać *one needs also to sing*
subjunctive mood/Konjunktiv	19-G2. M aber so spaßeshalber **könnte man** das durchziehen # oder? *but one could do it just for fun # right?*
lexical hedge/understater	39-E3. F let's go and have a **little** lie down in the bed
diminutive (morphological)	28-P3. F weź ją zamknij tam w **kąciczku** *take-and-close it in the corner-DIMINUTIVE*
modal adverbial	40-E3. F **may be** we should go and have a chat over there # shouldn't we # in case it's shown # . so that nobody sees it
permission request	2-G4. M kommt # lasst uns alle zusammen machen # ehrlich *come on # let us do it all together # really*
polite pessimism	41-E3. F are you **not** coming into the pool
conditional	42-E3. F **if you didn't** hold that pad that far away from me # maybe **I'd** reach it
complex hedge (incl. subjectivity marker)	43-E3. M I know # but just need to make sure that it gets `done # **that sort of thing** 44-E3. F we should really get it out for him and just put it out # **or something** # shouldn't we 45-E3. M **I think** we should possibly put ourselves into . categories of people that are worse # . if they are honest # they go first # and sod this boy girl thing
POSITIVELY POLITE	
	ENHANCING INFORMALITY/CONFIDENCE
colloquialism	46-E3. M promise me your bed and your baccy
nickname (referential)	29-P3. M gdzie jeszcze # **Barbi** dajcie **Barbi** od razu *where is NICKNAME # give me NICKNAME at once*

humour incl. humorous augmentative, humorous euphemism	11-E3. M so are we going to set up a little camp # **Camp David like**
	20-G2. F Walter # wenn du schon genug **Tiere** getötet hast # spielen wir noch mal Backgammon? (reference: flies)
	21-G2. M aber so spaßeshalber könnte man das durchziehen oder? wenn ich heute Abend ins **Bettchen** ´gehe *but one could do it just for fun right? when I go to bed-DIM tonight*
solidarity plural	30-P3. M nie **puszczamy** bąkow # dobra? *we don't fart # okay?*
	ENHANCING IMPOSITIVENESS
expletive (vulgarism)	22-G2. F du hast hier noch keinen Finger gerührt also # **Klappe** und mach nach *you haven't moved a little finger yet so # shut up and do the same*
augmentative	23-G2. M sei doch nicht so ein Spielverderber # . **hau** sie **um** oder lass sie . gewinnen *don't be such a fun killer # knock her over or let her win*
lexical intensifier	47-E3. F can I just say one thing # . I think that when you wash up # you should **really** wash up properly # . because so far # we had to rinse everything we used #
semantic/syntactic intensifier	31-P3. M słuchajcie # **już dawno zamknęliśmy** ten temat[4] *listen # we **have** already **closed** this theme **a long time ago** (an appeal to stop discussing a new theme currently under discussion)*
repetition	32-P3. M koniec gry na dzisiaj # _ **koniec gry** # *end of the play for today # _ end of the play*

Table 5. Types and examples of internal modifiers accompanying requestive speech acts.

[4] A categorical note is introduced by the use of the past tense.

Appendix 3. Frequencies of directive activities: participant structures.

REQUESTIVES	E3E		E4E		G2E		G4E		P3E	
Beneficiary	%	Interval	%	Interval	%	Interval	%	Interval	%	Interval
1) -S.+H.+EXT	1%	238.5	0%	266	1%	195.0	1%	116.0	0%	314.0
2) -S.-H.+EXT	2%	90.3	3%	66.5	11%	17.7	7%	21.1	9%	12.1
3) +S.-H.-EXT	38%	4.8	10%	16.6	40%	4.9	23%	6.1	24%	4.6
4) +S.-H.+EXT	4%	45.2	8%	20.5	7%	27.9	8%	17.8	13%	8.7
5) +S. +H. -EXT	36%	5.0	32%	5.3	21%	9.3	32%	4.4	21%	5.3
6) +S.+H.+EXT	18%	10.0	46%	3.7	20%	9.8	29%	4.9	32%	3.6
TOTAL		1.8		1.7		2.0		1.4		1.1

Appendix 3-1. Mean intervals in minutes between requestive utterances from particular beneficiary configurations and their ratio to the whole pool of requestives in the **early period** of the programme (between weeks 1 and 2).

REQUESTIVES	E3L		E4L		G2L		G4L		P3L		P1L	
Beneficiary	%	Interval	%	Interval	%	Interval	%	Interval	%	Interval	%	Interval
1) -S,+H,+EXT	0%	xxx	1%	322.0	1%	255.0	0%	xxx	4%	21.6	2%	81.3
2) -S,-H,+EXT	5%	47.7	5%	53.7	3%	85	6%	31.3	11%	8.4	10%	22.2
3) +S,-H,-EXT	33%	7.5	22%	11.5	25%	9.8	35%	5.1	30%	3.0	22%	5.5
4) +S,-H,+EXT	10%	25.1	8%	32.2	18%	14.2	4%	47.0	18%	4.9	5%	30.5
5) +S, +H, -EXT	34%	7.1	36%	7.0	38%	6.5	26%	6.7	18%	5.0	30%	7.2
6) +S,+H,+EXT	18%	13.3	29%	8.7	15%	17	30%	5.9	20%	4.4	33%	4.4
TOTAL		2.4		2.5		2.5		1.8		0.9		1.2

Appendix 3-2. Mean intervals in minutes between requestive utterances from particular beneficiary configurations and their ratio to the whole pool of requestives in the **late period** of the programme (between weeks 3 and 6).

REQUESTIVES	E3		E4		G2		G4		P3	
Beneficiary	%	Interval	%	Interval	%	Interval	%	Interval	%	Interval
1) -S,+H,+EXT	1%	374.0	0%	588.0	1%	225.0	1%	210.0	2%	30.5
2) -S,-H,+EXT	4%	57.5	4%	58.8	7%	32.1	6%	24.7	10%	5.5
3) +S,-H,-EXT	35%	6.2	16%	13.4	33%	6.8	28%	5.6	26%	2.1
4) +S,-H,+EXT	7%	29.9	8%	25.6	12%	18.0	6%	24.7	15%	3.6
5) +S, +H, -EXT	35%	6.2	34%	6.2	30%	7.5	30%	5.2	20%	2.7
6) +S,+H,+EXT	18%	11.9	38%	5.4	17%	12.9	29%	5.3	27%	2.6
TOTAL		2.2		2.1		2.2		1.5		1.0

Appendix 3-3. Mean intervals in minutes between requestive utterances from particular beneficiary configurations and their ratio to the whole pool of requestives – pooled for the **early and late** periods.

Appendix 4. The influence of the stage of the programme upon politeness choice: the ratios of negatively polite head acts for particular series in early and later period of the acquaintance.

HEAD ACT POLITENESS - INFLUENCE OF PERIOD: ALL REQUESTIVES

df=1	EARLY	LATE	x^2	significance	TOTAL
G2	16%	14%	0.0	insignificant	15%
G4	16%	13%	0.4	insignificant	15%
E3	30%	18%	6.6	$p<0.01$	23%
E4	20%	19%	0.2	insignificant	20%
P1	xxx	8%	xxx	xxx	8%
P3	7%	8%	0.1	insignificant	7%

HEAD ACT POLITENESS - INFLUENCE OF PERIOD: INITIATING REQUESTIVES

df=1	EARLY	LATE	x^2	significance	TOTAL
G2	17%	15%	0.0	insignificant	16%
G4	21%	15%	1.0	insignificant	18%
E3	39%	24%	6.3	$p<0.025$	31%
E4	24%	22%	0.2	insignificant	23%
P1	xxx	9%	xxx	xxx	9%
P3	8%	10%	0.4	insignificant	8%

HEAD ACT POLITENESS - INFLUENCE OF PERIOD: INHIBITIVE REQUESTIVES

df=1	EARLY	LATE	x^2	significance	TOTAL
G2	14%	7%	1.7	insignificant	12%
G4	3%	0%	0.3	insignificant	2%
E3	5%	7%	0.2	insignificant	6%
E4	3%	4%	0.0	insignificant	4%
P1	xxx	0%	xxx	xxx	xxx
P3	4%	3%	0.1	insignificant	4%

Appendix 5. Subtypes of modifiers in proposals (occurrences per 100 utternaces); interlingual comparison.

INFORMAL

SUPPORTIVES	ENG	GR	PL
interaction markers	9,7	9,8	23,7
starter (turn-initial)	5,5	8,7	15,8
vocative	0,7	0,0	1,8
interj./other	2,1	4,3	2,6
verb. cognosc.	0,0	0,0	0,0
imp. v. sens.	0,0	0,0	4,4
summons/link	2,8	4,3	7,0
address non-initial	4,1	1,1	7,0
pet name	0,0	1,1	0,9
colloquial	2,8	0,0	2,6
nickname/hum.	1,4	0,0	3,5
cajoler (v. cogn. non-init.)	0,0	0,0	0,9
supportive moves	3,4	1,1	0,0
compliment	0,0	0,0	0,0
appreciation	0,0	0,0	0,0
other	3,4	1,1	0,0
SUBTOTAL:	**13,1**	**10,9**	**23,7**

INTERNAL MODIFIERS

	ENG	GR	PL
colloquialism	4,1	7,6	9,6
nickname (non-voc.)	0,7	0,0	5,6
solidarity plural	0,0	4,3	0,0
humour	2,1	5,4	1,8
SUBTOTAL:	**6,9**	**17,4**	**17,0**
INFORMAL:	**20,0**	**28,3**	**40,7**

IMPOSITIVE

	ENG	GR	PL
starter (turn-initial)	5,5	12,0	7,9
other imp.	4,8	10,9	4,4
neg. particle	0,7	1,1	3,5
	8,3	13,0	10,5
emphasizer	2,1	4,3	2,6
grounder	2,8	3,3	0,9
specifier	2,1	5,4	5,3
steer/preparator	1,4	0,0	1,8
SUBTOTAL:	**13,8**	**25,0**	**18,4**
IMPOSITIVE:	**22,1**	**33,7**	**28,9**

NEG. POLITE

	ENG	GR	PL
tag	8,3	4,8	4,8
IFID (bitte)	0,0	0,0	0,0
any sup. move	7,6	2,2	0,0
SUBTOTAL:	**15,9**	**7,0**	**4,8**
depersonalisation	0,7	1,1	5,3
subjunctive	2,1	6,5	1,8
lexical hedge/dim.	11,7	19,6	0,9
modal adverbial	1,4	0,0	2,6
permission request	0,0	0,0	0,0
polite pessimism	2,1	2,2	0,0
conditional	2,1	1,1	0,0
hedge	2,8	5,4	0,0
morph. diminutive	0,0	3,3	1,8
SUBTOTAL:	**22,8**	**39,1**	**12,3**
NEGATIVE:	**38,6**	**48,9**	**18,4**

NEUTRAL

	ENG	GR	PL
summon/link	31,7	18,5	24,6
summon/link	27,6	14,2	21
voc. initial	2,1	3,3	2,6
voc. other	2,1	1,1	0,9
	26,2	9,7	10,5
steer/preparator	6,9	0,0	3,5
grounder	17,2	5,4	6,1
specifier	2,1	4,3	0,9
SUBTOTAL:	**57,9**	**28,3**	**35,1**
NEUTRAL:	**57,9**	**28,3**	**35,1**

Appendix 6.

Appendix 6-1. Subtypes of modifiers in initiating requests: interlingual comparison.

INFORMAL SUPPORTIVES

	ENG	GR	PL
interaction markers	13,5	15,4	29,6
starter (turn-initial)	7,2	8,6	17,8
vocative	0,9	2,1	5,7
interj./other	6,0	4,1	2,3
verb. cognosc.	0,0	0,0	2,8
imp. v. sens.	0,0	0,0	2,1
summon/link	0,3	2,4	4,9
address non-initial	5,7	6,5	11,3
pet name	0,3	1,7	3,6
colloquial	3,5	2,1	2,1
nickname/hum.	1,9	2,7	5,7
cajoler (verb non-initia)	0,6	0,3	0,5
supportive moves	0,3	1,7	1,0
compliment	0,0	0,7	0,3
appreciation	0,0	0,0	0,5
other	0,3	1,0	0,3
SUBTOTAL:	**13,8**	**17,1**	**30,7**
INTERNAL MODIFIERS			
colloquialism	3,5	6,5	5,9
nickname (non-voc.)	0,3	0,3	3,4
solidarity plural	1,6	0,3	0,3
humour	2,5	5,1	4,9
SUBTOTAL:	**7,9**	**12,3**	**14,4**
INFORMAL:	**21,7**	**29,5**	**44,6**

IMPOSITIVE

	ENG	GR	PL
starter (turn-initial)	4,4	6,5	6,4
other imp.	3,1	2,4	5,2
neg. particle	1,3	4,1	1,3
supportive moves	7,9	16,4	12,1
emphasizer	1,9	5,5	5,4
grounder	3,8	7,2	3,4
specifier	0,9	1,4	1,3
steer/preparator	1,3	2,4	2,1
SUBTOTAL:	**12,3**	**22,9**	**18,6**
augment./expletive	1,6	2,7	2,6
lexical intensifier	0,9	10,6	3,9
sem./synt. intensif.	0,0	0,3	0,8
repetition	11,3	8,2	8,8
SUBTOTAL:	**13,8**	**21,9**	**16,0**
IMPOSITIVE:	**26,1**	**44,9**	**34,5**

NEG. POLITE

	ENG	GR	PL
	7,5	11,9	4,4
tag	2,2	4,1	2,5
IFID (please)	5,3	7,9	1,9
	3,8	2,1	0,8
other sup. move	3,8	2,1	0,8
SUBTOTAL:	**11,3**	**14,0**	**5,2**
depersonalisation	0,6	1,7	2,1
subjunctive	1,3	2,7	1,3
lexical hedge/dim.	11,0	28,4	4,4
modal adverbial	0,3	1,0	1,3
permission request	0,0	0,7	0,0
polite pessimism	0,0	0,7	0,3
conditional	1,9	1,7	0,5
complex hedge	1,9	1,0	0,3
morph. diminutive	0,0	0,0	2,1
SUBTOTAL:	**17,0**	**38,0**	**12,1**
NEG. POLITE:	**37,4**	**63,7**	**16,5**

NEUTRAL

	ENG	GR	PL
	28,3	27,7	17,3
summon	2,5	2,7	1,0
link	6,6	10,6	10,3
voc. initial	13,5	8,9	4,4
voc. other	5,7	5,5	1,5
	6,6	7,9	7,2
steer	1,6	2,1	1,8
grounder	4,7	5,1	5,4
specifier	0,3	0,7	0,0
SUBTOTAL:	**34,9**	**35,6**	**24,5**
NEUTRAL:	**34,9**	**35,6**	**24,5**

Appendix 6-2. Subtypes of modifiers in inhibitive requests: interlingual comparison.

SUPPORTIVES

INFORMAL

INFORMAL	ENG	GR	PL
interaction markers	12,8	21,3	23,4
starter (turn-initial)	7,9	14,6	14,5
vocative	0,0	3,4	5,5
interj./other	5,5	7,9	0,7
verb. cognosc.	0,0	1,1	0,7
imp. v. sens.	0,0	0,0	4,1
summons/link	2,4	2,2	3,4
address non-initial	3,7	6,7	8,3
pet name	0,6	3,4	1,4
colloquial	2,4	2,2	2,8
nickname/hum.	0,6	1,1	4,1
cajoler (verb non-initial)	1,2	0,0	0,7
supportive moves	0,0	0,0	0,0
compliment	0,0	0,0	0,0
appreciation	0,0	0,0	0,0
other	0,0	0,0	0,0
SUBTOTAL:	12,8	21,3	23,4
INTERNAL MODIFIERS			
colloquialism	3,0	7,9	9,7
nickname (non-voc.)	0,6	1,1	2,8
solidarity plural	0,6	1,1	1,4
humor	3,7	7,9	2,1
SUBTOTAL:	7,9	18,0	15,9
INFORMAL:	19,5	40,4	44,8

IMPOSITIVE

IMPOSITIVE	ENG	GR	PL
interaction markers	4,9	7,9	6,9
other imp.	0,0	3,4	2,8
neg. particle	4,9	4,5	4,1
supportive moves	14,6	25,8	19,3
emphasizer	6,1	6,7	8,3
grounder	6,7	11,2	7,6
specifier	0,6	0,0	0,0
steer/preparator	1,2	7,9	3,4
SUBTOTAL:	19,5	33,7	26,2
augment./expletive	14,0	11,2	6,2
lexical intensifier	0,0	12,4	3,4
sem./synt. intensif.	1,2	0,0	2,8
repetition	16,5	1,1	16,6
SUBTOTAL:	31,7	24,7	29,0
IMPOSITIVE:	51,2	58,4	55,2

NEG. POLITE

NEG. POLITE	ENG	GR	PL
interaction markers	8,5	10,1	9,0
tag	1,8	5,6	5,5
IFID (please)	6,7	4,5	3,4
supportive moves	3,0	6,7	1,4
other sup. move	3,0	6,7	1,4
SUBTOTAL:	11,6	16,9	10,3
depersonalisation	1,2	3,4	1,4
subjunctive	1,2	3,4	1,4
lexical hedge/dim.	6,7	21,3	3,4
modal adverbial	0,0	3,4	1,4
permission request	0,0	1,1	0,0
polite pessimism	0,0	0,0	0,7
conditional	1,8	2,2	0,7
complex hedge	1,8	1,1	2,1
morph. diminutive	0,0	0,0	0,7
SUBTOTAL:	12,8	36,0	11,7
NEG. POLITE:	24,4	52,8	22,1

NEUTRAL

NEUTRAL	ENG	GR	PL
interaction markers	23,2	28,1	15,2
summon	1,2	2,2	0,7
link	2,4	11,2	6,2
voc. initial	14,6	10,1	5,5
voc. other	4,9	4,5	2,8
supportive moves	8,5	10,1	9,0
steer	1,2	0,0	2,1
grounder	7,3	9,0	6,9
specifier	0,0	1,1	0,0
SUBTOTAL:	31,7	38,2	24,1
	0,0	0,0	0,0
NEUTRAL:	31,7	38,2	24,1

Appendix 7-1. Head Acts of initiating requests.

The figures refer to the percentages of requests realised by particular types of head acts. Mild hints (off-record requests) may have occurred more frequently but gone undetected as their directive intention is non-transparent per definition.

G2 REQ INI	Realisation	Preference	Performative	Suggestory	Deontic	Competence	mild hint	strong hint	TOTAL
interrog	5.1%	0.0%	0.0%	0.0%	0.0%	1.7%	0.0%	0.8%	7.6%
declar	3.4%	5.9%	0.0%	0.0%	4.2%	2.5%	0.8%	1.7%	18.6%
imper	56.8%								56.8%
infinit	0.8%								0.8%
ellipsis	8.5%								8.5%
vocative	7.6%								7.6%
TOTAL									118
		impositive:		90%					

G4 REQ INI	Realisation	Preference	Performative	Suggestory	Deontic	Competence	mild hint	strong hint	TOTAL
interrog	4.6%	2.3%	0.0%	0.0%	1.1%	1.7%	0.6%	0.0%	10.3%
declar	7.3%	2.9%	0.6%	0.0%	5.7%	4.0%	1.1%	0.6%	20.7%
imper	62.1%								61.4%
infinit	2.3%								2.3%
ellipsis	4.0%								4.0%
vocative	0.6%								0.6%
TOTAL									174
		impositive:		84%					

G REQ INI	Realisation	Preference	Performative	Suggestory	Deontic	Competence	mild hint	strong hint	TOTAL
interrog	4.8%	1.4%	0.3%	0.0%	0.7%	1.7%	0.3%	0.3%	9.5%
Declar	5.1%	4.1%	0.3%	0.0%	5.1%	3.4%	1.0%	1.0%	20.1%
Imper	59.5%								59.5%
Infinit	1.7%								1.7%
Ellipsis	5.8%								5.8%
Voc	3.4%								3.4%
TOTAL									294
		impositive:		86%					

Head acts of various types in the German series G2 and G4: initiating requests.

E3 REQ INI	Realisation	Preference	Performative	Suggestory	Deontic	Competence	mild hint	strong hint	TOTAL
interrog	5.9%	3.9%	0.0%	0.0%	0.0%	16.4%	0.0%	2.6%	28.9%
declar	2.0%	1.3%	0.0%	0.0%	3.9%	2.6%	0.7%	0.7%	11.2%
imper	53.9%								53.9%
infinit	0.0%								0.0%
ellipsis	4.6%								4.6%
vocative	1.3%								1.3%
optative	0.0%								0.0%
TOTAL									152
		impositive:	71%						

E4 REQ INI	Realisation	Preference	Performative	Suggestory	Deontic	Competence	mild hint	strong hint	TOTAL
interrog	0.6%	2.4%	0.0%	0.6%	0.0%	10.8%	0.6%	3.0%	18.0%
Declar	2.4%	2.4%	0.0%	0.0%	5.4%	3.6%	1.2%	1.8%	17.4%
Imper	59.6%								59.3%
Infinit	0.0%								0.0%
Ellipsis	3.0%								3.0%
Voc	2.4%								2.4%
Optative	0.0%								0.0%
TOTAL									166
		impositive:	80%						

E REQ INI	Realisation	Preference	Performative	Suggestory	Deontic	Competence	mild hint	strong hint	TOTAL
interrog	2.8%	3.1%	0.0%	0.3%	0.0%	13.5%	0.3%	2.8%	23.0%
Declar	2.5%	1.9%	0.0%	0.0%	4.7%	3.1%	0.9%	1.3%	14.5%
Imper	56.9%								56.9%
Ellipsis	3.8%								3.8%
Voc	1.9%								1.9%
TOTAL									318
		impositive:	76%						

Head acts of various types in English: initiating requests.

P1 REQ INI	Realisation	Preference	Performative	Suggestory	Deontic	Competence	mild hint	strong hint	TOTAL
interrog	3.8%	0.8%	0.0%	0.0%	0.0%	2.3%	0.0%	0.0%	6.9%
declar	5.3%	1.5%	0.0%	0.0%	6.9%	0.8%	0.8%	3.1%	18.3%
imper	67.9%								67.9%
imp-decl	0.8%								0.8%
infinit	0.0%								0.0%
ellipsis	5.3%								5.3%
vocative	0.0%								0.0%
optative	0.8%								0.8%
TOTAL									131
		impositive:		92%					

P3 REQ INI	Realisation	Preference	Performative	Suggestory	Deontic	Competence	mild hint	strong hint	TOTAL
interrog	4.3%	0.4%	0.0%	0.0%	0.0%	1.9%	0.8%	1.2%	8.2%
declar	2.7%	1.2%	4.7%	0.0%	2.3%	0.4%	0.8%	2.3%	14.4%
imper	65.4%								65.4%
imp-decl	0.4%								0.4%
infinit	2.7%								2.7%
ellipsis	7.8%								7.8%
vocative	0.8%								0.8%
optative	0.4%								0.4%
TOTAL									257
		impositive:		92%					

P REQ INI	Realisation	Preference	Performative	Suggestory	Deontic	Competence	mild hint	strong hint	TOTAL
interrog	4.1%	0.5%	0.0%	0.0%	0.0%	2.1%	0.5%	0.5%	7.7%
declar	3.6%	1.3%	3.1%	0.0%	3.9%	0.5%	0.8%	2.6%	15.7%
imper	66.2%								66.2%
imp-decl	0.5%								0.5%
infinit	1.8%								1.8%
ellipsis	7.0%								7.0%
vocative	0.5%								0.5%
optative	0.5%								0.5%
TOTAL									388
		impositive:		92%					

Head acts of various types in Polish: initiating requests.

The figures refer to the percentages of requests realised by particular types of head acts.

G4 REQ INH	Realisation	Preference	Performative	Suggestory	Deontic	Competence	mild hint	strong hint	TOTAL
interrog	0.0%	0.0%	0.0%	0.0%	0.0%	0.0%	0.0%	2.1%	2.1%
declar	2.1%	2.1%	0.0%	0.0%	10.6%	2.1%	0.0%	6.4%	23.4%
imper	55.3%								55.3%
infinit	4.3%								4.3%
ellipsis	10.6%								10.6%
vocative	4.3%								4.3%
TOTAL									47
		impositive:		98%					

G REQ INH	Realisation	Preference	Performative	Suggestory	Deontic	Competence	mild hint	strong hint	TOTAL
interrog	0.0%	0.0%	0.0%	0.0%	0.0%	2.2%	0.0%	2.2%	4.5%
declar	1.1%	3.4%	0.0%	0.0%	7.9%	4.5%	0.0%	11.2%	28.1%
imper	47.2%								47.2%
infinit	6.7%								6.7%
ellipsis	11.2%								11.2%
vocative	2.2%								2.2%
TOTAL									89
		impositive:		93%					

Head acts of various types in German: inhibitive requests.

E3 REQ INH	Realisation	Preference	Performative	Suggestory	Deontic	Competence	mild hint	strong hint	TOTAL
interrog	0.0%	0.0%	0.0%	0.0%	0.0%	3.6%	0.0%	4.5%	8.9%
declar	1.8%	7.3%	0.0%	0.0%	4.5%	0.0%	1.8%	6.4%	21.8%
imper	56.4%								56.4%
infinit	0.0%								0.0%
ellipsis	8.2%								8.2%
vocative	4.5%								4.5%
TOTAL									110
		impositive:	94%						

E4 REQ INH	Realisation	Preference	Performative	Suggestory	Deontic	Competence	mild hint	strong hint	TOTAL
interrog	0.0%	0.0%	0.0%	0.0%	0.0%	1.9%	0.0%	1.9%	3.7%
declar	1.9%	0.0%	0.0%	0.0%	0.0%	0.0%	1.9%	0.0%	3.7%
imper	77.8%								77.8%
infinit	0.0%								0.0%
ellipsis	13.0%								13.0%
vocative	1.9%								1.9%
TOTAL									54
		impositive:	96%						

E REQ INH	Realisation	Preference	Performative	Suggestory	Deontic	Competence	mild hint	strong hint	TOTAL
interrog	0.6%	0.0%	0.0%	0.0%	0.0%	3.0%	0.0%	3.7%	7.2%
declar	1.8%	4.9%	0.0%	0.0%	3.0%	0.0%	1.8%	4.3%	16.9%
imper	63.4%								63.4%
infinit	0.0%								0.0%
ellipsis	9.8%								9.8%
vocative	3.7%								3.7%
TOTAL									164
		impositive:	95%						

Head acts of various types in English: inhibitive requests.

P1 REQ INH	Realisation	Preference	Performative	Suggestory	Deontic	Competence	mild hint	strong hint	TOTAL
interrog	0.0%	0.0%	0.0%	0.0%	0.0%	0.0%	0.0%	0.0%	0.0%
declar	8.3%	4.2%	4.2%	0.0%	0.0%	0.0%	0.0%	8.3%	25.0%
imper	70.8%								70.8%
imp-decl	0.0%								0.0%
infinit	0.0%								0.0%
ellipsis	4.2%								4.2%
vocative	0.0%								0.0%
optative	0.0%								0.0%
TOTAL									24
		impositive:	100%						

P3 REQ INH	Realisation	Preference	Performative	Suggestory	Deontic	Competence	mild hint	strong hint	TOTAL
interrog	0.0%	0.0%	0.0%	0.0%	0.0%	2.5%	0.0%	3.3%	5.9%
declar	0.8%	3.3%	2.5%	0.0%	0.8%	0.0%	1.6%	2.5%	11.8%
imper	65.3%								65.5%
imp-decl	0.0%								0.0%
infinit	1.6%								1.7%
ellipsis	10.7%								10.9%
vocative	3.3%								3.4%
optative	0.8%								0.8%
TOTAL									121
		impositive:	96%						

P REQ INH	Realisation	Preference	Performative	Suggestory	Deontic	Competence	mild hint	strong hint	TOTAL
interrog	0.0%	0.0%	0.0%	0.0%	0.0%	2.1%	0.0%	2.8%	4.9%
declar	2.1%	3.5%	2.8%	0.0%	0.7%	0.0%	1.4%	3.5%	14.0%
imper	66.4%								66.4%
imp-decl	0.0%								0.0%
infinit	1.4%								1.4%
ellipsis	9.8%								9.8%
vocative	2.8%								2.8%
optative	0.7%								0.7%
TOTAL									145
		impositive:	97%						

Head acts of various types in Polish: inhibitive requests.

Appendix 8. The distribution of impositives and negatively polite head acts.

"P-" signifies impositiveness and "N-" signifies negative politeness. "Other" is a waste-bin category for rarely occurring forms such as the vocative, the infinitive (for Polish and German) and the optative (for Polish). The category "imperative" in Polish comprises imperative and imperative-declarative constructions.

Appendix 8-1. Proposals

	G4	G2	E3	E4	P1	P3
POSITIVE POLITENESS						
imperative	16%	23%	18%	20%	27%	31%
P-declarative	53%	40%	39%	33%	55%	47%
ellipsis	4%	7%	7%	11%	0%	10%
other	2%	0%	2%	3%	9%	4%
TOTAL POS-HA	**74%**	**70%**	**67%**	**67%**	**91%**	**93%**
NEGATIVE POLITENESS						
N-interrogative	16%	23%	27%	25%	7%	6%
N-declarative	10%	7%	6%	8%	2%	1%
TOTAL NEG-HA	**26%**	**30%**	**33%**	**33%**	**9%**	**7%**

Appendix 8-2. Initiating and inhibitive requests.

FORM/POLITENESS	INITIATING REQUESTS			INHIBITIVE REQUESTS		
	ENGLISH	GERMAN	POLISH	ENGLISH	GERMAN	POLISH
imperative	57%	60%	67%	63%	47%	66%
P-declarative	10%	15%	14%	14%	24%	13%
P-interrogative	3%	0.3%	0.5%	4%	2%	3%
other	6%	11%	10%	13%	20%	14.5%
TOTAL POS-HA	**75.5%**	**87%**	**91.5%**	**94.5%**	**93%**	**97%**
N-interrogative	20%	9%	7%	4%	3%	2%
N-declarative	4%	4.5%	1%	2%	3%	1%
TOTAL NEG-HA	**24.5%**	**13%**	**8.5%**	**5.5%**	**7%**	**3%**

LINCOM Studies In Pragmatics

In this series: